explorer

INDONESIA

Fiona Dunlop

AA Publishing

Written by Fiona Dunlop
Original photography by Dirk Buwalda
Edited, designed and produced by AA Publishing
Maps © The Automobile Association 1996
Distributed in the United Kingdom by AA Publishing, Norfolk House, Priestley Road, Basingstoke, Hampshire, RG24 9NY.

The contents of this publication are believed correct at the time of printing. Nevertheless, the publishers cannot be held responsible for any errors or omissions or for changes in the details given in this guide or for the consequences of any reliance on the information provided by the same. Assessments of attractions, hotels, restaurants and so forth are based upon the author's own personal experience and, therefore, descriptions given in this guide necessarily contain an element of subjective opinion which may not reflect the publishers' opinion or dictate a reader's own experiences on another occasion. We have tried to ensure accuracy in this guide, but things do change and we would be grateful if readers would advise us of any inaccuracies they may encounter.

A CIP catalogue record for this book is available from the British Library.

ISBN 0 7495 1030 7

Published by AA Publishing (a trading name of Automobile Association Developments Limited, whose registered office is Norfolk House, Priestley Road, Basingstoke, Hampshire RG24 9NY. Registered number 1878835).

Origination by L C Repro Ltd
Printed and bound in Spain by Graficas Estella S.A.

Cover (front): terraced fields, Bali
Cover (back flap): stone-carvings, Batubulan, Bali
Page 2(a): coconuts, Timor roadside
Page 2(b): Gianyar, Bali
Page 3: temple umbrella, Besakih, Bali
Page 4(a): taxis, Bandung, Java
Page 4 (b): Balinese temple rules
Page 5(a): ikat design, Flores
Page 5(b): tea pickers, Puncak Pass, Irian Jaya
Pages 6/7: Gunung Merapi, Java
Page 8: paddy-fields, East Java

Fiona Dunlop has a taste for the tropics and a fascination for developing countries that lure her away from her Parisian home whenever the opportunity arises. Other books written by Fiona in the AA Explorer series include *Singapore & Malaysia*, *Mexico*, *Costa Rica* and *Paris*. Before her total immersion in journalism she was also involved in the worlds of fashion and art, and writes on cultural life in Paris for various magazines and newspapers.

How to use this book

This book is divided into five main sections:

❏ Section 1
Indonesia Is
discusses aspects of life and living today, from Islam to crafts and politics to population issues

❏ Section 2
Indonesia Was
places the nation in its historical context and explores those past events whose influences are felt to this day

❏ Section 3
A to Z Section
covers places to visit, arranged by island or group of islands, with suggested drives. Within this section fall the Focus-on articles, which consider a variety of topics in greater detail

❏ Section 4
Travel Facts
contains the strictly practical information that is vital for a successful trip

❏ Section 5:
Hotels and Restaurants
lists recommended establishments in Indonesia, giving a brief résumé of what they offer

How to use the star rating
Most places described in this book have been given a separate rating:

▶▶▶   **Do not miss**

▶▶   **Highly recommended**

▶   **Worth seeing**

     Not essential viewing

Map references
To make the location of a particular place easier to find, every main entry in this book is given a map reference, such as 176B3. The first number (176) indicates the page on which the map can be found; the letter (B) and the second number (3) pinpoint the square in which the main entry is located. The maps on the inside front cover and inside back cover are referred to as IFC and IBC respectively.

ATTENTION

I. THOSE WHO ARE NOT ALLOWED TO ENTER THE TEMPLE ARE:
1. LADIES WHO ARE PREGNANT
2. LADIES WHOSE CHILDREN HAVE NOT GOT THE FIRST TEETH
3. CHILDREN WHOSE FIRST TEETH NOT FALLEN OUT YET
4. LADIES DURING THEIR PERIOD
5. DVOTEES GETTING IMPURE DUE TO DEATH
6. MAD LADIES / GENTLEMEN
7. THOSE NOT PROPERLY DRESSED
II. ALL DVOTEES ENTERING THE TEMPLE SHOULD MAINTAIN CLEANLINESS AND ENVIRONMENTAL CONSERVATION

Contents

Quick reference

This quick-reference guide high-lights the elements of the book you will use most often: the maps; the introductory features; the Focus-on articles; the walk and the drives.

Maps

Indonesia Is

Quick reference

Kester Freriks
Kester Freriks was born in Jakarta, Indonesia, but he and his family were forced to repatriate to Holland in 1957. Since then his home has been in Holland but his heart in Indonesia, and he has visited often. He has written short stories, novels and a biography of the Dutch author, Maria Dermout, who wrote about the East Indies. He also contributes to a leading Dutch newspaper, *NRC Handelsblad*.

8

My Indonesia

by Kester Freriks

Once, together with thousands of other Dutch people, I was compelled to leave my native country of Indonesia. And now, like so many others, I return there time and time again. For I'm in love; in love with that garland of islands around the equator; in love with my Indonesia.

Many return seeking not the Indonesia of today, but the Indies of the past, the nostalgic old colonial world. In truth, however, the old Indies don't exist any more. You may look for them in the city outskirts, where the colonial houses, with their characteristically steep roofs, are to be found. Here you can sit out on the porch enjoying the cool of the evening and listening to the sounds of a tropical night. But where once horse-drawn carts rode by, now cars speed past with a fanfare of noisy exhausts, blaring horns and drivers screaming through open windows.

Nor is my Indonesia that of Yogyakarta or Bali – which to me smack of the East displayed for the benefit of the West. If I were to leave for Indonesia tomorrow, I would head straight for a little roadside restaurant, or *warung*. These *warungs* are both kitchen and table, and the dishes are served from buckets standing on the street. The flickering gaslight plays on the faces of the people gathered round and, as Indonesians eat in silence, I am able to gaze intently at the hands of the woman who so carefully prepares the food; smiling, lithe, elegant in her sarong.

Then I would travel further afield, to the Dieng Plateau in Central Java, where the clouds hover over those massive and ancient Hindu temples. I would go in, make my offering of flowers and coins, say my three prayers out loud. The grey stones would shut out the world, and I would feel I was truly at the heart of a mystic, secret Indonesia.

INDONESIA IS

■ **The Indonesian archipelago lies at the aquatic crossroads of Asia and Australasia where the Indian Ocean meets the Pacific, and offers a unique diversity of landscapes, flora and fauna, ethnic groups, religions and cultures. Thousands of islands are rolled into one giant nation that is bisected by the Equator.....■**

From Indonesia's western tip at Aceh in Sumatra to its eastern border with Papua New Guinea is a distance of some 5,000km, while its northern extremity lies some 2,000km from its southernmost island boundary. In between lie six seas and 13,677 islands (recently rounded upwards to 17,000), of which 6,000 are uninhabited and two fall into third (Borneo) and fourth (Sumatra) positions in the world's largest island stakes. These mind-boggling statistics serve only to indicate the infinite richness of Indonesia's offerings, from its Javanese crafts to Komodo's very live dragon, Bali's spiritual serenity and luxury hotels, Kalimantan's virgin rainforest and Irian Jaya's still isolated Papuans. Travelling through this country is ultimately a stimulating journey through time – something you will always lack.

Top: 1815 map. Below: a mosaic of fish-ponds in West Sumatra

Regional diversity Indonesia can be broken down into eight regions: the five largest islands of Sumatra, Java, Kalimantan (Borneo), Sulawesi and Irian Jaya; the tiny though socio-culturally significant island of Bali; and the archipelagos of Nusa Tenggara and Maluku. Two-thirds of the country's 190 million inhabitants are squeezed into Java, the centre of the nation's economic and political life, while many outer regions offer endless empty landscapes. Religions vary from the Hindu-Buddhism of the Balinese to orthodox Islam among Sumatra's Acehnese, devout Christianity in North Sulawesi, Maluku and East Nusa Tenggara, and animism among Irian Jaya's residents. In many cases, the acquired Muslim and Christian religions are simply nominal covers for deeply rooted animist traditions.

Betel-nut-chewing ethnic groups flourish in the outer islands and their fantastic architecture is usually the

Outriggers take on distinct personalities at the resort of Canda Dasa in Bali

first sign of local traditions and pride. Most astonishing are the carved creations of Sumatra's Batak and Minangkabau tribes, the temples of Bali, the boat-like roofs of Sulawesi's Toraja houses and the diverse village architecture of East Nusa Tenggara. History has also left its mark, above all in Java, where the hundreds of Hindu-Buddhist temples count the astounding Borobudur complex among their number.

Natural riches Indonesian landscapes vary from the spectacular smoking cauldrons of the volcanic chain which twists in an east–west arc from Sumatra to Maluku, to luminous-green paddy-fields, tropical rainforests and the dry savannah of the eastern regions. Between them stretch endless seas of aquamarine, sapphire and turquoise, edged by white sands that are a delight to surfers, divers, snorkellers and swimmers. Indonesia's geographical diversity offers the entire gamut of holiday occupations, whether strenuous trekking up volcanoes or through leech-infested nature reserves, visiting Stone Age villages or simply lazing the day away beneath a coconut palm. While ducking and diving the tropical downpours,

visitors also have the opportunity to see some of Indonesia's unique wildlife in the form of orang-utans, Komodo dragons, Sumatran tigers or the elusive birds of paradise.

Living culture Indonesian crafts and culture continue to thrive and provide a recurrent theme to any itinerary. Java's royal *kraton* (palaces) offer an insight into the ways of the archipelago's former dynasties, while many of Kalimantan's more isolated Dayaks carry on their democratic longhouse traditions. Dances performed by moonlight in a Balinese temple setting or gory buffalo sacrifices made for a Torajan funeral are just two of the many cultural offerings that now attract nearly 4 million tourists to Indonesia each year.

While exoticism is guaranteed, once you travel beyond the boundaries of the hard-trodden Java–Bali–Tana Toraja trail, infrastructure does not always meet demands. This relatively young nation (it officially achieved independence in 1950) is still developing, not without inherent difficulties created by its socio-religious diversity or acquired traits such as corruption. Hotels reach sublime heights in Bali, but expect them to dive in quality the further east you go. And although internal transport is improving as more national airlines are set up, sometimes the only choice is a long, bumpy road.

■ 'Unity in diversity': the Indonesian national slogan announces one of the country's greatest attractions. Scattered across the archipelago are hundreds of ethnic groups that only just manage a semblance of unity through the general use of the Indonesian language.....■

A journey through the Indonesian archipelago winds through a mosaic of cultures, customs, religions and languages that would put even the Tower of Babel to shame. The country's 190 million inhabitants compose some 300 ethnic groups and speak over 500 languages and/or dialects. This multi-ethnicity dates from prehistory when the first immigrants arrived from China and intermarried with the archipelago's Austro-Melanesian inhabitants. Trade also played a major role, inspiring exchanges with India, China, the Arabian Gulf, Polynesia and, much later, Portugal and the Netherlands. Settlers not only brought new blood but also new customs and religions (Hindu-Buddhism, Islam, Catholicism, Protestantism), creating today's complex socio-religious fabric which is heaven for tourist literature and hell for central government.

Flux Indonesia's largest ethnic groups are the Javanese (60 million), the Sundanese of West Java (22 million), the Madurese (7 million) and the Balinese (2.7 million). Nor are these populations static, for their deeply rooted peripatetic habits have long kept coastal Indonesians on the move. From the 15th century onwards, Muslim traders (Bugis and Makassarese from Sulawesi, Banjarese from South Kalimantan, and Acehnese and Minangs from Sumatra) contributed to the spread of Islam throughout the archipelago and beyond.

Last pockets However, behind the coastline lies another story. For millennia, Indonesia's vast scale, mountainous interiors, dense jungles and extensive seas maintained effective natural barriers between the numerous ethnic groups. This has left some communities surprisingly intact, even at this late date in the 20th century. Irian Jaya's Danis in particular offer the most extraordinary contrast due to their late 'discovery' only six decades ago and their Papuan blood, which bears no relation to ethnic groups across the rest of the archipelago. Animist practices continue to survive amongst the Dani, despite extensive missionary activity and an increasing Javanese presence. Certain islands of Nusa Tenggara contain similarly isolated communities where crafts, village structures and life-cycle rituals embody well-defined beliefs, the most fascinating being that of Sumba. Travel to Pulau Seram in Maluku, to Boawae in Flores or the Mentawai Islands off Sumatra and you will witness animistic ways of life that survive in rural – and impoverished – tranquillity.

Alfuro mother and child on Pulau Seram, Maluku

On the tribal trail Sulawesi's animist Toraja and Bali's Hindus offer the best marketed and most easily accessible rites, architecture and traditions, closely followed by Sumatra's Bataks and Minangkabau and Kalimantan's Dayaks, although the latter groups are suffering from increasing commercial erosion. Economic interests and improved communications generally spell disaster for ethnic traditions, which is why the unique Badui tribe of West Java has chosen voluntary isolation from the rest of the region and why Kalimantan's semi-nomadic Punans are a disappearing race in a land where timber and mineral concerns rule all. Ironically for the 'unity in diversity' epithet, the sense of Indonesian identity is strongest in more developed regions, whereas isolated and consequently more traditional communities identify first

The Tenggerese make up Java's last Hindu community

and foremost with their ethnic label and *adat* (traditional law). That said, change is fast approaching in the form of satellite television...

Bahasa Freedom of worship is theoretically guaranteed by the constitution and for decades religious conflicts have been rare. However, Christians (who represent 9 per cent of the population) are now feeling threatened by the rise of Islamic extremism and by their reduced representation in government. Muslims, in their turn, feel that Christians wield excessive media and economic power. Yet one factor manages to blanket all these differences – language. The adoption in 1928 of Malay (the traders' *lingua franca*) as the national language, or *Bahasa Indonesia* (see sample opposite),can clearly be seen as a milestone in the path towards unity, whatever minority problems continue to simmer beneath the surface.

13

■ **Since President Suharto assumed the reins of Indonesian power in 1966, this vast nation has made giant steps forward in every domain and presents a relatively stable face to the world. However, the prospect of Suharto's retirement in 1998 is inspiring a growing power struggle and there are few who can predict the nation's future direction.....■**

President Suharto's preferred sobriquet, 'Father of National Development', encompasses wide-ranging achievements in education, health, welfare, agriculture, communications and industrialisation over the last 25 years. Political continuity and economic flexibility have laid the foundations for a new confidence and Indonesia is now able to flex its political muscles within ASEAN (the Association of South East Asian Nations) and even advocate free trade among the nations of APEC (Asia-Pacific Economic Cooperation). Full democracy may still lie over the horizon, but meanwhile a complex chess game is being played out between military faithfuls to *Pancasila*, the revered national philosophy, who have seen their political power eroded, ICMI (a powerful lobbying association of Muslim intellectuals led by the ambitious Minister of Research and Technology, Bacharuddin Habibie), Chinese-owned business interests and Suharto's own burgeoning family assets.

First steps General Suharto first came to prominence in 1965 when, aged 44, he stepped into the power vacuum following the failed *coup d'état* which toppled Sukarno. Within a few months he had secured himself full powers, these being made official in 1968 when he became president. Suharto's true role in the messy and tragic period of 1965–6 is unclear, but what is certain is that he steered Indonesia towards political maturity by reversing Sukarno's isolationist stance.

Ending confrontation with Malaysia and rejoining the United Nations and ASEAN, Suharto embarked on a foreign policy outlined years before by Mohammed Hatta, namely 'rowing between two reefs'. but it was not until the 1980s that Indonesia finally shed its aloofness and encouraged trade and foreign investment. Suharto has now normalised relations with China (broken off in 1965), fearlessly counters US criticism of Indonesia's human rights record and, in 1994, announced a new target of quadrupling real per capita income by 2020 through industrial development.

Advances The contrast with the days of Sukarno's Old Order are enormous. Per capita income has multiplied tenfold since 1970, population growth has been reduced to 1.7 per cent, infant mortality, previously 12.7 per cent, now stands at 7 per

tion of population, power and industrial investment in Java, nor the outmoded political structure. Suharto's Indonesia could be a dynamic society on the road to real democracy and industrialised status or alternatively the arena for increased socio-political unrest and authoritarianism. Only time will tell.

Problems Governing such a vast, multi-ethnic country is not without its problems. The acronym SARA is used to describe threats to national security, namely sectarianism, racialism, tribalism and religious differences, and thus justify repression. Separatist movements in Aceh, Irian Jaya and even southern Maluku ferment, while international pressure has finally led Suharto to concede that the status of East Timor needs to be re-examined (its annexation is still not recognised by the UN).

Since 1985 some 10,000 non-governmental organisations have played increasingly active roles, forcing the government's hand on numerous issues within the official policy of *keterbukan* ('openness'). But the snake sometimes bites its own tail, as happened when Suharto himself was prosecuted for transferring money from a reforestation fund to IPTN, the state aeronautics venture managed by Habibie. In June 1994 increasing nervousness led to the banning of three news publications for their criticism of Habibie, seen by some as a possible successor to Suharto who is now aged 75. Even the army protested, but to no avail.

Independence celebrations stress socio-economic achievements

cent and life expectancy has risen to 62 years. Once classed as a war-scarred nation of hungry rice farmers, Indonesia today boasts an annual growth rate of 7 per cent. Compulsory education launched in 1984 ensures that 94 per cent of children aged between 7 and 12 attend school, and in 1994 the leaving age was extended to 15.

Yet all these positive indicators cannot alter the top-heavy concentra-

15

■ **The nations of Southeast Asia, economic dragons to some and tigers to others, are on the move and on the make. Sprinting along in the vanguard is Indonesia, its sights fixed on industrialised status in the next century and increasingly well equipped to achieve this goal. High-tech industries are considered to be Indonesia's key to the future.....■**

Ambitions run high in this fast-emerging market where deregulation and de-bureaucratisation have become the latest keys to entering the free trade door after years of protectionism. Indonesia can now boast a healthy state of affairs in which manufactured goods have overtaken oil and gas in the export table and opened up new markets. Growth bounds along at 7 per cent, inflation remains under 10 per cent, foreign investment tripled between 1993 and 1994 and, not least, rice production has tripled since 1969, leaving surplus to export. According to one recent survey based on World Bank regional forecasts, Indonesia

Rubber (top and below) was once an essential export product but has now been overtaken by oil and liquefied natural gas

could step into fifth place in the world by 2020.

Natural riches Blessed with extensive natural resources, Indonesia still relies substantially on oil (it is the world's 15th largest producer) and liquified natural gas (it is the number one world exporter) to supply 30 per cent of its export earnings. It is also heavily dependent on timber (it lies second in the world export table for plywood) and coal (it is the third largest exporter and has tripled production since 1989). Irian Jaya's Freeport copper mine is the world's fifth largest, while the state-owned Krakatau steel plant in West Java is the largest in Southeast Asia.

However, such riches do not last forever. It is thought that Indonesia will be a net importer of oil by the year 2000 if new oil-fields are not found. Gas may last a few decades longer but Indonesia's forests, which are being logged at an alarm-ing annual rate of 1.7 million hectares, may survive only another decade. Long-term energy hopes are being pinned on coal, much of which is virtually sulphur-free (and therefore non-pollutant), with reserves estimated to last another 500 years.

Boom As a result of these diminishing natural resources, economic policies have turned to developing the manufacturing sector. By the mid-1980s investment was booming and huge factories in the industrialised cities of Jakarta, Surabaya, Bandung, Medan and Semarang now churn out clothes, shoes, toys and electronic goods. An example of this success is the textile industry, which from 1987 to 1992 multiplied its exports twelvefold.

Today Indonesia is concentrating on high-tech industries such as aeronautics and shipbuilding, both perceived as the archipelago's weapons in the economic struggle with more landlocked Asian economies and as a means of creating jobs in other sectors. Diversification continues with tourism, which has stepped in as Indonesia's third largest foreign exchange earner, growing at an annual rate of 20 per cent. And in a land where over two-thirds of the population is rural-based, agriculture plays an important economic role, with rubber, rattan and coffee forming the top plantation crops.

Handicaps Corruption, bureaucracy, overpopulation, unemployment and the scattered landmass are the nation's main drawbacks to growth. Indonesia is classed top in the Asian

Despite restrictions on logging, annual plywood exports earn Indonesia US$3 billion

corruption stakes, a habit exemplified by the 1994 BAPINDO (National Development Bank) scandal which involved an illegal loan from a state bank to the tune of Rp860 billion (US$430 million). National banks are plagued by bad debts while the national debt itself stands at over Rp180 trillion (US$90 million), by far the largest of the ASEAN countries. Meanwhile, foreign aid pours in (1994 saw Rp10.4 trillion of US$5.2 billion), although it is often accompanied by criticism of rights and conditions.

❏ One of the keys to Indonesia's success is Chinese business acumen. Some 80 per cent of the country's economic activities are controlled by Chinese businessmen, a minority group which represents only 3 per cent of the population. Joint ventures with foreign companies are on the increase, with foreign capital attracted by recent deregulation to the sectors of power generation, oil refining, toll roads and ports. ❏

17

■ **Indonesia is home to the largest Islamic community in the world, visually symbolised by the countless mosque domes that pepper the towns and countryside. Until now, the nation has maintained a relatively moderate profile, but attitudes, whether stemming from governmental or grassroots levels, seem to be changing.....**■

Veils, Ramadan and daily prayers at the mosque form a well-known side to Islam, a religion which has played a significant role in Indonesia's social structure and economy since the fall of the Majapahit empire in the 15th century. Today, some 87 per cent of the population is estimated to be Muslim, this proportion rising to 95 per cent in certain regions, but these followers of Islam are by no means united in their goals. Many are only nominally Muslim, combining Islamic rituals with a deeply rooted mysticism which dates from pre-Islamic days,

Medan's Mesjid Raya, focal point for North Sumatra's more orthodox Muslims

while only a hard core supports more orthodox attitudes in line with the worldwide rise of fundamentalism. One of independent Indonesia's main principles was religious tolerance, yet there are signs of an increasing 'Islamisation' of government attitudes.

Moderation Indonesian Muslims are Sunnites, and since many conversions were originally made by Gujarati Indians, Islam was initially a flexible, partly Hinduised force. With the rise of nationalism in the 1920s, orthodoxy moved in and resulted in the first mass political party, Syarikat Islam. However, at Independence moderation prevailed and produced a particularly ambiguous tenet of

18

Pancasila (Indonesia's 'Five Principles'), namely 'belief in God, with the obligation for adherents of Islam to carry out Islamic law'. After the anti-Communist massacre of 1965–6 devout Muslims hoped to fill the political vacuum left by the destruction of the Communist PKI (Perserikatan Komunis di Indonesia) party, but this was not to be, and instead they turned to education, welfare and religious conversions. As a consequence, commitment and faith deepened on the one hand, but provoked an aversion to Islamic zealotry on the other.

Volte-face? Compared with neighbouring Malaysia and certainly with the Middle East, Indonesian Islam is low key. Muslim Indonesians can have only two wives (with the consent of the first) compared to the more usual four elsewhere, and women have a far more autonomous role with only a minority donning the veil. There are no Islamic banking laws and alcohol is widespread. Until recently, a national lottery added to the list of Islamic no-nos (gambling is banned by the Koran), but this has now been dismantled, pointing to a new official attitude.

In 1991 Suharto himself, not known for his religious fervour, followed every self-respecting Muslim on the hadj, or pilgrimage to Mecca. In 1993, when a French couturier embroidered a Koranic verse on one of his creations, who officially protested? Indonesia. More serious, 1993 also saw a government reshuffle which, though apparently bureaucratic, actually left the 40 ministerial portfolios almost entirely controlled by Muslims.

Roll on One of the protagonists behind this changing attitude is the Minister of Research and Technology, Bacharuddin Habibie, who some see as Suharto's successor. Apart from his influential government role, Habibie is also president of the very powerful ICMI (Ikaran Cendekiawan Muslim Indonesia; an association of Muslim intellectuals). It is now almost impossible to obtain a high-level government post without

Veils can't always conceal the innate Indonesian spirit

belonging to this association, whose ponderings are widely diffused to the public through the violently anti-West and, naturally, pro-Habibie newspaper, *Republika*.

At the same time, a growing Muslim middle class is turning to religious symbols and prayer as an antidote to material social changes. Perhaps most symbolic of the change is the number of hadj pilgrims: in 1993 they numbered 123,000; by 1994 the total had climbed staggeringly to around 158,000. Islam is certainly not a declining force in Indonesia.

❑ Indonesia's ethnic and regional diversity inevitably has pockets of staunchly Muslim societies. Foremost among these is the province of Aceh in north Sumatra, the first region to be converted in the 13th century and accorded a special politico-religious status at Independence. Together with South Kalimantan (93 per cent Muslim) and, to a lesser extent, the island of Madura, this is where the muezzins wail most audibly, calling the faithful to prayer. ❑

■ **Indonesian cuisine uses vitamin-packed ingredients which arrive on the plate straight from the soil or sea, and which are always accompanied by piles of fluffy rice. Tropical fruits, highland vegetables and ultra-fresh seafood are the common lot, these presented in varying styles from region to region.....■**

Lying as it does at a sea-route crossroads between India, China and the Arabian Peninsula, Indonesian cuisine is a healthy amalgam of all these influences. Although each region has its speciality – ranging from buffalo-blood soup or dog's meat in Sulawesi to sago cakes in Maluku, fruit-bats in North Sumatra and roast dragonflies in Bali – the national dishes lie firmly within the rice and vegetables tradition. If you develop a taste for *nasi goreng* (fried rice mixed with vegetables and pieces of chicken) or its noodle variant, *mie goreng*, you will never go hungry in Indonesia.

Some of the most authentic regional food is served at *warungs*, makeshift roadside stalls that leap into action at nightfall. In the hissing light of kerosene lamps, cooks steam, fry and dish up to locals seated on wooden benches. Prices are derisory but quality is variable – the tip is to follow the crowds.

Nasi Indonesia's staple diet of cooked rice (*nasi*) was combined with successive dishes of vegetables and meat by the Dutch to form the extremely popular and hearty *rijstaffel* ('rice table').

❑ Indonesians are great food grazers, and markets always abound in stalls selling a variety of cakes (*kueh*), pancakes (*apam*, usually stuffed with nuts, or *martabak*, an Indian import which can also be savoury), palm sugar and coconut delicacies or, in Maluku, sago-based inventions. ❑

Usually comprising 12 dishes, the *rijstaffel* is echoed in today's Padang restaurants which, although originally from West Sumatra, have invaded the nation. Here, a large selection of dishes is placed on the table and you eat at will, paying only for what you have consumed. Padang food is notoriously spicy compared with more subtle Javanese and Balinese dishes in which the chilli heat is tempered with liberal dowsings of coconut milk. Ginger, saffron, lemon grass, cardamom, tamarind and turmeric commonly enliven chicken (*ayam* means chicken or bird, and sometimes you wonder), beef, goat's meat or, less frequently, pork (*babi*). A more unadulterated carnivore speciality is satay, skewers of marinated and barbecued meat served with a peanut sauce and a neat mound of steaming rice.

Meatless dishes
Vegetarians thrive in Indonesia. Peanut sauce comes into its own again in *gado-gado*, where it smothers steamed bean sprouts and vegetables. *Cap cai*, a Chinese-inspired

Padang food offers a tantalising buffet of spicy dishes

dish of stir-fried vegetables, is equally common, while *tahu* (tofu, a soyabean cake) is whipped up in a variety of guises as a *warung* snack. Aquatic creatures, whether freshwater fish netted in flooded paddy-fields or salt-water varieties such as tuna, lobster, shrimp, squid or sea cucumbers, are not scarce in this maritime nation. *Ikan bakar* (baked fish) is particularly delicious in South Sulawesi and on Irian Jaya's northern coast. For a real treat try one of Sulawesi or Maluku's coconut crabs, whose flesh absorbs the flavour of their coconut diet.

Washing it down Despite Islam, Indonesia is fairly relaxed in its attitude towards alcohol. Beer – usually the locally produced lagers, Bintang and Anker – is found everywhere, but stronger stuff can be had in the outer islands in the form of *tuak* (a fermented palm-wine alcohol) or, in Bali, *brem*, which is brewed from rice and, taken one stage further, distilled into *arak*. Fizzy soft drinks are now part of the culture, but bottled mineral water (*aqua*) is also sold on every street

from Sumatra to Irian Jaya. Theoretically, drinking water (*air minum*) that is served in restaurants is boiled, but don't count on it. *Kopi* (coffee), served with grounds floating on the surface, is made from the excellent locally grown beans, and Indonesian *teh* (tea) is served universally. Fresh tropical fruit juices abound, but best of all is *kelapa muda* (young coconut milk).

Eating in the traditional way

■ **A rare common thread binding together the islands of the archipelago is the crafts tradition. Indonesian dexterity is astounding, using materials that range from precious metals to simple palm leaves, and producing items from *ikat*-weavings to baskets or delicate woodcarvings.....**■

Few countries in the world can rival Indonesia's wealth of crafts, a legacy of the pre-Christian Indochinese Dongson culture and subsequent Indian, Chinese and Arab influences. The handicrafts are as varied as the country's myriad cultures, ranging from primitive woodcarvings to elaborate weaving, plaited palm leaves and rattan- or bamboo-ware, spiritually imbued gold and silver jewellery, and cowrie-shell necklaces. What is common to all these, however, is a seemingly innate sensitivity to colour and form which retains its own individuality, at the same time adapting to influences from the West.

Textiles Lustrous *songket* brocade incorporating gold or silver threads into intricate designs was originally developed in Muslim-influenced coastal regions, but today it is only handwoven extensively by the Minang people of West Sumatra and Lombok's Sasaks. Equally rich are Sulawesi's silk-weavings and a

Metallic threads woven into silk produce songket

tie-dye technique that is unique to Banjarmasin in Kalimantan, but Indonesian textiles come into their own in the fields of batik (see pages 94–5) and *ikat* (see pages 194–5), both of which have been developed with industrialised methods into a booming commerce. Although Lampung's stunningly woven ship cloths have practically disappeared (see panel on page 136), handwoven *ikat* still thrives in the islands of East Nusa Tenggara, and its timeless motifs in rich, earthy colours are much appreciated by contemporary Western tastes. Batik, whether handpainted with traditional Javanese motifs or rolled off a factory machine, is a national passion and is worn by men and women alike.

Plant-based crafts Countless ingenious techniques of splitting, folding, plaiting, knotting and weaving parts of plants have existed for centuries to make containers, mats and even houses. Bamboo, rattan, water-rushes, *Pandanus* (screw pine), sago, coconut and *lontar* palms are all exploited to the full and transformed into elaborate functional objects which are often further decorated by dyeing, staining or painting.

In Palembang baskets are coated in lacquer to create food-containers, and in Lombok intricately woven baskets are beaded and palm-leaf boxes studded with shells. Some of the most complex basketware designs are produced by Kalimantan's nomadic Punans, while the most ephemeral are the delicate coconut-palm envelopes that are created for Balinese Hindu offerings.

Woodcarving Prized by museum collections throughout the world, Batak (Sumatra), Asmat (Irian Jaya)

Wayang golek *(wooden puppets) are a speciality of West Java*

and Nias (Sumatra) woodcarvings are masterpieces of primitive art made for specific spiritual functions. These regions now produce endless copies of traditional sculptures, usually out of durable tropical hardwoods. The centre of recent change is Bali, where forms have developed from the purely mythological and divine to figures that represent anything from ducks to banana palms. Technically, these are masterful, but visitors may prefer the more classic talents of the *wayang golek* puppet-makers and mask-carvers, or the totems and shields once carved out of mangrove wood with cassowary bones and shells by the Asmat (see page 252). Kalimantan's Dayaks are also talented carvers in the purist 'primitive' tradition, while in contrast the elaborately gilded furniture and screens of Java, Madura and Bali incorporate abundant floral, vegetal and mythological elements.

Metalwork The Bronze Age culture is thought to have arrived in the archipelago from Indochina with the Dongson (8th to 2nd centuries BC), metalwork techniques gradually spreading to copper, silver and eventually gold. Small objects are made with the lost-wax method (using a wax and resin mould), while filigree techniques displayed in magnificent silver jewellery have long been a tradition of Sumatra's Acehnese and Minangkabau cultures. For Bataks, every piece of jewellery has a spiritual significance and a jeweller's tools were once coated in sacrificial blood before he started work. The inlaid handles and scabbards of the sacred *kris* (a curved sword or dagger) stimulated superb workmanship in Java and Bali, and the jewellery towns of Kota Gede near Yogyakarta in Java and Celuk in Bali still make these along with other exquisitely crafted traditional ornaments.

Fine silver filigree jewellery produced at Kota Gede

■ **Dazzling brocade-clad beauties and fearsome masked demons vie for attention in centuries-old enactments of myths and legends that every Javanese or Balinese knows by heart, yet can't resist returning to watch again and again.....■**

Music, dance and theatre still form an integral and essential part of Javanese and Balinese cultures. Their source lies in the flowering of pre-Islamic Javanese culture in the 8th to 13th centuries, which gradually integrated folklore, religious cults and court rituals to produce an extraordinary and unique hybrid. Sumatra, Maluku, Kalimantan, Sulawesi and other islands also have their dance traditions, but these are more spontaneous and less refined. Common to all is the gamelan orchestra which, despite varying instrumental compositions from region to region, produces an inimitably Indonesian sound.

Gamelan Gamelan orchestras consist of a minimum of 40 percussion instruments, this number rising to over 80 in a full-scale orchestra. Bronze gongs, drums, xylophones, string instruments and bamboo flutes produce rhythmical and haunting sounds which reach heights of dynamism in Bali where they are characterised by 'masculine' and

Balinese legong *dancers start at five and retire at 14*

'feminine' sounds and a faster tempo. Western musicians have been caught in this hypnotic net, not least Debussy, whose *Nuages* was inspired by the gamelan rhythm. Balinese village orchestras and Javanese court gamelan are called upon for every major festivity, so visitors to these regions won't miss the ethereal, sometimes even monotonous sounds.

Bumblebees Where there is gamelan there is dance, a spiritual expression developed as an offering to the gods and depicted in the bas-reliefs of ancient Javanese temples. Classical dancing is rigidly choreographed and executed, an arduous discipline which concentrates as much on extreme suppleness as moments of meditative stillness. Since being a royal monopoly of the rival courts of Yogyakarta and Solo (Surakarta), it has developed into a popular dramatic art, reaching heights of inventive fantasy in Bali where adolescent dancers may enact the flirtation of bumblebees (*oleg tambulilingan*), or perform the popular *legong* (an archetypal expression of feminine grace) or the bewitching *kecak* trance dance, held only by nocturnal torchlight in the open air and accompanied by hypnotic chanting.

Unfortunately, the onrush of tourism in Bali has caused many troupes to sacrifice quality for *potpourri* shows designed for short – and foreign – concentration spans. Ubud and surrounding villages form the performance epicentre where several shows are staged nightly.

From magic to epic Not all dance depicts voluptuous charm, as masked demons or armed warriors may leap on to the stage and some legends are pure burlesque. One of the most astonishing performances is the magical east Javanese *kuda kepang*, in which dancers enter into the movements of a black hobby-horse in a trance and even munch grass. A modern development in music and dance is *jaipongan*, a Sundanese (West Java) speciality, while the performing arts academies of Yogya and Solo both explore new choreographic expressions.

Never far from the classical repertoires are dance-drama extracts and interpretations of the Hindu epics, the *Ramayana* and the *Mahabharata*. Yogyakarta stages numerous performances, both at the superlative setting of Prambanan's open-air theatre, with smoking Gunung Merapi and the full moon as a backdrop (June to October), and in its city theatres. In Solo, whose gliding technique is regarded by rival Yogya dancers as sloppy (inversely, the Solonese find their cousins too stiff), nightly performances are held at the Sriwedari Park.

Strong make-up and dazzling costumes play to the gods

❏ *Wayang kulit* (shadow plays) and *wayang golek* (wooden-puppet plays, mainly limited to West Java) are Indonesia's other, equally enthralling sources of entertainment, as well as providing didactic lessons in a certain moral code. See pages 108–9 for details. ❏

These may be *wayang orang* (or *wayang wong*), where the accent is more on lengthy dialogues than actual dance. In East Java there is the magnificent open-air theatre of Candi Wilwatika near Pandaan, whose natural volcanic-ring setting is another popular venue at full moon during the dry season.

■ **Bewitching multi-coloured, multi-textured and multi-formed coral landscapes await travellers who plunge beneath the surface of Indonesia's turquoise and emerald seas. The archipelago is dotted with some of the world's best diving spots, where the uninitiated can also paddle about in shallower waters.....■**

The world's largest archipelago occupies the centre of the Indo-Pacific region, its tropical waters a natural nursery for blossoming coral gardens and home to thousands of spectacular fish, crustaceans, sponges, crayfish and marine plants. These coral reefs are most common around the coastlines of smaller islands where they act as a natural barrier; if destroyed, there would be hugely damaging effects on the ecological balance and on tides. Marine tourism in Indonesia is still in its teething stage, a frustrating situation for serious divers in search of equipment. One solution is to pack a snorkel and mask in your baggage, a sure way to avoid missing the aquatic treasure troves that await discovery.

Vulnerability Coral is a living organism made up of millions of tiny polyps, cup-shaped creatures forming a ring of tentacles around a mouth. Many corals resemble plants, but they are in fact carnivorous organisms related to the sea anemone and jellyfish, and feed on microscopic plankton caught in their tentacles. The soft, palpitating,

In a country where 81 per cent of the total area is sea, you stand a good chance of spotting a dolphin

velvety sponges and twisted graphic branches of coral colonies all make up a delicate interactive ecosystem which controls coastal erosion but which is also highly sensitive.

Dynamite-fishing, although now heavily policed, has destroyed large sections of coral reefs, leaving an unfortunately familiar sight of lifeless, grey coral skeletons. A surfeit of divers and anchored boats also has a negative effect as ignorance of the reef's vulnerability is still widespread. When snorkelling, always make sure you avoid standing on or breaking coral as you could set off a damaging chain reaction.

A classic example of human short-sightedness is the reef off Bali's Candidasa (see page 147), where pillaging for lime has irreversibly changed tidal patterns and resulted in a vanished beach. But nothing can pre-empt natural disasters such as the tidal wave which swept over eastern Flores in December 1992, destroying some 40 per cent of Maumere's famed reef.

Electric flashes Darting in and out of the waving sea fans, staghorns, tube sponges and underwater valleys are shoals of technicoloured tropical fish, luminously spotted and striped as in

26

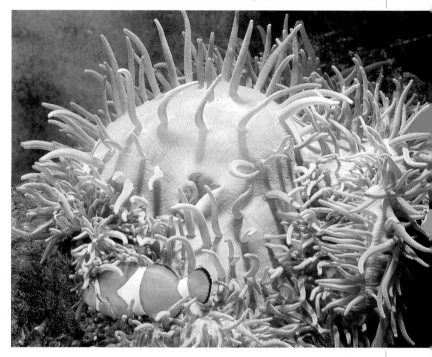

the butterfly, parrot, angel, tiger or clown fish, or sweepingly opaque as in the manta-rays. Deep-divers may encounter lobsters, barracudas, groupers, giant Napoleon wrasses, snappers, the mysterious flashlight fish or even a shark (usually the innocuous reef shark), and turtles flipper along just above the starfish-studded bottom. Dolphins are common sightings, especially around Sulawesi and Maluku. Outside the rainy season visibility can often exceed 30m, and water temperatures may reach a bath-like 30°C.

Superior dives Easily accessible destinations with good diving facilities are Bali (particularly Pulau Menjangan and Nusa Lembongan – see pages 145 and 157), Lombok's popular Gili Islands (see page 178), the Seribu Islands north of Jakarta (see page 54), and Pulau Bintan in the Riau Archipelago (see page 137), best reached from Singapore; added interest lies here in the form of numerous World War II wrecks.

Head further afield to Flores and plunge into Maumere's outlying reefs

A clownfish brushes past the waving tentacles of a sea anemone

(see page 174), where 70m visibility offers a close-up on nearly every known species of reef and tropical fish – or at least it did before the big wave. Sulawesi offers the burgeoning dive centre of Manado near the magnificent marine reserve of Pulau Bunaken (see page 205), and a lesser known centre at Donggala near Palu (see page 199) which offers fabulous diving trips up the untouched northwest coast of the island.

Further east still are the increasingly popular reefs surrounding the tiny islands of Banda (see page 233), which offer excellent though small-scale facilities that are earmarked for future development. The marine reserve at Ambon (see page 234), which also has a diving shop, has suffered from extensive fish-bombing and offers only passing interest. Indonesia's scuba tour ends at Pulau Biak in Irian Jaya (see pagea 250–1), where trips can be arranged to explore the reefs of the idyllic Padaido Islands.

INDONESIAN PLANNED PARENTHOOD ASSOCIATION

RESPONSIBLE YOUTH

■ **The fourth most populous nation in the world has been forced to confront its problems with radical policies of transmigration and family planning. These policies, inspired on the one hand by a startling imbalance in population density and on the other by massive unemployment, have met with conflicting success.....■**

Java, splitting at the seams of its rice-fields, claims 60 per cent of Indonesia's population, a density of 814 people per sq km, while at the other end of the scale Irian Jaya, about three times the size of Java, is home to only 0.92 per cent of Indonesia's 190 million inhabitants. Attempts to alleviate Java's overcrowding started with the Dutch in 1905, when large numbers of Javanese were shifted to Sumatra's Lampung province. In 1969 the *transmigrasi* policy moved into top gear and in 25 years relocated 1.6 million families, well below its ambitious targets and hardly keeping up with the population growth of Java and, to a lesser extent, Bali and Lombok. Between 1989 and 1994 over 500,000 families moved, usually landless peasants or homeless city-dwellers, and improvements were made to the disastrous infrastructure of existing settlements.

Top: campaigning for planned parenthood. Below: Irian Jaya has the country's lowest population density

Bye bye baby Far more successful is the family planning policy that was initiated in 1970 when population growth stood at 2.3 per cent. Educational and motivational campaigns spearheaded by trained field workers have encouraged voluntary sterilisation and an increased use of contraceptives, the result being that Indonesia has now reduced its annual population growth to 1.7 per cent, although high infant mortality rates (70 per 1,000 births, compared with Malaysia's 14 per 1,000) also keep the figure low.

Much of the success of the family planning policy is due to its emphasis on the 'small-but-happy-and-prosperous-family' norm, encouragement to practise self-help family planning through grassroots services, and educational targeting of young, unmarried people. A trend towards later marriage is another factor: the average marriage age now stands at just over 22 years. Indonesia's birth control programme has been recognised throughout the developing world as a model in this field.

INDONESIA WAS

■ **In the beginning was *Homo erectus*, who may possibly have evolved in Java. As he left the cave and developed a system of agriculture, so societies became more organised and an animist, megalithic culture emerged that still has not completely disappeared from some more remote parts of Indonesia.....■**

In the murky depths of the origins of man, Java plays a significant and still controversial role. It has long been assumed that *Homo erectus* evolved from the ape in Africa about 1.8 million years ago, gradually spreading to Asia. This theory is backed up by fossils found at Sangiran and Mojokerto in Central Java, which were estimated to be between 900,000 and 1 million years old. However, a palaeontological bombshell was dropped in early 1994 when two respected researchers at Berkeley, California, announced that these fossils were in fact 1.6 and 1.8 million years old respectively.

This new theory does not correspond so neatly with the climatic changes of that period, when global cooling was replacing tropical forests with savannah – an easier ground for humans to move on from Africa to Asia, presumably in a quest for food. An alternative argument counters that *Homo erectus* may have evolved in Asia and not in Africa, before moving to Java – and so the theorising goes on.

New waves Moving on a million years or so, remains discovered in cave sites in Sarawak, the Philippines and eastern Java indicate that humans of Australoid appearance, from whom modern Australian Aborigines and Melanesians are descended, were inhabiting southeast Asia by about 30,000 years ago.

Today's Javanese-type people, however, are of much later, Mongoloid descent. Their ancestors, part of the vast Austronesian family, seem to have arrived a mere 4–5,000 years ago, from the mainland to the north. With this neolithic culture came settled agriculture and

❏ 'In this idyllic seclusion of the vast jungle, in this bit of forgotten Paradise, lies Aur Duri and here, to our surprise, we found the remains of a mysterious culture, columns with carved capitals, beautifully chiselled and decorated with flowers. One might say enormous kris hilts, with leaf motifs, volutes, and human faces. Sometimes they stand in a row, sometimes near a stone platform.'
– From the archaeologist FM Schnitger's still unique overview of Sumatra's classical age, *Forgotten Kingdoms in Sumatra* (1939). ❏

improved technology. Fine polished stone tools (adzes and trapezoid axes), baskets and pottery have been found in Java dating from this era. But it was the Vietnamese Dongson culture, which probably appeared in Indonesia around 800BC, that brought bronze and iron to this part of the world. The most impressive legacy of the Dongson are their gigantic bronze thunder-drums. Used to invoke rain, they were elaborately decorated and no doubt attractive to the first Indian traders.

Magic and megaliths Essential among these pre-Hindu societies were animist practices, led by tribal leaders and shamans who communicated with the spirit world. For early Indonesians every object, animate or inanimate, had its own life force and the afterlife held as much sway as the land of the living. Carved megaliths such as dolmens, menhirs, tombs, troughs and urns formed the core of their life-cycle ceremonies, these often accompanied by buffalo sacrifices, while magic affected their every move.

Relics abound in Sumatra (Danau Toba, Pulau Nias, Aur Duri, Kerinci, Pasamah) and Sulawesi (Toraja) where sophisticated forms of animist culture developed – but when? Conjecture about age remains strong in this field due to limited archaeological research, but academic concepts have evolved and now accept that separate societies could produce similar elements or traits without necessarily interconnecting. These deeply rooted 'supernatural' beliefs are essential to an understanding of Indonesia's history as they influenced every subsequent culture, whether Buddhist, Hindu, Muslim or Christian, created a subtle form of resistance against the Dutch, and still survive today in remote parts of Nusa Tenggara, Maluku, Sulawesi, Kalimantan and Sumatra.

The island of Nias (left) has many prehistoric relics, including this carved megalith at Bawamataluo

■ Maritime trade and rice were the catalysts for the rise of Indonesia's early dynasties, whose Indianised structures reflected the adoption of Buddhism or Hinduism. Kingdoms rose and fell as gold bars were tossed nonchalantly into the ocean – the ultimate royal status symbols.....■

For centuries Asia saw a continuous flow and interchange of culture and goods that crisscrossed the seas between the great land masses of India, Indochina and the Indonesian archipelago. By the first centuries AD, however, a gradual change was taking place. Indian traders brought with them what was to become the spiritual and social basis for a series of Hindu-Buddhist dynasties that were to control much of Java and the outer islands for well over a millennium.

Above and below: bas-reliefs on Candi Siva, Panataran, thought to date from the mid-9th century

Apart from religion, the Indians also brought models of political institutions, sophisticated art and architecture, Sanskrit and an agricultural system capable of dealing with vast tracts of fertile land. Rival dynasties rose and fell, intermarrying and overlapping in a patchwork of regional domination that defies any neatly definable chronology.

Buddhist dominance East Sumatra lays claim to Indonesia's first significant commercial kingdom, that of the Buddhist Srivijaya. It was established near Palembang in the 7th century AD and survived until the early 14th century. The key factor for Srivijaya's wealth was its maritime control, this extending as far as Siam and coastal Borneo. However, the heavy taxes imposed on all ships using the Strait of Melaka also spelled its downfall. Far more visible in terms of its monumental legacy (Borobudur) is an offshoot of Srivijaya established in Central Java, the Sailendra kingdom. This dynasty spanned two centuries, its end coinciding with the eruption of Merapi in AD928 or 929.

Siva's comeback Parallel to and a close rival of Sailendra was the Hindu Sanjaya kingdom, soon known as Mataram, which brought about a Sivaite revival incarnated in the staggering Hindu temples of Prambanan. After its emergence in the 9th century, Mataram's influence soon covered Central and East Java, but it came into disastrous conflict with Sumatra's Srivijaya over control of the spice trade and only saw a resurgence of its power when the pacifist king, Airlangga (ruled 1016–49), married a Srivijayan princess.

Airlangga's significant reign brought a synthesis of Hinduism and

Buddhism, and nurtured a specifically Javanese culture which left indelible marks on the island of Bali. However, on his death this great kingdom was split in two, and some 200 years of conflict followed between the East Javan dynasties until Kediri finally succeeded in gaining the upper hand in 1222.

❏ Borobudur, Mendut, Kalasan, Sari and Sewu figured among Sailendra's formidable artistic and cultural achievements, and were financed quite simply from the fertile soil of the surrounding volcanoes. ❏

Greatest hour A brief but frenetic burst of temple-building took place when Kediri's victorious king, Ken Arok, established his new capital at Singosari, near Malang. Doomed to a short life, Singosari's end was precipitated by megalomaniac demands from the illustrious Chinese emperor, Kublai Khan. After refusing to capitulate, Singosari's greatest king Kertanegara was killed in 1292 and his heir took off to found the

Some 30,000 workers laboured for several decades to construct the temple complex of Borobudur

Majapahit Dynasty. Over two centuries of unprecedented wealth and influence followed, controlled by Indonesia's greatest pre-Islamic state. From the Majapahit capital of Trowulan in East Java, political dominance covered much of Java, Sumatra, Bali, eastern Nusa Tenggara and Borneo, while trade links reached across most of Asia.

A socio-cultural zenith peaked under the reign of Hayam Wuruk (1350–89), guided by his astute prime minister, Gajah Mada, whose name is still honoured in countless streets across Indonesia. The 98 songs of the Majapahit epic poem *Nâgarakertâgama* (1365) have given historians much to ruminate over, but what is certain is that Majapahit festivities were unrivalled and that Hinduism and Buddhism were symbolically united in the king. By the early 15th century, Majapahit's influence throughout the archipelago began to decline in the face of Melaka's surging maritime status and the gradual rise of Islamic states.

■ **Although Islam was slow to reach Indonesian shores and slow to spread, it nevertheless brought a major change to the region's socio-economic structures. Intermarriage and booming east–west trade routes together promoted the inexorable advance of the word of Muhammad, former god-kings were displaced and a new social order emerged.....■**

As with the penetration of Hindu-Buddhism, so Islam's arrival cannot clearly be defined. Java and Sumatra's rugged mountainous interiors impeded contacts, leaving individual states dependent on their maritime highways – the natural path of Islam. Sea-trading Arabs, Muslim Chinese and Gujaratis from India produced a gradual infiltration and assimilation from the late 13th century until the early 16th century, while some members of Javanese royalty had already converted during the Majapahit's reign. Within two centuries, intermarriage, evangelising and new ports had led to the establishment of Islam, hard-core Hindu-Buddhists had fled to

The old mosque in Kota Ambon, Maluku, where Islam first arrived with Arab traders

Bali, and Indonesia was left with its modern-day pattern of cultures.

Allah's stepping-stones Northern Sumatra is thought to have been Islam's first stepping-stone into Indonesia, a fact noted by Marco Polo in 1292 when he stopped in Aceh on his return from China. Aceh's strategic trading position soon transformed it into one of the most powerful states of the Malay–Indonesian area, and even today this staunchly Muslim state has a special political status within the republic. With the landmark conversion of neighbouring Melaka in 1414 and the blossoming of commerce with Europe, the process of Islamic conversion speeded up, spreading down East Sumatra through Palembang to West Java, where Banten later developed into a Muslim fiefdom. The spice trade then spread Islam to Maluku's Ternate, Tidore and north Ambon, as well as parts of coastal Borneo.

The most influential Islamic state in Indonesia was Demak, one of several trading sultanates along Java's north coast which pumped their riches from the spice trade between Maluku and Melaka. In 1478 Demak overcame the dwindling Majapahit Dynasty, leaving Java's interior to a number of powerless, agriculturally based kingdoms, and by the mid-16th century had established itself through military expansion as far as Surabaya and Malang. The last of the great Javanese kingdoms which also witnessed early Dutch manoeuvring was that of Mataram, a Muslim state which, under the devout and ambitious Sultan Agung (ruled 1613–45), extended its influence across Central and East Java.

Why Islam? This momentous period saw extensive Muslim evangelising, much stimulated by the nine legendary *walis* (Islamic saints) whose tombs in Demak (see page 75), Cirebon (see page 74) and Kudus (see page 82) remain major pilgrimage destinations today.

❏ Aceh legend relates that its ruler (Sultan Malik as-Salih) first converted as the result of a dream in which Muhammad appeared to him, spat in his mouth (thus transferring knowledge of Islam) and named him 'Sultan'. On awaking, he discovered that he could read the Koran, speak Arabic and that he had magically been circumcised. Soon after, a ship arrived, sent by the Caliph of Mecca to fulfil a prophecy of Muhammad, and Aceh's sultan was duly installed according to Islamic custom. ❏

Indonesia is now the largest Muslim nation in the world

Historians still argue over why this new religion was so attractive. Hypotheses point to the role of Sufism, a mystical branch of Islam which dominated the Islamic world after Baghdad fell to the Mongols in 1258, but there is no evidence of Sufi evangelisation. What is certain is that although Islam had little impact on existing Javanese philosophy, it radically altered social customs, replacing cremation with burial, introducing circumcision and offering a convivial structure (same God, same prayer times) that was suited to the new cosmopolitan trading centres. The Hindu gods of old, dwelling in lakes and volcanoes, were too static, too closely linked with a sedentary agrarian society whose social hierarchy and caste languages were inappropriate to the burgeoning new race of self-made men.

■ **Like red rags to bulls, spices used as medicine and for flavouring and preserving meat magnetised European maritime efforts for well over a century. Portuguese ballads and Catholicism are the only survivors of their initial control, soon superseded by the superior strategies of the Dutch.....■**

New navigational techniques and faster, more seaworthy vessels brought the Portuguese into the Asian arena at the turn of the 16th century. From Goa in India they forged eastwards to capture Melaka in Malaysia in 1511, thus successfully disrupting the existing trade network. But their aspirations did not stop there; compasses were soon set for the source of the region's riches, the fabled Spice Islands of Ternate and Tidore, blossoming with clove trees, and Banda and Ambon, thriving on nutmeg. In 1512 a Portuguese fleet arrived in Maluku, the start of over a century of conflict

Below: Melaka in Malaysia (1611), jewel in the spice trade crown.
Spices are still all-pervasive – Top: cinnamon; right: ginger sweet paper

between European powers intent on bypassing Arab and Asian middlemen in a most lucrative trade.

Portuguese supremacy Europeans operating in this far-flung region were more often than not adventurers or desperadoes, and the Portuguese were no exception. A treaty made with the Muslim sultan of Ternate led to intermarriage and the spread of Catholicism – above all in Ambon where the Jesuit preacher, Francis Xavier, converted extensively in the 1540s. The Spanish threat was dispelled by the 1529 Treaty of Zaragoza, and for the rest of the century the Portuguese were left to their own debatable devices.

Euro ambitions Although Sir Francis Drake loaded his hold with Ternate

the 1620s when Dutch dominance of the region was forcefully established.

Dutch monopoly The turning point for the Dutch came in 1619 when Governor-General Jan Pieterszoon Coen decided on Jayakarta (Jakarta) as the ideal base for focalising VOC interests and administration. Despite local resistance backed by the English, he reduced the town to ashes, and his ruthlessness was a key factor in imposing the Dutch monopoly on the spice trade, something the less-organised Portuguese never managed.

VOC rulings were brutally imposed on the region, the sultans of Ternate and Tidore were pensioned off, spice trees outside Dutch control were destroyed and, in an attempt to control smuggling, most of the population of Banda was massacred or deported, to be replaced by Dutch colonists using slave labour. The record was hardly impressive.

Francis Xavier (1506–52) left a permanent mission in Ambon

cloves during his 1577–80 circumnavigation of the globe, it was not until 1600, when Elizabeth I granted a charter to the East India Company, that the English seriously entered the spice fray. This coincided with Dutch ambitions, spurred into action by Cornelius de Houtman's 1596 expedition to Banten and Jacob Van Neck's fleet which reached Maluku three years later. In 1601 a total of 14 Dutch expeditions reached Maluku, and 1602saw the founding of the VOC (Vereenigde Oost-Indische Compagnie, or United East India Company). The commercial race had begun in earnest.

The next few years saw the Portuguese surrender to the VOC in Ambon, while Ternate and Tidore fell to a Spanish fleet based in the Philippines. From their trading post in Banten the English also moved into Maluku, stimulating fierce Anglo-Dutch competition. Conflicts alternated with co-operation until

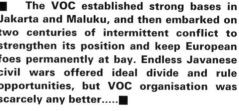

■ **The VOC established strong bases in Jakarta and Maluku, and then embarked on two centuries of intermittent conflict to strengthen its position and keep European foes permanently at bay. Endless Javanese civil wars offered ideal divide and rule opportunities, but VOC organisation was scarcely any better.....■**

Although the VOC's concerns were commercial and not territorial, the company was drawn into a ferment of regional conflicts and rebellions which lasted on and off for the next 150 years. Local allies supplied food, men and the use of strategic ports, but the almost permanent state of internal war finally succeeded in bankrupting what was essentially a mismanaged and corrupt company. Famines, wars and epidemics also contributed to a decimation of the Javanese population, which only fully recovered in the late 18th century.

Local powers Three main powers dominated the archipelago in the early 17th century: Aceh, which under Sultan Iskandar Muda (ruled 1607–36) led aggressive expansionist campaigns before calming down into an Islamic centre of learning; Mataram, whose Yogyakarta-based warrior king Sultan Agung (1613–45) led devastating campaigns throughout Central and East Java; and the sultanate of Gowa in Makassar. The VOC's new base at Batavia (Jakarta) also looked suspiciously at neighbouring Banten, a trading kingdom which prospered on pepper.

The first to experience the VOC chop was the dynamic maritime kingdom of Gowa, whose sabotage of the Dutch spice monopoly and campaign to impose Islam on its Bugis neighbours led to serious

❑ Batavia (Jakarta) was not left unscathed by troubles. In 1740 a suspected plot provoked a massacre of some 10,000 Chinese traders. Survivors fled eastwards, attacking VOC coastal ports, and eventually won the support of Mataram – but the alliance was doomed when the Madurese stepped in to support the VOC. ❑

confrontation from 1609. The VOC finally succeeded in shattering Gowa's power in 1669, leaving South Sulawesi under the virtual dictatorship of the Dutch ally, the Bugis Prince Arung Palakka, until his death in 1696. Palakka's merciless campaigns inspired an exodus of Bugis and Makassarese throughout the archipelago, simultaneously unleashing piracy and spreading Islam. Meanwhile, the VOC had moved into North Sulawesi, establishing forts and converting Minahasans to Christianity.

Divide and rule As spices gradually lost their commercial status to pepper, textiles, coffee and tea, the VOC's foothold in fertile Java became of paramount importance. Mataram's golden era was disintegrating under the next tyrannical king. Internal revolts, famine and the eruption of Merapi in 1672 coupled with

doom-laden prophecies all culminated in a major rebellion in 1675 which spread from Madura. VOC and Bugis allies reversed this tide but dynastic struggles recurred, exploding again with the First Javanese War of Succession (1704–8) and the Second War in 1719–23. Crises, intrigues and warfare continued sporadically until 1757 when the Mataram kingdom was partitioned, thus creating the separate, weakened courts of Yogyakarta and Surakarta.

Vicious circle With each treaty, the VOC's role as ally to warring Javanese royalty won the company more territorial and commercial gains, and by the mid-18th century it controlled most of Java, directly or indirectly. After the overthrow of Banten in 1682 (again facilitated by an internal *coup*) when the English retreated to Bengkulu, pepper was added to the Dutch monopoly list of spices, opium and textiles. Yet profits were non-existent: military demands were enormous, the VOC was

A Dutch East Indies colony c 1650. Amsterdam's East India House (opposite, top) masterminded a strategy to disrupt inter-island trade. Below: VOC emblems

undermanned, inefficient and corrupt, and most personnel died of disease or alcoholism.

Caught in a vicious circle, the company made increasing demands on the Javanese, provoking further rebellion. This necessitated more expense to enforce control and in turn created more VOC needs. The turning point came in 1795 when France invaded the Netherlands and Napoleon's younger brother was placed on the Dutch throne. A government investigation into the VOC revealed its total bankruptcy. The company was dissolved and in 1808 Herman Daendels was appointed governor-general of the Dutch East Indies. Daendels' far more structured administration relegated the chaotic days of the VOC to history.

■ **Cheap manpower and natural resources sharpened Dutch interest in their colony, while new arms and transport technology helped consolidate their power throughout the archipelago. The Indonesians, still divided and actively assisting the Dutch by subjugating one another, tasted little of the new prosperity.....■**

Top: Prince Diponegoro
Above: Herman Daendels,
Governor-General from 1808

After the leisurely pace of change which had characterised the previous two centuries, the 19th century saw an acceleration and strengthening of Dutch colonial status, so that by 1908 the borders of Indonesia (minus Irian Jaya) had been defined. Defensive on the one hand and aggressive on the other, colonial rule evolved from straight-faced exploitation to a more paternalistic approach. Profits soared as mineral resources joined agricultural wealth, and manpower multiplied, infrastructures were improved, missionaries flocked in, education and health care were eventually introduced, and a new class of get-rich-quick expatriates joined the more settled planters and administrators.

Anti-feudal Governor-General Daendels' short administration (1808–11) was significant in transforming the tone. By creating a centralised bureaucracy, introducing *adat* (traditional law) courts, stamping out corruption and reducing the powers of local *bupati* (regency nobles), Daendels laid the foundations for a more streamlined system, at the same time alienating Dutch officials and Javanese aristocracy.

Daendels' attitude was echoed by his successor, the young and idealistic Stamford Raffles who headed the British East India Company's interim rule (1811–16), a move made at the request of the Dutch King Willem V who had taken refuge from Napoleon in England. New policies reflected a concern for peasants' welfare and led to greater intervention in local affairs. Raffles' rule also saw a symbolic event in 1812 when, in reaction to a royal plot, the British actually attacked, ransacked and thus humiliated Yogyakarta's court.

Last princely stand The last Javanese princely revolt was embodied by the Java War (1825–30) when the rebel Prince Diponegoro, convinced of his mystical calling, profited from aristocratic dissent at the abolition of the land-leasing system and led uprisings throughout Central and East Java. Diponegoro's mobile guerrilla tactics confounded the Dutch but he was eventually captured and exiled, although only after 200,000 people had died. This spelled the end of the Javanese élite, confirmed their submission to the Dutch, and initiated the powerless rituals and blossoming of culture which were to characterise the courts of Yogyakarta and Surakarta.

Iniquities From 1830 onwards there followed an unopposed period of classic colonial exploitation. The key was *Cultuurstelsel*, a policy introduced to provide the ailing Netherlands greater revenue and, theoretically, also benefit villagers, but which was in essence a tax in the form of compulsorily grown export crops. Hazy systems of assessment provided opportunity for corruption and were in any case unprofitable for an expanding population. The system did work briefly for the Netherlands: by the 1850s Javanese produce (sugar, coffee and indigo) averaged 25 per cent of Dutch state revenue. But iniquities were blatant and this, combined with

famines and epidemics, painted a miserable picture.

Growing opposition from Dutch liberals finally ended forced labour, the system was dismantled and private enterprise was implemented in the 1860s. This, together with improved communications with Europe (steamboats had begun operating through the new Suez Canal), announced a golden era for the Europeans, and their population and profits multiplied. The Javanese, still required to pay land tax, were little better off, but it would take several decades for their discontent to become focused.

Outer islands Dutch colonial attention was not only riveted on Java. The outer islands represented a security problem and in 1816 the few surviving Dutch posts were hardly impressive. For a further century the Dutch obstinately pursued a goal of consolidating their power throughout the archipelago. Negotiations, manipulations, treaties and/or prolonged struggles took place (the bloodiest being Sumatra's Aceh Wars and the Paderi Wars), finally bringing success in Kalimantan (1863), then Lombok (1894), Sumatra (1903), Sulawesi (1905), Nusa Tenggara (1907), Bali (1908) and, a late outsider, Irian Jaya in 1928. Feudal systems, head-hunting, cannibalism and piracy were abolished, but simultaneously an educated Indonesian class was emerging, united against a common enemy and only recently aware of its new territorial boundaries.

Jakarta's statue of Prince Diponegoro of Mataram at Medan Merdeka commemorates Java's first great freedom fighter

■ Hand in hand with expanding economic horizons came a growing sense of national identity, this spreading from a select few educated Indonesians to the peasant masses. The Japanese occupation served as an essential catalyst for the protracted struggle for independence, and by the end of World War II the structures and mentalities were already in place.....■

Conditions for the average peasant in early 20th-century Dutch East Indies were scarcely any better than those of a century earlier. Tin, oil, rubber and coffee had become valuable exports, but discontent among the 37 million Indonesians was growing. A new Dutch approach did emerge with the Ethical Policy, a theoretical landmark in colonial morality that unfortunately was outbalanced on the one hand by Dutch bigotry and on the other by an increasingly reformist Islamic zeal among the native population. Tensions rose and new nationalist political parties sparked off repression, but it was not until the Japanese occupation that a serious challenge to the colonial system emerged.

Ethical Policy Dutch humanitarian concerns had grown since the publication in the 1860s of books such as *Max Havelaar*, a denunciation of the oppressive system by a former colonial officer. Expanding entrepreneurism brought international interests to the outer islands; by

Surabaya suffered greatly from Japanese bombing in 1942

1907 Royal Dutch Shell was operating intensively in Sumatra and Kalimantan, and by 1930 44 per cent of plantation crops were devoted to the new money-spinner – rubber. A growing need therefore arose for modernity, welfare and peace.

In response to this need, the Ethical Policy of 1901 offloaded colonial guilt and introduced three concepts: education, irrigation and transmigration. The introduction of the policy was not unconnected with a widening cleavage between over-populated Java and the less pressurised, more prosperous outer islands. Dissent against the regime was a logical product of a hungry Javanese population subjected to artificial amalgamations of villages, ineffective social policies and with no control over their conditions.

Nascent forces The first 'native' political party to emerge was the Indische Partij (Indies Party), formed by a Eurasian in 1912, followed soon after by the Syarikat Islam (Islamic Union) which, through the forceful oratory of leader HOS Cokroaminoto, gained a massive following. From 1920 the influential PKI (Perserikatan Komunis di India, or Indies Communist Party) initiated strikes, only to disintegrate temporarily after a major 1926 rebellion. Regional ethnic parties, Islamic schools and trade unions proliferated, resulting in heavy handed government reactions. Despite the Dutch attempt to stifle the rumbling dissent, the notion of 'Indonesia' gained ground, especially after 1927 when one Achmed Sukarno founded the Partai Nasional Indonesia. The following year a flag was designed, a national anthem sung and the phrase 'one nation – Indonesia, one people – Indonesian, one language – Indonesian' coined.

Rising sun World Depression in the 1930s sorely affected the Indonesian economy and this, together with the effects of Dutch repression, slowed the independence movement. However, in 1942 another force appeared: the Japanese. Dutch military forces collapsed and 170,000 Dutch were interned, about a third of

The Japanese campaign for 'Great East Asia Co-prosperity' merely camouflaged a desire to replace Dutch colonialism with Japanese imperialism

whom later died. In some cases Indonesians actively assisted the invaders, whose initial tolerance of nationalist sentiments aimed to destroy any Western influences and mobilise men to aid Japanese victory. Into an increasingly chaotic arena stepped Mohammed Hatta, Sutan Sjahrir and Sukarno, all able negotiators and highly motivated by years of political imprisonment.

By late 1943, as Japanese fortunes were turning, so was their attitude. Hundreds of thousands of 'economic soldiers' were recruited from villages and rice requisitioning was enforced. Anti-Japanese peasant resistance, underground networks and new youth and military groups all created a climate of conflicting goals, but Sukarno's proposals finally won the day, and in July 1945 preparations were made to grant Indonesia full independence. However, Japanese ambitions were cut short, for in August the atomic bombs dropped on Hiroshima and Nagasaki resulted in their unconditional surrender. On 17 August, in a last-minute attempt to pre-empt the return of colonial rule, Sukarno read out the Declaration of Independence.

■ **Although most Indonesians were convinced by the notion of independence, the aftermath of occupation saw renewed violence, both at the hands of the increasingly desperate Dutch and also the *Pemuda* youth movement. Sukarno initially represented a more moderate path, but the tone soon changed.....■**

44

The year 1945 saw a strangely complex situation in the unilaterally declared independent Indonesia. Theoretically, Sukarno was president and Hatta vice-president, backed up by a constitution, but with no political reality. It took five years for this dream to materialise, the fragmented nation becoming a stage for endless struggles between rival factions. And nor did external interests represent a consensus: the Netherlands obstinately manoeuvred to recover its former colony, but its British, Australian and American allies later actively supported Sukarno's goal.

The republic Indonesia remained in a state of suspended animation until late 1946 as British, Indian and Australian troops rounded up the Japanese occupiers and released surviving Dutch internees. The blackest moment occurred at Surabaya where massive local resistance resulted in a terrible massacre (see panel on

Dutch troops countering guerrilla action in Malang, 1947

page 97), clearly demonstrating how little a return of the Dutch was desired. From that moment on, the Indonesians had a symbolic rallying cry and the British became far more circumspect in their attitude.

For the next few years the uncertain and violent climate continued, while poor communications, internal divisions and ethnic differences fragmented the independence movement. Brutal Dutch police actions, massacres and guerrilla warfare eventually culminated, in 1949, in a US-backed round-table conference at The Hague. Here, a federal solution was finally adopted and sovereignty (except for Irian Jaya) transferred to the new state. A last hiccup occurred with resistance to the new federation from East Sumatra and eastern Indonesia, and on 17 August 1950 a new constitution and the Republic of Indonesia at last came to life.

Democracy? Sukarno was confronted with political chaos, poverty, regional and religious splits, low literacy levels and authoritarian

Sukarno and independence

In December 1949 Queen Juliana signed the transfer of sovereignty

☐ Fundamental to the new republic were, and still are, the five principles of *Pancasila* devised by Sukarno which represent a synthesis of Western democratic ideals, Marxism, Islam and *adat* (traditional law). They are: belief in one supreme God; a just and civilised humanity; unity of Indonesia; democracy guided by unanimity; and social justice. ☐

traditions. For seven years he led a democratic experiment which, despite tremendous advances in education and the landmark acceptance of *Bahasa Indonesia* as a national language, eventually dissolved in a morass of corruption, disunity and social injustice.

Increasing Islamic extremism and unrest in Sulawesi and Sumatra, Indonesia's most lucrative region, as well as dissent within the army, inspired a volte-face in 1959 when Sukarno introduced his 'guided democracy', a euphemism for virtual dictatorship. Balancing his power between the army and its popular rival, the Communist PKI party, and on the one hand looking to the Soviet Union for arms and on the other to China for support, Sukarno's rule became increasingly precarious. *Konfrontasi* (confrontation) with Malaysia over Borneo and with the Dutch over Irian Jaya erupted in 1962, and the following year, in one of his typically stirring speeches, Sukarno told the USA to 'go to hell'.

Crisis By August 1965 Indonesia had severed all remaining links with capitalist institutions, power was increasingly divided and the chaotic economy saw hyper-inflation hovering around 100 per cent. On the night of 30 September Sukarno's regime was blown sky-high by an ill-planned *coup* which saw the assassination of six senior generals. General Suharto stepped in, rapidly taking command and restoring order in the capital (see page 14), but political tensions in the countryside exploded into mass anti-Communist violence, essentially targeting PKI supporters and Chinese, who were suspected of masterminding the *coup*. Unknown numbers (possibly around 500,000), mainly in Java and Bali, were killed and thousands of political arrests were made. Sukarno's reign thus ended in a tragic bloodbath, power was transferred to General Suharto and the beleaguered nation faced its next 'new order'.

Monument to Surabaya's role in the struggle for independence

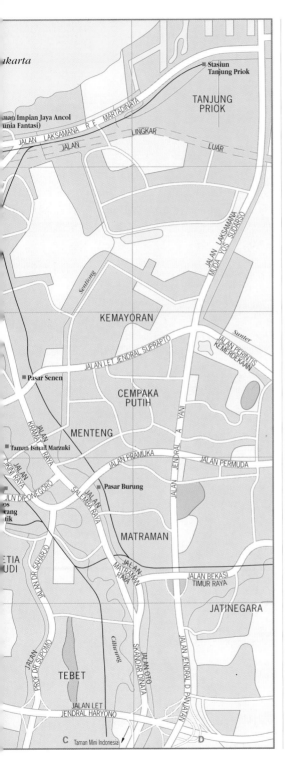

akarta

Stasiun Tanjung Priok

TANJUNG PRIOK

man Impian Jaya Ancol
unia Fantasi)

JALAN LAKSAMANA R E MARTADINATA

LINGKAR

JALAN

LUAR

JALAN LAKSAMANA MUDA YOS SUDARSO

Sentiong

KEMAYORAN

Sunter

JALAN PERINTIS KEMERDEKAAN

JALAN LET JENDRAL SUPRAPTO

Pasar Senen

CEMPAKA PUTIH

JALAN A YANI

JALAN KRAMAT RAYA

MENTENG

Taman Ismail Marzuki

JALAN PRAMUKA

JALAN PERMUDA

JLN DIPONEGORO

AKIN RAYA

JALAN JENDRAL A YANI

os rang tik

JALAN SALEMBA RAYA

Pasar Burung

ETIA UDI

MATRAMAN

JALAN DR SAHARJO

JALAN MATRAMAN RAYA

JALAN BEKASI TIMUR RAYA

JATINEGARA

Ciliwung

JALAN OTO SKANDAR DINATA

JALAN JENDRAL D PANJAITAN

JALAN PROF DR SUPOMO

TEBET

JALAN LET JENDRAL HARYONO

C   Taman Mini Indonesia

D

A young dancer in traditional dress

Jakarta The 23km road from Jakarta's airport into the city centre takes the visitor through all the highs and lows of this sprawling, anarchistic metropolis whose population approaches 9 million. Like so many other Asian capitals, Jakarta is in a state of transition, optimistically looking forward to the next century while simultaneously dragging a mammoth socio-economic burden. Slums and beggars coexist with gleaming post-modern high-rises and shopping centres, while broad avenues chock-a-block with paralysed traffic mount flyovers that overlook teeming backstreets and precarious hovels. In the middle of it all is Jakarta's noisy, polluted centre, where most of the hotels and monuments are concentrated. Yet the city has improved its face considerably over the last two decades, and a few days judiciously spent here can add considerably to an understanding of the nation as a whole.

Batavia The city stepped into history in the 14th century as a small harbour named Sunda Kelapa under the Hindu kingdom of Pajajaran. In the early 16th century Portuguese ships appeared on the horizon in search of the legendary Spice Islands, but it was to the Muslim Demak sultanate, led by Prince Fatahillah, who renamed it Jayakarta ('Great Victory'), that the town fell in 1527. Dutch and English merchants soon established themselves, becoming inextricably enmeshed in local and imperial power struggles. Confrontation came in 1618, and the following year Jayakarta was stormed by the Dutch fleet commanded by Jan Pieterszoon Coen. From the ashes rose Batavia, property of the VOC (United East India Company – see page 37), which was to remain virtually impregnable for the next 350 years.

The 'Queen of the East', as Batavia was known, soon expanded over the low-lying marshes, its booming commercial concerns attracting Indonesian and Chinese immigrants. Epidemics and massacres (in particular the 1740 massacre of some 10,000 Chinese prior to their settlement in Glodok) changed the urban layout and forced development south, away from the pestilential canals of Kota. More recent changes came during World War II when the city fell to the Japanese, who renamed it Jakarta (a shortening of Jayakarta), while Sukarno's subsequent era produced little other than a string of ugly monuments.

North to south The centre of Indonesia's industrial, administrative, political and cultural life lies between the district of Kebayoran Baru in the southwest (itself focused on the lively social and commercial centre of Blok M) and Medan Merdeka in the north. Between the two lies the pleasant central district of Menteng, with its tree-lined streets and colonial buildings, edged by the great north–south axis of Jalan Jend Sudirman and its modern blocks. Beyond Medan Merdeka is the old town of Kota, home to several museums and far more atmospheric.

Adjoining Kota are the port of Sunda Kelapa, the Chinatown of Glodok and, to the northeast, the huge recreation park of Ancol and the main harbour of Tanjung Priok. Far away to the south are two destinations for visitors with children: the zoo and the Taman Mini Indonesia. This is also the less polluted area where wealthier inhabitants choose to have their homes.

Inhabitants Despite efforts to prevent further migration to the capital, Jakarta still attracts rural Indonesians; it is estimated that nearly half the capital's 9 million inhabitants were born outside the city. In amongst this melting pot of cultures is a specific indigenous group with distinct characteristics, the *orang betawi* ('Batavia race'). Their language and customs are still alive in districts such as Condet, Mampang, Kebon Jeruk, Pasar Minggu and Jagakarsa.

In the inner city, immigrants once grouped together in one-storey houses densely packed into a maze of narrow lanes which bore their regional identities (for example, Kampung Bali or Kampung Makassar), but today inhabitants mix much more. A stroll around any of these enclaves, complete with crowing cocks and flourishing gardens, gives an enlightening close-up on a semi-rural way of life which continues under Jakarta's shiny new veneer.

'Operation Cleansing'
In a re-enactment of an early 19th-century clean-up, Jakarta's authorities are now intent on making the city a safer place in which to live. Crime and often fatal violence have been on the increase in the last few years, and reached such a peak in early 1994 that a police operation sprang into action to ease citizens' fears. Around 16,700 personnel from the police, army, navy and air force formed a special unit to attempt to prevent escalating street crime. East Jakarta was pinpointed as the area with the nation's highest crime rate, and criminals were said to be mainly in the 20–30-year-old age group. With 2.5 million young people entering Indonesia's job market annually, Jakarta's problems are far from resolved and the social time bomb keeps ticking.

49

Traffic thunders down Jalan Thamrin to Jalan Jendral Sudirman, the commercial axis of the city

National Archives Building

This superb building lies half-way between Medan Merdeka and Kota at Jalan Gajahmada 111. It was built by Governor-General Reiner de Klerk in the 1760s, subsequently changing hands several times before being transformed into the National Archives (Arsip Nasional). The ornate design incorporates a Dutch layout with elaborate Javanese wood-carvings, and as such is a rare example of the period. An interesting collection of Dutch furniture is on display.

Medan Merdeka

No visitor can miss this 1 sq km hub, which lies half-way between the old city of Kota and the towering modern blocks of Jakarta's central business area stretching south from Jalan Thamrin down Jalan Jendral Sudirman. Jalan Thamrin is lined with banks and airline offices, as well as the popular Sarinah department store, opposite which is the visitor information centre (Jalan Thamrin 9).

On the eastern side of Medan Merdeka stands the unmistakable **Gambir railway station** and, one street back, the luxury **Borobudur Hotel**, with its hive of travel agents, airline offices and quality shops. On the southern side of the square, **Jalan Jaksa** and its narrow side-lanes cater for all the needs of budget travellers. The northern flank of Medan Merdeka is dominated by the neoclassical **Istana Merdeka**, built as the residence of Batavia's Dutch governor-general and now the official but uninhabited presidential residence. Immense crowds gather here each year on Independence Day to echo the cries of '*merdeka*' ('freedom') which greeted the raising of the Indonesian flag on 27 December 1949.

Mesjid Istiqlal (Istiqlar Mosque)   46B3

Jalan Veteran 1

This imposing modern mosque dominates the northeastern corner of the square and was built in 1978. Its immense white dome accommodates 100,000 worshippers, for the moment making it Southeast Asia's largest mosque. Non-Muslims can visit outside prayer times if suitably attired. Opposite stands the neo-Gothic Catholic Cathedral, dating from the late 19th century.

Monas (National Monument)   46B3

If ever there was an imposing symbol of national aspirations, this is it. Some 137m of white Italian marble rise to a giant flame coated in 35kg of gold leaf to create an obelisk which is also known unofficially as Sukarno's Last Erection. It was he who commissioned this monument in 1961, just four years before his downfall. The base of the monument houses a museum that features 48 dioramas of Indonesian history (hardly enthralling, but popular with

The bronze elephant outside the Museum Nasional was presented by the King of Thailand in 1871

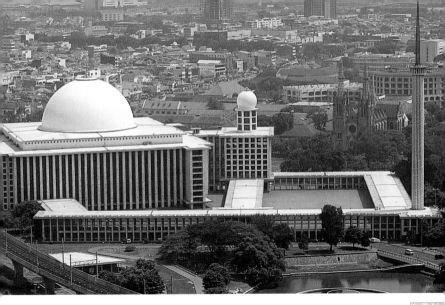

local schoolchildren) while a viewing platform at its summit (accessible by lift) offers sweeping views of the city. Avoid the queues by going early (*open*: Monday to Friday, 8:30–5; Saturday and Sunday, 8:30–9). Facing the obelisk is an equestrian statue of Prince Diponegoro, the hero of 19th-century resistance against the Dutch (see page 40).

▶▶▶ Museum Nasional (National Museum)   *46B3*
Jalan Merdeka Barat 12

The oldest and most fascinating museum in Jakarta lies on the west side of Medan Merdeka. Founded in 1860, the Museum Nasional's elegant, colonnaded façade shelters a wide-ranging collection of Hindu-Buddhist sculptures, textiles, bronzeware, Chinese ceramics and ethnographic artefacts. Rooms are arranged around an open courtyard which displays Javanese stone temple sculptures and some impressive bronze Buddhas.

The Chinese ceramics collection is very comprehensive, as is the recently reorganised ethnographic section. For those travelling beyond Java the latter offers a good introduction to cultural artefacts (of Bali, Kalimantan and Irian Jaya), as well as displaying models of traditional regional architecture. Similarly, the textile collection gives a good preview of the diversity of batik, *ikat* and *songket* designs. (*Open*: Tuesday to Sunday, 8:30–2:30.)

▶ Museum Tekstil (Textile Museum)   *46B3*
Jalan KS Tubun 4

Although not strictly within the Merdeka area, this museum lies only a short distance to the west near the Tanah Abang railway station and market. The grand old 19th-century mansion housing the museum was first owned by a Frenchman and later by the Turkish consul, before eventually passing into municipal hands. Although somewhat disappointingly displayed considering Indonesia's wealth of textiles, the collection contains over 327 examples of *ikat*, batik, *pelangi* (tie-dye) and *songket*, plus a small workshop showing the batik-making process. (*Open*: Tuesday to Sunday, 9–2; Friday, 9–11.)

Hard to miss in central Jakarta is the dome of the state mosque, Mesjid Istiqlal

Jakarta's boom
Jakarta's property boom began in earnest in the early 1980s and is currently in a state that brokers compare to Hong Kong of the 1970s. While the market today remains focused on office space, it is predicted that residential property will catch up in the next few years. In 1994 over 1,000 apartments entered the market, and with demographers forecasting a population of 11 million by the year 2010, this figure will certainly rise. The market for offices, exemplified by the shining post-modern towers lining Jalan Jendral Sudirman, is now glutted, rents being depressed at just Rp26,000–32,000 (US$13–16) per sq m for prime locations.

At the centre of Kota this old colonial building, where VOC problems were discussed and prisoners confined and executed, now houses the Museum Sejarah Jakarta

Si Jagur cannon
On the north side of Taman Fatahillah stands a sturdy bronze Portuguese cannon, Si Jagur, which was once exhibited at the Old Batavia Museum. However, problems arose when locals began to view it as a fertility symbol, childless women making offerings and climbing astride it. It is now positioned on a pedestal high enough off the ground to prevent such antics.

Kota

The centre of old Batavia focused on an area stretching from the port of Sunda Kelapa south along the Ciliwung river. The term *kota* ('city') was used to denote a walled area within which only the Dutch and a privileged élite could live; beyond it lay the kampungs for Indonesian, Chinese and Indian inhabitants. Today, only a few stones of the wall remain, but Kota and Glodok (the latter is a bustling Chinatown bordering the filthy canal to the south-west) harbour an atmosphere and monuments that have little to do with the rest of high-rise Jakarta.

At the centre of Kota, immediately north of the railway station, lies the **Taman Fatahillah**, an open square centred on a fountain, and bordered by three museums and shaded by trees. The square and buildings were all restructured and restored in the early 1970s. A 15-minute walk north takes you to Batavia's former lifeline, the harbour of **Sunda Kelapa**, and, to the east, the vast recreation park of **Taman Impian Jaya Ancol**.

► ▬▬ **Gereja Portugis (Portuguese Church)** *46B4*
Jalan Pangeran Jayakarta 1
Bus: P1, P11
Just east of Kota railway station on the corner of Jalan Jembatan Batu stands this reminder of Dutch slavery (also called Gereja Sion). Built in 1693, the elegant little

church catered for a community of Eurasian slaves brought from Portuguese settlements in India; 'convert and be free' was the message. The exterior is modest but houses a well-proportioned whitewashed interior that is enlivened with baroque elements, an impressive organ and immaculate black ebony pews.

▶ **Museum Bahari (Maritime Museum)** *46B5*

Jalan Pasar Ikan 1
Mikrolet: M15 from Kota's bus terminal

A large complex of shuttered warehouses dating from the 18th century which stands just west of the river mouth houses the Maritime Museum, offering a relevant background to the maritime origins of Kota. The cool interior displays numerous models of traditional boats from all over Indonesia, occasionally alongside the real thing. Navigational instruments, cannon, fishing equipment and, above all, old maps and some well-documented photos give a far clearer idea of the capital's history than does the Jakarta History Museum (see page 54).

Menara Syahbandar, the sturdy watchtower overlooking this pungent street (the fish market is near by), was built in 1839 on the site of a former fortress and can be climbed for a good panorama of the port and old city. (*Open*: Tuesday to Sunday, 9–3; Saturday, 9–noon.)

▶ **Museum Keramik (Ceramic Museum)** *46B5*

Jalan Pos Kota 2
Bus: P1, P11

Kota's only example of neoclassical architecture now houses a fine art gallery and the Ceramic Museum. The building was first constructed as the Court of Justice in the 1860s and then transformed into a museum in 1976. Despite their illustrious setting, the contemporary Indonesian paintings and sculptures are not of major interest, while the Chinese and Southeast Asian ceramics (16th to 20th centuries) are particularly badly displayed. (*Open*: Tuesday to Sunday, 9–4; Friday, 9–3.)

A detail of Pallas Athena from a screen once used by the Council of the Indies (now in the Museum Sejarah Jakarta – see over)

Early Portuguese presence in the archipelago is symbolised by the Si Jagur cannon on Kota's main square

53

JAKARTA

Time chimes by
The four-year restoration process of Jakarta's old *stadhuis* (City Hall), completed in 1974, involved a curious correspondence with a London clockmaker. Years of neglect had left the clocktower chime mechanism out of order, but hopes were raised when the authorities realised that it had a lifetime guarantee which dated from 1810. After contacting the illustrious old firm of Swaithes & Taylor, whose archives still contained the original bill of lading, the clock was flown to London, duly repaired and finally reinstated in its tower in full working order.

Pasar Seni at Taman Impian Jaya Ancol

Island ruins
The remnants of an early Dutch maritime presence can also be seen on the islands of the Pulau Seribu group that lie closest to the mainland. On Onrust you can explore the ruins of an 18th-century shipyard and on Kelor there is an old fort. Bidadari (home to a popular day-trip resort) and Cipir also claim historical remains of the Dutch East Indies period.

▶▶ **Museum Sejarah Jakarta (Jakarta History Museum)** *46B4*

Jalan Taman Fatahillah 1
Bus: P1, P11
This fine old colonial building originally served as Batavia's City Hall and was built in 1710 to replace an earlier edifice. A celebrated early 19th-century inhabitant was Prince Diponegoro, who was imprisoned here by the Dutch before being banished to Manado.

Although the museum was inaugurated barely 20 years ago it already looks tired, and the first-floor windows that remain open to the elements do little to preserve some exceptionally fine VOC furniture. Portraits of governors, old maps, engravings, porcelain and a dimly lit prehistoric section complete this poorly maintained and badly labelled museum. (*Open*: Tuesday to Thursday, 9–2; Friday, 9–11; Saturday, 9–1; Sunday, 9–3.)

▶▶▶ **Museum Wayang (Shadow-Play Museum)** *46B4*

Jalan Pintu Besar Utara 27
Bus: P1, P11
This very Dutch-looking building dating from 1912 formerly housed the collection of the Old Batavia Museum before being inaugurated as a puppet museum in 1975. The rather dusty setting is redeemed by its 3,000-odd exhibits. Masks, musical instruments and old photos form a background to the kernel of the collection, a riveting display of *wayang golek* (wooden puppets) and *wayang kulit* (buffalo-hide or goatskin puppets) from Indonesia, Thailand, Malaysia and China. Casts of thousands peer out from the showcases, including 1916 versions from Cirebon, fresher looking contemporary puppets, and a magnificent and expressive Cantonese crowd dating from the 17th century. Shortened forms of the normally lengthy *wayang kulit* shadow plays are performed every Sunday morning. (*Open*: Tuesday to Sunday, 9–2.)

▶▶ **Pulau Seribu** *46B5*
The 'one thousand' islands (a wildly exaggerated figure as they actually number 128) that lie scattered across the Java Sea north of Jakarta have become a favourite weekend destination for city-dwellers. Many are uninhabited and some are privately owned, but most have beautiful white-sand beaches and offshore coral reefs. Those which are closest to Jakarta can be visited on a day-trip by taking a speedboat or ferry from the Ancol Marina, but for really clear waters and true tropical paradise settings you should head further out to Putri, Melintang, Sepa, Pelangi, Perak or Papa Theo. These are best reached by a short aeroplane ride to Pulau Panjang, from where a ferry service operates to other islands. Cottage accommodation mainly targets the affluent, but the best rates are available with package deals booked in Jakarta that can also include scuba-diving.

▶▶▶ **Sunda Kelapa** *46B5*
After serving as an essential trading gateway for the Hindu Pajajaran kingdom in the 15th century, Sunda Kelapa became a strategic feature in the spice trade and

was coveted by the Portuguese, the English and the Dutch until Batavia was finally founded in 1619. Today the harbour still functions as a berth for *pinisi*, the majestic tall-masted Bugis schooners that continue to ply the seas of the archipelago laden with agricultural and industrial products.

► **Taman Impian Jaya Ancol
(Jaya Ancol Dreamland)**   *46B5*

Jalan Laksamana R Martadinata
Bus: 64, 65

Invaded at weekends yet virtually deserted during the week, this 551-hectare recreation park offers an endless whirl of predictable fishing, boating, swimming, bowling, golfing and eating facilities. Added to these are hotels, a drive-in theatre, nightclubs and massage parlours. Of most interest to foreign visitors are the Pasar Seni, an art market with a good range of Indonesian handicrafts, and the open-air theatre which stages regular traditional and contemporary performances. (*Open*: daily, 24 hours.)

Hitch a bike ride
Unique to Jakarta and in particular to the Kota/Glodok area, is the *ojek sepeda*, which must be the cheapest form of transport available. It consists quite simply of a bicycle and a rider who will take a passenger for a small fare (though hard bargaining is required by foreigners).

The port of Sunda Kelapa still sees over 9,000 cargo ships annually

✳ *Walk* Around Glodok

See map on pages 46–7.

This short walk around the southern part of Kota takes you through lively Glodok, Jakarta's Chinatown. Wander through a maze of narrow lanes, pass shopping centres, negotiate open-air markets and stroll alongside canals to reach the capital's oldest Buddhist temple.

Start from the square in front of Kota railway station and walk south down Jalan Pintu Besar. After about 300m, turn right at the large market building of **Pasar Glodok** and into Jalan Pancoran, a lively street market.

Walk straight on past a Chinese shopping centre on your right towards the canal (Kali Besar). At the bridge, turn sharp left to walk south beside the neglected and dirty waterway. Street vendors abound, smoke rises from food-stalls, and the building façades are a mix of dilapidated early 20th-century stucco and the occasional modern glitz.

At the second bridge, turn left along Jalan Kemenangan III. This residential street makes a welcome change from the intense commercial activity of the canal area. Follow it around a bend and you will see, on your right, a courtyard backed by a Chinese temple. This is the **Dharma Jaya**, Jakarta's oldest Buddhist temple (mid-17th century) yet still very much in use. The ornate interior houses numerous altars devoted to gods of justice, travel, marriage and wealth. If you are lucky enough to be accompanied (the local Chinese are only too happy to show off their temple) you will be taken to a brand new prayer hall where electronically activated curtains open to reveal a kitsch Buddhist garden of heavenly delights.

Continue along Jalan Kemenangan III and turn left at the end to return to the Pasar Glodok. Cross the main road (Jalan Pintu Besar) under the market bridge and stop for lunch or dinner in one of the small restaurants on Jalan Pinangsia.

South Jakarta

▶ **Lubang Buaya**   *47C1*

A short distance east of Taman Mini Indonesia (see below) lies the Pancasila Sakti Monument, a memorial to the seven army officers killed here during the fateful 1965 *coup*. Statues of the heroes stand near a dried-up well into which their bodies were thrown, but more graphically memorable are the dioramas in the adjoining museum.

▶ **Ragunan Zoo**

Jalan Kebon Binatang Raya, Ragunan
Bus: P19

Jakarta's zoo is laid out in a lush tropical park situated several kilometres south of the centre in the Pasar Minggu area. Some 3,600 indigenous animals, from the Komodo dragon to tapirs, *banteng* (wild oxen), orang-utans, a Javanese tiger and flocks of brilliantly coloured birds (including birds of paradise), await the Sunday crowds. (*Open*: daily, 9–6.)

▶▶▶ **Taman Mini Indonesia**
        (Miniature Indonesia Park)   *47C1*

Jalan TMI Pintu 1
Bus: P16, then red minibus 01-02

The offerings of this 160-hectare park (12km southwest of the city centre) may sound banal, but they do give an excellent overview of Indonesia's richly diverse cultures. Some 27 regional pavilions surround a central lake and a map of the archipelago, and are encircled by countless recreational facilities as well as specialist museums, temples, churches and a mosque. Visitors can get around the park by cable-car, train or bus.

Priorities should include the **Museum Indonesia**, a grandiose traditional Javanese structure of carved wood and marble set in a pond of lotus flowers. Displays include colourful ethnic costumes, *wayang* puppets, an entire gamelan orchestra and, on the upper floor, regional artefacts. Of the regional pavilions, each built in traditional style, those representing West Sumatra, North Sumatra, South Sumatra, Lampung and Irian Jaya are particularly interesting. All contain souvenir and handicraft shops. Dance and music performances are held at weekends. (*Open*: daily, 9–5.)

Taman Mini Indonesia is a showcase for the archipelago's numerous architectural styles

57

Bird park
Located in the far corner of Taman Mini is the strikingly designed Bird Park with its walk-in aviaries. The giant domed enclosures, one of which tops 30m, contain man-made ecosystems where birds and vegetation thrive in an almost natural environment. Some 250 species of birds, including 22 that are endangered, flutter freely and are, of course, much tamer than their wild brethren.

A Bengal tiger at Ragunan Zoo

Ondel *masks at TIM offer an escape from high-tech Jakarta*

Hard Rock
A new destination for Jakarta's youth and homesick Westerners alike is yet another version of the global Hard Rock Café. It is located in the Sarinah Building, and lays on a programme of live rock music every evening between 5pm and 8pm. Even if you are not into hard rock (also pumped out in video form on a big screen and on restaurant monitors), it is a great spot for people-watching.

Accommodation Jakarta is relatively expensive compared with the rest of Indonesia and unfortunately there is a shortage of good, mid-range hotels. Most luxury hotels are situated around or south of Medan Merdeka along Jalan Thamrin and Jalan Jendral Sudirman, each one trying to outdo its neighbour in terms of architectural innovation and facilities. For the moment the most audacious is the **Grand Hyatt**, rising above the Plaza Indonesia shopping centre, but it is surpassed in style by the **Borobudur**, with its enormous lush park and classic comforts.

There is another cluster of mid-range hotels near the Taman Ismail Marzuki, as well as in the Menteng area south of Medan Merdeka. Backpackers home in on the Jalan Jaksa labyrinth which offers the full range of budget accommodation, from flea-ridden *losmen* (budget inns) to more up-market establishments such as the Djody or, even better, the Cipta Hotel on Jalan Wahid Hasyim.

Nightlife Cultural evenings can be spent happily at the **Taman Ismail Marzuki** (often shortened to TIM) on Jalan Cikini Raya, a short distance southeast of Medan Merdeka. Performances, ranging from Balinese dance to Western jazz, take place on most nights. Blok M, Jakarta's lively southern socio-commercial centre, has two jazz cafés, **Jamz** (Jalan Panglima Polim Raya 11) and **Prambors Café** in the basement of Blok M Plaza. For an inebriated expat ambience, go to **Jaya Pub** in the Jaya Building at Jalan Thamrin 12, or the more up-market **O'Reiley's** at the Grand Hyatt where live music combines with bar food and a giant video screen to create an Irish-American pub atmosphere. The Hyatt Aryaduta also has a popular bar, **The Tavern**, with live Asian rock music and occasional theme nights (don your camouflage and helmet for 'Commando Night'). Hip-hoppers should head for the **Pitstop**, a popular disco in the bowels of the Sari Pan Pacific Hotel with live Filipino rock. Finally, the latest in sound and lighting systems keeps Jakartan youths bopping at **Big Fire**, located in the Plaza Indonesia.

OPEN THEATRE
PURAWISATA
YOGYAKARTA

No. 021078

NIGHTLY PERFORMANCE
20.00 - 21.30 WIB

Ramayana Ballet

Food and drink

In recent years Jakarta has undergone a culinary revolution, and any number of oriental and Western cuisines are now on offer in every shopping centre and luxury hotel.

Indonesian Cheap Indonesian food in all its guises is best sampled at night markets or, in the central area, at numerous small restaurants in the popular **Jalan HA Salim**, parallel to Jalan Jaksa and its mainly Westernised offerings. **Jalan Kendal** (south of the Hotel Indonesia) and **Jalan Pecenongan** (3km north of Medan Merdeka) both have concentrations of night *warungs* (food-stalls), particularly strong on Chinese and seafood specialities. The faint-hearted should head for the more hygienic food-courts of the **Sarinah** and **Pasar Raya** department stores. The latter is situated at Blok M, a burgeoning enclave for a wide variety of mid-range restaurants. Satay-addicts will appreciate the excellent **Sate House Senayan**, while those with rupiah to spare should not miss the **Oasis**, an up-market restaurant in a 1920s colonial mansion which serves unbeatable *rijstaffel*.

Rest of Asia If the novelty of *gado-gado* fades, Jakarta has plenty of Japanese, Chinese, Korean and Thai alternatives. Apart from the exquisitely prepared but wildly expensive food at the Hilton and Borobudur hotels' Japanese restaurants, the **Kikugawa** and the **Tokyo Garden** both offer quality and value. Szechuan cuisine is dished up at the Mandarin Oriental's **Spice Garden** as well as at the enormous **Summer Palace** in Cikini. Chinese dishes also figure on the menu at the **Café Batavia**, a stylish café-restaurant located in isolated splendour on Kota's Taman Fatahillah and open 24 hours.

Seafood The waters of Indonesia yield bountiful harvests, and the capital's restaurants offer everything from king prawns to jellyfish salad, though local favourites remain sweet and sour gourami, fried squid and charcoal-grilled fish. The **Kuningan**, **Nelayan** and **Ratu Bahari** are all reasonably priced, popular seafood restaurants.

Private initiative is thick on the ground

Euro-nostalgia
Classic French cuisine is served at Le Bistro, an intimate restaurant with a provençal-cum-Montmartre décor, but if you fancy pasta or pizza there is a much wider choice – including Pizza Hut. Infinitely more refined is the Hyatt Aryaduta's Ambiente restaurant, but for a relaxed family setting try Pinocchio's at the Wisma Metropolitan II.

59

Mobile food-stalls or warungs

Shopping

Shopping in Jakarta should only be considered as a last-minute necessity as prices are higher and the range incomparable to, say, that of Bali. Street markets provide atmosphere and occasional rustic bargains, while the Kota area is the place to go if you are looking for cheap electronic goods.

Shopping centres Sleek new malls dot the city, each offering anything from video discs to Cartier watches, jeans and *ikat*. Most central is the **Plaza Indonesia**, located beneath the Grand Hyatt on Jalan Thamrin, while dominating southern Jakarta is **Blok M**, a high-tech universe packed with designer labels, handicraft shops and household goods. Less confusing for foreign visitors are the **Sarinah** and **Pasar Raya** department stores, the former in the central hub and the latter close to Blok M. These make an easy destination for picking up clothing, batik or even handicrafts at reasonable prices.

Markets For a glimpse of grassroots city life, try sampling the colourful atmospheres of **Pasar Cikini**, **Pasar Minggu**, **Blok A**, **Pasar Tanah Abang**, **Pasar Baru** or **Glodok**. All disgorge food in every state and guise alongside cooking utensils, clothes, textiles and general household goods.

More oriented towards tourist tastes and budgets are the handicraft and antique markets of Jalan Surabaya, Ancol and Taman Mini Indonesia (see page 57). The **Jalan Surabaya** 'antique' market is located southeast of Medan Merdeka in a side-street crammed with stalls, the owners of which are exceptionally alert to passing trade and can be seen actively ageing their goods. That said, this is a hive of temptation, offering basketware from Lombok, Sumatran jewellery, inlaid Javanese *kris* swords or woodcarvings from Irian Jaya. In amongst the wealth of handicrafts and under layers of contrived dust are a few authentic Dutch relics; hard bargaining is essential for anything here.

In the Taman Ancol complex, the **Pasar Seni** offers a wide range of regional handicrafts and also has craftspeople demonstrating their various skills. For real antiques head for shops in either Jalan Kebon Sirih Timur or along Jalan Majapahit.

60

Blok M shopping mall is a favourite with local shoppers

The art of the deal
Sharp bargaining tactics are essential for making purchases at Jalan Surabaya and at thousands of other handicraft outlets all over the country. At Jalan Surabaya you can easily aim to pay 30–50 per cent of the asking price, best achieved early in the morning or late in the evening. Humour and feigning uncertainty over the purchase are the basic tactics. If the vendor agrees to your offer, you must buy – otherwise you will undergo a severe loss of face.

Antiques and handicrafts at Jalan Surabaya

Practical points

Getting about

Despite the huge variety of transport on offer in Jakarta, getting around the 650 sq km capital is no picnic. Add to that severe traffic problems and an itinerant host of beggars and pickpockets, and you have an intimidating situation. Yet fear not. Taxis are readily available (except during tropical deluges) and mostly run on meters, although drivers do not necessarily know their way around. **Bluebird** is commonly regarded as the most reliable firm (tel: 314 3000/325607), followed by **Royal City Taxi** (tel: 850 0888), but avoid President taxis. Next step down are the little orange *bajaj* (motorised three-wheelers) which clatter around town; they are unmetered and hence require heavy bargaining before you jump in, but they are convenient for short distances.

If you need to take a bus aim for the *patas* (express) routes, identified by the P before the number. These are less crowded than normal buses (often double-deckers) due to their higher prices. *Mikrolets* (pale blue minibuses) squeeze ten passengers into a tiny space but can be useful for otherwise inaccessible routes. All buses post their flat-rate prices inside. Beware of pickpockets on all forms of public transport and try to stick to the marginally safer *patas* routes. *Becaks* (trishaws) are banned from the city centre, but you may come across the odd survivor in Glodok or in a far-flung suburb.

Getting out

For information about the Sukarno-Hatta Airport, see page 255. A city air terminal is located on the ground floor of Plaza Indonesia, with check-in facilities, airport transfers and luggage assistance (tel: 335 6608). Trains heading east through Java leave from the renovated **Gambir** station, which has regular connections with Bogor and Bandung as well as Yogyakarta, Solo and Surabaya along the southern route. Deluxe night trains for Yogya, Solo and Surabaya depart from **Kota** station in the north of town. **Tanah Abang** station serves West Java, including Merak (the port for boats heading to Sumatra), while **Pasar Senen** serves the northern route of Cirebon, Semarang and Surabaya.

Jakarta's bajaj are noisy and dirty, but nevertheless a convenient way to get around

Bus onwards

Three city bus terminals cover Java: Kalideres serves the west, Cililitan the south (including Bogor and Bandung) and Pulo Gadung the centre and east. All are on the edge of the city and have connections with city buses into town. Tickets for long-distance buses can be bought at travel agents. Travel times are easily comparable to and sometimes faster than the equivalent journey by train.

Suburban becak

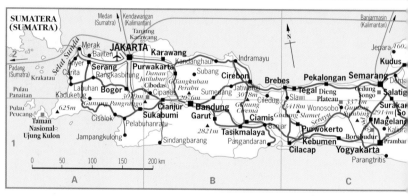

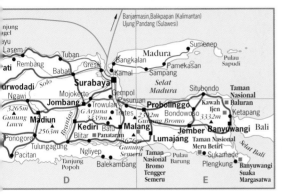

Banjarmasin,Balikpapan (Kalimantan)
Ujung Pandang (Sulawesi)

njung
gel
ayu
Lasem
ati   Rembang   Tuban
              Babat   Gresik   Bangkalan   Madura   Sumenep
urwodadi   Solo   Kamal   Pamekasan   Pulau
Ngawi   Surabaya   Sampang   Sapudi
         Mojokerto   Gempol   Selat
3265m   Jombang   Trowulan Pasuruan   Madura   Situbondo   Taman
Gunung   G.Arjuna Tretes 2392m Bondowoso Kawah   Nasional
Lawu   Madiun   3339m   Gunung Bromo Ijen   Baluran
     2563m   Kediri   Batu   3332m   Ketapang
Ponorogo   Blitar Panataran Malang   Jember Banyuwangi   Bali
          Tulungagung   Lumajang   Taman Nasional   Selat Bali
Pacitan   Ngliyep 3676m   Meru Betiri
                 Tanjung   Gunung   Taman   Pulau   Sukamade
                 Popoh   Balekambang Semeru Nasional Barung Plengkung Banyuwangi
                              Bromo   Suaka
              D   Tengger   E   Margasatwa
                              Semeru

Javanese agriculture evolves with altitude. High up in the Dieng Plateau potatoes and cabbages replace rice

Dextrous pineapple preparation

Java The scenically rich island of Java forms the cradle of the nation's history and culture, as well as the pivot of modern Indonesia's political and economic forces. The strength of its aristocratic past, linked inextricably with spiritual concerns, is such that the island could only be viewed through rose-tinted cultural spectacles with the occasional upward glance at one of its 121 volcanoes. Yet it is hard not to notice the effects of an urgent population problem. An estimated 100 million of Indonesia's 180 million inhabitants are concentrated on this fertile 132,000 sq km island and they leave no land uncultivated. Photo opportunities of endless paddy-fields abound, and although life may be hard, smiles are prolific.

Java caters for every mood. Visitors can meditate on sublime landscapes or temples, plunge into the cultural life of the island's cities, trek through nature reserves or collapse on one of the south coast beaches. One thing is sure, however, you will never be alone. The Javanese (who encompass the Sundanese of West Java and the Madurese of the island of Madura) are exceptionally friendly, inquisitive people and their communicative talents greatly enliven lengthy bus or train rides.

Past kingdoms Java's history started with 900,000-year-old Java Man and culminated with Independence in 1949. Between the two came a string of powerful dynasties, first established in the 8th century, from the Hindu-Buddhist kingdoms of Sailendra, Kediri, Singosari and the omnipotent Majapahits to the first Muslim kingdom of Demak, which called itself Mataram and was founded in 1511. Relics of these prosperous but volatile kingdoms are found in the temple structures of Borobudur, Prambanan,

Gedung Songo, Panataran, Trowulan and around Malang, as well as in the mosques of Demak, Cirebon, Banten and Kudus.

Although Dutch control was practically total by the end of the 18th century, it did not destroy the influence and significance of local sultans, whose presence is particularly visible today in the *kraton* (palaces) of Yogyakarta, Surakarta (Solo) and Cirebon. The highest concentration of colonial relics is found in West Java, from the superb botanic gardens of Bogor and Cibodas to the wealth of art deco architecture in Bandung.

Sulphurscapes Java is crossed from east to west by a chain of volcanoes, 30 of which are still active, their towering cones swathed in clouds and sporadically spitting smoke and ashes. All have spectacular surroundings, whether these are neatly terraced lower slopes or moonscape summits, the latter increasingly protected as national parks. Their bubbling, sulphurous hearts should be a priority on any Javanese itinerary. Bromo is the favourite, but you should not ignore the craters of Dieng, Kawah Ijen, Papandayan and Merapi.

No less strenuous are jungle treks which can be made through nature reserves at Ujung Kulon, Meru Betiri, Pangandaran or Baluran, or from any number of verdant hill-resorts to waterfalls or hot springs. And in this deeply spiritual land it is rare not to stumble upon an ancient temple, tomb or shrine shrouded in tropical vegetation.

Living culture Far from being dead, Javanese culture is a refined expression which has radiated from the courts of Yogyakarta and Solo to permeate the Javanese soul. *Ramayana* and *Mahahbarata* performances are held regularly in these two cultural centres, whether in dance-drama form or enacted by shadow puppets. Soft and melodious gamelan music forms a semi-constant accompaniment throughout Java in hotels, *kraton* and at remote village celebrations. Batik, worn throughout the archipelago, has its origins in Java and wildly diverse styles are produced in Yogya, Solo, Cirebon, Pekalongan and Garut. In essence, Javanese culture is as unpredictable as the countless ceremonies and festivals which highlight its continuing links with a culturally diverse past.

Agro-tourism
Indonesia's three largest industrial cities are found on Java – Jakarta, Surabaya and Semarang – all of which have become environmental black spots. Yet almost 70 per cent of the island's population remains rural, working with pre-industrial methods (buffalo- or even hand-drawn ploughs are a common sight), laboriously sowing rice or transporting superhuman loads of produce up steep hillsides on foot. And when it is not rice, it is corn, coffee, tea, cloves or rubber. In East Java an attempt is being made to open up plantations to tourists; a pioneer in this domain is the Kaliklatak Plantation near Banyuwangi (tel: 0333 24896 or 24061), which even offers accommodation in cottages.

65

Transport offerings include horse-drawn dokars, seen here on the island of Madura

Chinatown

An overdose of 1920s architecture could drive the unwary visitor west of the centre. Here is the start of Chinatown, an area of two-storey shophouses, narrow lanes, idle *becaks* (trishaws) and vociferous caged birds. The Pasar Baru (New Market) on Jalan Oto Iskandar Dinata is the heart of this market district. Follow any of the streets radiating west from here to gain a glimpse and smell of the ingredients of Chinese and Indonesian cuisine. On Jalan Kelenteng stands the main Chinese temple, typically resplendent in golds and reds.

► **Baluran, Taman Nasional** *63E1*

Baluran National Park's 25,000 hectares offer good wildlife-spotting opportunities and are easily accessible from Banyuwangi, in the far east of Java. To the north of Gunung Baluran, extensive savannah is roamed by *rusa* deer, *banteng* (wild oxen) and feral buffaloes, and terminates on a rocky coastline interspersed with mangroves and the odd fish farm. To the south and west secondary forest harbours numerous monkeys and peafowl, while to the east white beaches overlook the Bali Strait.

Poaching is a major problem, particularly in the dry season (May to October) when the streams dry out completely and four-wheel drives move in. Entrance to the park is from Wongsorejo, and basic accommodation is available 12km in from here at Bekol.

►► **Bandung** *62B1*

This large, prosperous business city was long regarded as a major jewel in the Dutch colonial crown. Completion of the railway line to Jakarta in the early 1880s announced a golden era, aided by the refreshing high-altitude climate. Bandung flourished until World War II, but in 1946, when confronted with the return of the Dutch, its citizens chose to set fire to their city. Luckily for architectural enthusiasts they only managed to destroy the southern part of the city, consisting mainly of kampungs, leaving the northern boulevards and colonial monuments intact.

Central sights The town radiates from the central *alun-alun* (town square) on Jalan Asia Afrika, an area rich in activity and sights, the latter including the **Great Mosque** (rebuilt in 1989), the **Pendopo** (1867), now the mayor's residence, and the art deco **Gedung Merdeka**, originally a social hot spot that in 1955 housed the watershed congress on colonialism attended by 29 African and Asian leaders. A short distance east stand two remarkable relics of Bandung's pre-war boom: the **Savoy Homann Hotel**►► and the **Grand Preanger Hotel**►. The former is also home to the very active local heritage society, which

Bandung's Savoy Homann Hotel dates from the 1880s but was entirely rebuilt in pure art deco style by AF Aalbers in 1938

The sun rises over a fisherman and his floats in Baluran

produces an excellent publication giving detailed information on the city's historic buildings.

Running north from the Savoy Homann to the railway line is **Jalan Braga►►**, once described as the 'Fifth Avenue of Indonesia' and high on the colonial place-to-be-seen ladder. Today its shops offer little of interest, but much of the fine original 1920s architecture remains. Beyond the railway lies **Taman Merdeka**, a grassy park ending at the City Hall (1929) which is bordered by several other monuments to 1920s and 1930s modernism.

Stretching northeast from Taman Merdeka is a peaceful area combining 1920s garden suburbs with wide boulevards and green squares, and dominated by the landmark **Gedung Sate** (1917). This eclectic mammoth now functions as West Java's governor's office and also houses the Philately Museum. Opposite is the **Geological Museum►►** (Jalan Diponegoro 57), which exhibits the skeletons of prehistoric rhinos and elephants alongside fossilised trees and a 156kg meteor that dropped on to Java in 1884. Outstanding in historical terms is the skull of Java Man (see page 30).

North of centre Bandung is home to over 25 colleges of higher education, and continues to thrive on an intellectually and politically active reputation. Most celebrated is the **Bandung Institute of Technology (ITB)►►**, situated to the north of the city. It was built in 1920 to an innovative Indo-European design by Maclaine Pont and remains Indonesia's most prestigious technical university. The verdant campus grounds and creeper-shrouded 'winged' buildings stand out in startling contrast to Bandung's geometric art deco architecture.

More prosaic tastes are catered for in Jalan Cihampelas, home to an extraordinary stretch of shops devoted to jeans – hence its nickname of **Jeans Street**. Garish giant effigies of King Kong, Superman and Rambo compete here to attract customers. Moving northwards towards the visible and still active volcano of Tangkuban Perahu (see panel), you may spot the spectacular forms of **Villa Isola►►**, 6km from the city centre, another of Bandung's tropical art deco jewels which commands panoramic views over the city from its lovely gardens.

Steaming craters
Many of the high peaks surrounding Bandung are volcanic, so there is no shortage of hot springs in the area. Most spectacular are the craters of Tangkuban Perahu ('Capsized Boat'), 30km north of town, rife with colourful legends and a favourite local weekend destination. Escape the crowds at the first crater by walking around the rim to the second, or follow a steep path down to the active part of the crater where jets emit sulphurous steam. A further 6km to the north among the tea plantations of Ciater is a popular spa fed by hot water from Tangkuban Perahu. Restaurants, bungalows and two large pools which are good for a mineral soak provide suitable distractions here.

JAVA

Rubber-mad
By smuggling rubber seeds out of Brazil in a stuffed crocodile, an unprincipled or enterprising (depending on one's viewpoint) Englishman was to spell the downfall of the Amazonian rubber economy and the rise in fortune of Indonesia and Malaysia. After transiting at Kew Gardens, the seedlings were taken to Singapore's Botanic Gardens where the botanist Henry 'Mad' Ridley campaigned obsessively – and successfully – for their adoption by planters in the region.

Bogor's raison d'être, the Botanical Gardens, assemble tropical plants from all over the world

▶   **Banten**   62A2

About 150km west of Jakarta lies the ghost of what was once one of Java's most powerful sultanates, now a small, neglected port. At the peak of its power under Sultan Agung (1651–83); this prosperous bastion of Islam controlled the lucrative spice trade, but the arrival of the English and Dutch soon put paid to its supremacy.

Today, the old town (Banten Lama) offers an impressive 16th-century mosque in Hindu-Islamic style, the **Mesjid Agung**▶▶, still used today and whose towering minaret can be climbed. Close by lie the ruins of a fortified palace, the **Istana Surosowan**, destroyed by the Dutch in 1832. Fronting this is a modest museum which displays artefacts and weapons, while beyond the mosque to the northwest stand the ruins of **Fort Spellwijck** (1682), abandoned in the early 19th century. Far more animated is an 18th-century Chinese temple, still in use.

Bird-lovers will relish **Pulau Dua**▶▶, home to flocks of breeding migratory birds between April and August. These, together with the permanent winged population, make the island one of Indonesia's richest bird sanctuaries. Access is via a causeway or by 30-minute boat ride from Karanghantu Harbour.

▶   **Blitar**   63D1

This pleasant but nondescript town is sanctified above all for **President Sukarno's tomb**, which attracts hordes of Indonesian pilgrims. The elaborate mausoleum within marble walls is located north of the centre on the road to the Hindu temple ruins of Panataran (see page 89). Although Sukarno died in 1970, it was not until 1979 that his unmarked grave was transformed into this monumental affair which has since spawned rows of souvenir stands. Otherwise, Blitar's main attractions (including a good hotel-restaurant) centre around Jalan Merdeka and the *alun-alun* (town square), the latter lined with immense banyan trees.

▶▶   **Bogor**   62A2

Bogor's location 60km south of sweltering Jakarta in the foothills of the mountains inspired its growth as a colonial hill-station, appropriately named Buitenzorg ('Without Worries'). Today the town is famed for its superb **Kebun Raya (Botanical Gardens)**▶▶▶ (*open*: 8–4). The 87 hectares of undulating landscaped park completely monopolise the town centre, and were established in 1817 by botanists from London's Kew Gardens under the aegis of Sir Stamford Raffles. Thousands of species of plant life from all over the tropical globe can be found here, including towering centennial trees, palms, *Pandanus*, rattan, bamboo, cacti and giant water lilies. Extensive experiments took place here with cash crops (tea, coffee, tobacco and quinine), not least being those on the infamous *Hevea brazilliensis* (rubber tree).

Meandering through the middle of the gardens is the Ciliwung river, while in the northwestern corner stands the elegant **Istana Bogor**, fronted by a vast lawn on which deer roam. This was the first palace built for the Dutch governor-general (in 1745), although the present edifice dates from 1850. The last semi-permanent resident was Sukarno, who was held here under house arrest between 1967 and 1970. Today the palace is used for state guests and major conferences, such as the 1994 APEC summit (it cannot be visited). On a more nostalgic note you can see a modest memorial to Olivia Raffles, first wife of Sir Stamford, which stands at the path crossroads near the entrance.

West of the southern entrance to the gardens is the **Museum Zoologi (Zoological Museum)**►► (*open*: daily, 8–4; closed Friday lunchtime), replete with hundreds of models or stuffed versions of local birds, insects and animals. Particularly impressive is a huge skeleton of a blue whale (over 27m long) which was beached on the south coast of Java in 1916. Across the road lies a busy market area, while to the north of the gardens radiate tree-lined streets of old colonial villas. Bogor's proximity to Jakarta (it is only an hour away by either train or bus) makes it a popular destination with weekend visitors, so make sure you time your visit accordingly.

Gongs

If gamelan music is starting to take its grip, you may be interested in visiting one of the few remaining gong foundries in West Java. Located at Bogor's Jalan Pancasan 17 (follow Jalan Empang from the Ramayana Theatre opposite the Zoological Museum), it produces both the sonorous metal gongs and the carved wooden stands from which they are suspended.

Banten's Mesjid Agung is dated 1556

The Bodhi tree

A cutting taken from the Bodhi tree under which Buddha attained 'benevolence' was presented to a Sri Lankan temple in 234BC. Over 2,000 years later, during the festival of Waisak (held in memory of Buddha's birth) in 1934, a cutting of this second tree was planted on the eastern side of Borobudur temple by a Buddhist priest. A statue of Buddha now sits beneath it and during Waisak (celebrated annually at full moon in May) it becomes a focus for Buddhist offerings.

▶▶▶ Borobudur   62C1

Borobudur is arguably Southeast Asia's finest Buddhist monument after Cambodia's Angkor Wat. It was built over 75-odd years between the late 8th century and the mid-9th century, and its majestic scale and surroundings alone create a startling vision. No fewer than 504 statues of Buddha and some 2,500 panels of magnificently carved stone reliefs adorn the terraces of its tiered levels. Yet 25 years ago the temple was on the point of collapse, a crumbling remnant of ten centuries of abandon, tropical decay, earthquakes and pillaging; the benefit of interventions by Sir Stamford Raffles in 1814 (who actually uncovered the ruins) and Theo Van Erp in 1907 had been erased. This moved Unesco to start a Rp50 billion (US$25 million), ten-year restoration programme that was completed in 1983.

New developments inevitably included tourist facilities, a museum and a pristine park, thus multiplying the site's attractions. These, combined with Borobudur's proximity to Yogyakarta (42km southwest), ensure constant throngs of visitors, so to gain some sense of Buddhist nirvana it is best to stay overnight in the village and be at the gates at dawn (*open*: daily, 6–5:30). Views in the intensifying light through early morning mists and against the volcanic backdrop are quite spectacular.

Structure Seen from the air, Borobudur looks like a giant tantric mandala. Its nine levels are modelled on the Buddhist cosmos, which consists of three worlds: *kamadhatu*, the lower sphere of human desires; *rupadhatu*, the transitional sphere of form; and *arupadhatu*, the sphere of formlessness and celestial enlightenment. The first stage is illustrated at the base of the temple in panels concealed

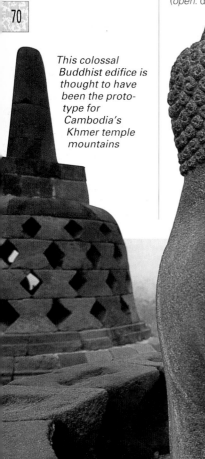

This colossal Buddhist edifice is thought to have been the prototype for Cambodia's Khmer temple mountains

by a stone platform, constructed for technical reasons or, more probably, to hide the depictions of the effects of good and evil. Only a small section has been opened up on the south side. Above this rise four tiered galleries of form, faced on both sides with intricate reliefs depicting Buddhist texts and the life of Buddha. The fifth gallery links the sphere of form with that of formlessness; reliefs are absent and rings of stupas (bell-shaped domes) are visible above.

On leaving the square, 'earthly' terraces you rise into the open, circular terraces of the higher spheres. Here even depictions of Buddha were considered inappropriate, and the 72 statues stand inside trellised stupas (although two have been left exposed and thus meditate openly over the valley). Crowning the three circular terraces is the huge central stupa, untrellised and symbolically empty, repre-senting the nothingness of nirvana.

Itinerary By entering through the main eastern gateway and circulating clockwise, you will follow the prescribed Buddhist route. A total of 5km of Mahayana Buddhist scenes accompany you, but remember not to turn right – if you do, you pay tribute to the spirits of the underworld. A small museum is sited at the exit from the central temple area, but it is worth seeing beforehand as it documents the restoration process and displays statues etc that could not be reinstated. The hive of souvenir and refreshment stalls at the main entrance is best avoided – better nourishment and friendlier service can be found in the village.

Triad of temples The interest of Borobudur does not stop at the central temple. This is actually the culminating tem-ple of a row of three aligned east–west across the valley. The oldest, **Candi Mendut**▶▶▶, lies 3km east and has a superb 3m statue of a seated Buddha flanked by two Bodhisattvas, all carved from single blocks of stone. The roof is missing, but the exterior façade reliefs are exquis-itely carved. Closer to the village centre and the confluence of the rivers Elo and Progo stands the smaller **Candi Pawon**▶, faced in equally fine reliefs but empty inside.

Over 2 million blocks of andesite stone were carved and then transported to the temple site by horses and elephants

Life of Buddha
Buddha is thought to have been born in 560BC, (making him a contempo-rary of Confucius and Pythagoras) in the shadow of the Himalayas in present-day Nepal. Although his father, raja of the Sakya kingdom, gave him the surname of Gautama, his followers later called him Siddharta, meaning 'he who has fulfilled his destiny'. At the age of 29, Buddha decided to renounce his princely married life and undergo six years of hardship and meditation in the pursuit of wisdom. Dissatisfied with Hindu philosophy, he finally attained enlightenment in solitude under a Bodhi tree at Gaya in the Indian state of Bihar. In a famous sermon delivered near Benares, Buddha expoun-ded the principal doctrines of Buddhism and spent the rest of his life (he died at the age of 80) preaching.

JAVA

Mystical dawn mists

▶ ▶ ▶ Bromo Tengger Semeru, Taman Nasional
63E1

Sunrise over Bromo's smouldering crater may have become a fixture in every tourist itinerary but it still remains an awesome sight. The 2,392m Mount Bromo and its partner, extinct Mount Batok, are the result of a massive ancient eruption. The calderas now form the focal point of the 58,000-hectare national park, which also includes Java's highest peak, the 3,676m Gunung Semeru to the south.

Access to the park is easiest by minibus from Probolinggo or Pasuruan to the north, but tours can also be arranged from Malang and even from Surabaya. If changing buses at Probolinggo, beware of the numerous sharks who haunt the bus station – they pose as official tourist-office representatives but are hard bent on hotel and bus commissions. Accommodation is available at nearby Tosari and Ngadisari, and also right on the

caldera's edge at Cemoro Lawang. All hotels around Bromo arrange early morning jeep trips (sometimes starting at 2:30am) to Cemoro Lawang, a factor which can cause pre-dawn traffic jams in high season.

Fire god Bromo's local Tenggerese inhabitants form one of Indonesia's smallest ethnic groups. They are believed to be the descendants of Hindus who fled Central Java in the 15th century at the fall of the Majapahits and chose to live on these remote slopes to avoid the spread of Islam. These small, peaceful people, swathed in sarongs against the cold mountain air, live by farming the steep and fertile slopes, but Bromo's growing popularity with tourists now also provides them with pony-trekking work. The Tenggerese religion blends Hinduism with animism, Mount Bromo itself figuring prominently as the embodiment of their fire god. The annual ceremony of Kasada sees thousands of Tenggerese ascending Bromo to pray and throw offerings into the crater, while a modern temple in the 'sand sea' below serves their daily needs.

Crater views The nature of the landscape here is spectacular and varied, from densely terraced green slopes along the winding approach roads to the early morning mists that roll across the valley or the caldera itself. After brooding in the soft dawn light, the contours of the steaming crater of Bromo gradually sharpen as the sun rises, a phenomenon best viewed from **Mount Penanjakan**, situated a few kilometres to the west. Jeep trips are arranged to this viewpoint (a short climb is also involved), which offers fewer crowds and allows you to accomplish the sand-sea trail and crater close-up in relative peace later in the morning.

Most visitors choose to see the sunrise from the crater edge, an experience agoraphobics should avoid. Ponies ferry the weary hundreds across the sand sea, leaving the more energetic to stagger along by torchlight in the early morning mist. The final stage involves climbing 250 steep concrete steps to the narrow edge of the crater, overlooking a cavernous and sulphurous heart that belches steam continuously. Temperatures can hover around freezing point before dawn, so make sure you take sufficiently warm clothes with you.

▶ **Carita** 62A2
This seaside resort on Java's west coast is accessible in under 3 hours from Jakarta, a factor which has contributed to its recent rapid development (weekends are crowded and expensive). Carita is situated 7km north of Labuhan and offers a long, white sandy beach lined with coconut palms, reasonable swimming and surfing, as well as some snorkelling on the reef. Bungalow and hotel development has not, however, enhanced its charms.

The resort's main claim to fame is its view of the infamous **Krakatau** volcano, which rises out of the Sunda Strait between Java and Sumatra. Boat trips can be arranged through hotels in Carita (at a price and, occasionally, at a risk), but much depends on Krakatau's mood: early in 1994 volcanic activity became so intense that landings were suspended. The main port for ferries to Sumatra is Merak, 50km or so to the north.

Krakatau devastation
When Krakatau erupted on 27 August 1883, the explosion was heard from Sri Lanka to Perth and was the loudest ever recorded on Earth. Its strength has been estimated as equivalent to 2,000 Hiroshima bombs and the resultant massive waves affected even the English Channel. Over 36,000 people died and 163 villages were destroyed along the coasts of Java and Sumatra, while three-quarters of the island itself collapsed into a chasm beneath the sea. Since then another island has emerged, Anak Krakatau ('Krakatau's Child'), first visible in 1928 and still growing. Although it often shoots out rocks and smoke, Anak Krakatau can be visited at quieter moments. Boats land on its east coast, from where visitors can hike up to the caldera.

73

Bromo's sand sea can be crossed on foot or on horseback, but there is no alternative to climbing the steps

This extraordinary royal chariot, the Kareta Paksi Haga Liman, *is housed in the stables of Cirebon's Kraton Kasepuhan*

Topeng *dance performances are usually held on Sunday mornings at the Kraton Kasepuhan*

74

► Cibodas   62B2

Cibodas is Indonesia's oldest nature reserve (founded in 1889) and remains famous for its fine and rich montane flora specific to its altitude of 1,200–3,000m. The Cibodas Botanic Gardens, situated 46km south of Bogor over the brow of the Puncak Pass and just off the main Jakarta–Bandung road, offer a beautiful display of flowering shrubs, as well as the possibility of an arduous climb up **Mount Gede** (2,958m) or **Mount Pangrango** (3,019m). These adjoining volcanic peaks (together constituting a newly created national park) harbour natural forest formations (sub-montane, montane and moss or cloud forest) which are regarded as the finest examples left in Java, and which share genera with the European Alps. The open meadow just below Gede's crater edge claims an everlasting plant, *Anaphalis javanica* or Javan edelweiss, while at lower altitudes the slopes are dominated by oaks, chestnuts and laurels. Lower still are pitcher plants and begonias, as well as a mass of luxuriant epiphytes. Accommodation can be found at **Cipanas** (1.5km south of the entrance to the gardens) or at a guest-house in the gardens themselves.

►► Cirebon   62B2

Cirebon's location 272km east of Jakarta, at the crossroads of West and Central Java, gives it a fascinating mixture of Sundanese and Javanese cultures that is further injected with strong Chinese influences. This industrialised port is well off the mainstream tourist itinerary, but its royal past, thriving batik industry and nickname of 'shrimp city' all hold obvious interest.

Of the four *kratons* (palaces) still inhabited by their former sultans, the largest and most striking is the **Kraton Kasepuhan►►**. Situated in the southeast of town, this *kraton* dates from the early 16th century, when it marked Cirebon's adoption of Islam, but was rebuilt in 1677. Part of the restored palace can be visited by the public (open: daily, 8–5), and reveals an eclectic mixture of European

furnishings and various Asian architectural styles. A rather dusty museum occupies the main courtyard, behind which lie the graceful palace rooms. Opposite the museum stands an extraordinary relic, a 17th-century gilded carriage in the shape of a symbolic creature with wings that flapped as it moved (see panel). Across the square stands the wooden **Mesjid Agung** mosque (1480), whose elegant tiered form is one of Java's oldest.

Kraton Kanoman▶ lies closer to the town centre and is fronted by a colourful outdoor market. Less well preserved, and even verging on the decrepit, it also has a small museum and carriages, as well as a live population of chickens and kite-flying children. The walls are inlaid with Chinese and European plates, as are those of the Kraton Kasepuhan.

It is impossible to visit Cirebon without having a close look at its distinctive style of batik, heavily influenced by a large Chinese community (which has also dotted the town with temples). The motifs include dragons, tigers, rocks and clouds executed in a bold style traditionally only by men. The centre of this industry is **Trusmi**, 6km west of town. Shops along Jalan Karanggetas (near the Pasar Pagi market) also stock a good selection.

▶ Demak   62C2

Demak was once the capital of Java's first Islamic sultanate, this reaching its apogee during the 16th century before power moved south to the Mataram kingdom. It has lost its port status due to silting of the coast and today lies inland, 25km east of Semarang in Central Java, but none the less remains an important pilgrimage destination. The **Mesjid Agung▶▶**, which dominates Demak's central square, is Java's oldest mosque and dates from 1478. It is said to have been founded by the nine *walis* (saints) who first brought the Muslim faith to Java. As such it draws throngs of devotees and has encouraged rows of souvenir stands to set up outside the walls. The mosque itself is made entirely of wood, with four central teak pillars (reputedly constructed by four of the *walis*) supporting a typical tiered roof.

Triad of cultures
One of the most curious exhibits at Cirebon's Kraton Kasepuhan is an ornately carved wooden carriage, designed to symbolise Java's three main spiritual influences of Buddhism (the dragon body), Hinduism (an elephant's trunk grasping a trident) and Islam (the mobile wings).

Cirebon wedding

Volcanic eruptions

■ **In a land where an active volcano is rarely far away, the threat of eruption has governed people's lives for centuries. Thousands of victims have perished under layers of volcanic ash, but the seats of ancient gods and ancestral spirits still seem unappeased.....■**

Divine punishment?
Every century Bali's most spectacular festival is held at Besakih, the mother-temple on Mount Agung's slopes. During the last celebration, in 1963, however, Agung erupted dramatically. Was this divine punishment? It was interpreted as such by the Balinese, who redoubled their offerings to avert further devastation. When Agung started rumbling ominously again in 1984, even President Suharto rushed to participate in a ceremony in which 80 animals were sacrificed.

Top: Mt Bromo, Java
Below: Krakatau
erupting in 1883

Indonesia has the densest concentration of volcanic activity in the world. Some 110 volcanic centres (containing a total of 132 active volcanoes) unleash an eruption on average every three years, while earthquakes and tidal waves have proven equally unmerciful. The 5,000km volcanic chain sweeps down Sumatra's west coast, cuts across Java, continues through Nusa Tenggara, and then curves up through Maluku and past Sulawesi to the Philippines, creating a succession of dramatic landscapes, crater lakes and perfect smoking cones. Off-balancing the loss of human life, the volcanic ash has created some of the most fertile tracts of land on this planet.

Record-breakers During the past two centuries two of Indonesia's 'big bangs' have set world records. When Gunung Tambora (on the island of Sumbawa – see panel on page 189) erupted in 1815, it left 12,000 immediate fatalities, a further 40,000 people dying in the ensuing famine. Three days of darkness followed the disaster, brilliant orange sunsets painted the skies of the world and northern hemisphere temperatures dropped to such an extent that 1816 popularly became known as the 'year without a summer'.

In 1883, the notorious Krakatau (located between Java and Sumatra – see page 73), blew itself out of the sea, hurling an estimated 8.5 cu km of debris into the stratosphere. It was the loudest explosion ever recorded on Earth, and was heard from Sri Lanka to Perth – although Tambora is said to have released 50 times more energy. The follow-up 40m-high tidal wave killed 36,000 people, devastated most of the adjoining coastlines and swept huge blocks of coral several kilometres inland. And 45 years later Krakatau gave birth – to Anak Krakatau. This baby volcano has been growling steadily ever since, regularly giving vent to its fury by emitting showers of molten lava, ash and smoke.

Living memory Such earth-shattering fireworks displays have also taken place within living memory. Volatile Merapi, which towers over Java's famed Buddhist temple of Borobudur, has a deadly track record, engulfing several hundred villages in 1954 and again in 1973, 1979, 1984 and 1994; today, it continues to threaten major future action. Bali saw its holy mountain, Agung, explode in 1963 to leave behind a calamitous 1,600 victims, while Java's highest peak, Semeru (3,676m), erupted in 1978 and 1979. Earthquakes and resultant tidal waves wiped out northeastern Flores in December 1992 (over 2,000 were killed), as well as an area covering the coasts of East Java and western Bali in June 1994 (some 250 people

died). In February 1994 Sumatra's southernmost province of Lampung was hit by an earthquake measuring 6.5 on the Richter scale, the disaster killing nearly 150 people.

Gods or tectonic plates? When two tectonic plates of the Earth's rigid surface collide, the result is either a violent volcanic eruption or a powerful earthquake. Yet for the deeply mystical Indonesians, their ring of fire is a consequence of the wrath of the gods. Volcanoes played an essential role in ancient Javanese cosmology, and the island's summits were believed to be the seats of gods and ancestral spirits. Krakatau's eruption was put down to its spirit, Orang Atjeh, who was offended by pirates raping and abducting women from the island shores.

The fire god of Bromo, in East Java (see page 73), still holds powerful sway over the local Hindu Tenggerese inhabitants. An annual ceremony brings thousands of them in a pre-dawn torchlit procession to the crater edge, from where they throw fruit, flowers, money and even chickens into the sulphurous depths. Other Javanese volcanoes have even seen voluntary human sacrifices, while Bali's Agung, Lombok's Rinjani, Ternate's Gamalama and Banda's Api all have powerful, fiery souls. Western science is still not capable of predicting seismic activity, so the act of making offerings can hardly be considered *de trop*.

The tidal wave after the 1883 Krakatau eruption was so massive that it beached this steamer in the jungle

Degree of restlessness
'Every volcano in Java has its own legends, firmly believed in by every native. Of the terrible Gunung Kloet, for instance, they say that there sleeps beneath the triple craters a giant prince with the head of a buffalo, and that whenever he stirs or turns over in his sleep there is an eruption, serious or slight according to the degree of his restlessness. But if ever it should happen that he wakes up completely and rises from his hard couch, then the whole of Java and its people will be overwhelmed in a disaster a thousand times more terrible even than the eruption of Krakatau.'
– From *Javanese Panorama* by HW Ponder (1942).

A devastating scene in Maumere, Flores, three days after the 1992 tidal wave

Candi Bima is stylistically unique among Dieng's temples as it lacks a plinth

Dieng magically blends rural scenes such as this with crater lakes and ancient Hindu temples

▶ ▶ ▶ **Dieng Plateau**   62C1

With a Sanskrit name meaning 'Domain of the Gods', Dieng has a lot to prove. This scenic plateau is home to Java's oldest Hindu temples (7th to 8th centuries), of which only eight remain from an estimated 400, all dedicated to the god Siva. However, Dieng Plateau holds more of interest than mere ruins. It lies at an altitude of 2,000m in a saucer rimmed by volcanoes and offers spectacular walks to sulphurous lakes, steaming craters and peaks perfectly angled for both sunrise and sunset.

Access to this region is usually from Yogyakarta, 137km southeast, or from Pekalongan or Semarang to the north. The nearest town with decent facilities is Wonosobo, 26km south of Dieng along a slow, vertiginous road which winds through picturesque terraced slopes. Hardy souls should consider staying in Dieng itself to profit from the clear early morning light before the inevitable rains and mists move in – but remember that nights are cold and hot water unheard of up here.

Temples Six of the remaining *candis* (temples) are clustered in the marshy fields in front of the village and can be reached along paths that lead from the north or from the west. Although lost in the scale of the plateau and architecturally unremarkable, they nevertheless represent the heart of what was once a holy city which flourished until the 12th century, before being abandoned like Borobudur (see pages 70–1).

Each of the small stone shrines has a particular decoration, but most striking is **Candi Bima**▶▶, a lone temple situated about 1km south along the road from the museum. Its pyramidal tower and niches carved with heads show close links with temples from the Indian state of Orissa, although they are constructed on a far smaller scale. The small museum houses diverse sculptures found all over the plateau. Another isolated but unimpressive temple, **Candi Dvaravati**, lies a short distance up a path leading off the main road in the village.

Crater lakes Dieng's thermal strength is such that a geothermal station has been built to tap the energy of the hot geysers and mud-pools of **Kawah Sikidang** crater, which is situated about 1km from Candi Bima. A short distance from here lies one of Dieng's most beautiful sights, **Telaga Warna** ('Lake of Many Colours'). The lake is rich in

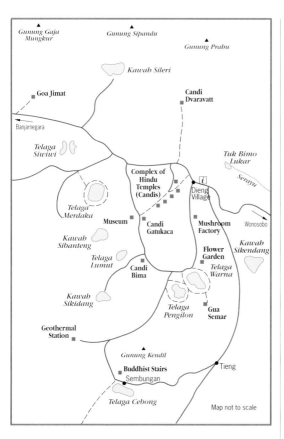

Map not to scale

Gunung Gaja Mungkur

Gunung Sipandu

Gunung Prabu

Kawah Sileri

Goa Jimat

Candi Dvaravatt

Banjarnegara

Telaga Siwiwi

Tuk Bimo Lukar

Serayu

Complex of Hindu Temples (Candis)

Dieng Village

Telaga Merdaka

Museum

Candi Gatukaca

Mushroom Factory

Wonosobo

Kawah Sibanteng

Flower Garden

Kawah Sikendang

Telaga Lumut

Candi Bima

Telaga Warna

Kawah Sikidang

Telaga Pengilon

Gua Semar

Geothermal Station

Gunung Kendil

Buddhist Stairs

Tieng

Sembungan

Telaga Cebong

79

minerals and edged by mud-pools, its hues running the gamut of greens and blues, these changing with the weather. A path leads around the lake to **Gua Semar**, a cave apparently even used by Suharto for meditation.

Other sights in this southern part of Dieng include a Japanese-owned mushroom factory, a brilliantly coloured flower garden and the 2,600m peak of **Sembungan**, a favourite summit from which to watch the sunrise. The village here is Java's highest, and its ruddy-complexioned inhabitants live in notably primitive conditions.

Deep within
'The mysticism of concrete things on that island of mystery called Java...Down in its soul it had never been conquered, though smiling in proud contemptuous resignation and bowing submissively before its fate. Deep in its soul...it lived in freedom its own mysterious life, hidden from Western eyes, however much these might seek to fathom the secret – as though with a philosophic intention of maintaining before all a proud and smiling tranquillity, pliantly yielding and to all appearances courteously approaching – but deep within itself divinely certain of its own views...'
– From *The Hidden Force* by Louis Couperus (1900).

Heading northwest
Longer hikes to the northwest of the plateau lead through immaculately cultivated fields to Dieng's own Death Valley, or Goa Jimat, which lies beyond the bubbling crater of Kawah Sileri. Sunset is particularly spectacular when viewed from Mount Sipandu, one of five peaks to the north.

Geysers provide a useful energy source

The beautiful site of Gedung Songo was considered sacred for its volcanic slope and the sulphur springs at its base

Siva
Three gods dominate the seemingly endless Hindu pantheon: Brahma (the creator), Vishnu (the preserver) and Siva (the destroyer and reproducer). All three are often depicted with four arms, and each is associated with an animal 'vehicle' upon which he rides. At Gedung Songo and at Dieng the *candis* are dedicated to Siva (also spelt Civa or Shiva), possibly because of the volatile and destructive nature of this volcanic region. Siva rides on the back of a bull, the goddess of the Ganges in his hair, with a third eye on his forehead and carrying a trident. Another incarnation of Siva is as Nataraja, the cosmic dancer who created the world.

▶▶   **Garut**   62B1

Garut lies 65km southeast of Bandung and makes a scenic stop-off on the main road east, although hard-bitten hikers should stay longer. The region is rich in lakes and hot springs (the most popular is Tarogong, 5km to the north), but above all it is the mountain peaks that beckon. **Papandayan** (2,622m), **Telagabodas** (2,201m) and **Galunggung** (2,168m) tower above Garut in active splendour. Papandayan was born in 1772 in a volcanic explosion that killed over 3,000 people, while Galunggung's eruption in 1982 projected rocks so high that a passing Boeing 747 was hit and forced to make an emergency landing. Garut also claims the first Hindu temple to be discovered in West Java, the 8th-century **Candi Cangkuang**▶▶ which, although very simple in design, is stunningly sited on a lake about 15km north of town.

▶▶   **Gedung Songo**   62C2

Gedung Songo ('Nine Buildings') is composed of nine small temple complexes scattered over the slopes of Mount Ungaran, and is located 3km from Bandungan, itself 33km south of Semarang. These little-visited Hindu temples are not the easiest to reach, but their spectacular mountainside location overlooking a fertile plain and bubbling sulphur springs is one of the most inspiring in Java. Even Mount Merapi and Mount Merabu are visible through the transient mists. All the temples are believed to have been built between the 8th and 9th centuries, and all are dedicated to Siva, god of destruction. They vary greatly in their state of preservation; group 3 has been particularly well restored, and group 6 displays an interesting stepped pyramidal roof. Horses can be hired to tour the ruins, but avoid visiting at weekends as this is a favourite time with locals.

▶   **Gunung Semeru**   63D1

This is Java's highest peak (3,676m), an active volcano also called Mahameru and forming part of the Bromo Tengger massif (see page 72) in East Java. For those content merely to gaze at this giant cone (which has been spouting columns of dust and ash since 1940), the best viewpoint is from Piket Nol, to the east of Lumajang. Climbers aiming for the top usually start from the lakeside village of **Ranu Pane**, already at 2,200m and accessible by bus and *bemo* (minibus) from Malang via Tumpang and from Gubug Klakah.

If you leave Ranu Pane at dawn you can spend the following night at the crater lake of Ranu Kumbolo before starting on the final leg to the summit. It is a hard hike, best undertaken outside the rainy season (May to October) but the vast panoramas and varied landscapes easily make up for this.

▶ **Jepara** 62C2

This small town in northeast Java is famed for one thing: traditional woodcarving. Jepara was a major trading port in the 14th century, and was therefore influenced by numerous cultures – from Indian to Cambodian and Chinese – all of which permeated local carving styles. As Islam discouraged the representation of humans or animals, Jepara's craftsmen were forced to develop a highly stylised form. Entire houses, huge panels and doors, chests, chairs and chess sets are intricately carved with floral motifs, scroll patterns, carved *nagas* (sacred snakes), vines and leaves. Hundreds of workshops line the access road to Jepara from Kudus, while many villagers sell equally impressive examples of this craft from their houses.

▶▶ **Kaduketug** 62A2

The territory of the Baduy, Java's last 'primitive' ethnic group, lies 25km south of Rangkasbitung in West Java. Operating a reverse attitude to 'progress', the Baduy have firmly opted out of the 20th century and refuse any of technology's offerings. In 1985 Suharto promised to maintain their desired isolation from the outside world and gave them, as a symbolic gesture, 500 concrete markers to outline their territory. The village of Kaduketug is the only Baduy village outsiders can enter; beyond it lies a completely closed and self-sufficient community. A permit must be obtained in Rangkasbitung at the Kantor Sosial Politik Kabupaten to enter Kaduketug; note that this can take up to a week to process.

Black and white Baduy
The 10,000 or so Baduy are divided into two groups: the Baduy luar (black Baduy) and the Baduy dalam (white Baduy). Some 40 hamlets of the former protect three villages of the inaccessible inner group. The black Baduy, usually dressed in black with navy blue turbans, practise slash and burn cultivation, growing rice and fruits such as pineapples and durians. The white Baduy have a priestly role related to their animist beliefs and the sacred area of *Domas*, which lies in the forest at the source of the river Ciujung. Their priests, or *puun*, are said to possess supernatural powers.

81

Jepara's wood-carving trade was revived in the late 19th century at the initiative of the teenage daughter of the local regent

Djarum clove cigarettes (kretek)

Alternative ferry
The most obvious access to Madura is by the 24-hour Surabaya ferry, but another daily service could help to avoid back-tracking. The picturesque port of Kalianget, at the far eastern end of Madura, offers a daily service to Situbondo, convenient for visiting Bromo or making the Bali connection at Banyuwangi. The ferry leaves at 7am and takes 7 hours.

Traditional wedding costume of east Madura

▶▶ **Kawah Ijen** 63E1

The Ijen Plateau extends over much of the rocky mountainous region northwest of Banyuwangi in the eastern corner of Java. The crater (*kawah*) lies at 2,300m and forms a twin volcano with the now extinct Mount Merapi. At its heart is a steaming, sulphurous lake of a milky green hue, rich in minerals and occasionally spouting furious jets of acid. More astonishing even than the sight of this jade-green inferno is that of locals far down at the crater's edge collecting blocks of sulphur (loads can reach 70kg), which they then carry laboriously up to the crater rim and down the mountain to a factory.

Kawah Ijen's difficult access preserves it from the crowds. The easiest approach is from the east via Bondowoso, Sempol and Wonosari; from Banyuwangi take a *bemo* (minibus) to Jambu, from where it is a 5- to 6-hour, 21km walk to the crater.

▶ **Kudus** 62C2

The fact that Kudus was founded by a Muslim saint has put it on a par with nearby Demak (see page 75) as a pilgrimage destination. Crowning this devotion is the **Mesjid Al-Manar**▶▶ (1546), a mosque that incorporates both Hindu-Javanese and Islamic architectural features. The lofty red minaret can be climbed for sweeping views of the old town, whose narrow, winding streets of whitewashed and carved houses give an impression of the Middle East, this further strengthened by the orthodox inhabitants (women are heavily veiled and men wear topis). This is the only Javanese town to have kept an Arabic name (Al-Quds means 'holy'), and is also known for its role in the *kretek* (clove cigarette) industry. The national addiction to this cigarette is fuelled by several major manufacturers in Java, of which the Chinese-owned Djarum brand controls about 25 per cent of the market. The Djarum factory is situated in the new town east of the River Serang and can be visited.

▶▶ **Madura** 63E2

The 5,000 sq km island of Madura is easily accessible from Surabaya, 30 minutes by ferry across the narrow strait. It is renowned for its bull-races, which take place from August to October (see panel), but also offers a unique history, some good beaches and a beautiful rural setting. The island's 3 million inhabitants, mostly cattle-breeders, farmers and fishermen, are devout Muslims. Although reputed by the Javanese to be aggressive, the Madurese are in fact an exceptionally friendly race and only too pleased to see the occasional tourist taking time to visit their island.

History Madura was initially governed by several royal houses before being incorporated forcefully into Sultan Agung's powerful Mataram kingdom in 1624. Sporadic rebellions continued over the years, even after Madura had been ceded to the Dutch in the early 18th century, and thus the Madurese earned their bellicose reputation. By the late 19th century the power of the four ruling *bupati* (regency mayors) had become purely symbolic.

Island sights The most rewarding way to explore Madura is by car (see pages 84–5), although frequent buses connect Surabaya with the main towns of the south coast where most of the population is concentrated, as well as the beaches of the north coast. Reasonable accommodation is available in Bangkalan, Camplong, Pamekasan and **Sumenep**, the latter making an ideal base. This peaceful provincial town harbours a magnificent yellow and white 18th-century mosque, the **Mesjid Jamik►►►**, which dominates the main square. Beyond the square lie an old *kraton* (palace) and taman sari (pleasure garden), fronted by a small **museum** housed in an old carriage-house. Exhibits include a 300-year-old Chinese bed and examples of Madurese carved wooden furniture.

On a hilltop outside town is **Asta Tinggi►►**, the elaborately conceived royal cemetery. Stretching northeast of Sumenep around the point is a string of fishing villages interspersed with fine, white, sandy beaches: Lombeng and Salopeng are particularly beautiful and often deserted, although at Lombeng Madurese continue a curious tradition of sleeping while buried in the sand.

Kerapan sapi
Bull-racing (*kerapan sapi*) has been a Madurese tradition since the 16th century, when it evolved among farmers. Breeding stud bulls soon became big business and today's bull is unique to the island. The local bulls are descended from wild *banteng* cattle, and are hardier than water-buffalo and far more powerful than their doe-eyed appearance suggests.

Preliminary heats start in August, the bulls decked out in fantastically decorative tack and even shaded from the sun with ceremonial parasols. Racing takes place in pairs, the bulls joined by a carved wooden yoke and the jockey perched precariously on a sled behind. Speeds of up to 50kph have been recorded, and illicit bets intensify the tension.

The 18th-century Mesjid Jamik at Sumenep, Madura

Drive Madura

The island of Madura is rarely visited by tourists outside the bull-racing season (August to October), yet it also offers rural activities, fishing villages, superb beaches and relics from a rich royal past. This drive can be done in a long day but merits two.

From the port of Kamal drive north to the small town of **Bangkalan**, whose main grassy square is dominated by a graceful white mosque, the Mesjid Agung, and main street by gold shops. This is a major destination during the bull-racing season, but otherwise the town holds little of interest. From here the main road veers southeast through corn and paddy-fields punctuated by coconut palms and huge clumps of bamboo. Traditional kampungs of stilt-houses with peaked tiled roofs emerge from often idyllic pastoral land-scapes, where buffalo-ploughs and cow-hides stretched out to dry in the sun remind you of Madura's *raison d'être* – bulls. Stop at the town of **Blega**, 38km from Bangkalan, to visit the large and colourful market fronted by armies of *becaks* (trishaws) and *dokars* (horse-drawn carriages).

Keep on the main Pamekasan road as it hits the coast near the beach of Camplong, and drive through the fishing village of **Bandaran**, squeezed between the road and the sea where hundreds of brightly painted boats and outriggers are moored. Mangroves also line the shore until, 52km beyond Blega, the road reaches **Pamekasan**. This neat town, with its

The fishing fleet prepares to leave

stop as you can watch the carvers at work. **Sumenep** itself has several historic attractions (see page 83), as well as a sleepy provincial charm that is reflected in its shady streets lined with whitewashed houses sporting yellow or green shutters. Beach-lovers should continue east to Jurangan, the closest point to **Lombeng**, where casuarina trees edge a long stretch of white sand. Close by, at Legung Pasir, is the village of sand-sleepers (see page 83). An alternative is to head 20km north to the pretty village of **Ambunten** where the architecture has been strongly influenced by Chinese settlers. Here, too, is the superb beach of **Slopeng**, with its rolling dunes and lofty palm trees.

The road running along the arid north coast is less frequented than the southern route and takes you through several small fishing villages before you arrive at **Tanjungbumi**. This, together with Ambunten, is the main centre of Madurese boat-building and is also the hub of local batik-making. Another beautiful beach, Pantai Siring Kemuning, lies outside the village. After passing Klampis in the island's northwestern corner, the road veers south to Arosbaya and, a few kilometres further south, passes a turning that leads inland to **Air Mata**. This terraced royal cemetery stands in a superb location overlooking the river valley and it is worth negotiating the rough access road to reach it. From Arosbaya it is about 30km back to the port of Kamal.

85

tree-lined streets, is Madura's administrative centre. From here the road passes endless palm groves, fields and salt-flats, while the outlying islands of Pulau Raja and Genteng gradually come into view.

Before you reach Sumenep you will drive through the village of **Kardulur**, a major woodcarving centre worth a

Beaches
The drama of East Javanese landscapes and their ruins may inspire a break for the coast. Three beaches offer respite: Balekambang, known locally for its Hindu sea festival held at Javanese New Year; Ngliyep, a magnificent rocky beach which sees Malang inhabitants offering a goat's head to the waves during an annual ceremony; and Sendang Biru. The latter offers the best beaches – opposite is the island of Sempu, accessible on foot at low tide or by hired boat at other times, which has a superb, sheltered stretch of white sand.

Ears need to be finely tuned at Malang's Pasar Burung

►► Malang
63D1

This former Dutch hill-station, situated at a cool altitude and rimmed by volcanic peaks, makes a pleasant base for exploring a wealth of historic and natural sights in the surrounding hills and plain. Malang lies at the heart of numerous 13th-century Singosari ruins, and is located immediately west of Bromo Tengger Semeru National Park and 50km or so north of some reasonable beaches. Accommodation here is of a high standard and, despite its lack of monuments, this burgeoning university city of over 600,000 inhabitants has plenty of character.

City sights The Brantas river that meanders peacefully through the centre of Malang divides the northern residential district neatly from the lively southern commercial district. **Jalan Tugu**, a generous grassy roundabout edged with centennial mahogany trees, is the colonial heart of the northern part of the city. To the east of Jalan Tugu lies the art deco railway station, and on its southern side is the elegant **Balai Kota (Town Hall)**. From here, Jalan Tumapel winds down through a night-market area to the riverbank, home to the enormous and melodious **Pasar Burung (Bird Market)**►► and the adjoining **Pasar Bunga (Flower Market)**.

Across the river, Jalan Basuki Rakhmat offers banks, travel agents, restaurants and textile shops, as well as the odd ancient wood-panelled tobacconist or shoe shop. This road leads south to Malang's main social hub, the *alun-alun* (town square), where most of the population seems to gather every evening. A few metres from the graceful old mosque stands an overrated colonial hangover, the **Toko Oen**, once a gastronomic haunt for Dutch coffee- and tobacco-growers but devoid of character (apart from the pre-war furniture and fittings) since it was targeted by local business interests.

Immediately south, on Jalan Pasar Besar, lies the gigantic central market and its commercial satellites. At the end

A Kala monster on Candi Kidal represents Devouring Time

Ever upwards
Malang's surroundings also harbour some relaxing hill-resorts. Some 15km to the northwest, on the slopes of legendary Mount Arjuno, lies Batu. It is at the centre of an orchard region famed for its apples and is a favourite weekend retreat. The temple of Songgoriti stands by hot springs just outside town, while the pool at Sengkaling offers a relaxed, landscaped setting. The source of the Brantas river (which flows down to Malang) lies above Batu beyond the smaller hill-resort of Selekta. To the west of Malang looms one of Java's sacred mountains, Gunung Kawi, site of a revered royal tomb which attracts streams of Indonesian pilgrims.

87

of this street stands the symbol of Malang's large Chinese community, the **Eng Ang Kiong Temple▶**. Tiled courtyards, a sweeping roof, ornate murals, pillars writhing with dragons and numerous altars all create a colourful and striking setting.

Singosari temples Part Buddhist, part Hindu, these finely tapered stone shrines consist of large, square platforms surmounted by one or more 'cells', originally topped by a pointed, pagoda-style roof. Today's remaining temples vary considerably in their state of conservation or restoration but all date from the 13th century. Two particularly interesting examples stand 18km east of Malang near the village of Tumpang.

Candi Jago▶ was dedicated to the third Singosari king, Visnuwardhana, the only ruler of this dynasty not to suffer a violent death. Although very dilapidated, it shelters an eight-armed (though headless) statue of a deity and finely carved bas-reliefs of the *Mahabharata* epic are still visible. A few kilometres from Tumpang, in the village of Rejokidal, stands the superb and atmospheric ruin of **Candi Kidal▶▶**, built as a memorial to the second Singosari king, Anusapati. The elaborately carved central cell is mounted on a massive moulded plinth replete with bas-reliefs of *garudas* (mythical eagles), and is surmounted by a huge pyramidal tower, today sprouting abundant vegetation.

Candi Singosari▶▶, 10km north of Malang in the village of the same name, is thought to be the burial site of the last Singosari king. Now well restored, it is a good example of a four-celled temple, each cell fronted by a goggle-eyed *kala* (demon) head. Only one statue remains inside – a bearded and turbanned representation of Siva as Agastya. The neat grass compound displays other fragmented artefacts from the temple, including two massive *dvarapala*, the monstrous temple guardians.

Garden break A day-trip around the Singosari temples can easily take in **Kebun Raya Purwodadi (Botanical Gardens)▶▶**, a few kilometres north of the villages of Singosari and Lawang. Entrance from the main road is through a huge stone gateway dramatically backed by the Bromo Tengger massif, often shrouded in cloud. These beautiful gardens are home to a collection of rare xerophytes (dry climate plants) and a waterfall.

The mid-13th-century Candi Kidal, one of the Singosari group near Malang

Of tigers and turtles

Two centuries ago most of Java was inhabited by Javanese tigers (*Panthera tigris sondaica*). However, merciless hunting in the 19th century took its toll and by World War II the tiger survived only in the most remote forested regions of Java's south coast. Since then the Indonesian government and the World Wide Fund for Nature have tried to ensure that at least a handful of survivors are protected.

Turtles are doing somewhat better. Full-moon nights at certain times of the year bring these creatures out of the sea to bury their scores of eggs deep in the sand of Sukamade Beach. The eggs are collected and reburied in hatcheries, safe from the acquisitive paws of leopards and poachers.

Crossing the river in the Meri Betiri reserve

▶▶ Meru Betiri 63E1

This 50,000-hectare reserve lies southeast of Bromo Tengger Semeru National Park on the south coast of Java's eastern tip. From the main road linking Jember with Banyuwangi, a rough and very pot-holed 60km side-road (often flooded by rivers during the rainy season) winds painfully through rubber, coffee and cocoa plantations and dense jungle to end finally at Rajegwesi Bay, site of a rest-house. Coffee plantations occupy much of the surrounding low land while thick forest covers the higher parts, these terminating in precipitous headlands.

At Sukamade Beach there is a large turtle hatchery where four species of turtles come ashore to lay their eggs – over 2,500 have been tagged since the beach became a protected area in 1972. Meru Betiri is, however, known above all as the final refuge of the nearly extinct Javanese tiger. If you don't spot one of the estimated four or five that remain, you may see a black panther or leopard, or even a rare *Rafflesia* flower.

▶ Mojokerto 63D2

The town of Mojokerto (situated 42km southwest of Surabaya) is really only of interest as a stop-over on the way to the Majapahit ruins of Trowulan (see pages 102–3). It has a few relics dating from the Dutch era, the most obvious being the canals and red-tiled roofs of the old houses, as well as a good archaeological museum on Jalan Yani, the **Museum Purbakala▶**. Some fine Majapahit pieces include statues and bas-reliefs from Trowulan, dominated by a superb statue of Vishnu astride the *garuda* eagle. The main commercial street of Mojokerto is appropriately named Jalan Majapahit; this is where you will find restaurants, shops, a night market and, in the side-streets, the odd hotel or guest-house (see Hotels and Restaurants, page 273).

▶▶ Panataran

This is the largest of East Java's temple complexes and the only one which approaches the scale of Central Java's Prambanan, its courtyard design a forerunner of later Balinese temples. The site is located 10km north of Blitar on the lower slopes of Mount Kelud, and is now recognised as having been the state temple of the Majapahit Dynasty. Stone inscriptions from the site indicate that it lasted from the late 12th century to the mid-15th century, but most of the surviving buildings were constructed during Majapahit's golden era under the reign of King Hayam Wuruk (14th century). Although modest in size, Panataran has been well restored and sits in a pretty rural area.

Temples The asymmetrical lay-out consists of three gently terraced courtyards surrounded by a wall, with steps at the back leading down to a small bathing-pool. At the entrance are two huge *dvarapala* (temple guardians), behind which stands a large platform carved with fine bas-reliefs. This is all that remains of the meeting-halls and is backed by a small restored *candi*. The date over its entrance (1291) has led to its name – the **Dated Temple**.

The next level contains the superb **Naga Temple** which, although roofless, displays nine remarkably carved female figures holding up the undulating form of a *naga* (sacred snake) which twists around the *candi*. In the final courtyard stands Panataran's most impressive structure and **principal shrine**, which looks east across fields towards the mountains, home to the gods. All that remains of this monument to Siva are three superimposed terraces, their base carved with superb bas-reliefs illustrating the *Ramayana*. If you climb to the top you will see an astonishing frieze depicting alternating *garudas* (eagles) and lions, while the intermediary terrace is carved with high-reliefs of the Krishna stories.

Behind this structure, which is surrounded by the remains of four smaller shrines, is a path leading down to the king's *mandi*. The pool is lined with stone and rather crudely carved with lizards, bulls and dragons.

The main shrine of Panataran, once the state temple of the Majapahit Dynasty

Big game and surf
More animal sightings can be made at the extreme southeastern tip of Java in the Banyuwangi Selatan Reserve, also known as Blambangan. This remote peninsula is best reached by bus from Banyuwangi to Grajagan, then by boat to Plengkung. The long, white beach of Plengkung is considered one of the world's best for surfing, and basic beach-huts serve the needs of an international band of big-wave enthusiasts. Turtles also favour this coast, while inside the reserve there are plenty of leaf-monkeys, *rusa* deer, leopards, wild pigs and *ajak*, a rare Indonesian species of wild dog. For more information about this reserve and Meru Betiri, contact the Perlindungan Hutan dan Pelestanan Alam (PHPA, or Directorate General of Forest Protection and Nature Conservation) office in Banyuwangi (tel: 0333 41118).

A quiet moment at Pangandaran's warungs

Cilacap backwaters
Visitors travelling from Pangandaran to Yogyakarta (or vice versa) can enjoy a relaxing alternative to the lengthy overland bus trip. A peaceful 4-hour boat ride covers part of the distance, winding through mangroves and stopping at lagoon villages between Kalipucang and the busy port of Cilacap to load and unload. Usually packed to the gunwales, the boat offers plenty of distractions and, above all, delicious snacks which are hawked by locals. There are four morning departures in both directions, but it is far easier to buy a combined bus–boat–bus ticket from agencies in Pangandaran or Yogyakarta, this ensuring immediate connections at either end. It is also possible to travel directly to Wonosobo (for Dieng) instead of Yogya. The entire trip takes a full day.

▶▶ **Pangandaran** *62B1*

Java's second beach resort is located 88km southeast of Bandung on a narrow isthmus which terminates in a nature reserve. The low-key development is mostly aimed at slim wallets, the wide palm-lined beaches are extensive enough never to be really crowded and local fishermen ensure endless supplies of fresh seafood. Pangandaran is only a day's journey from Yogyakarta and so offers a pleasant break from city-touring, although on public holidays it gets very crowded.

Three parallel roads run south down the peninsula with the main cluster of accommodation situated along the west beach. Restaurants, souvenir stalls, bike-rental shops and coconut palms monopolise this stretch while a short walk away the quieter east beach favours fishing boats and a fish market. A helpful tourist office located at Jalan Kidang Pananjung 201 offers an imaginative range of nature tours in the region.

Pangandaran ends at the **Pananjung Reserve**▶▶, a headland of tropical jungle inhabited by barking deer, wild oxen, monkeys, iguanas, flying foxes and countless insects. Secluded sandy coves dot the coast here and offer good snorkelling on the west side. Guides can be hired from the tourist office, but beware of unofficial pretenders who lurk around the park entrance.

▶ **Parangtritis** *62C1*

Parangtritis lies 28km south of Yogyakarta on the Indian Ocean and is the number one weekend beach destination for overheated city-dwellers. The waves and currents here are unwelcomingly strong, sometimes even fatal, and it is much safer to swim in the freshwater pools near the village. Despite these negative factors, Parangtritis's rolling sand-dunes and dramatic cliffs make a striking setting, and walks along the clifftops offer some fabulous views. One path west of town leads down to a cave network which is a favourite for meditation. Parangtritis is also the focus of an annual ceremony in honour of Nyai Loro Kidul (see panel opposite).

▶ **Pekalongan** 62C2

The small coastal town of Pekalongan, lying virtually halfway between Cirebon and Semarang, is famed above all for its batik but otherwise holds little of interest. Jalan Mansyur and Jalan Hayam Wuruk are the main commercial streets where Pekalongan's intricate, pastel-coloured batik designs are sold, although there are plenty of itinerant vendors all over town. A small **Batik Museum** (*open*: Monday to Saturday, 9–1) is located at the intersection of these two streets, while at the village of **Kedungwuni** (9km south of town) visitors can watch work in progress at Oey Soe Tjoen's workshop.

▶ **Pelabuhanratu** 62A1

This picturesque fishing village lies in a horseshoe-shaped bay and is gradually developing into another of Java's Indian Ocean resorts. The much-improved road running due south from Jakarta speeds capital-dwellers to the coast within 3 hours, so avoid visiting the resort at weekends and during public holidays. Some 15km of wide, sandy beaches backed by tropical forest and rocky cliffs offer plenty of opportunities for hiking, while the hundreds of local fishermen, whose boat-lamps twinkle in the bay at night, ensure a copious supply of excellent seafood. The large fish market in the centre of Pelabuhanratu holds both morning and evening auctions – lively and pungent events.

Swimming is dangerous (the sea goddess Nyai Loro Kidul is also very active here), but an alternative soak is offered at the hot springs at **Cisolok**▶▶, 16km or so to the west. The most popular beach is **Pantai Citepus**, a generous sandy expanse ending in paddy-fields and lined with plenty of souvenir stalls and restaurants. Most of the better accommodation is situated on the beach that lies towards Cisolok.

Goddess of the South Seas
The aura of this goddess is such that male swimmers off Java's south coast are advised not to wear green – the goddess's favourite colour – unless they want to risk ending their days in her watery palace.

Reputed to have originally been a West Javanese princess, she was cursed by her father because of her megalomania and told that her kingdom would be limited to the South Seas. Reincarnated as the strikingly beautiful but malevolent Nyai Loro Kidul, she remains a much-respected deity. Pelabuhanratu ('Harbour of the Queen') is said to have been where she leapt into the ocean. Spectacular annual festivals honouring this seductress take place here and at Parangtritis; offerings relegated to the waves range from food to toenail-cuttings, locks of hair, old clothes and flowers.

Taking a ride along the black sands at Parangtritis

JAVA

Buddhist variant
A different type of 9th-century Buddhist shrine is embodied by Candi Sari, located about 3km west of Candi Prambanan. This rectangular, three-storeyed block is surmounted by rows of small stupas, with 'blind' windows flanked with finely carved statues.

▶▶▶ **Prambanan**   62C1

Java's largest temple complex and Indonesia's most extensive Hindu site lies 17km northeast of Yogyakarta on the road to Solo. Spectacular carved pinnacles tower out of the plain, echoed by the sharp peak of volatile Mount Merapi which looms ominously to the north. The entire site has now been extensively landscaped and restored and, like that at Borobudur, includes recreation facilities, a museum and two theatres.

At the heart of the complex and nearest the entrance stands the main group of *candis* (temples), dominated by the 47m-high Candi Siva, while many others lie scattered around the fields in varying states of ruin. Particularly fascinating is Candi Sewu, one of Prambanan's three Buddhist temples and now restored to its original splendour. *Becaks* (trishaws) can easily be hired in the village to visit some of the more distant temples.

History Prambanan's path to glory started in the 8th century with the establishment of the powerful Hindu Mataram Dynasty in the north and the Buddhist Sailendra Dynasty in the south. It is thought that the temple complex and its incorporation of Buddhist and Sivaite elements in both structure and carvings may have resulted from an alliance through marriage of these two dynasties. The colossal temple complex was probably constructed shortly before the kings retreated from Central to East Java in AD930. After being abandoned for centuries, a huge earthquake in the 16th century reduced Prambanan to ruins and exposed it to plundering. Restoration, started under the Dutch, was only completed on the main complex in 1993.

Lara Jonggrang The central temple complex, Lara Jonggrang (named after a princess who, according to legend, was turned to stone for refusing to marry a giant), originally incorporated no fewer than 232 temples. The plan, representing the cosmic mountain as at Borobudur (see pages 70–1), centres on a square court containing the eight principal temples and is dominated by the magnificent, towering Candi Siva. Six diminishing levels lined with stupas (bell-shaped domes) encompass lavishly carved terraces which recount the story of the *Ramayana*, best followed by walking clockwise from the eastern stairway. An inner chamber at the foot of the eastern entrance contains a massive statue of Siva, reincarnated again in the southern chamber as the pot-bellied teacher, Agastya. The western sanctuary contains a striking representation of Ganesh, the elephant god, while Siva's consort, Durga, can be found in the northern sanctuary.

Candi Siva is flanked to the north and south by similar scaled-down versions, dedicated respectively to Vishnu and Brahma, the other two members of the Hindu trinity. *Ramayana* scenes continue on the façades of **Candi Brahma**, while bas-reliefs on **Candi Vishnu** relate the *Mahabharata*

One of the colossal raksasa *demons which protect Candi Sewu from evil spirits*

story of Krishna. Facing these temples are three pavilions, of which the central shrine, Candi Nandi, contains a powerful statue of Siva's bull-emblem.

Impressive Candi Lara Jonggrang

Northern temples To the north of Lara Jonggrang, a path leads across lawns to the prettily designed museum. On display is a large collection of artefacts, statues, ritual platters and ceramics, as well as photos of the restoration process. Paths lead north from here past the less interesting **Candi Lumbung** and **Candi Bubrah** to reach impressive Candi Sewu and, further east, Candi Plaosan.

The Buddhist monument of **Candi Sewu** ('Thousand Temples') was probably built in the late 8th century and originally incorporated 249 temples. Its square central temple displays a unique interior of finely carved niches and is surrounded by a passage leading to four shrines. Four rows of 240 smaller shrines surround the main body, again echoing the cruciform pattern of the Buddhist cosmos. **Candi Plaosan**, also recently restored, is thought to date from the 9th century. It consists of two central chambers surrounded by 116 stupas and 58 smaller shrines, and is renowned for its outstanding Bodhisattva sculptures – some are exhibited in the museum.

Buddhist cosmos
The Buddhist universe consists of a main continent surrounded by seven alternating oceans and seven mountain ranges. At the centre of the main continent stands the sacred Mount Meru, and in the four cardinal directions of the sea lie four islands, one of which (Jambudwipa) is inhabited by humans. Above this hovers the eighth mountain range, Mount Besi ('Iron Mountain'), symbolising the boundary between the cosmos and emptiness. The overall square lay-out is reflected in Buddhist monuments such as Borobudur and Candi Sewu.

Scenes from the Hindu epic, Ramayana, *carved on the terraces of Lara Jonggrang*

■ **Batik is an easily recognisable Javanese craft which has developed from regal origins into a mass-produced cloth. Motifs and colours change according to the region, while quality veers from individual hand-painted pieces to industrial bales of screen-printed viscose.....■**

94

Court dress

Solo's Pasar Klewer is one of Java's best sources of batik as the city itself is known for its textile innovation. Among countless traditional designs, you may come across batik edged with strips of velvet (in black, green, blue, turquoise or pink) and bordered with gold or silver braid, as well as broad lengths of plain material ranging in colour from salmon-pink to vermilion. These cloths are worn by Solonese men as their 'court dress', the stiff border keeping the sarong and shirt firmly in place.

A batik worker using the **cap** *(stamp) method*

Batik is still the preferred cloth for sarongs and *kebayas* (fitted women's blouses) in rural areas; it can be found in every market-place in Indonesia as towering piles of sarong-lengths, or spotted on the backs of women work-ing every paddy-field. Yogyakarta and Solo (Surakarta) are the two main centres of production, each with its own distinctive style, and are closely followed by Cirebon (notable for its Chinese-influenced motifs), Pekalongan (intricate floral motifs) and, to a lesser extent, Madura (coarser designs) and Garut. Although some experts once thought that India or the Middle East were the source of this technique, it is now believed that batik is a purely Javanese creation. It is by no means a static craft, and although traditional designs are still produced there is constant innovation in patterns and colours.

Methods Originally all batik was hand-painted using a *canting*, or small copper ladle with a narrow spout through which hot wax is dribbled on to the cloth. The dried wax produces colour-resistant areas and lines that escape the dyeing process. Several stages of wax-dribbling and dye-ing (producing progressively darker tones) are carried out to achieve the final design, after which all the wax is scraped off and the cloth boiled. If the wax is not applied properly and cracks, dye seeps into the reserved area and creates a marbling effect, seen as a sign of inferior quality although this is also used in some cases as a motif in

itself. Batik (literally meaning 'to dot' in Javanese) produced in this time-consuming way is known as *batik tulis* ('drawing') and is the reserve of women; it is easily recognisable by the irregular, free-hand nature of the motifs and the strong wax odour of the cloth.

In the mid-19th century a new technique known as *cap* ('stamp') was introduced and began to be used by men. Wax is applied using a copper stamp embossed with the desired pattern, so creating a repetitive design and considerably speeding up production. Batik which combines both *tulis* and *cap* techniques is known as *kombinasi*. A third evolution in this craft came in the 1950s when industrialised methods and the use of chemical dyes brought batik cloth from the domain of clothing into household furnishing. This type of cloth can be distinguished from *batik cap* by the fact that the colour is only printed on one side. More recently still, batik has been adopted as a technique for producing one-off 'paintings', rarely as tasteful as the original *tulis* cloths and targeting the tourist market.

Blossoming motifs Batik motifs form a synthesis of neolithic, Hindu-Javanese, Islamic, Dutch, Chinese and Japanese influences, and over 3,000 of them can be classified roughly into geometric designs (*ceplokan*) and non-geometric ones (*semen*). *Ceplokan* motifs include circles, crosses, stars, polygons, diamonds or a diagonal S (traditionally reserved for the sultan and his family), and may also incorporate stylised designs of flowers or fruit.

However, it is the flowing *semen* motifs that blossom as they depict landscapes, plants and animals. This is where the batik painter's imagination breaks loose, as in Cirebon batik, where waves and clouds roll across the cloth, sometimes complemented by mythical figures. The Javanese proverb, 'Those who can't dance, can't make batik' becomes clear, as do the meanings of the titles of the designs: *Melancholic Bird*, *Sad Rain*, *Swimming Under the Crescent Moon* or even *State of Mind of the Virgin Forest*. Colours also vary, from the subtle creams, indigos, ochres and reds which dominate Yogya's formal batik to the browns and umbers of Solo, Pekalongan's pastel palette, and Garut's bold and exuberant tones.

Batik tulis is made with a canting, *a type of wax pen with a bamboo handle and a small copper bowl containing the liquid wax*

Batik courses
Batik courses can be followed in Yogya or Solo where private workshops and institutes cater for foreign adepts. The Batik Research Centre (Balai Penelitian Kerajinan dan Batik) at Jalan Kusumanegara 2 in Yogya organises month-long courses and will also advise on reliable teachers for shorter, private courses. Solo offers a more limited range but fewer sharks – enquire at the tourist office for information.

The invention of the copper stamp revolutionised the batik industry and broke women's monopoly of it

63D2

Local transport
Surabaya is actually quite easy to get around. *Becaks* (trishaws) and metered taxis are plentiful and Bus 1 links Jalan J B Rachmad in the centre to the port in the north. Bus 2 runs along Jalan Sudirman, connecting the zoo, museum and southern bus station at Joyoboyo with the centre. Two daily express trains connect Surabaya with Jakarta, while two others go to Banyuwangi, the port for boats to Bali. There are three railway stations – Gubeng (centre), Pasar Turi (west) and Semut or Kota (north).

Island escape
If you are looking to escape to a very remote coral island, head 16km north of the city to the ugly industrial satellite town of Gresik, where a new jetfoil service crosses to Pulau Bawean on Wednesday and Saturday at 9am. The 2-hour crossing spirits visitors to an idyllic beach and island lake where basic accommodation is available.

Surabaya's Kalimas harbour has barely changed in its 600 years of existence

▶▶ Surabaya

The burgeoning city and port of Surabaya sits on Java's northwestern coast opposite the island of Madura. Although hardly a peaceful holiday retreat, it does make an interesting stop-over for a couple of days. All the highs (skyscrapers) and lows (beggars) of Jakarta are found here without the capital city's daunting scale.

Surabaya's dynamism dates from the days of the Majapahit kingdom, when the Kalimas river, a branch of the 300km Brantas river, was the trading lifeline. Despite the growth of big business, the port still plays an active role in East Java's economy.

Orientation The interest of Surabaya is concentrated at the heart of its immense sprawl, bordered by the zoo and museum to the south and the harbour to the north. Halfway between the two, around Jalan Pemuda, lies a buzzing commercial district where hotels, shopping centres, banks, markets and *warungs* (food-stalls) cater for most needs. To the north lies a mixture of crumbling art deco colonial buildings, Javanese-style administrative buildings, riverside shacks, a Chinese quarter and a fascinating Arab quarter.

City sights The Kebun Binatang (Zoo)▶ is said to be the most complete in Southeast Asia (*open*: daily, 7–6), with a vast crowd of panthers, Komodo dragons, snakes and even orang-utans, mostly housed in open enclosures. Immediately opposite on Jalan Raya Diponegoro is the **MPU Tantular Museum**▶ (*open*: Tuesday to Thursday, 8–2; Friday, 8–11; Saturday and Sunday, 8–1), with a small display of ethnographic and archaeological artefacts. Further north, along Jalan Sudirman and beside the river, is a lively market area which includes a flower market.

At the western end of Jalan Pemuda stands the stately residence of the governor of East Java, once that of the Dutch governor. Close by, in a shady enclosure under a holy *waringin* (banyan) tree, is a 14th-century statue, **Joko Dolog**▶▶, brought by the Dutch from Trowulan to Surabaya. It has an awkward, short-necked body and was created as a memorial to the last Singosari king.

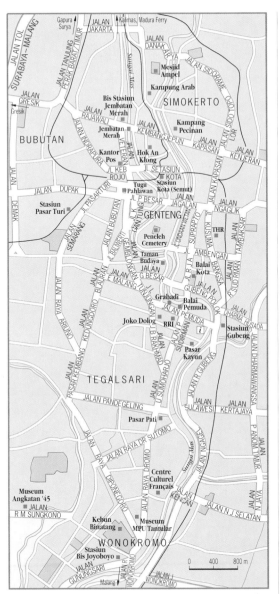

One of Surabaya's wide-ranging gastronomic offerings

To the harbour Kampung Arab▶▶▶, best reached along Jalan Sasak, is an old quarter of narrow lanes with a market offering a temporary trip to an Arab kasbah – wailing music, korans, prayer-mats and glittery bangles create a unique atmosphere. Nearby **Mesjid Ampel** is East Java's oldest mosque and contains the tomb of one of the nine original *walis* (Muslim saints).

Surabaya's traditional dock, **Kalimas▶▶**, lies on the east side of the port. Scores of majestic Bugis schooners (*pinisi*) are moored at the wharf, which is also where the Madura ferry docks. The west side of the port, the **Gapura Surya**, is for large ocean-going vessels.

Heroes' monument
Surabaya's main city square is graced by a rocket-shaped monument that was erected to commemorate the city's struggle against British forces in November 1945. After the Japanese surrendered, their commander giving his arms to the Indonesian resistance, Islamic groups made renewed moves to counter the return of the Dutch rulers. British troops (in support of the Dutch) landing in Surabaya were vastly outnumbered by these Indonesian forces, and their proposed ceasefire soon failed. British air and military reinforcements renewed their attack on the city which, after three weeks of bloody fighting, led to the capitulation of the Indonesians. Hari Pahlawan ('Heroes' Day') is commemorated every year on 10 November.

Entertainment
Apart from the excellent nightly *wayang orang* dance-drama performances at the Sriwedari Park, Solo offers gamelan performances on Saturday mornings and classical Javanese dance on Wednesday mornings, both at the Pura Mangkunegaran. At ASKI (the performing arts academy) near the university campus occasional dance performances are held, as they are at the local broadcasting station (RRI) near the railway station. The tourist office has details on events, but if you visit during a quiet period go to the palatial Kusuma Sahid Prince Hotel at Jalan Sugiyopranoto 22, where gamelan concerts are held nightly, occasionally enlivened by dance-drama.

Solo's smaller palace, the Pura Mangkunegaran, houses numerous antiques

►►► **Surakarta (Solo)**   *62C2*

Central Java's second royal city may lack the liveliness and scale of Yogyakarta, but its clean, well-maintained centre makes it a far more peaceful place to stay. Tree-lined streets, a handful of palaces and museums, a rich cultural and spiritual life, and a thriving batik industry are the attractions, while the beautiful rural surroundings offer walks through verdant valleys and hills to temples and waterfalls.

Surakarta, more commonly known by its original name of Solo, was founded in 1745 as the new capital of the Mataram kingdom by Pakubuwono II after he had been deposed and then reinstated by the Dutch. However, his son's weakness led to the break-up of the kingdom, at the same time announcing a renaissance of the arts which was supported by an array of new rulers. Culture still thrives at Solo's two academies of performing arts, and inhabitants continue to respect their king.

Orientation Solo is sliced east–west by a wide avenue, Jalan Slamet Riyadi, which, apart from banks, hotels and shops, also oddly possesses a railway track that is used by cargo trains once a day. To the north lie the airport, railway station and bus station, elegant old villas and the Pura Mangkunegaran, while to the south is the central market area, the main mosque, *kraton* (palace), museum and amusement park. Getting around the centre is best done by *becak* (trishaw), well suited to the slow pace of this friendly city.

Palaces The Kasunanan Palace, also called the **Kraton Surakarta Hadiningrat**►►► (*open*: Sunday to Thursday and Saturday, 8:30–2), stands behind the *alun-alun* (town square) and is visited only with a guide. Half the palace was destroyed by fire in 1985 and subsequently

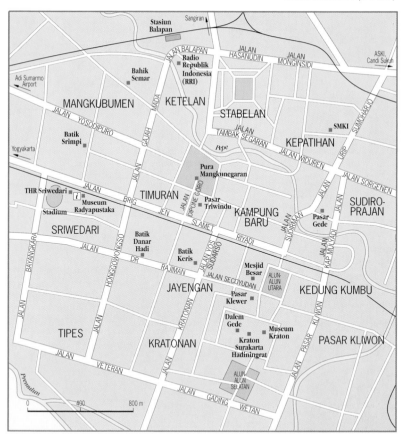

restored. As a result, parts of it distinctly resemble a theatre-set, but a regal aura still remains. Two elegant pavilions (1745) front the main walled body of the *kraton*. Visitors are led through the well-stocked museum (exhibiting Hindu and Buddhist statues, *wayang* puppets, royal heirlooms, carriages, weapons and antique furniture) to a magnificent tree-lined court-yard fronted by a flashily restored pavilion where gamelan orchestras rehearse. Most spectacular here is the **Panggung Songgo Buwono**, an octagonal 'tower of the universe' built in 1782 as a place for the kings of Solo to meditate and meet with Nyai Loro Kidul, the goddess of the South Seas (see panel on page 91).

Although less impressive externally, the mainly 19th-century **Pura Mangkunegaran▶▶** (*open*: Monday to Thursday, Saturday, 8–2; Friday, 8–11; Sunday, 9–1) houses an exquisite collection of antique jewellery. Some of the pieces date from the 8th century and even include a male chastity case, as well as some superb *kris* swords and diverse *objets d'art*. These are exhibited in the inner chamber behind a huge marble *pendopo* (pavilion) with an intricately painted ceiling. About 100 retainers remain, but the royal family is rarely in residence – one princess owns a Jakarta discothèque and the prince is a businessman in the capital. Again, visits are by guided tour only.

Pasar Klewer market specialises in batik

JAVA

Unique Candi Sukuh

Keep going
From Candi Sukuh an undulating path leads to an impressive waterfall at the hill-resort of Tawangmangu, a 2-hour hike away. Superb panoramas make this a very pleasant walk. More bucolic landscapes are visible on the vertiginous road to Candi Ceta, about 7km north of Candi Sukuh (car required). This recently restored, stepped *candi* was the last Majapahit temple to be built, and again occupies a spectacular site.

Becaks are plentiful

Cultural life Three important destinations are grouped together at Jalan Slamet Riyadi 275: the very informative tourist office; the museum; and the **Sriwedari Amusement Park** where *wayang orang* (dance-drama) performances are held nightly at 8pm. The atmospheric **Museum Radyapustaka►►►** (*open*: Tuesday to Thursday, 8–12:30; Friday to Sunday, 8–11) is Indonesia's second oldest, built in 1890, and displays some important Mataram artefacts, a remarkable collection of *wayang* puppets, weapons, gamelan instruments, furniture and a library of ancient Javanese philosophy and literature.

Solo's main batik factory can be visited, or the products can be bought at the **Pasar Klewer►►**, a labyrinthine treasure trove on Jalan Secoyudan. Antique-lovers should visit the small **Pasar Triwindu►** on Jalan Diponegoro, although note that valuable pieces are scarce.

Excursions In an area of barren hills 18km north of Solo is the archaeological site and museum of **Sangiran►**, a paleontologist's dream. This is where, in 1890, Eugène Dubois uncovered the fossilised remains of Java Man (*Pithecanthropus erectus*), thereby suggesting the existence of man in Indonesia some 800,000 years ago (a still disputed estimation). Excavation continues today and a small museum exhibits some assorted finds.

More accessible to the uninitiated is the unique 'erotic' temple, **Candi Sukuh►►►**, high on the slopes of Mount Lawu, 35km east of Solo. Access on foot from the bus-stop at Nglorok is painfully steep, so try to visit by car. The site dates from the mid-15th century, the last years of the Hindu Majapahit kingdom, and was apparently related either to sex education or to a fertility cult. Offerings are still made here by local Hindus. The stepped, truncated pyramid strangely resembles Mayan constructions in Central America, but such comparisons end at the curling snake carved on its summit. More erotic images abound in the surroundings, from a bas-relief female *yonis* and male *lingams* to a headless man grasping his penis. The shady site is lined with panels of carved animals, two *garuda* (mythical eagle) statues and stone turtle gods.

Candis

■ **Central and East Java offer a wealth of both crumbling and immaculately restored temples, from lone structures to elaborate complexes. Inspiration for these** *candis* **came from India along with Hinduism and Buddhism, but the Javanese artisans soon developed their own style.....**■

The term *candi* refers to a square structure based on the Indian type of single-celled shrine that is surmounted by a pyramidal tower culminating in a stupa, and fronted by a portico. Later *candis* had external cells added on to the other three walls. All the shrines served as a focus for cults and housed one or more statues of gods which were often identified with royal personages. The total structure symbolised the cosmic Mount Meru, itself representative of the Hindu-Buddhist universe (see panel on page 93). Although the word *candi* originates from *candika* (the name of Dewi Durga, Siva's consort, incarnated as the goddess of death), and some later East Javanese *candis* appear to have been royal funeral monuments, their basic function was for worship.

Three spheres The three elements of the shrine (stepped plinth, cell and pyramidal roof) echo the symbolic division of the Hindu-Buddhist universe into a lower sphere of mortals, an intermediary sphere of the purified where icons are placed for worship, and the upper sphere of the gods. Façades, steps and niches are often ornately carved; a recurring sight is the ferocious-looking guardian spirit, whether in relief or as a statue. Today's *candi* names bear no relation to their original function as they usually stem from a local geographical feature or commemorate a popular epic hero.

Early examples Java's oldest surviving *candis* date from the 8th to 9th centuries and were dedicated to Siva: notable are those on the Dieng Plateau (see pages 78–9) and at Gedung Songo (see page 80). The star of this epoch was, of course, the central Buddhist temple of Borobudur and the ornately carved Candi Mendut (see pages 70–1), both dating from around AD800. From then on there was an increasing emphasis on decorative motifs and a generalisation of three-dimensional significance. Candi Kalasan, located between Prambanan and Yogya, is a superb example, as is the larger Candi Sewu complex (see page 93). Towering over all these *candis* are those of Prambanan itself (see pages 92–3), dedicated to the Hindu trinity and dating from the early 10th century.

East Java
As kingdoms moved eastwards, so too did the *candis*. East Java's examples are more linear than the extravagant volumes of the Central Javanese style, and have a proliferation of decorative elements. Candi Sawentar, Candi Kidal and the Singosari group (all dating from the 13th century) demonstrate more massive plinths, multiplied cells and a shifting of the horizontal bands of moulding. Hinduism and Buddhism were by then intimately linked, the loss of direct contact with India no doubt leading to a strengthening of Javanese architectural conceptions.

Below: Candi Plaosan at Prambanan
Left: Candi Kawi

Spiritual springs
If you are driving between
Tretes and Surabaya, a
short detour can be made
to the village of Gempol.
Here lie the springs of
Behalan, the oldest relic in
the region and pre-dating
the Singosari and
Majapahit temples. Only
one pool remains of this
structure, built during the
reign of Airlangga in the
11th century. Water flows
into a pool through two
fountains carved in the
forms of Laksmi and Dewi
Sri, the wives of the Hindu
god Vishnu. An inscription
dated 1049 suggests that
this may also be the burial
place of Airlangga. A
superb statue of Vishnu
astride his *garuda* (mythical eagle) was found here
and is now displayed at the
museum in Mojokerto.

▶ **Tretes** 63D1

Tretes is a popular East Javan hill-resort on the slopes of
Mount Arjuno, half-way between Malang and Surabaya.
The town itself has little to offer (although it does manage
to attract convoys of wealthy Surabayans at weekends),
but there are some pleasant trails to the **Kakek Bodo
Waterfall** and through the lush hills. Spectacular scenery
is assured from a newly opened road which winds its way
steeply up through protected forest to the village of
Cangar, known for its hot springs, then descends to the
orchards of Batu (see panel on page 87) through a patchwork of fertile hill plantations.

The 14th-century **Candi Jawi▶▶**, located at Pandaan on
the main Surabaya road, stands surrounded by pools against
a backdrop of mountain peaks. It represents a perfect example of Hindu-Buddhist syncretism prevalent in the Singosari
temples, embodied in a Sivaite structure crowned by a
stupa. In Pandaan itself, outdoor performances of East
Javanese dance are held between May and October.

▶▶ **Trowulan** 63D1

The ruins of Java's most powerful empire are found
scattered around the town of Trowulan, 10km from
Mojokerto. At the height of their power during the mid-
14th century, the Hindu-Buddhist Majapahits controlled
much of the Indonesian archipelago as well as parts of
modern-day Malaysia. Their wealth was based on agriculture and on the control of the spice trade, and their capital
at Trowulan flourished gloriously before falling to the
Muslim advance from Demak in 1478. This marked the
exodus of Javanese Hindus to Bali.

Start your visit at the **Museum Pengunjung▶▶▶**
(*open*: daily, 7–4; Friday 7–11), located about 1km
south of the main Mojokerto road. The excellent
display (with captions in English) exhibits detailed
descriptions and photos of the main sites, as well
as major artefacts that have been recovered from
the ruins. Considerable information is also given
about the Singosari temples, forerunners of
those built by the Majapahits.

*Tretes, a favourite
weekend getaway for
stressed Surabayans*

Diametrically opposite the museum lies the **Kolam Segaran**, a 375m-long pool that is a symbol of the Majapahits' wealth. Banquets apparently ended with gold dishes being tossed unceremoniously into its depths. Two other sites lie southeast of the museum: **Bajang Ratu▶▶**, a pyramidal-roofed gateway which is now fully restored; and **Candi Tikus▶▶**, once a ritual bathing-pool. The latter's name, meaning 'rat', derives from the lair of creatures found nesting there when the site was first excavated in 1914.

On the other side of the main Mojokerto road stand **Candi Berahu▶**, a complex construction of four cells presently under restoration, and, just beyond it, **Candi Siti Inggil▶**. Further north and lying off the main road is **Wringin Lawang▶▶**, a temple cut vertically in half. A trip to Trowulan is completed by a brief visit to the old museum, now an archaeological store and office, whose overgrown garden houses several major statues and artefacts.

▶▶▶ Ujung Kulon, Taman Nasional   62A1

This national park of over 60,000 hectares covers the westernmost point of Java as well as the islands of Peucang, Panaitan and Handeuleum. Its peninsular form, surrounded by sea on three sides and with a barrier of mountains to the east, has ensured the survival of several animal species that disappeared long ago from the rest of heavily populated Java. This is the last refuge for the Javanese rhinoceros, although visitors are more likely to see wild pig, barking deer, *banteng* (wild buffalo), leopards, leaf-monkeys, gibbons and macaques. Large tracts of lowland rainforest survive, although much was wiped out by the tidal wave that followed Krakatau's eruption in 1883 and which left hundreds of trees fossilised.

Well-maintained trails criss-cross the forest and pass grassy plains, clumps of palms, ginger and bamboo before reaching the sandy beaches of the dramatic west coast. The entire walk across the peninsula from Taman Jaya in the north is about 45km long. There is deep-diving off Tanjung Layar and good snorkelling around the offshore islands – in particular Panaitan's extensive coral reefs.

Hikers at Ujung Kulon may well see leopards

Park practicalities
Access to Ujung Kulon is from the port of Labuhan, either by boat to the islands and the mainland headquarters of Taman Jaya or by jeep direct to Taman Jaya. Permits need to be obtained at the PHPA office in Labuhan (Jalan Perintis Kemerdekaan 43), which also arranges guides and accommodation at its island rest-houses. Hiking is only advisable in the dry season (April to October) as the trails become impossibly boggy at other times of the year.

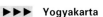

▶ ▶ ▶ **Yogyakarta**   *62C1*

Cultural hits
Performances of classical dance are held at the sultan's palace on Sundays at 10:30am, and of gamelan music on Mondays and Wednesdays. Nightly *wayang kulit* (shadow plays) are performed at the Sonobudoyo Museum at 8pm and daily at 3pm at the Agastya Art Institute (Jalan Gedongkiwo 237). On Saturday the latter switches to *wayang golek* (wooden-puppet plays). Glamour, glitter, farce, acrobatics and grace are rolled into one enthralling *Ramayana* performance held nightly at 8pm at the Purawisata (Jalan B Katamso), a 'people's' theatre attended mainly by tourists. Most inspiring of all, however, is the *Ramayana* held at Prambanan's open-air theatre at each full moon from May to October.

This booming cultural capital of over 3 million inhabitants owes its special territorial status to the decisive role it played in the struggle for independence, led by its enlightened Sultan Hamengku Buwono IX. Not only did he offer asylum to members of the new republican government (notably Sukarno and Hatta) between 1945 and 1949, but he also lent parts of the *kraton* (palace) to the first university founded for and by Indonesians. At independence the sultan played an important ministerial role under Sukarno and later became vice-president under Suharto. His funeral in 1988 was attended by over a million people, proof of the extreme devotion he inspired.

Today, the life of this aristocratic city still revolves around the central *kraton*. Although fascinating for these reasons, Yogyakarta nevertheless still faces the big-city problems of pollution, overcrowding, poverty and, as a result of its popularity with tourists, irritating commercialism.

Early days The founding of Yogyakarta (more commonly shortened to Yogya) dates from 1755 when Prince Mangkubumi split off from Solo's Mataram kingdom and chose to build his new *kraton* in the village. Adopting the title of sultan, the prince reigned under the name of Hamengku Buwono I, the first of a new dynasty which continues today under Hamengku Buwono X.

Rebellion against Java's foreign overlords arose sporadically. In 1812, during the short period of British rule, a plot was uncovered and colonial vengeance taken by sacking the *kraton* and exiling the guilty sultan. His brother was given a new title, Paku Alam, as well as land to establish a new *kraton* in Yogya which survives today, although it is hardly comparable to the main *kraton*. Far more destructive was the war of 1825–30, declared by Prince Diponegoro against the Dutch but which ended in bloody defeat (see page 40).

Dancers prepare for a performance at Yogya's kraton

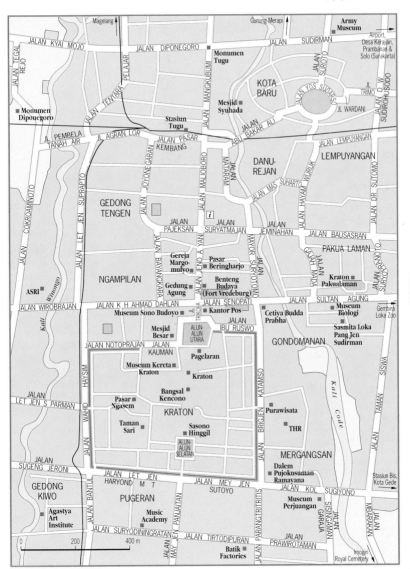

Kraton The spiritual, political and geographical heart of Yogya is the walled *kraton*, a town within a town whose 30,000-odd inhabitants all take part in palace activities. Quiet, tree-lined streets and squares, a 'water castle', a bird market and, of course, the shady courtyards of the palace itself all lie within this square kilometre of whitewashed walls. The main northern entrance leads to the *alun-alun*, a large grassy square edged with 64 banyan trees (a symbolic figure derived from Muhammad's age at his death) and with two more in its centre which represent the sultan's union with his subjects. On the west side of the *alun-alun* stands the Javanese-style **Mesjid Besar (Great Mosque)** and, to the north, the **Museum Sono**

The Taman Sari pleasure palace

Double function
Besides Taman Sari's function as a place for contemplation, relaxation and even voyeurism (from the tower the sultan would watch his wives and concubines bathing, and then summon whichever one appealed), the 'water castle' was also constructed as a unique defence system. In the event of an attack, the sultan and his family could flee through the underground passageways, then the water-gate would be opened and water allowed to flood the area – hopefully drowning the enemy.

A ferocious guardian spirit at the Taman Sari

Budoyo▶▶ (*open*: Tuesday to Thursday, 8–1:30; Friday, 8–11:15; Saturday and Sunday, 8–noon) which displays Javanese arts and crafts and Balinese crafts and sculptures. The courtyard is lined with Hindu statues dating from the 8th to the 10th centuries.

Sultan's abode The palace▶▶▶ itself (*open*: Monday to Sunday, 8:30–2; Friday, 8:30–1), part residence for the present sultan and his army of ageing retainers, and part ceremonial areas, is composed of a series of interconnecting courtyards, halls and open *pendopo* (pavilions). Visits are only by guided tour and include the new museum devoted to the life of Hamengku Buwono IX.

Every courtyard leads ultimately to the central **Bangsal Kencono (Golden Pavilion)**, whose four teak pillars are carved with motifs symbolising Java's three religions: Hinduism, Buddhism and Islam. Even if individual displays are nothing spectacular, it is above all the timeless atmosphere of the *kraton* which leaves an indelible impression. The pressure of Yogya's furious traffic and its batik-vendors evaporates in this universe peopled by lizards and turbanned palace guards who languidly rake the sands of the South Seas that are scattered over the courtyards.

Regal amusement To the west of the palace lies the Pasar Ngasem (Bird Market)▶, a labyrinth of narrow lanes filled with decorative cages, and which is particularly animated in the morning. Behind this is the **Taman Sari**▶▶ (*open*: daily, 9–4), a Portuguese-inspired 'water castle' built in 1765 for the pleasure of the sultan's family and his concubines, but now very much a faded splendour (see panel). The dilapidated canals, stagnant pools, tunnels, towers and ramparts all merge to the south in a maze of lanes which has become the centre for Yogya's pushy batik-painters.

Up Malioboro Jalan Malioboro leads north from the *alun-alun* into Yogya's main commercial area, a last historical monument, **Fort Vredeburg**▶, standing to the east. This

1790 building (heavily restored) houses a poor museum composed entirely of dioramas illustrating the history of the city. Opposite stands the **Gedung Agung**, the former Dutch governor's residence and now a state guesthouse. Far more lively is the **Pasar Beringharjo (Central Market)**▶▶, which seethes with optimistic vendors and pickpockets. Batik thrives here as nowhere else, but it is more judicious to make purchases at any of the textile stores outside where prices are fixed (usually).

The tourist office is near by at Jalan Malioboro 16, but beware of being told that it is 'closed' and being offered a tour of a batik gallery instead. The side-roads here are packed with budget and mid-range hotels, while top hotels lie on Malioboro and beyond the railway track.

Peripheral sights East of the centre along Jalan Sultan Agung stands the **Pakualam Palace**▶, a rather disappointing affair consisting of an overgrown courtyard, a ceremonial *pendopo*, and a small museum displaying old photos and royal memorabilia alongside some extravagant carriages. Some 5km southeast of Yogya lies the village of **Kota Gede**▶▶, once the capital of the 16th-century Mataram kingdom and site of a **royal cemetery** (*open*: Monday, 10–noon; Friday, 1:30–4). Walled gardens contain ponds of lotus flowers as well as an ancient yellow turtle believed to possess magical powers. Today, however, Kota Gede's fame stems from the numerous silver workshops which line its main street and attract busloads of tourists.

A further 10km south on a beautiful wooded hilltop site stands **Imogiri**▶▶ (*open*: Monday, 10–noon; Friday, 1–4), the royal cemetery of Mataram which was founded in 1645 by the great Sultan Agung. A total of 345 steep steps lead up to this imposing spiritual monument. Behind the walls are buried 24 sultans from Yogyakarta and Surakarta, each greatly revered and enjoying an afterlife perfumed with incense. As at Kota Gede's cemetery, traditional Javanese dress must be worn if you wish to enter the tombs – this is available for hire. Views sweep across the surrounding countryside and south to the Indian Ocean.

Fire Mountain
A dominant feature of the landscape to the north of Yogya is active Mount Merapi (2,911m), about 30km from town. White smoke curls out of its magnificent cone incessantly to form a hovering cloud, and when sulphur fumes become excessive the summit is closed to climbers. The wide, sandy plateau of the cone contains several small fire-spewing craters and is best viewed from the mountain resort of Kaliurang. Here, accommodation and guides are available for the 4-hour trek to the crater or arduous 6-hour climb to the summit. Closer at hand (an hour's trek away) is an observation point with spectacular views which are at their optimum in the morning. Many climbers attack the summit from the village of Selo on the northern flank, this being a safer and marginally easier route.

107

Over 10,000 birds from all over the archipelago vie for customers at the Pasar Ngasem

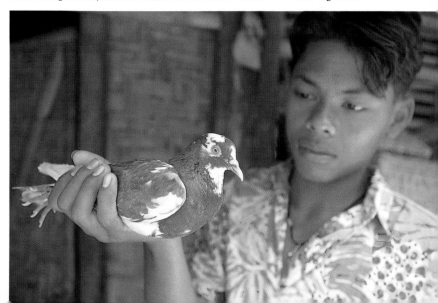

■ **Central to Javanese culture is the art of shadow plays, a legacy from pre-Islamic days and probably even pre-dating Hindu times. These marathon magical performances are still held for specific ceremonies, and most characters from the *Ramayana* and *Mahabharata* epics are household names.....■**

Curious vocabulary

'Among the volumes of *wayang* plays you may find too an interesting textbook called *Uger Pedalangan* containing the rules for *wayang* showmanship. The vocabulary of this curious art is a rich one, but none the less the *dalang*, or showman, must be able to express by a distinct intonation every mood and emotion, whether love, farce, tragedy, triumph, contempt, and so on; and the slightest departure from the accepted tone would be resented by any native audience. Each of these tones has a name, *prenesan, banolan* etc, and the *dalang's* art of expressing them...is called *lakon.*'
– From *Javanese Panorama*, by HW Ponder (1942).

The dalang *(puppet master) plays a versatile, semi-mystical role*

Wayang literally means shadow, but it has come to be used more generally to mean theatre – whether *wayang kulit* (shadow play), *wayang golek* (wooden-puppet play) or *wayang orang* (dance-drama enacted by men and women). *Wayang kulit* is present throughout much of Asia, its origins remaining as shadowy as its form. Some believe it to date from pre-Hindu days, but what is certain is that by the 11th century it was flourishing in Java, and that by the 17th century puppet designs had been standardised and used articulated arms.

The ease with which this art form spread in rural Java and Bali is due above all to its mobility: the *dalang* (puppet master) needs only a trunk of puppets and a white cotton screen, for an accompanying gamelan orchestra already exists in every village. In pre-colonial Java, *wayang kulit* was an important pedagogical tool to spread the ethics of court culture to remote villages.

The performance *Wayang kulit* puppets are made from stiff buffalo-hide cut in the shape of a particular character, carved and painted with details, and then attached to articulated arms and a stick. For a full repertoire of Javanese legends and the Hindu epics, the *Ramayana* and the *Mahabharata*, a puppeteer needs some 200 puppets, and a complete performance will take all night, finishing at dawn. On one side of the screen sits the *dalang* and his army of puppets, while on the other is the orchestra. Spectators choose either to watch the flickering shadow play from the orchestra side or to watch the

master and his cast. Whatever the story, the play is presented in three acts: first, the characters and their motivations are presented, the initial rupture taking place; second, there is a sequence of meditation in which the hero meets his sage and the philosophical message is conveyed; and third, a great battle takes place, ending with the victory of order and balance.

Pivotal role The *dalang*'s role is far more complex than that of a simple puppeteer. His talents not only include extreme stamina, directing the gamelan orchestra, manipulating the puppets and projecting the voices of numerous different characters, but also poetic, comic and dramatic improvisation. Above all, the *dalang* becomes a medium for the gods, playing an intermediary mystical role for which he undergoes certain rites. Audiences know the stories by heart, so the art lies in their interpretation, this being modified for each performance.

Epic tales The central theme of the *Mahabharata* is a power struggle between two royal families, the Kurava and their cousins, the Pandava. Rivalry and the division of a kingdom leads to a series of bloody battles in which Arjuna, the Pandava prince, is given moral encouragement to fight his relatives by Krishna, an incarnation of the god Vishnu. Advice comes in the form of the chanted Bhagavad Gita, a key Hindu text which elaborates on the indestructibility of the soul. By the end of the *Mahabharata* many of the great heroes have been killed, but the Pandavas, representing enlightenment and refinement, win the day over the Kuravas, who incarnate the forces of greed and destruction.

Vishnu reappears in the other great epic, the *Ramayana*, in which he is embodied by the hero, Prince Rama, who is severely tested by the antics of the ogre, King Rawana. Aided by Hanuman, the monkey-god, Rama sets off to search for his wife, Sita, who has been abducted by Rawana. Finally, after endless trials and tribulations, Rama manages to rescue Sita and so the essential cosmic harmony is restored.

Puncturing buffalo-hide puppets at a Yogya workshop

The 'tree of life'
The *gunungan* ('tree of life') is an important puppet design in *wayang* as it is used to indicate scene changes as well as representing every aspect of life. Its elaborate shape resembles a stupa with, at its base, two fierce demons surmounted by two *garudas* (mythical eagles) and, in the branches of the tree, a group of snakes, monkeys and other animals.

An eerie presence...

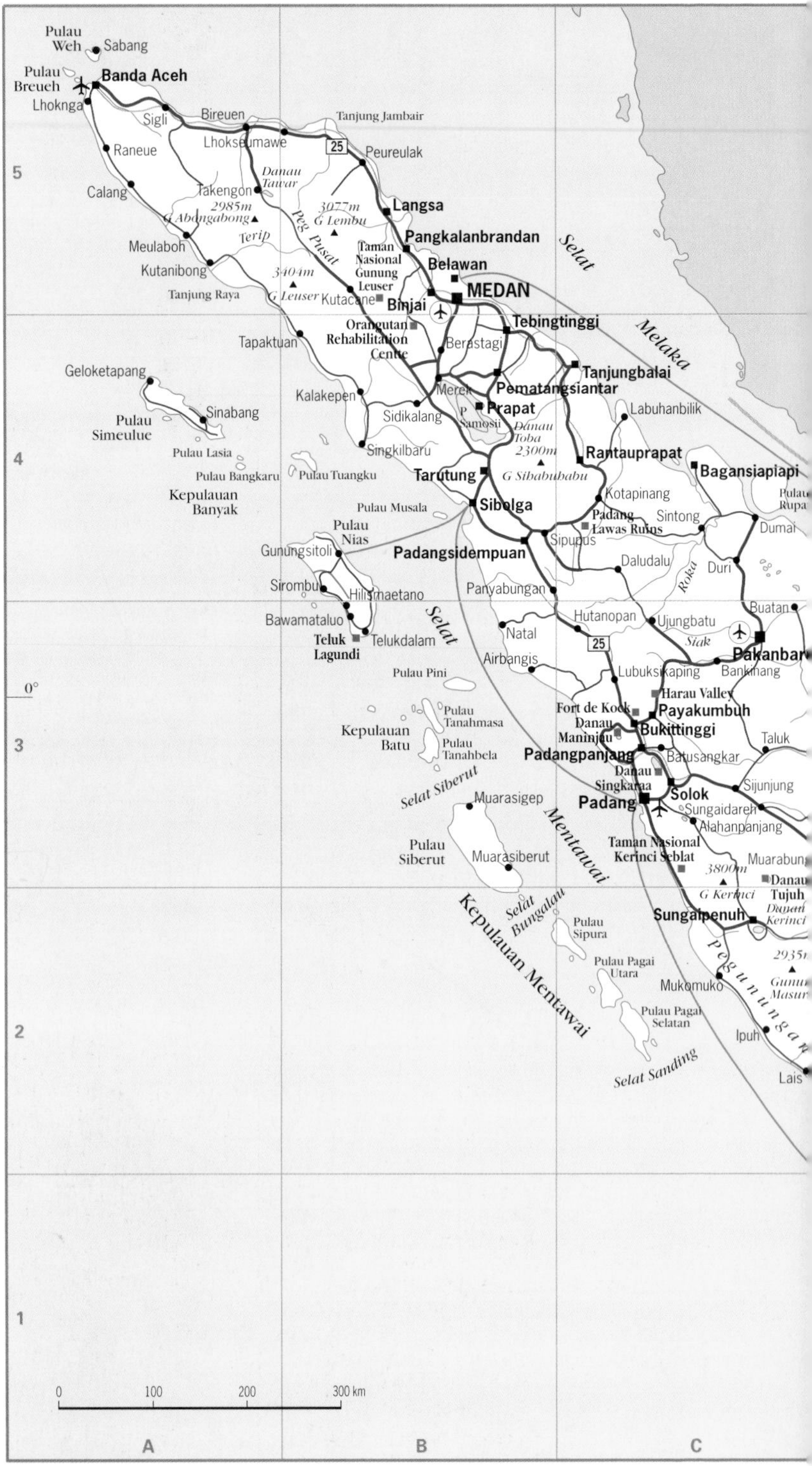

SUMATRA

Pulau Weh — Sabang
Pulau Breuch — Lhoknga — **Banda Aceh**
Sigli — Bireuen — Tanjung Jambair
Raneue — Lhokseumawe
Calang — Takengon — Danau Tawar — Peureulak — 25
5 — 2985m — 3077m — **Langsa**
G Abongabong — G Lembu
Meulaboh — Terip — **Pangkalanbrandan**
Kutanibong — Taman Nasional Gunung Leuser — **Belawan**
Tanjung Raya — 3404m — **MEDAN**
G Leuser — Kutacane — **Binjai**
Orangutan Rehabilitation Centre — **Tebingtinggi**
Tapaktuan — Berastagi
Geloketapang — Merek — **Pematangsiantar** — **Tanjungbalai**
Kalakepen — **Prapat** — Labuhanbilik
Sinabang — Sidikalang — P Samosir — Danau Toba 2300m
Pulau Simeulue — Singkilbaru — **Rantauprapat**
Pulau Lasia — G Sibabubabu — **Bagansiapiapi**
4 — Pulau Bangkaru — Pulau Tuangku — **Tarutung** — Kotapinang — Pulau Rupa
Kepulauan Banyak — Pulau Musala — **Sibolga** — Padang Lawas Ruins — Sintong — Dumai
Pulau Nias — Sipurus — Daludalu — Duri
Gunungsitoli — **Padangsidempuan** — Rokai — Buatan
Sirombu — Hilismaetano — Panyabungan
Bawamataluo — Teluk Lagundi — Telukdalam — Natal — Hutanopan — Ujungbatu — Siak — **Pakanbar**
0° — Pulau Pini — Airbangis — 25 — Bangkinang
Lubuksikaping
3 — Kepulauan Batu — Pulau Tanahmasa — Fort de Kock — **Harau Valley** — **Payakumbuh**
Pulau Tanahbela — Danau Maninjau — **Bukittinggi** — Taluk
Padangpanjang — Batusangkar
Selat Siberut — Muarasigep — Danau Singkana — **Solok** — Sijunjung
Pulau Siberut — Muarasiberut — **Padang** — Sungaidareh — Alahanpanjang
Taman Nasional Kerinci Seblat — Muarabun — Danau Tujuh
Selat Bungalau — 3800m — Danau Kerinci
Pulau Sipura — G Kerinci — **Sungaipenuh**
2935m — Gunu Masur
2 — Pulau Pagai Utara — Mukomuko — Iputi
Pulau Pagai Selatan
Selat Sanding — Lais

Selat Melaka
Selat
Mentawai
Kepulauan Mentawai
Pegunungan

1

0 — 100 — 200 — 300 km

A — B — C

(MAL)

Kepulauan
Anambas

Pulau
Bengkalis

ulau
adang

Pulau
Tebingtinggi

Selat Singapura

(SGP)

Pulau
Batam

Pulau
Bintan

P. Kundur

Pulau Mendol

Kepulauan
Riau

Kepulauan
Badas

Sungaiguntung

Kampar Kana

Pulau Sebangka

Equator

Sakeanlosong

Tembilahan

Pulau
Lingga

Kepulauan
Lingga

Rengat

apura

Indragiri

Pangkalankosai

Pulau
Basu

Dabo

Pulau
Singkep

Kualatungka

Selat Berhala

Tanjung Jabunk

Muara
Jambi

Simpang

Batangbar

Tanjung

Belinyu

Jambi

Pelawan

Pulau
Bangka

Muaratembesi

Muntok

Kelapa

Pangkalpinang

Bangko

Bayunglineir

Lalan

Sarolangun

Gresik

Selat Bangka

Surulangun

Koba

383m

25

Talangbetutu

Batubetumpang

Seblat

Sekayu

Musi

Palembang

Toboali

Pulau
Lepar

Selat Gasper

Muaraaman

ubuklinggau

Sungaigerung

Tebingtinggi

Perabumulih

Tanjungraja

Bengkulu

Muaraenim

Kayuagung

3159m

Lahat

Betung

Mesuji

G.
Dempo

Pasemah

Baturaja

Tanjung
Lumut

anjung
erbau

Pagaralam

Martapura

Dintiteladas

Barisan

Manna

Menggala

Tebarumbayan

Kotabumi

Seputih

Surabaya

Bandingagung

Way Kambas
Elephant Reserve

Bintuhan

Danau
Ranau

Bukitkemuning

Metro

Tridatu

Pulau
Enggano

Krui

Kotaagung

Tanjungkarang

Ngaras

Banding

Telukbetung

Bakauheni

Selat Sunda

Tanjung Cina

Serang

JAKARTA

Rangkasbitung

Bogor

JAWA (JAVA)

D

E

SUMATRA

112

Muara Jambi

One of Sumatra's more easily accessible archaeological sites lies only 27km northeast of the city of Jambi, although getting there includes negotiating rough dirt roads and continuing by boat along the Batanghari river. This major 10th- to 13th-century Melayu site covers about 12 sq km, and contains eight brick temple compounds and some 27 mounds of earth (*menapos*), thought to be the ruins of ancient dwellings. The site is crisscrossed by moats and is also home to a man-made lake. It has been proved to be a Mahayana Buddhist compound and the dwellings are thought to have been inhabited by priests. Restoration of the temples has been in progress since the 1970s and the site, though scattered, is very impressive.

Minangkabau roofs sweep out of the morning mists near Bukittinggi

Sumatra The fourth-largest island in the world is home to the Batak and Minangkabau peoples, orang-utans and immense mineral wealth. It is one of the most difficult regions of Indonesia to travel around, yet you soon forget any hardships when you see its spectacular, relentlessly green and mountainous landscapes. This is a destination for nature-lovers, trekkers and mountain climbers, the numerous crater lakes allowing for post-jungle soaks. The main points of interest lie within the majestic Bukit Barisan mountain range, which forms a continuous ridge down the west coast and is relatively accessible from the parallel Trans-Sumatran Highway.

Drawbacks Sumatra's attractions are also its detractions. Distances over this 475,000 sq km island are enormous and airports thin on the ground. As a result, travellers rarely veer from the main north–south trail between Medan and Padang, and often skip South Sumatra altogether. This has resulted in the growth of large, commercialised centres at Danau Toba and Bukittinggi, while Banda Aceh, in the north, and Bengkulu, to the southwest, are rarely visited. Similarly, major logistical feats are needed to reach the archaeological sites at Padang Lawas, Muara Jambi and the Pasemah Plateau, whereas the crashing surf and megaliths of Pulau Nias, now accessible by plane, appear on most itineraries.

Sumatra's other negative aspect is its climate: 85 per cent of the island has a dry season that lasts just two months (June to July), and the Equator, which bisects the island just north of Bukittinggi, creates further climatic anomalies. As a consequence, many of Sumatra's roads become mud-baths between October and April.

History Sumatra's past dynasties, far fewer than those of neighbouring Java, were dominated by the maritime kingdoms of Srivijaya (7th to 14th centuries), Melayu (7th to 13th centuries) and Aceh (16th to 19th centuries). More relevant today is the fact that Islam first penetrated Indonesia through Aceh in the 9th to 10th centuries, and from there spread south through Muslim trading states down the east coast. European colonial powers started eyeing the island's rich natural resources in the 1600s, when the Dutch and the British set up rival trading posts. However, it took another 250 years or so and heavy losses before the Dutch finally subdued the entire island.

Society What it lacks in historical relics, Sumatra makes up for in its patchwork of ethnic groups, many of which cling firmly to their identities and traditions. Squeezed between the fervently Muslim and independently minded Acehnese in the north and the unique Minangkabau of West Sumatra are four types of Christian Bataks around Danau Toba, with yet another group based on Pulau Nias and the Mentawai Islands. Menhirs and megaliths, superb woodcarvings and startling village architecture have now entered the clear light of tourist itineraries, the result being that authenticity is often hard to find.

The 20th century and corrugated-iron roofs may have arrived, but the 4 million Minangs have not abandoned their matrilinear society, and nor has the national spread of their Padang restaurants faltered. Their fertile region mirrors that of the neighbouring Bataks, who display an equal wealth of magnificent architecture and crafts. In contrast, heavily populated southern Sumatra, a victim of excessive transmigration from Java, has lost its traditions. Another facet of Sumatran society is visible in Palembang and Medan, both influenced for centuries by Chinese immigrants.

Untouched wilderness About 40 per cent of Sumatra is still clad in tropical forest, although logging has left its indelible mark – particularly in the south. Sumatra's greatest offering lies in the huge tracts of rainforest and mountains that are now protected as nature reserves. The Gunung Leuser National Park, Kerinci Seblat Reserve, Way Kambas and numerous smaller reserves all offer basic facilities and give the opportunities of exploring magnificent landscapes, trekking to volcanic craters or meeting an orang-utan in the wilds.

An inhabitant of Aceh, which since 1967 has enjoyed 'special territory' status

Who said noses?
Travellers through Indonesia will often encounter references being made to the noble proportions of Western noses. A Sumatran joke on this subject develops the nose complex even further: as Western countries are excessively polluted, their inhabitants have to clean their noses daily, creating a certain nasal prominence. On the other hand, in Indonesia, where electricity is rare, people tend to bump into trees at night and therefore flatten their best feature!

SUMATRA

A display of rencong, traditional Acehnese daggers

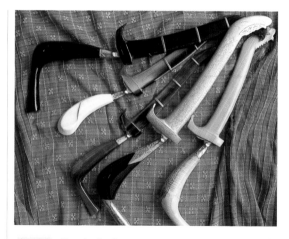

Acehnese beaches
For those desperate for the waves, Banda Aceh offers several alternatives. Remember, though, that this is a strongly Islamic state where women bathe fully dressed, so keep your bikini for other more tolerant destinations. Top of the list is Lampu'uk, a beautiful stretch of white sand about 13km southwest of town. Lhoknga is another popular weekend destination, and is well supplied with *warungs* (food-stalls) as well as boats for snorkelling trips. The surf is rough here and currents strong, so beware. To the east of Banda Aceh on the Strait of Melaka is the black-sand beach of Ujung Bate, rife with ghostly legends.

The Mesjid Raya Baiturrahman was built by the Dutch to replace an older mosque they destroyed during the Acehnese Wars

▶ **Banda Aceh** 110A5

This prosperous town, situated at the northern tip of Sumatra, is the capital of one of Indonesia's most orthodox states and is a continuing thorn in central government's side. An active separatist movement (Aceh Merdeka, meaning 'Free Aceh') rears its head sporadically, inciting a merciless response from the army and leaving an unknown number of victims. The main issue is the immense revenue generated by Aceh's large reserves of natural gas, discovered in 1971. Production now represents one-third of Indonesia's oil and gas exports, but brings little benefit to Aceh's mainly rural population and disappears mostly into the coffers of central government instead.

The second major issue relates to Islamic extremism, and it is not a new one. In the 17th century the brilliant Sultan Iskandar Muda transformed this trading centre into a booming cosmopolitan cultural city which controlled much of West Sumatra, as well as parts of Peninsular Malaysia. Aceh remained protected under a treaty with the British until 1871, when the Dutch entered the fray and, in a protracted and bloody attack, finally succeeded

in capturing the city and annexing the province. In 1967 continuing dissatisfaction led to Aceh being declared a 'special territory'.

Sights Dominating the town centre is the **Mesjid Raya Baiturrahman►►**, built in 1879 by the Dutch to appease the Acehnese and an elaborate hybrid of Arabesque and Mogul styles. The mosque can be visited outside prayer times, its minarets offering good views over the town and river. Immediately behind the mosque lies the Chinese quarter and a handicrafts market. To the southeast, on Jalan Alauddin Mahmudsyah, is the **Aceh Museum►►**, with displays of local artefacts, weapons, handicrafts and ceremonial clothing. In the same complex is the **Rumah Aceh**, a superb reconstruction of a traditional aristocratic home fronted by a huge Chinese cast-iron bell. The tomb of Sultan Iskandar Muda, several cannon and the graceful residence of the Acehnese governor all lie within what was formerly a palace compound.

Further south, on Jalan Teuku Umar, lie two historic sights. On the river bank is the **Gunongan►►**, a palace and pleasure garden built by Sultan Iskandar Muda for his aristocratic Malay wife. This strange 17th-century theme park contains a bizarre pinnacled white structure whose actual function or symbolism is still open to speculation. Was it an observatory? Did it represent the hills of her homeland? Or was it meant as a phallic symbol? Far clearer in its function is the impeccably maintained Dutch cemetery of **Kher Khoff►►**, which lies across the road. Some 2,200 elaborate graves stand as reminders of the bloody Aceh War which dragged on until the early 20th century, and whose victims included Ambonese and Javanese fighting for the Dutch.

►► Bengkulu   111D2

Bengkulu lies in faded colonial splendour very much off the beaten track on the southwest coast of Sumatra. It is a unique relic of Britain's only trading presence in Indonesia (1685–1824) and of Raffles' memorable Residency (1818–23). This small, sleepy port retains a lot of character, and for the moment has been ignored by Indonesian developers. The town's main historic monument is the massive and well-maintained **Benteng Marlborough►►** (1715), whose elaborate fortifications include a tunnel running straight out to sea. On the hill behind stands another British monument, built in memory of Resident Thomas Parr who was assassinated by Bugis officers in 1807. In front of this is the large market of **Pasar Barukoto** which overlooks Bengkulu's seafront Chinatown and the ruins of the former British Residency. Those interested in the plight of Sukarno, who was held in Bengkulu by the Dutch in the 1930s, will want to visit **Rumah Bung Karno►** on Jalan Sukarno-Hatta, which offers relevant memorabilia. The tourist office is close by.

On the promontory's southern edge is **Pantai Panjang**, a 7km-long clean, sandy beach with reasonable swimming, recreation facilities and accommodation at Nala. For a beautiful lake setting, head 8km out of Bengkulu to **Danau Dendam Tak Sudah** (meaning 'Endless Grudge Lake'!), whose surface is carpeted with brilliantly coloured water orchids in season.

Raffles' last days
When Stamford Raffles was appointed lieutenant-governor of Bencoolen (as Bengkulu was called by the British), he had just spent five successful years governing Java. Bencoolen, ravaged by earthquakes and bad government, was altogether different.

Raffles' first acts were to abolish slavery and close down the gambling dens. His next was to discover the enormous flower that is named after him, the *Rafflesia*, and by 1819 he had founded Singapore. But tragedy soon occurred: Raffles' four children all died and he went into a deep depression. On leaving Bencoolen in 1823, his ship caught fire and sank, destroying all his belongings. He died just two years later, on his 45th birthday.

115

Sir Stamford Raffles

The high fertile lands around Berastagi produce a wealth of fresh fruit and vegetables

Jungle orchestra
As you lie in your bungalow surrounded by the dense Sumatran jungle, it could be worth meditating on the origins of the sounds permeating your dreams. Frogs offer an easily identifiable concerto when the males sing loud and strong for mates – at the risk of being eaten by snakes. Cicadas actually spend 17 years of their lives underground, surfacing only for a few weeks to sing for a partner; their buzzing sounds are made by the rapid and repetitive bending of their abdominal plates. Hear high-pitched whoops? Then you could be listening to male and female white-handed gibbons singing complex duets to defend their territory. Entire families of furry *siamangs* (black apes) may also tune up to protect their ground from neighbours.

►► **Berastagi**   *110B4*

The small North Sumatran town of Berastagi holds no interest in itself, but its location on a 1,400m-high plateau makes it a favourite base for trekkers. Lorries may hurtle down its one main street, but as you head out to hot springs, waterfalls and craters you enter a spectacular landscape. Two volcanoes dominate the area – Mount Sinabung (2,417m) and Mount Sibayak (2,100m). The latter, now extinct, can be climbed in 3 hours and Mount Sinabung can be climbed in about 6 hours, but longer jungle treks can easily be arranged with local guides; the tourist office (at the main crossroads by the market) will advise. This region is also remarkable for its traditional Karo Batak houses, visible in the nearby villages of Lingga, Peceran and Cingkes.

►►► **Bukit Lawang (Orangutan Rehabilitation Centre)**   *110B4*

The Orangutan Rehabilitation Centre of Bohorok lies some 75km from Medan at the end of one of Sumatra's infamous bone-shaking roads and just outside Bukit Lawang. This low-key tourist settlement is surrounded by the Gunung Leuser National Park's dense jungle and crossed by the fast-flowing Bohorok river.

Guests and orangs alike congregate at the rehabilitation centre at feeding time (8am and 3pm), at the far end of the village and a 30-minute walk from the tourist settlement. Comic primate performances are not guaranteed but crowds are, particularly at weekends. Get permits from the PHPA office at the entrance to the village (a passport is required for this). A visit to the adjacent visitor information centre is well worthwhile. An informative film (c1975) about the early days of the centre is shown here on Monday, Wednesday and Friday evenings.

Bukit Lawang's popularity has also spawned more strenuous activities, from jungle trekking to white-water rafting and inner-tubing (floating or being flung downriver while seated in an inner tube – this can be dangerous during the rainy season). And, as at Berastagi, there is no shortage of willing guides.

Orang-utans

■ **The sight of a furry orange orang-utan swinging from lianas through the canopy of the tropical rainforest has long appealed to man. But although the adults may resemble shaggy sumo wrestlers and the babies bring paternal or maternal instincts to the fore, the 'man of the forest' is fast disappearing.....■**

The orang-utan, one of the planet's endangered species, lives only in Sumatra and Borneo. Its solitary and elusive nature makes it hard to track down, but sanctuaries at Bohorok (Bukit Lawang – see opposite) and Tanjung Puting (southern Kalimantan – see page 228), as well as at Sepilok in Malaysia's Sabah and at Semenggoh in Sarawak, offer some exceptional close-ups.

Man's ancestor? The orang-utan's endearingly human gestures and expressions long convinced scientists that this member of the ape family provided the missing link in man's evolutionary tree. In the 18th century a certain James Burnett even believed that they merely had an accidental speech impediment, supporting his theory by escorting his pet orang-utan, suitably attired in jacket and tie, to society dinner parties. Today, however, scientists are more concerned with saving this primate from extinction: logging of the orang-utan's natural habitat and the Sumatran fashion for keeping the animals as pets has created havoc with their numbers. There are an estimated 10,000 to 20,000 alive today, a number much boosted by the efforts of the rehabilitation centres which retrain them for life back in the forest after years of caged existence.

Personalities Adult males tend to live alone, choosing to spend their 30-odd years in swampland and lowland dipterocarp forest near rivers. A female gives birth to a total of three or four young which remain dependent on her for their first five years, but if her basic diet of fruit, leaves, bark and insects is depleted she does not hesitate to abandon them – one of the reasons why so many of the rehabilitation centre's inmates are helpless young.

Beware
Although the behaviour of orang-utans may seem entrancing, their strength should not be under-estimated. Biruté Galdikas, who set up the Tanjung Puting sanctuary in Kalimantan in 1971, relates how she has several times escaped attempts on her life by potential protégés. The ape's strength comes into its own when pushing dead trees on to over-curious spectators, or even stripping tourists of their brightly coloured clothes. However, they are particu-larly renowned for spraying the unsuspecting with their urine and throwing their own dung, so keep a distance and be wary of their apparent charm.

Orang-utans are occasionally sighted in riverside trees outside the Bohorok centre, Bukit Lawang

The reconstructed sultan's palace of Pangaruyung

▶▶▶ Bukittinggi
110C3

The small highland retreat of Bukittinggi lies 90km north of Padang on the Agam Plateau and is encircled by the ever-visible volcanoes of Sago, Singgalang and Merapi. The town is situated at the heart of the Minangkabau region and makes a stimulating base for discovering traditional villages, crafts and superbly diverse landscapes. The climate is cool, the atmosphere relaxing, the Minang people friendly and tourist facilities sufficiently developed to allow access to this fascinating culture (see pages 130–1).

Town sights The town centre rises up on either side of the main road, Jalan Jend A Yani, which has a monopoly on budget hotels, tour agencies and restaurants. At the southern end stands Bukittinggi's symbolic clock-tower, the **Jam Gadang**, which was erected by the Dutch in 1827, and, rather oddly, incorporates a Minangkabau roof. Uphill from here is the start of the sprawling **market** area, particularly lively on Wednesdays and Saturdays when local villagers come to buy and sell a vast range of goods.

Beyond the Mesjid Raya and along the ridge of the hill lies the park of **Taman Bundokanduang**, of more interest for its museum than its rather forlorn zoo inmates. The well-established **museum▶▶▶** (*open*: daily, 7:30–5), built in traditional style, offers a good introduction to local culture. Displays include Minangkabau artefacts, ornaments, models of traditional houses, *songket* and musical instruments. A footbridge leads from the museum over Jalan Jend A Yani to the site of a Dutch fort on the hill opposite. **Fort de Kock** dates from the 1820s, but today only offers sweeping panoramas over the town.

To the canyon At the southern end of town lies Panorama Park, a popular promenading area containing a labyrinth of tunnels used by the Japanese in World War II as hide-outs and for propelling Indonesians to their death in the canyon below. Opposite, on Jalan Panorama, is the **Museum Perjuangan (Military Museum)▶**.

The long grave
The sleepy little village of Pariangan offers several intricately carved Minangkabau houses fronted by their obligatory rice-barns. Although in many places traditional multi-family houses have been abandoned in favour of small one-family houses, this village continues in its own sweet way. It also boasts a long grave, said to be that of Tantejo Gurhano, a prominent protagonist in Minangkabau art and culture. Villagers offer you a stick to measure the grave (it is over 20m long); in one direction the stick fits 46 times, in the other direction it fits 47 times. Work that one out!

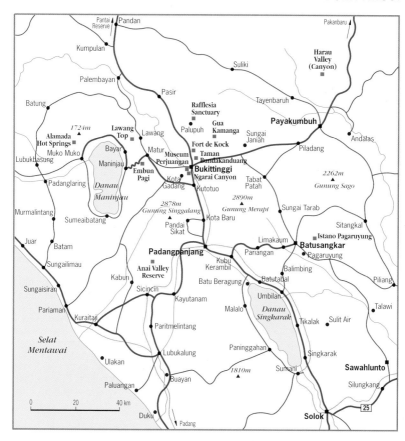

The massive chasm of the **Sianok (Ngarai) Canyon** slices through Bukittinggi's rocky cliffs and the foothills of Mount Singgalang, and can be crossed by descending a trail which starts at the end of Jalan Teuku Umar. Allow 2 hours to reach the village of **Kota Gadang▶▶**, the Minangkabau centre for silver jewellery, and take a guide as the trail is not always clear.

Out of town Tours of Bukittinggi's surroundings include the beautiful Danau Maninjau (see page 120), bullfights at Kota Baru on Tuesdays and Saturdays, *songket*-weaving and woodcarving at Pandai Sikat, the *Rafflesia* sanctuary near Palupun, and the fertile Harau Valley (see page 127). To glimpse surviving Minangkabau village traditions, allow a day to explore the **Batusangkar region▶▶▶**, east of Bukittinggi. Rolling landscapes of rice or corn offer peaceful foregrounds to the swooping winged roofs of Minangkabau communal houses and rice-barns. The villages of **Balimbing** and less-visited **Pariangan** offer outstanding architectural examples, some 300 years old (see panel opposite). At **Pangaruyung** stands a magnificent replica palace, the Istano Silinduang Bulan, but more impressive still is the Istano Pangaruyung, a reconstructed sultan's palace now converted into a museum. Between these edifices lie menhirs, some carved in Sanskrit.

Hunters
A common sight in Minangkabau territory is that of men leading around well-groomed dogs that sport studded collars. These are not family pets but specially bred hunting dogs, much cosseted so that they are all the better to track down wild boar. The hunter himself will inevitably have a *parang* (dagger) stuck into his belt, used to deliver the final fatal blow. In the nature and game reserve of the Harau Valley, hunters gather once a week to track down boars (these are not protected due to their destructive habits). Dogs are even hired out for the day from the local market for this occasion.

The Maninjau crater lake offers cool, relaxing surroundings with banks that sometimes descend a precipitous 600m

Minangkabau shopping
The region around Bukittinggi offers some enticing buys, from the fine filigree silver jewellery or embroidery made at Kota Gadang, to the intricate basketwork of Paya Kumbuh (near the Harau Valley), the exquisite and pricey, labour-intensive *songket* woven at Pandai Sikat and the pottery and hardware items made at the blacksmith's village of Sungai Puar. Bukittinggi's market offers a good overview of the region's offerings and there are a number of antique and souvenir shops along the main street. As always, bargain hard.

►►► **Danau Maninjau** *110C3*

This is another of Indonesia's stunning crater lakes, one of the largest in the world, and lies 38km west of Bukittinggi. Access from Bukittinggi is via the Lawang Top, which offers panoramas of the deep blue lake 800m below. From here the road winds down through jungle and terraced paddy-fields to the lake resort of Maninjau. Water-skiing, boating, swimming and fishing are the main activities here, and there is also plenty of good hiking along jungle trails or to the Alamada Hot Springs. Traditional local dances are sometimes staged at the village of Matur overlooking the lake. Maninjau is now beginning to rival Danau Toba in the backpacker popularity stakes, but none the less it still manages to remain low key.

►► **Danau Ranau** *111D1*

This vast lake, still pristine and undeveloped, lies lost in the Bukit Barisan mountain range of South Sumatra. Although a favourite with domestic tourists for its watersports, hiking, cool climate and hot springs, few foreign visitors make it here as the lake lies well off the Trans-Sumatran Highway. Most accommodation and facilities are concentrated on the northern shore at **Bandingagung**, which looks across to Mount Seminung soaring 1,880m above the lake's southern shore. The quickest access is from Martapura by bus, but the longer southern route from the port of Tanjungkarang via Bukitkemuning is more scenic as it meanders through undulating foothills and traditional Lampung villages.

► **Danau Singkarak** *110C3*

About 30km southeast of Bukittinggi is another large mountain lake. Singkarak offers rural landscapes and limited lakeside accommodation, although it is far from the magnificent spectacle of Danau Maninjau. Access from the east (via Batusangkar) offers a view of the river that feeds the lake, much of the latter's eastern shore edged with paddy-fields. A ferry service connects Singkarak with villages on the opposite shore. At Solok, a few kilometres south of Singkarak, there are some stunning examples of richly carved and painted Minangkabau architecture as well as two smaller lakes, Danau Dibawah and Danau Diatas.

■ **Bamboo is one of the planet's most versatile plants, a fact that has been recognised and exploited to the full by Southeast Asian villagers for centuries. Bamboo grows quickly in bushy riverside groves and is economical to use, its only problem being its lack of durability.....■**

Some 31 species of bamboo grow in Indonesia and, until very recently, this essentially tropical plant was the national building material. In the 1950s, 35 per cent of houses were built entirely of bamboo and a further 35 per cent constructed from a mixture of bamboo and timber. Since then, concrete has made its inroads, contributing to the negative association of bamboo with poverty in the minds of the local people. However, the extreme versatility and accessibility of bamboo (it grows naturally from Sumatra to Sulawesi) and an increasing interest in its applications among contemporary architects may see a reversal of this trend.

Multi-purpose product A Chinese scientist once calculated that bamboo had 1,386 uses, not including the traditional Asian umbrella and modern aeroplane fuselages. It is both waterproof and insect-proof while offering gentle ventilation, and is therefore ideal for tropical dwellings. Nor is it hard to come by. Bamboo shoots develop into full 30m canes in a month, making it the fastest growing plant after grass. Its low weight, high resistance to tension, compression, flexibility and ease of processing further augment its attractions.

Plaiting The skilled craft of splitting and plaiting cane to make *bilik* (bamboo walls) is widespread throughout the Indonesian archipelago, but the most sophisticated designs can be seen in Sumatra's Batak country and in Sulawesi's Tana Toraja. Canes of up to 10m are cut lengthwise with a sharp *parang* (dagger) into narrow, pliable strips which are interwoven, sometimes into extremely intricate patterns that are then given further relief by paint. Most *pasar* (markets) stock stacks of these large sheets and a common rural sight is of a figure half obscured beneath his future house wall.

Decorative bamboo poles in Bali

Facts and figures

● In AD552 silkworm eggs were smuggled in bamboo tubes from China to Constantinople, thereby precipitating the downfall of the Silk Road.

● Four centuries earlier the Chinese had already invented a bamboo pipeline to transport natural gas.

● Bamboo's superior resistance to timber and iron is renowned: its fibres resist 40kg/sq mm before snapping; timber resists only 5kg/sq mm; and iron resists 37kg/sq mm.

● Records of bamboo growth over 24 hours start at 91cm, recorded in London's Kew Gardens in 1855, and reach a staggering 121cm, recorded in Kyoto in 1956.

Bringing home a bilik

SUMATRA

Lake Toba's depths plunge to over 400m while the undulating shores offer superb vistas

▶▶▶ Danau Toba   *110B4*

The immense and beautiful 1,700 sq km volcanic lake of Toba is Southeast Asia's largest lake and one of the world's highest at an altitude of over 900m. It was formed 75,000 years ago by an almighty eruption which left the island of Samosir sitting in its middle, and has since become North Sumatra's main tourist destination. Natural beauty aside, Lake Toba is also home to the Batak people, who have left magnificent traditional houses, tombs and stone-carvings on Samosir and around the lakeshore. Unfortunately, a profitable tourist industry has developed out of this, hitting heights of commercialism at the main lake resort of Prapat.

The shores It is hard to miss **Prapat** on the lake's eastern shore as this is Toba's main bus and ferry hub. The small town is a favourite haunt for the Medan weekend set but has developed a hard edge with unsmiling locals and a plethora of overpriced hotels, tourist shops and watersports facilities. The setting may be attractive, but foreign visitors will find a more welcoming atmosphere across the water on Samosir.

In the hills southeast of Prapat a picturesque cluster of traditional Batak villages centres on **Jangga▶▶**, famous for its *ulos*-weaving with decoration of broken lines. To the north, in a stunningly beautiful region of pastures, cornfields and pine forests, lies the village of **Haranggaol▶▶**, a centre for the Simalungan Bataks. Ferries leave here for Samosir island. Near by, at Pematang Purba, are the gardens of the **Simalungan Palace▶▶**, containing a massive royal longhouse built of teak and raised on piles which could accommodate up to 24 of the chief's wives. The thundering 108m waterfall of **Sipisopiso** at Tongging forms a grand finale at the end of the lake and also offers superb panoramas.

The island The large, mountainous island of Samosir has been a favourite with backpackers for many years and offers a peaceful rural setting, good hiking, swimming and numerous Batak relics. On the west coast lies the island capital of **Pangururan**, connected to the mainland by a bridge. Just outside this nondescript town you can plunge into an intensive sulphur cure at the hot springs of Mount Belirang. On the northern tip of the island is the village of **Simanindo▶▶**, where a former chief's house has been transformed into an ethnological museum next to a well-conserved group of Batak houses and some enigmatic sculptures of Batak deities. Traditional Batak dance performances are held here every morning.

Foreign travellers tend to head for the golden triangle of Ambarita, Tuk Tuk and Tomok on Samosir's east coast. Regular ferries connect these villages with Prapat, about 30 minutes

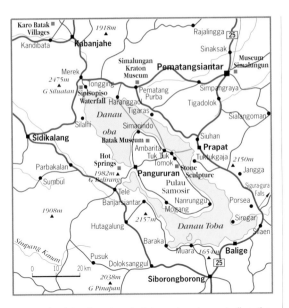

Batak *pustaha*
Among the multitude of intriguing Batak artefacts that are churned out for the tourist trade you are likely to encounter the *pustaha*, folded bark manuscripts covered with Batak script. These concertina-shaped books of beaten bark from the *alim* tree were used by soothsayers for oral instructions in the art of divination, magic and medicine, and were handed down from master to apprentice. The texts contain notes on agricultural procedures, oracles and charms, as well as recipes for potions and poisons.

across the lake. Low-key hotels and restaurants line the shores of the relaxed **Tuk Tuk Peninsula**, good for swimming and canoeing but without any culture. **Ambarita**, immediately north, is home to an impressive circle of 300-year-old stone chairs which stand behind a row of immaculate Batak houses near the jetty. To the south is **Tomok**, with its outstanding circle of carved seated figures, coffins, the tomb of King Sidabutar and a modest Batak museum in a traditional house. These sights have now unfortunately been invaded by endless rows of souvenir-stalls and their aggressive owners.

Lake ferries shuttle regularly between Prapat and the island of Samosir

■ **The Batak are famed for their extraordinary stone- and woodcarvings, their architecture and their jewellery, whose divine functions have mostly disappeared in the wake of Christianity. Pockets of animist *adat* (traditional) culture manage to survive, but cannibalism is definitely a thing of the past.....■**

Jewellery

As in other regions of Indonesia, Batak jewellery was imbued with both spiritual and temporal significance. Besides indicating the wearer's social status, jewellery was used by the *datu* in healing ceremonies. Among the Karo Batak, ornaments worn by bride and groom were also used in rituals to call back wandering souls of sick people. This was based on the belief that the temporary union of complementary opposites (male and female) produced protective powers. Batak jewellery was principally cast by the lost-wax method in silver or brass, and often incorporated as a talisman the head of the mythical *singa* monster, with its long, protruding tongue.

Traditional Batak headgear combines fabric and foliage

North Sumatra, a land of volcanoes and high plateaux with the immense Lake Toba at its heart, has been home to the Batak for millennia. The Batak (a general term meaning 'pig-eater' coined by the Muslims) consist of six major cultures: the Toba Batak, who live in the centre of this rugged terrain; the Karo and Simalungan, who live in the north and northeast; the Dairi-Pakpak, who inhabit the northwest region; and the Angkola and Mandailing, who can be found in the south.

The Bataks' unique, deeply mystical cultures resisted external influences until the early 19th century when the Dutch and English, competing for control of Sumatra's rich agricultural and mineral resources, started penetrating the region. By the mid-19th century the Dutch had gained control of important districts from their Minangkabau and English rivals, and in 1864 the first Christian mission was founded. The next 40 years saw the Batak fight desperately to preserve themselves from foreign domination, but the Dutch and Christianity won the day, and today the Batak form a fervent Christian group of some 3 million sandwiched between their Muslim neighbours – the orthodox Acehnese to the north and the Minangkabau to the south.

Batak cosmogony Of the six groups, visitors are most likely to come into contact with the Toba Batak on Samosir island and on the lake shores, and with the Karo, who are concentrated around Berastagi. Myths of Batak origins vary, but all regard Lake Toba as their ancestral homeland. Traditional Batak religion recognised a tripartite division of the universe into upper, middle and lower worlds, respectively the realms of the gods, men and malevolent spirits. Their supreme god was Mula Djadi, universal creator and progenitor of three further deities.

Every human was believed to have two souls: the spirit of the living person (*tondi*), and the potentially harmful spirit released upon a person's death (*begu*). For the *begu* to be appeased and reach the higher spirit form, it was essential for the deceased's family to make ritual offerings and prayers. Even more important was the expertise of the *datu* (spiritual mediator), who played a crucial role in invoking divine protection. The main tools of the *datu*'s trade, now reproduced endlessly as tourist souvenirs, consisted of a *pupuk* (a ceramic container for 'magic' organic substances applied to objects and sculptures), an elaborately carved ritual staff called a *tunggal panaluan*, and the essential divination book, the *pustaha* (see panel on page 123). The *datu* also consulted divination calendars and charts inscribed on bamboo tubes or bones.

Cannibals The Bataks were renowned for their skill in warfare and for their stunning array of weapons and firearms, but they still relied heavily on supernatural forces to ensure victory in battle. No conflict was initiated without consulting the *datu*, who determined an auspicious date for combat by consulting his *pustaha*. However, it was the end of a battle that saw the Bataks' most gruesome custom – cannibalism, which persisted among the Toba and Pakpak into the 20th century. Captured enemies were regarded as inhuman and, as such, excellent gastronomic fare. The victim would be tied to a stake and cut apart by the victorious warriors who roasted his flesh for consumption.

Cosmic replicas Batak homes re-created the cosmos, with upper, middle and lower areas protected by the *singa*, a mythical monster whose carved head adorned the front of the nobleman's house. Most villages consisted of only about ten houses, those of the Toba Batak built with dramatic carved, saddleback roofs, and those of the Karo sporting a monumental hipped, gabled form. Village enclosures were often fortified with high embankments planted with bamboo, and houses were aligned according to spiritual criteria.

The *sigalegale*
One of the many Batak funerary rituals featured an almost lifesize puppet known as the *sigalegale*. This was designed to chase evil spirits away from the grave, but today is used more often in wedding ceremonies. The large, carved banyan-wood puppet has articulated limbs and is dressed in traditional costume of turban, loose shirt and sarong. It is then mounted on a wheeled platform and made to dance to the accompaniment of gamelan music, flute and drums. The most sophisticated *singalegales* can weep, smoke cigarettes and even poke out their tongues.

125

Sophisticated Batak construction and carving techniques linger on...just

SUMATRA

Rafflesia arnoldii, 1m in diameter, on the vine it parasitises

Mitred leaf monkey

Forest products

The biologically rich rainforests of Indonesia offer an abundance of products whose value is only too easily recognised by locals and corporations alike. Non-timber forest products include rattan, resins, medicinal plants and animal products. Resin (a secretion obtained from hardwoods) and gums are both used as raw materials for plastics, adhesives, inks and paints. Essential oils such as canaga, citronella and cloves are used in the cosmetics and pharmaceutical industries, as are seed oils such as castor oil. Rainforest plants produce a quarter of all pharmaceutical ingredients and 70 per cent of them have been identified as potentially useful treatments. In 1989 Indonesia's non-timber forest products netted Rp626 billion (US$313 million) in revenue.

▶▶ **Gunung Leuser, Taman Nasional**   *110B5*

Southeast Asia's largest national park (946,000 hectares) lies northwest of Medan in the Bukit Barisan mountain range. The park is a largely wild area of primary rainforest and swamp forest harbouring some rare and endangered species. The highest point is Gunung Leuser, which peaks at 3,500m and is situated in the largest section of the park, to the west of the cultivated Alas Valley. Here, too, are the magnificent gorges of the upper Alas, as well as the Mamas Valley with its undisturbed wildlife and vegetation.

Natural salt-licks all over the park attract elephants, tigers, mouse deer and orang-utans. *Siamangs* (black apes), gibbons, long-tailed macaques and leaf-monkeys abound, as does a rich bird community which includes hornbills and argus pheasants. There are some 3,500 species of flora, including the giant *Rafflesia* flower, while each hectare of lowland forest proliferates with 60–130 tree species. The drawback is the abundance of leeches, which are eminently at home in the humid rainforest environment.

The park headquarters are at **Kotacane** where permits are issued and basic accommodation is available. Jungle treks with guides can last anything from a day to a week, or you can raft down the Alas river; expeditions can be organised through tour agents in Medan. An alternative way into the park is from the Orangutan Rehabilitation Centre of Bohorok at Bukit Lawang (see page 116).

►► Harau Valley 110C3

If you follow a scenic, verdant road 37km northeast of Bukittinggi you will reach a spectacular stretch of sheer granite cliffs washed by a 150m waterfall which plunges into a deep, clear pool. This is the Harau Valley with, at its heart, the nature and game reserve of Cagar Alam Harau, a relatively modest area of 315 hectares which harbours *siamangs* (black apes), tapirs, bears, wild goats and tigers. The exotic products of an orchid garden is a popular local crowd-puller, but the reserve's main interest lies in its excellent hiking and rich wildlife.

►► Kerinci-Seblat, Taman Nasional 110C3

This gigantic 1,484,650-hectare nature reserve is home to Sumatra's highest peak, Mount Kerinci (3,800m), and spans the borders of four provinces in southwest Sumatra. Most of the reserve is situated above 400m and so offers a cool contrast to the steamy coast. The easiest and most scenic access is via Padang along the coast road to **Sungaipenuh**, which lies at the heart of a 70km-long valley. Sungaipenuh offers limited accommodation, the PHPA office for permits, local guides and a particularly ornate mosque, said to be over 400 years old.

From Sungaipenuh trails lead to the high-altitude marsh of Danau Bentu and the wilder, more remote southern half of the reserve around Mount Seblat. Away from the settlements of the valley wildlife becomes more varied as you enter lowland and then montane forest, with alpine vegetation on the higher slopes. The crater lake of Danau Tujuh is impressive, but try the arduous 2-day climb of Kerinci to see the view from this home of the gods. The best base for this feat is the village of Kersik Tuo.

Sumatran tiger

Sumatran tiger
The population of the elegant yellow *Panthera tigris sumatrae* has been declining steadily and is now estimated at around 400, half the number that existed five years ago. This is a direct result of resettlement projects in Sumatra, of increasing deforestation and of commercial motives – tiger hides are still seen as a status symbol amongst wealthy Javanese. In an attempt to prevent extinction, a tiger sperm bank was set up in 1994 near Bogor, in West Java.

Logging
Illegal logging by local inhabitants (many are transmigrants from Java) is an ongoing problem in Kerinci-Seblat, affecting up to 30,000 hectares. Ironically, it was the local communities who made the first moves to protect their forest in 1927, applying their traditional law to Temedak Forest in a move to halt deforestation for cash crops.

SUMATRA

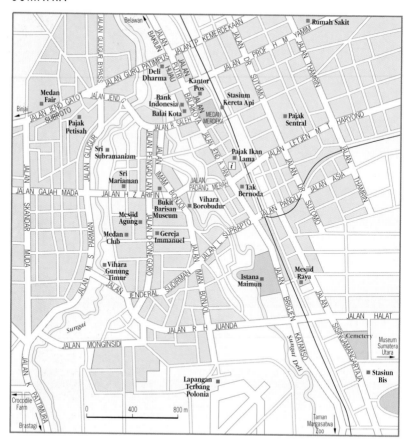

▶▶ Medan

110B5

Far from being the noisy, polluted, aggressive bastion of Islam that it is made out to be, North Sumatra's capital has a distinctive character and rhythm. The city is an obvious gateway to Sumatra, whether by boat from Pulau Pinang in Malaysia or through its international airport, and offers a modest introduction to the region's culture. Beyond lies the rural Sumatra of plantations, hill towns and nature reserves, so make the most of the city's urban offerings.

Battlefield Medan actually means 'battlefield', a reference to its role as a point of friction between the sultanates of Deli and Aceh in 1630. By 1682 it had been established as a trading centre, but it was under Dutch control from 1886 onwards that the commercial boom really got going. Rubber, coffee, tea and tobacco from local plantations were all exported through Medan's port of Belawan. Since then, the discovery of oil and natural gas has further stimulated the regional economy. However, Medan's battlefield role seems far from over. In April 1994 several days of strikes by over 20,000 workers escalated into widespread violence, much of it targeting the local Chinese. Troops eventually quelled the socio-economic storm, but racial tensions and huge discrepancies in wealth remain.

Sights Medan's centre radiates from **Medan Merdeka**, a large grassy square lined with fine old colonial buildings (visit the superb 1911 Post Office) and shaded by huge trees. From here the main road of Jalan Jend A Yani runs south past some badly maintained but striking colonial buildings (including the tourist office at No 107) towards Medan's monuments.

The massive black-domed **Mesjid Raya**►► is one of Indonesia's largest mosques, designed in solid though distinctive Moorish style for Sultan Makmun Al-Rasyid in 1906. Diametrically opposite stands the richly decorated **Istana Maimun**►►►, still partly inhabited by 25 descendants of the last sultan. This elegant colonnaded palace was built by Capt TH Van Erf in 1888, and incorporates Italian marble and Baccarat chandeliers in a lavish Moorish-style interior. Old photos, the sultan's carved ironwood throne (higher than his wife's!) and some 16th-century Dutch furniture are the main offerings. The rather neglected garden contains a replica of a Toba Batak house, a symbolic gesture to a sultan's Batak wife. About 3km from here is the traditionally styled **Museum Sumatera Utara**►►, which exhibits an interesting collection of North Sumatran cultural artefacts, from Batak calendars, masks and *ulos* weavings to superb totemic statues from Pulau Nias (see pages 134–5).

Peripheral sights Medan's cosmopolitan community has also left its mark in temples scattered over town. Sumatra's oldest Tamil temple, the **Sri Mariaman** (1884), is a typically polychromatic affair replete with Hindu deities, and is situated on the corner of Jalan Teuku Umar and Jalan HZ Arifin. Chinese temples are more numerous, the oldest dating from 1870 (just off Jalan Pandu) and the largest, the **Vihara Gunung Timur**, located in Jalan Hang Tuah. The latter, a huge, modern Buddhist and Taoist complex, lies in a tree-lined district of large villas that provide a good indication of the prosperity of Medan's Chinese community.

Shopping
A treasure trove of textiles from all over the archipelago is concentrated in a labyrinth of stalls at the Pajak Ikan Lama in Jalan Perniagaan, just behind the tourist office. On Jalan Jend A Yani itself a string of antique/souvenir shops offers varying standards of merchandise, but the sharp-eyed visitor may still spot a bargain. About 2km east of here, on Jalan Dr Sutomo, is the enormous central market (Pajak Sentral), where goods range from fish to basketware. Beware of the pickpockets who operate intensively here.

The astonishing Istana Maimun

■ The Minangkabau people, who are concentrated in the centre of West Sumatra, constitute one of Indonesia's most economically successful ethnic groups. Their unique matrilineal society may be one of the reasons for this, but their democratic system of thought has also nurtured extreme resourcefulness and adaptability..... ■

Women's treasure trove
Massive bracelets, superb gold filigree head-dresses and glittering *songket* weavings are usually part of a Minangkabau family's heirlooms. Men have the responsibility for ensuring the safety of such treasures – but who holds the key to the safe in this matriarchal society? The woman of course!

Certain sarongs are decorated with four gold stripes which symbolise the necessary qualities of these superwomen: serenity, wisdom, frugality, and good management of house and land.

Top: the replica royal palace at Pangaruyung, near Bukittinggi, built to traditional Minangkabau design
Below: Minangkabau wedding costume

The fertile highlands and luxuriant jungles of West Sumatra are home to nearly 4 million Minangkabau, an ethnic group that probably arrived in the region some 3,000 years ago. Although their early wealth stemmed from mountain gold mines, these resources had dried up by the late 18th century, and the Minangs turned to developing sophisticated agricultural techniques for salt, coffee and pepper instead. Today, their spicy Padang restaurants are known all over the archipelago. Many Minangs have also played important political roles – most notably the independence leader Mohammed Hatta – it is said that their business acumen is second only to the Chinese.

Matriarchy Above all else, the Minangkabau are unique in Indonesia for their matrilineal society, which emigrants also took to Malaysia's state of Negeri Sembilan. In this system, inheritance, titles and family names are passed down through the female line. Women are the family heiresses and retain the right to live in the family houses even after marriage, the eldest holding the most powerful role in the household. Men have no rights over women other than to expect marital fidelity, and a mother's eldest brother rather than her husband will supervise her children's education and advise on their marriage. While a woman can demand that her husband fulfil his marital obligations, a man cannot demand the same of his wife. Young men are encouraged to leave their mother's house at an early age to go walkabout (*merantau*), and it is this which is thought to be the reason for Minangkabau peripatetic habits.

Paderi Wars Although the Minangkabau are now solidly Muslim, this was not always the case. Conversion came gradually, starting in the 16th century, but became more generalised as a result of the protracted Paderi Wars (1803–38). These were instigated by fundamentalist Muslims from the Agam Plateau who were named Paderis after their port of embarkation for Mecca, Pedir. The hadjis were inspired by the new Wahabite reformist zeal that had swept Arabia, and took a dim view of Minangkabau matriarchy, gambling, drinking, tobacco-smoking, betel-nut-chewing and opium-taking. An impassioned and ruthless civil war soon erupted to eradicate these habits.

In 1815 the Minangkabau royal family was murdered, but further military confrontations followed when anti-Paderi *adat* (traditional) chiefs signed a treaty with the Dutch in 1821. Dutch sovereignty found itself pitted against a formidable enemy led by the Imam Bonjol, but managed to cut the Minangkabau trade lifeline and, in 1838, carried off a final colonial victory. The result of this momentous period was that a division was created between commitment to Islam and Minangkabau *adat* laws and social organisation.

Architecture The extravagant Minangkabau architecture is a superb symbol of this people's ethnic confidence. Majestically sweeping roofs ending in buffalo-horn gables surmount the rectangular *rumah gadang* ('big house'), itself raised on piles. Inside is a row of family rooms (up to seven) fronted by a communal living area. The houses are intricately carved and, like those of the Toraja (see pages 208–9), fronted by equally ornate rice-barns as well as the male sleeping quarters.

Unique to Indonesia, the Minangkabau matriarchal society gives women a prominent role

SUMATRA

Mentawai Islands
From Padang's Muara Harbour, boats leave on Mondays, Wednesdays and Thursdays for the idyllic Mentawai Islands, 12 hours away across the rough Indian Ocean. An easier option is to join an organised tour from Padang or Bukittinggi. Of the four islands, Siberut offers the most interest, both scenically and atmospherically, and has recently been declared a National Biosphere Reserve by Unesco. The 18,000 inhabitants remained isolated from the rest of the world until missionaries found their way here in the early 20th century, and they still preserve an astonishingly pure way of life, living in communal longhouses and practising animism. Conditions are very basic but the rewards are genuine, whether you take canoe trips through tropical rainforest, visit remote villages, snorkel around the island's superlative coral reefs or merely experience the strength of this 3,000-year-old culture.

► **Meulaboh** *110A5*

Few travellers attempt the long, hard haul down Sumatra's northwestern coast from Banda Aceh, but those who do rarely forget its remoteness and dramatic shores. Meulaboh itself, about 230km south of Banda Aceh, is a peaceful seaside town that is popular with surfers and has some basic accommodation. Local villages specialise in embroidered and handwoven textiles which are rarely seen outside the region.

►► **Padang** *110C3*

This tropical staging post lies half-way up Sumatra's west coast and is the gateway to the Minangkabau region, the proud culture of these people announced by Padang's modern buffalo-horn buildings. Half a million inhabitants live in the provincial capital, which sprang on to the map in the early 18th century on the back of gold and pepper exports. Today its greatest asset is a palm-lined white beach where fiery sunsets, welcoming breezes and sizzling *warungs* (food-stalls) attract the evening crowds.

Padang's compact centre offers a rather uninspired introduction to Minangkabau culture at the imposing

Fishermen at Teluk Bungus near Padang, from where boats can be hired

Palembang's market activity at Pasar 16 Ilir spills on to the street

Adityawarman Museum► which, in true traditional style, is fronted by two rice-barns. A cultural centre across Jalan Diponegoro stages regular performances of music and dance. North of the museum is Padang's main administrative and commercial hub, this also being home to the white-tiled mosque and the elegant old **Balai Kota (Town Hall)**, now adjoined by a modern version. Here, too, sprawls the vast **Pasar Raya (Central Market)►►**, a maze of stalls selling specialised goods.

South of the museum towards the river and radiating from Jalan Niaga is Padang's Chinatown, an area of atmospheric old stucco shophouses and warehouses crowned by an impressive Buddhist temple, the **Kwan Im Bio►►** (1861), which rises in ornate splendour behind a lotus pond. Don't miss the weeping ceramic dragons on its roof. From the riverside fishing village, ferries cross to the opposite bank where a path leads over the headland through a Chinese cemetery and frangipani trees to the popular beach and fishing village of **Air Manis**, and beyond that the main port of **Teluk Bayur**. Further south still is **Teluk Bungus►►**, a once exquisite beach now partly marred by a giant sawmill.

Unloading bananas beside Palembang's lifeline, the Musi river

133

► Palembang   111E2

Although situated some 80km from the sea, Palembang possesses the strange status of being Sumatra's principal port. Ships loaded with rubber, timber, coffee, tin and, above all, oil ply the Musi river constantly through this prosperous but swampy region. Some 13 centuries ago Palembang was the capital of the great Srivijaya kingdom. This powerful Hindu-Buddhist maritime kingdom controlled West Java, the Malay Peninsula, eastern Borneo and the rest of Sumatra (see panel). Sadly, virtually nothing remains, although archaeological investigation continues. Today this heavily industrialised city of over a million inhabitants has little to offer the tourist, and visits are not helped by the sticky climate that is nurtured by the surrounding marshes.

The city centre is sliced by the Musi river, in turn spanned by the Ampera Bridge, with sights concentrated on the northern bank. The recently restored **Mesjid Agung►►** (1738) dominates the area just north of the bridge and vies with the mosques of Banda Aceh and Medan for grandeur. Close by stands the **Museum Budaya Sultan Mahmud Bandaruddin►**, a traditional wooden house which is home to European, Chinese and Srivijayan artefacts, as well as the tourist office and a crafts market in the garden. East of here, along Jalan Pasar 16 Ilir, lies the fascinating market area at the heart of Palembang's Chinatown, a labyrinth of houses leading down to and almost toppling into the river. Of the numerous Buddhist temples that are situated in the area, the **Klenteng Kwa Sam Yo►►** is the most rewarding for its descriptive murals.

About 5km north of town at Jalan Srivijaya stands the **Museum Negeri Sumatera Selatan►►**, which houses an extensive collection of ethnographic and archaeological pieces. Behind the museum stand two reconstructed *rumah limas* (traditional Palembang houses) which exhibit remarkable stone-carvings, some from the Pasemah Plateau near Lahat.

Srivijayan tentacles
Information about the Srivijaya kingdom has controversially been pieced together since Georges Coedès' first relevant publication in 1918. Some details were gleaned from carved stones found around Palembang, and others from ancient chronicles and travellers' accounts. What is certain is that by the 8th century the empire-building Srivijayans had sent an army as far as Cambodia, where rulers were forced to bow to the west in prayer as a tribute to the maharaja of Srivijaya. By the 9th to 11th centuries, Srivijaya had monasteries in Bengal and South India, and Palembang had become a flourishing city of learning, home to over a thousand Buddhist monks. Pilgrims from China would stop here to learn Sanskrit and the tenets of Buddhism before visiting the holy land of India. By the 13th century Srivijaya was in serious decline and in 1377 it bowed to Javanese conquest.

SUMATRA

Nias's traditional stone-jumping ritual – the initiation leap

Nias rites
One of Nias's crowd-pullers is stone-jumping (*fahombe*), an exercise formerly practised in preparation for war. Acrobatic warriors, sword in hand, would launch themselves from a slab to leap over a stone pedestal placed in the ceremonial square of a village. The stone sometimes reaches heights of 2.5m. Fearless as ever, the Niassans also confronted death eye to eye: the low stone tables seen in villages were used for laying out corpses which were only buried once their flesh had completely decayed. Their coffins were beautifully decorated, often carved with figures of birds and lizards. The fate of pigs was less honoured although their value was highly regarded by the hierarchical and ritualistic Nias society: up to a hundred would be slaughtered for major ceremonies and they were used as payment for such services as the making of ceremonial jewellery or the erecting of a monument.

▶▶ **Pulau Nias** *110B4*

The island of Nias, long isolated from developments in the rest of Sumatra, has now been catapulted firmly into the 20th century. Surf is the prime reason for its popularity, particularly the southern beaches on Lagundi Bay. However, this mountainous island, about 125km west of the port of Sibolga, also harbours some superb relics of an enigmatic megalithic culture. It is thought that the ancestors of today's 500,000 Nias Bataks emigrated from continental Asia during the Bronze Age. Although Arab traders mentioned the island in the 9th century it was not until the 17th century that outsiders, in this case Dutch, first established a trading post here. By the late 19th century missionaries began to arrive. Today, 80 per cent of the islanders are

Christian and their traditions have all but disappeared.

The quickest access to Nias is by plane from Medan, but many budget travellers choose to ride out the ocean waves in daily ferries (12 to 24 hours) from Sibolga which dock at the capital of **Gunungsitoli**. This town offers little in the way of cultural or hedonistic interest, although some traditional oval houses of the northern region are still in evidence. More useful is the port of **Telukdalam** in the south. Although this offers nothing to the visitor, it is near Nias's most interesting traditional villages as well as **Lagundi**'s perfect horseshoe bay, about 12km west. This 4km coral beach is now Sumatra's epicentre for surfers and shoestring travellers. Lined with *losmen* (budget inns), it offers reasonable swimming at its eastern end.

Southern villages For those more interested in the culture of the island, the villages in the hills of southern and central Nias have most to offer. These were usually built on defensive high ground surrounded by a wall and consisted of two rows of elevated, high-gabled houses overlooking a long paved street. Communal areas were located at the front of each house and private quarters at the back, with livestock scuffling around below. The chief's house was always the most ornamental, its high gable carved with animal heads and fronted by stone megaliths and benches which were used for village rites.

The rather touristy but easily accessible village of **Bawamataluo**▶▶▶ is approached by 480 stone steps and tight hairpin bends 14km northwest of Telukdalam. Its atmosphere may be far from *adat* (traditional) and even overtly commercial, but it boasts a remarkably carved chief's house, now partly a museum, and a wealth of intricately carved stone sculptures and megaliths. At **Hilismaetano**▶▶, a more recently built village, the soaring-roofed houses face the chief's house around a square which is used for stone-jumping rituals (performed

Mysterious remains
'One lies down in the sand and looks into the top of the coconut trees, like great, symmetrical windroses. The sun sinks into a blue sky full of little white clouds and from the vast deeps of the Indian Ocean great waves roll into the bay. Deep in the jungles of south-east Nias lie the mysterious remains of villages long deserted – great terraces and altars, double rows of pillars, crowned with figures of deer and rhinoceros-birds, mushroom-shaped stones on which graceful dancers once bent and swayed...'.
– From *Forgotten Kingdoms in Sumatra* by FM Schnitger (1939).

135

The village of Bawamataluo has a fascinating complex of 100-year-old houses

Modern dwellings are increasingly replacing the traditional structures of Nias villages

Lampung ship cloths
Lampung's tradition of fine ceremonial weavings is now all but lost and the few pieces woven today cannot compare with those exhibited in museums. The ship motif is a stylised interpretation of the route to death and the afterlife, often incorporated into a design of animals, houses or other wordly possessions. These magnificent, sombrely coloured weavings were traditionally used during ceremonies such as birth, circumcision and death.

on Saturdays – see panel, page 134) and traditional war dances. Megalithic stone benches and chairs, and stone- and woodcarvings are also abundant here. **Lahusa**, 40km northeast of Telukdalam, and the remote park of **Gomo**, which contains some fine old menhirs, make another rewarding excursion. Southern Nias has numerous villages and megaliths in varying states of decay, and treks through the forested hills with local guides will take you to more authentic settlements.

▶▶ Pulau Weh   110A5

This 150 sq km dot on the map opposite Banda Aceh makes a peaceful retreat from the Sumatran mainland and offers some good snorkelling, diving and swimming off its palm-lined beaches. A daily ferry connects Balohan, on Weh's south coast, with the port of Krueng Raya near Banda Aceh, and there are also daily flights between the two. Watch out for the island's rainy season, perversely the opposite of Sumatra's, from June to September.

The north coast town of **Sabang** makes the best base for reaching Weh's white sandy beaches (Pantai Kasih, Pantai Paradiso, and Pantai Sumur Tiga) and also for reaching

Pulau Rubia, which lies at the centre of a protected marine reserve to the west. Although much coral has been damaged by fish-bombing, there is still abundant marine life and excellent visibility. Inland is the Iboih Forest, a tropical reserve with good trails and wildlife.

▶ Riau Archipelago 111D4

Some 3,000 islands scattered strategically between East Sumatra and Singapore form part of Sumatra's Riau Province and are now being developed into a playground for bored Singaporeans. For centuries these islands were closely linked with the culture and destiny of Johor, Malaysia's southernmost state, and served as a favourite stop-over for ships on the Spice Route. They are now part of a triangle of development linked to the economic interests of Johor and Singapore.

Closest to Singapore is Pulau Batam, a burgeoning industrial and commercial centre dotted with luxury resort hotels; hydrofoils and ferries dock regularly at Sekupang, a short distance from the capital of Nagoya. Pulau Bintan holds more interest as its atmospheric port of Tanjung Pinang is the crossroads for boats and sampans from all over the archipelago. Pulau Penyegat, 6km away, offers Bugis ruins and royal tombs, while Pulau Tekulai and Pulau Soreh have some lovely beaches. Coral reefs are found around the islands of Mapor, Abang, Pompong and Balang.

▶ Takengon 110A5

Takengon lies on Danau Tawar in the shadow of the thickly forested Gayo Highlands and in the centre of the province of Aceh. The town itself has little to offer, but the surrounding hills provide excellent hiking to hot springs and up through Gunung Telong's moss forest. From the peak of Gunung Tetek panoramic views sweep over the mountains to the Strait of Melaka. The less energetic can explore the lake by boat. Accommodation in Takengon is basic.

Tanjungkarang 111E1

Ferries to and from Java arrive at the harbour of Bakauheni, where bus connections cover the 100km north to Sumatra's first major town. This confusingly has three names: Tanjungkarang, Telukbetung and Bandar Lampung, the latter now more commonly used for administrative purposes. Sumatra's only passenger trains run from Tanjungkarang station to Palembang or to Lubuklinggau, which is convenient for reaching Bengkulu. The provincial Lampung Museum has a reasonable display of superb local ship cloths, rarely seen elsewhere (see panel, page 136), and a small ethnographic and archaeological section. Beach-lovers should head for Merak Pelantung, which offers good swimming, watersports and accommodation.

▶ Way Kambas Elephant Reserve 111E1

This 130,000-hectare nature reserve on Lampung's swampy east coast is probably the best place in Sumatra to spot wild Sumatran elephants (see panels). Tigers, primates and wild pigs also thrive in these grasslands, while the flat marshes are excellent for bird-watching. Much of this area has suffered from logging and massive forest fires, and further environmental damage has been caused by transmigrants settling along its southern boundary.

The Sumatran elephant
The elephant (*Elephas maximus sumatranus*) starts its life weighing around 90kg but soon builds up to a weight of 5 tonnes. It grows from a height of about 1m to reach a shoulder height of 3m with a 1m-long trunk. For two or three years the baby elephant is breast-fed by its mother. Skin colour varies from grey to dark brown, and the ears and trunk often have areas of lighter pigmentation. The elephants' favourite habitat is primary and secondary forest or swamps where they can move around ingroups.

Visiting Way Kambas Elephant Reserve
Permits are issued at park headquarters at Tridatu, just north of Jepara, and from here boats or canoes can be chartered to negotiate the Kambas river and its tributaries through the reserve. An elephant training centre is located at Kadangsari. The easiest way to visit the reserve is by organised tour from Bandar Lampung, about 2 hours away by road.

Nias dancers

■ **The idyllically deserted palm-fringed beaches of the Riau Archipelago are deceptive, for as night falls out come high-speed motor boats manned by armed robbers intent on plunder. The politically sensitive issue of piracy is now being confronted by international shipping organisations and by the governments of Singapore, Malaysia and Indonesia.....■**

Tom Tiddler's ground

'At the end of a cruise pirates could repair to their strongholds, secure from attack, and there they would divide the spoils of the season, pass their days in cockfighting and their nights in opium-smoking – and plan fresh raids...

While the buccaneer was an outlaw, with the hand of every nation against him, the Malay pirate chief was a prince who might range where he wished, taking what he would. Rulers would placate him and even come to his bidding, and the seas over which he roved became a sort of Tom Tiddler's ground which traders crossed at their peril and, so far from picking up other men's gold and silver, frequently lost their own.'

– From *The Pirate Wind* by Owen Rutter (1930).

Right: a galleon under attack at the turn of the century. Today, local fishermen (top) are equally vulnerable, but the pirates board from high-speed motor boats

Piracy conjures up images of 17th-century galleons, fluttering skull and crossbone flags and marauding natives in polka-dot headbands clenching knives between their teeth. Not so. Today's pirates are a well-organised, high-tech lot and their activities are a continual cause for concern. A favourite target area is the Strait of Melaka, sandwiched between Sumatra, Singapore and Malaysia and the main seaway connecting the Indian Ocean with the South China Sea. Every year over 30,000 ships navigate its 830km length, which narrows into a strait only 17km wide at its southern end around the Riau Archipelago. This is a perfect maritime bottleneck for pirates in fast motor launches and allows easy escape into its numerous channels. Reported incidents peaked at over 100 in 1991, and although they have dropped since, local government sensitivity to the problem may disguise statistics.

Precedents Athough piracy has existed for centuries, it was not until the late 18th century that it became a large-scale operation. This was a direct result of colonialism: mercantile greed and trade monopolies (particularly the Dutch spice monopoly) deprived much of the local population of their living, and so provoked a high-seas guerrilla warfare against the 'white barbarians'. Piracy became an honourable occupation and offered a lucrative and exciting way of life that was encouraged by the political anarchy of petty states whose rulers sought improved status and fortune through it. From Manila to Sumatra and from Melaka to Sulawesi, no trading ship was safe from the sea-rovers and no coastal village immune from attack.

In the South China Sea and the Celebes Sea it was the ferocious Filipino Sulus and Sulawesi Bugis who ruled the waves, while the Strait of Melaka was a playground for Malay pirates from Johor and the Sumatran Acehnese. Pirate fleets consisted of up to 40 proas, each manned by 100 warriors or slaves. Every year some 500 Spanish subjects were sold into slavery, while the Dutch, who organised a system of cruising gunboats, met with little more success.

Ahoy there In the 1980s the situation escalated to such an extent that the International Maritime Organisation, a United Nations agency, set up a working group to look into the piracy problem. Its report stimulated concerted action from the Indonesian, Singaporean and Malaysian authorities who stepped up co-ordinated naval patrols.

Pirates

However, as one customs official commented, 'the chances of identifying pirates at night are as good as finding a coin in the ocean'. Many are fishermen, or disguised as such, and so impossible to detect.

Attacks generally take place at night when pirates, armed with anything from machetes to sub-machine guns, can board ships undetected from the stern. They are equipped with fast motor boats and hence have no trouble in overhauling ships which, when fully laden, are low in the water and therefore easy to board. Short attacks taking as little as 30 minutes carry off cash and easily transportable valuables, but in some cases the ship is held for a few days while the entire cargo is unloaded or, more extreme still, is permanently hijacked.

Apart from the danger to the crew, who may be the victims of a vicious attack, piracy also increases the navigational and environmental risks of collision and oil spillage. In some cases crews have been tied up and the ship left to steam uncontrolled at full power while the robbers make their escape; in others the captain and crew have been murdered. Precautionary advice, co-ordinated patrols and the SafetyNet system organised by the Regional Piracy Centre (which notifies all vessels in the area of a suspicious-looking craft) now seem to be winning this centuries-old battle – for the time being at least.

Into hibernation

'The reduction in the frequency of attacks in South-East Asia is, no doubt, due both to the current heightened international focus on the problem and to the preventive measures instituted by littoral states. Clearly, the decline in frequency is cause for satisfaction. But true victory can only be claimed if there is no upsurge in attacks once the preventive measures are withdrawn. What is more likely is that the menace has been driven into hibernation until opportunities reappear.'
– Mazlan Abdul Samad, Regional Manager of the International Maritime Bureau, *Straits Times* (29 June 1993).

BALI

LAUT BALI

Tanjung Bungkula
Kubutambahan
Sangsit
Singaraja Sukasada
Sawan
Pura Jagaraga

Tanjung Pasir
Pulau Menjangan
Labuhan Lalang
Banyuwedang
Pulaki
Ketapang
Gilimanuk
Cekik
Jayaprana Grave
Lovina (Kalibukbuk)
Seririt
Pengastulan
Celukanbawang
Gitgit
2096
Gunung Catu
Danau Buyan
Danau Tamblingan
Candikuning
Kebun Raya Bedugul
Danau Brata

Selat
Bali

Melaya
Sungiang
1386m
▲ *Gunung Merbuk*
Daya
Taman Nasional Bali Barat
1580m
▲ *Gunung Patas*
Bilukpob
Medewi
Yeh Sumbul
Pupuan
2276m
▲ *Gunung Batukau*
Pacung
Jatiluwih
Batukau
Penebel

Negara
Mendaya
Pulukan
Yehbatian
Yeh He
Pengambengan
Tanjung Perancak
Antosari
Soka
Tabanan
Pura Taman Ayun
Yeh Sunga
Mengwi
Krambitan
Klatingdukuh

Tanah Lot

JAWA (JAVA)

Legian
Kuta
Ngurah Rai ✈

0   10   20   30 km

Uluwatu
Bukit Badun

3

2

1

A

B

C

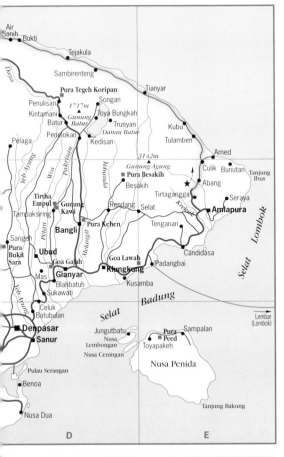

BALI

Cremations
Balinese funerals are joyful occasions celebrating the passage from this life to the next; the cremation of the body releases the soul so that it can be united with the supreme god. As these funerals are extremely costly affairs, many Balinese bury their relatives temporarily to await a mass cremation. After a festive banquet men rush to fetch the corpse and lift it into a bamboo tower which represents the cosmos. This is then carried to the cremation ground to the accompaniment of a sprinting gamelan orchestra and women bearing offerings. The corpse is transferred to a coffin and the entire tower structure set alight. The final procession carries the ashes to the sea or a river where they are scattered.

Bali The island of Bali, like the mask of Janus, has two faces: an outer shell of sensational monuments, now overrun with tourists and commercialism; and an inner core expressed by a continuing concern with harmony and spirituality in daily life. In a last desperate act of self-preservation, the Balinese have erected a solid barrier between the sacred and the profane, rarely allowing the two to meet. Visitors on a one- or two-week holiday will barely scratch the surface of this intriguing, dazzling culture, yet year after year tourists pour in, if only for a taste of what might have been.

Exodus to Eden In 1597 a small Dutch fleet, the first Westerners to land on Bali's shores, decided that they had stumbled upon the Garden of Eden and promptly refused to leave. The bewitching society they encountered has its roots in the 11th century when the first permanent Hindu Javanese links were established, but it was not until 1343, under the great Majapahit minister Gajah Mada, that Bali was brought directly under Javanese control. Gelgel became the capital of the flourishing Balinese kingdom which soon extended its power to Lombok and then, in the 15th century, received a new influx of Javanese fleeing the disintegrating Majapahit kingdom in the wake of Islam. Nobles, priests, artists, musicians and dancers formed this cultural exodus, thereby helping to mould the rich and complex Balinese society which exists today.

Western influx By the early 18th century Gelgel's domination had fragmented into rival courts, and in the 19th century the Dutch started manoeuvring in north Bali and Lombok, in 1908 finally gaining control of the whole island after the battle at Klungkung (see page 151). The 1920s and 1930s saw a new influx, that of Western artists and anthropologists (including Margaret Mead), once more mesmerised by this tropical Eden. Japanese occupation, followed by the bloodbath of the 1965 riots when Balinese threw off their veil of gentleness and murdered some 100,000 'Communists', were the preludes to today's imbalance where, on a yearly basis, tourists outnumber inhabitants.

Lay of the land About 70 per cent of Bali's 5,600 sq km is cultivated, leaving a wild pocket of forest and volcanic mountains in the north and west, but blanketing the rest of the fertile island in scenically terraced rice-fields. Heavy rainfall from November to April replenishes rivers and irrigation systems, while sea breezes and the mountains in the north provide relief from lowland humidity. The largest resort areas are concentrated along the white sandy beaches of the south at Kuta, Legian, Sanur and the élitist Nusa Dua, although the northern black-sand beaches at Lovina and, to a lesser extent, east of Singaraja are gradually siphoning off those budget travellers and divers who go in search of relative peace. The east coast resort of Candidasa, modest Padangbai and the 'haunted' islands of Nusa Penida provide outsider alternatives. Bali offers a wealth of possibilities for trekkers, from the Bali Barat National Park to the extraordinary volcanic peaks of

Bangli's Pura Kehen disappears into the aerial roots of a banyan tree

Twilight zone
'Cast out from the sunlit paradise that had seemed so compliant, I was borne back, so it seemed, into the night world of Bali, island of shadow plays and cock-fights, sacred daggers and full moon rites. This was the Bali where artists wait to be visited in dreams before they cover their canvases with swirling druggy patterns; where villagers place dead cocks on their doorsteps to placate evil spirits; where a menstruating woman is shunned even by her husband as a thing possessed. In Bali, when witches come out from the dark, gold-toothed monkeys are seen on deserted roads, and headless giants. In Bali – twilight zone of the unrational – I had seen a holy cave full of bats, and a temple in the sea guarded by a snake.'
– From *Video Night in Kathmandu* by Pico Iyer (1988).

Offerings to the gods

Agung and Batur or lakeside rambles at Batur and Bratan. Central Bali, which revolves around Ubud, is the hub of Balinese arts and crafts, and now spawns a virtually continuous line of craft shops down to Denpasar.

Temples Some 30,000 ornately carved temples pepper the land, these varying from the familiar silhouette of Tanah Lot's sea temple to the 1,000-year-old rock temple at Gunung Kawi and the numerous shrines of the mother of them all, Besakih. Processions, cremations and cere-monies are inseparable from daily life amongst 95 per cent of the population which continues to practise Hindu Dharma, a unique synthesis of Hinduism, Buddhism and ancestor worship. The offshoots of these deeply embed-ded beliefs – dances, music and crafts – have a high tourist profile and offer the best opportunity to observe this complex society without fear of intruding.

BALI

Demon gods flank the entrance to the Pura Kehen in Bangli

144

Jewellery
Although Celuk's jewellery can be extremely elaborate, its crafting was and in some cases still is extremely primitive. Artisans used a tree stump with a protruding iron spike as a pounding base, a bamboo stem to catch the filings and a manually operated gas pump for heating the metal. As with most Balinese crafts, gold and silver work is a hereditary trade and apprenticeship starts at a very early age. By the age of 12 the boys are already producing fine ornaments and soon are able to turn their hand to any commission.

Time and nature leave their marks: sculpture at the Pura Kehen temple, Bangli

▶ **Air Sanih (Yeh Saneh)** *141D3*

This village lies on Bali's relatively untouched north coast, about 15km east of Singaraja, and is popular for its cool spring-water pools set in a lush garden parallel to the beach. The discreet accommodation creates a peaceful enclave, and the village also makes a good base for excursions to inland temples (at **Jagaraga**'s temple of the dead, look out for the curious façade bas-reliefs depicting Dutch colonists, aeroplanes, cars and bicycles) or to the village of **Sawan**, famed for its manufacture of gamelan instruments, its dances and a bustling night market. Snorkelling off the beach and hiking in the hills are alternatives to these cultural pursuits.

▶▶ **Bali Barat, Taman Nasional** *140B3*

Over 70,000 hectares of Bali's forested and mountainous northwestern tip have been declared a national park, a brave move in this densely populated island. Entrance to the park is from **Cekik**, where information, permits and guides can be found at the PHPA office, or at **Labuhan Lalang** on the north coast. There is basic accommodation in both places. Hot springs and a temple are located at Banyuwedang while, immediately to the west at Teluk Terima, stands the royal grave of Jayaprana, an ill-fated 17th-century prince. Wildlife includes monkeys, leopards, and *rusa*, barking and mouse deer, while the rich birdlife includes a species exclusive to Bali, the white Rothschild mynah bird whose population numbers only a few hundred.

Also incorporated into the park is the uninhabited, mangrove-fringed **Pulau Menjangan▶▶▶**, which lies off the north coast. The exceptionally clear water, extensive coral reefs and an inspiring drop-off have made this protected area a divers' paradise. Access is by boat from Labuhan Lalang where snorkelling equipment can be hired, but divers should arrange their trip through one of the diving shops in Lovina.

▶ Bangli 141D2

This cool, peaceful hill town, half-way between Ubud and Gunung Batur, claims one of Bali's largest and most magnificent temples, the **Pura Kehen▶▶▶**. The 12th- to 13th-century edifice is terraced up a slope, its monumental entrance flanked by sculptures of elephants and the lower courtyard shaded by a huge banyan tree, as old as the temple itself. The middle courtyard is occupied by shrines, but more spectacular is the huge tiered *meru* (pagoda), with its superbly carved stone and wood base which dominates the final enclosure. Look out for the bas-reliefs of a tortoise captured by two snakes, the guarantors of world equilibrium. The *meru* is dedicated to Siva, supreme god of the mountain and of the world. In the northern corner of this courtyard stands an elevated stone throne, a sacred monument destined to receive Siva, Brahma or Vishnu.

A few kilometres west of Bangli and a short climb from the road is the hill of **Bukit Demulih**, offering breathtaking views over southern Bali from a viewpoint on the ridge. North of Bangli the countryside becomes wilder and less inhabited, punctuated by huge banyans, poinsettia and bamboo groves.

▶ Batubulan 141D1

The village of Batubulan lies firmly entrenched in the heavily populated hills north of Denpasar, and continues to produce the fine stone-carving for which it is famous. The pot-bellied *dvarapali* (demon gods) which guard every Balinese temple are particularly prominent amongst the crowd of stone divinities lining the main road. Not surprisingly there are some impressively carved temples in the vicinity: the gate of **Pura Puseh**, a few hundred metres east of the main road, intriguingly juxtaposes the Hindu pantheon with a meditating Buddha. Batubulan's craftsmen have more recently turned their skills to pottery and woodcarving, and nor are the performing arts forgotten – dance performances are held every morning and evening although the atmosphere is decidedly touristy.

A few kilometres northeast of Batubulan lies the silver- and goldsmith centre of **Celuk**, which produces some of the most stunning jewellery in Southeast Asia. Numerous workshops display intricately crafted filigree work beside inventive contemporary designs; bargaining is, as usual, the name of the game.

North versus south
The art of carving in north Bali is very distinctive from that of the south. Southern temples are generally intricately carved in grey sandstone, but remain restrained in comparison to the flamboyant northern temples whose dynamically rising gates are often covered entirely in carved motifs. The pink sandstone quarried near Singaraja in the north is extremely soft and enables carvers to let their imaginations fly, and you will sometimes even find burlesque caricatures of Dutch colonials incorporated into temple façades. Even more startling are the brilliant colours used to heighten the drama of the carvings.

145

Due to the friability of Balinese sandstone, sculptures have to be replaced regularly – keeping Batubulan's carvers in business

Another form of temple offering, made of split bamboo

Candikuning's gardens
Just south of Lake Bratan, between Candikuning and Bedugul, a turn-off climbs west up to the Kebun Raya (Botanic Gardens) on the slopes of Gunung Pohon. The high-altitude climate (1,200m) encourages a wide diversity of trees and shrubs as well as over 500 species of orchids. These gardens were set up in 1959 as an offshoot of Java's famous national gardens at Bogor and Cibodas but, though cool and tranquil, do not offer the same landscaping nor maturity of plants.

▶▶ **Besakih** *141D2*

The mother of all Balinese temples is situated 1,000m up the slopes of the great Gunung Agung. Besakih is both a royal sanctuary and the principal state temple of Bali, incorporating some 30 different *puras* (temple buildings) into its vast terraced complex, and as such attracts a continuous flow of pilgrims. Nor are tourists absent, but as they cannot enter the main temple courtyards (Pura Penataran Agung) they must be content with peripheral shrines and sublime views. The decidedly unspiritual approach is via a long, steep street chock-a-block with souvenir- and snack-stalls where prospective guides can be found aplenty; if you want one (and it is not essential), agree on a price first. Also make sure that you are correctly dressed before visiting the temple (see panel opposite).

Besakih is thought to have been established in the early 11th century by Maharesi Markandeya, who travelled from Java with 8,000 followers to establish a new settlement in Bali. It was much expanded following royal conflicts and the vagaries of the centuries, yet somehow, miraculously, escaped damage from Agung's recurring eruptions. The temple is graphically spectacular when it emerges from early morning mists (this is the best time to visit), the towering dark *merus* (pagodas) assuming their real significance as symbols of the sacred mountain.

▶ **Bukit Sari** *141D2*

About 10km northeast of Mengwi in the monkey forest of Sangeh lies the temple of Bukit Sari, built in the 17th century for the royal family of Mengwi. The *pura* (temple) remains a quiet, shady place enlivened by the numerous macaques that bound out of the surrounding nutmeg trees. *Ramayana* legend has it that the macaques' presence is a result of Rama's fight with the demons; aided by an army of monkeys, Rama attacked the land of the demons by throwing the Earth at it – one piece broke off and fell directly on Sangeh, together with the monkeys.

▶ ▁▁▁ Candidasa   *141E2*

Although it is named after an old hillside temple, Candidasa is now firmly established as a beach resort – but without a beach! Ironically, this magnificently sited fishing village on Bali's east coast suffers either from the rough surf of high tides that crash up to the hotel gardens, thereby making the beach inaccessible, or low tides which leave no water and a lot of broken coral underfoot. In a desperate attempt to improve the situation, a row of concrete jetties was built, but this has only succeeded in spoiling the bay and has even accelerated the erosion process. This said, if you are content not to swim in the sea Candidasa remains a fairly peaceful spot with a string of restaurants, homestays and hotels along the main coast road. More scenically sited accommodation is found in a banana grove off a slip road at the northern end of the village. Across the lagoon in the centre of the village is a Gandhi meditation centre.

▶▶▶ Danau Bratan   *140C3*

This is one of Bali's most beautiful sights and is situated high on the slopes of the 2,000m Mount Catur which dominates the north end of the island. The crater lake, rimmed by peaks, is considered home to the Balinese goddess of water and irrigation, Dewi Danu, to whom a magnificent lake temple is dedicated. This was built by the king of Mengwi in 1634 and occupies the lake shore beside two seemingly floating island *merus* (pagodas).

The dramatic watery site, with its backdrop of drifting clouds and mountains, is best seen early in the morning or late in the afternoon to avoid the inevitable tourist buses. Entrance to the temple is from the village of Candikuning, where impeccably tended gardens lead down past a gigantic banyan tree to the lake shore and temple. For those seriously enraptured by this mystical place, there are good walks around the lake, boats for hire and reasonable accommodation.

Hundreds of agile macaques inhabit the sacred forest of Bukit Sari

147

Temple etiquette
The more frequented sites issue entrance tickets and hire out yellow sashes to be worn around the waist, while in more obscure temples it is sufficient to give a donation and sign the ubiquitous visitor's book. Visitors should be respectably dressed (no shorts) and preferably in sarongs. The sash serves to cut the negatives forces emanating from the Earth, thus allowing the positive forces from the gods to predominate. Panels in front of temples also state that menstruating women should not enter. The reason for this is the Balinese belief that their vulnerable state attracts demon spirits who accompany them into the temple and thus destroy the harmony.

The tranquil temple of Ulu Danu at Danau Bratan

BALI

Out of Denpasar

Getting around Bali by public *bemo* (minibus) is no picnic, as most routes run via Denpasar and involve a cross-town trip to pick up a connection. An alternative is to use the tourist buses that offer regular services to main points around the island (Kuta, Sanur, Ubud, Padangbai, Candi Dasa and Lovina); tickets are advertised wherever tourists tread and services are reliable. For those determined to travel with the locals or to less frequented destinations, Denpasar's *bemo* terminals are as follows: Ubung on Jalan Cokroaminoto (north and west); Tegal, west of town (south); Suci on Jalan Hasanuddin (port of Benoa); Batubulan, on the Gianyar road northeast of town (centre, north and east).

The main building of Denpasar's Museum Bali is modelled on the Karangasem palaces of eastern Bali

▶ Denpasar

141D1

In 1958 the small but strategically placed village of Denpasar was declared capital of Bali, and has since swallowed up surrounding villages and paddy-fields to become a traffic-choked city of over 300,000 inhabitants. Urban planning has endowed the town with ring roads which bypass it, but it remains Bali's central transport hub and anyone travelling by bus will inevitably find himself or herself transiting here.

Denpasar's past role as royal capital of the kingdom of Badung ended in 1906 with a magnificent but tragic display of moral bravura when the king and his entire court committed *puputan*, a collective suicide, in the face of Dutch troops (see panel opposite). A monument to this event stands on Lapangan Puputan, a square adjoining Denpasar's main artery, Jalan Gajah Mada. On the east side of the square stands the capital's principal sight, the **Museum Bali▶▶▶** (*open*: Tuesday to Sunday, 8–5; Friday, 8–3:30), which was founded in 1931 with the help of Walter Spies, the German artist who put Balinese arts and crafts on the world map (see panel on page 164). The museum layout reflects traditional Balinese temple and palace design, with its ethnographic and archaeological collections displayed in courtyard pavilions. Some superb masks, dance costumes, puppets, double-*ikat* weavings and *kris* (swords) are part of the rich offerings, but information is only in Indonesian.

Next to the museum stands the more recent **Pura Jaganatha▶**, a temple whose central courtyard is surrounded by a lotus-filled moat. Across the road is the tourist office which provides information on dance and music events held at Denpasar's various arts academies. The **Werdi Budaya Art Centre▶** (*open*: Monday to Sunday, 8–4) offers a permanent window on Balinese crafts as well as holding regular performances in its open-air auditorium.

A rare dokar on the streets of Denpasar

▶ **Gianyar** 141D2

This uninspiring town 27km west of Denpasar is the manufacturing centre of Balinese textiles, these eventually finding their way to every souvenir-stall and hotel boutique on the island. Gastronomically it is famed for its succulent *babi guling* (roast suckling pig) which should be consumed when at its optimum before midday in the *warungs* (food-stalls) of Gianyar's market. The kingdom of Gianyar sided astutely with the Dutch during their conquest and thus avoided the fate meted out to other Balinese kingdoms. Although not open to the public, the royal palace (still inhabited) can clearly be seen behind its brick walls.

▶▶ **Goa Gajah** 141D2

This sacred grotto or 'Elephant Cave' lies just 3km east of Ubud embedded in cliffs overlooking the Petanu river. Access is via a steep staircase which descends past shady banyans to the main cave entrance. The surrounding rock is carved with figures, animals and the central mask of Boma, god of the forest. At the back of the oppressive T-shaped cave stands a statue of Ganesh, the elephant god, a cluster of phallic stone *lingams* and a series of niches thought to have been used by visiting pilgrims for meditation. In front of the cave are two excavated bathing-pools, below which more stairs lead down across fields to a group of Buddhist statues and a huge carved stone relief depicting *stupas* (bell-shaped domes).

▶▶ **Goa Lawah** 141D2

This fascinating temple is constructed around a bat cave and lies on the coast about 10km east of Klungkung. Legend has it that the cave forms the entrance to a labyrinth that ends far to the north in the temple of Besakih, and that an underground river in the system is home to the mythical snake of Naga Basuki. Whatever the truth of the matter, the cave temple creates a unique spectacle (and odour), leaving worshippers transfixed by the thousands of bats that zip in and out or roost on the rocks. Offerings are laid out in front of shrines dedicated to Naga Basuki and colourful processions often proceed down through the temple gardens to the beach.

Boma, god of the forest, overlooks the entrance to Goa Gajah

BALI

Lake trips
Boat trips around Lake Batur are organised from Kedisan, circuits including the stunningly sited village of Trunyan on the lake's eastern shore. This is a rare Bali Aga village inhabited by descendants of the island's pre-Majapahit peoples, However, their welcome is not euphoric and visitors cannot enter the temple, though they can visit the ghoulish cemetery. If you are lucky you may see Bali's largest statue, the 4m guardian of the village, Ratu Gede Pancering Jaget.

Mysticism fades into commercialism at Lake Batur

▶▶▶ Gunung Agung 141E2

Bali's 'navel of the world' rises 3,142m over the north-eastern corner of the island to form a highly visible and majestic landmark. Although the volcano has been venerated for centuries, this has not stopped it from occasionally exercising its wrath. The last major eruption occurred in 1963, leaving over 2,000 people dead, some 85,000 homeless and blanketing a quarter of the island in lava. Calmer days have returned, but if you make a circuit of Agung to the north you will see the aftermath of activity in sparse vegetation, lava rocks and bleak vistas.

It is possible to climb the volcano from the south, either from Besakih or from the village of Sorga which lies north of Selat. In both cases the tough climb takes about 5 or 6 hours and a guide is advisable.

▶▶▶ Gunung Batur 141D3

The dramatic crater lake below the 1,717m peak of Gunung Batur is one of Bali's tourist 'musts' and offers a wealth of activities, from boating to bathing in hot springs and trekking around and up the volcano. The spectacular 2- to 3-hour climb to the summit is fairly arduous, but the numerous trails from **Kintamani**, the commercialised lakeside village of **Kedisan** or the hot-spring village of **Toya Bungkah** are easy to follow. Routes are well trodden (even by drinks-vendors) and a guide is not essential, but do leave early in the morning to reach the cone before the clouds come down. Views over the steaming crater, the lake and as far as Lombok's Gunung Rinjani are breathtaking. There is no shortage of descent routes, and you can even continue to the north coast.

▶▶ Gunung Kawi 141D2

Half-way between Denpasar and Kintamani, just east of the village of Tampaksiring, another of Bali's fascinating rock temples nestles in an astonishing gorge setting. Down by the Pakrisan river the rock-face (Gunung Kawi, meaning 'Mountain of Poets') is hewn into oval niches containing stone pagodas, said to be the tombs of the first Balinese kings and probably created in the 11th

century before cremation became widespread. A short distance away is a network of man-made caves which were used by Buddhist monks for meditation. Access is via 220 steep and irregular steps, but the views easily justify the effort. Aim to visit in late afternoon to avoid the crowds.

▶▶▶ Klungkung (Semerapura) *141D2*

Some 300 years ago Klungkung became the capital of Bali's most influential dynasty which had moved here from neighbouring Gelgel. Rival courts subsequently sprang up throughout Bali, yet Klungkung remained the supreme royal authority. In the early 1900s Klungkung was the last stronghold of Balinese resistance against the Dutch, finally capitulating in 1908 after a heroic battle in which the king was killed. A towering new stone monument on the central crossroads commemorates the event and houses dioramas relating the story of the battle.

Opposite the monument lies the **Taman Gili▶▶▶** which contains the palace's two remaining pavilions set around a delightful lily pond beside a small museum. The corner pavilion, the **Kerta Gosa (Hall of Justice)**, is renowned for its painted ceiling depicting animal tales, punishments meted out in hell and an earthquake chart. These are painted in the naive Kamasan style, similar to *wayang* puppets in its effect. The same technique is used in the beautiful central pavilion, the **Bale Kambang**, where friezes depict battle scenes, Buddhist tales and astrological symbols. This floating pavilion is surrounded by stone statues, some of colonial figures. The modest museum is mainly devoted to the history of the Klungkung kingdom. Running east from the palace is Jalan Diponegoro, with numerous antique shops.

Klungkung's magnificent Kerta Gosa

Batur eruptions
Although Gunung Batur is not as impressive as Agung, it also has a heavy record of volcanic activity – witness the solidified lava flows on its slopes. This century the 1917 eruption left 1,000 dead and over 65,000 homeless, while a further eruption in 1926 completely destroyed the village of Batur and its temple. The replacement, Pura Batur, is now located at a safer distance, standing on the crater slope just south of Kintamani.

Balinese Hinduism

■ **Bali's deeply rooted cults of animism and ancestor worship were gradually infiltrated over the centuries by Hindu and Buddhist influences from India and Java, creating a flexible religion aimed at maintaining the balance between opposing forces. Harmony is achieved only by constant striving to keep evil spirits at bay and by placating the diverse manifestations of the supreme god.....■**

The Balinese are a deeply religious people whose belief somehow manages to resist external influences; even in the most Westernised enclaves of the island you will see delicately made palm-leaf and hibiscus offerings laid out in front of tourist shops. Daily devotions are taught from infancy, guided by priests who have studied the complex theology of Agama Hindu. The religion promotes one supreme god, Sanghyang Widi, plus the embodiment of the Hindu trinity of Brahma, the creator, Vishnu, the preserver, and Siva, the destroyer. A multiplicity of ancestral, wind, rice, fertility and sea spirits are also venerated as personifications of the same universal god. And then come the goblins, witches and giants of the night.

152

Temple festivals (odalan) produce extraordinary processions which combine brilliant colour with extreme serenity

Polar opposites The Balinese see nature as eternally polarised between night and day, high and low, right and left, the east of the rising sun and the west of the setting sun. Strength and weakness, and cleanliness and uncleanliness are further expressions of this duality in which each opposite illuminates the other. Balinese ritual strives unerringly to maintain a harmony and coexistence between these opposites.

From pre-Hindu times the Balinese have conceived of an ordered universe which stretches from the heavens above their mountains down to the depths of the sea, every aspect of nature having a rank, direction and place. Holiness is associated with height (the domain of the gods is Mount Agung), while anything that is harmful or destructive belongs to the underworld forces of the ocean, home to fanged demons and giants. Between the two extremes is the intermediary sphere of the fertile plains where the Balinese live. Man is perceived as a microcosm of this, with his three parts (head, body and feet) models of the three parts of the cosmic universe (heaven, man's middle world and the underworld).

Orientation This view has led the Balinese to develop a complex system

of spatial and spiritual orientation which governs the siting of every temple, shrine and home on the island. Orientation towards the holy mountain is called *kaja*, positioning away from it towards the sea is called *kelod*, toward the rising sun is *kangin* and towards the less sacred west is *kauh*. To these four points and their divisions is added the position of centre (*puseh*). Villages and house compounds are always aligned *kaja-–kelod*, with cemeteries and the *pura dalem* ('temple of the dead', dedicated to Siva) situated at the *kelod* end and the *pura puseh* ('navel temple', dedicated to Vishnu) at the *kaja* end. Balinese even sleep with their heads *kaja* or *kangin*.

Analogous to the tripartite structure of the cosmos and of man, the house is divided into three parts: the family temple (in the *kaja–kangin* corner), the living quarters in the middle and, very *kelod*, the more profane sections of kitchen, garbage and animal pen.

Spooks Witches (*leyak*), or the spirits of living persons who practise the art of black magic, are perhaps the most colourful creatures in the Balinese underworld. Their many nocturnal personalities (giants, gold-toothed monkeys and blood-sucking vampires, to name just a few) are only spotted by foreigners when they leap on to the stage during certain dances wearing elaborate and gruesome masks with flaming tongues and long wispy hair. Equally feared are the invisible earth demons, *bhuta* and *kala*, which haunt desolate seashores and shady woods yet, being essential for the balance of the universe, cannot be destroyed but only appeased through offerings.

Cremation towers are works of art, sometimes rising 15m

Caste system
The Balinese caste system was introduced several centuries ago by the Javanese, and is a much simpler and more relaxed affair than that of the Indians. The four castes start with the basic village working class, the Sudras (90 per cent of Balinese), followed by the nobility which is divided into three groups: the Brahmanas (the highest caste); the Satrias (to which former Balinese royalty belongs); and the Waisyas (the warrior class which includes merchants and craftsmen). Religious practice is coded according to each caste and even alters within castes depending on whichever ancestor is worshipped. The full name of every Balinese includes his or her caste, and three corresponding languages are used according to whom is addressed.

▶▶ **Krambitan** *140C2*

Some 8km southwest of Tabanan lies the cultural stronghold of Krambitan which boasts two royal palaces set off by gardens of beautiful flowering shrubs. These were an extension of Tabanan's court, whose rulers remained in constant conflict with the neighbouring Mengwi Dynasty. The end came in 1906 when the king and his son committed suicide in the face of the Dutch.

Krambitan's older palace, **Puri Anyar**, dates from the 17th century and now partly functions as a rather chic private hotel. **Puri Gede**, an 18th-century construction, is interesting above all for its family temple which houses a long row of ancestral shrines inlaid with Chinese porcelain. Performances of the *tertekan* exorcist dance to unique bamboo-instrument music are held in the village.

Kuta/Legian *141C1*

Kuta's proximity to Denpasar airport (Ngurah Rai) makes it hard to avoid when arriving in or departing from Bali. Many visitors wish they had never set foot here, while others revel in its commercial dynamism and endless nightlife. Kuta is Australia's Corfu, Cancun or Benidorm – in other words, the cheapest tropical paradise on the antipodean doorstep – and as such attracts regular streams of cruising bruisers out to get a suntan and get drunk. The first hotel opened in 1959 but it was not really until the 1980s that Kuta completely forwent its Balinese identity and assumed the anonymous, materialistic façade it sports today.

Surreal sights Aussie surfers skim through the waves, beach masseurs ply their trade, itinerant vendors snap open showcases of wristwatches on every street corner and young men hopefully mutter 'Transport, transport' or 'Hashish? Cocaine?' to promenading Westerners. Neon signs, McDonald's restaurants and kilometres of tacky shops, take-aways and bars dominate, but Kuta also has its beggars and, hard to believe in this commercial absolute, temples and daily offerings. It is difficult to recommend this budget resort, throbbing as it does with Western sounds and European and Aussie package tours, but a night spent here will provide a few interesting, if somewhat surreal sights and a day can easily be spent shopping – the choice of goods is endless, the range of quality huge and competition makes bargaining profitable.

Kuta alternative
If you are considering using Kuta as a one-night stop-over on your way to the airport, think again. The alternative lies at Jimbaran, just a few kilometres south of the airport on a picturesque crescent-shaped beach which is still used by fishermen. Development has started (and includes Bali's most luxurious hotel, the Four Seasons) so this peaceful little enclave may not last long, but for the moment the handful of up-market hotels is tasteful and mid-range accommodation is also available.

Succumbing to a beach massage

Anything and everything is sold in Kuta

North to south A 10km white-sand beach edged by crashing surf connects Kuta with adjoining Legian to the north, once a separate village but now swallowed up in one ribbonlike sprawl. Running parallel to the beach strip is Jalan Legian, an around-the-clock hive of hustling activity, and connecting the two in central Kuta is a labyrinth of *gang* (lanes). The mainly budget hotels in these backstreets offer some surprising havens of peace, while a distinctly upbeat buzz emanates from the video-bars and the latest-in-grunge boutiques. The smartest hotels are situated at the two extremes, either in north Legian or in Kuta's Kartika Plaza area (closest to the airport in the south). Public transport converges on Kuta's central crossroads (known as Bemo Corner) and there are plenty of bikes and motor cycles for hire along Jalan Legian – a bargain can always be found.

Activities If you have just arrived in Indonesia, don't think you can recover from jet lag on crowded Kuta Beach. This area probably claims more hawkers of every kind than potential customers, so know what you want. Swimming is not always safe in the rolling surf, but the psychedelic sunsets that brought the first hippies to Kuta back in the 1960s are memorable.

Nightspots change in popularity constantly. Discos and pubs where Aussies indulge in raucous beer-drinking contests are legion, while further up towards Legian there are even some impressively designed cocktail bars where the ambience approaches sophistication. Kuta can perhaps best be exploited by having leather clothes made to measure or by checking out some of the very inventive styles made here by local and foreign designers. A good selection of handicrafts from all over the island is sold in the resort, although time is required if you are keen to find the quality merchandise.

When even Kuta stops
Nyepi, or Balinese New Year, is held annually around March or April. This extraordinary event reduces the entire island to silence and inactivity – even Kuta screeches to a halt. Four principles rule: no light or fire is allowed (implying that the inner fire of desire should be purified through fasting and meditation); no physical activities are allowed; no travelling or locomotion is allowed; and finally no amusement or pleasure is permitted. This day thus produces an eerie and seemingly deserted island, most inhabitants staying indoors. A totally different atmosphere prevails on the preceding day (*Pengerupukan*) when the Balinese perform ceremonies to ward off evil spirits and hold nocturnal torch-lit processions.

Pura Taman Ajun, at Mengwi

Pura Peed
The three islands lying off Bali's southeast coast are swathed in myths and legends of malefic spirits, a result of their position amidst violent currents that have caused many a shipwreck over the centuries. Nusa Penida's temple of Pura Peed is dedicated to the king of demons, Jero Gede Mecaling, held responsible by Balinese for every misfortune that has assailed their island. The temple is surrounded by a wall encrusted with fossils, shells and coral while in an adjoining annexe stands a sacred tree carved with the demon's face. It is hardly spectacular as Balinese temples go, but nevertheless has a haunting atmosphere.

▶▶ **Lovina**   *140C3*

Bali's north coast resort offers a string of villages west of Singaraja that are known collectively as Lovina Beach. This unspoilt, scenic area stretches inland to the mountains, and offers essentially budget-oriented bungalow development. The coarse, black, volcanic sand may be unappealing (and difficult to wash off) but a reef keeps the water calm so swimming is possible. Restaurants and tour agents dot the main road while hotels and *losmen* (budget inns) are located along the turn-offs leading down to the beach.

Lovina centres around the village of **Kalibukbuk**, which lines a pretty curve of the beach and claims a temple, palm grove and fishing boats, as well as reasonable accommodation and restaurants. However, this is still Bali and you will be hounded on the beach by hawkers selling drinks and sarongs.

▶▶ **Mengwi**   *140C2*

From 1634 until 1891 Mengwi was the centre of a powerful kingdom originating from the Gelgel Dynasty (based at Klungkung), and today these kings continue to be venerated by their descendants at Mengwi's state temple, **Pura Taman Ajun**. The temple complex lies in spacious gardens surrounded by a moat and edged by a small lake, the recently created **Museum of Complete Cremation** (of little interest) standing on its west shore. From the royal *pendopo* (pavilion), the park rises gently past a ceremonial building to reach the third and most sacred walled enclosure which can be walked around but not entered. Inside, ten *meru* (pagodas) are aligned beside *palinggihs* (shrines which served to receive visiting deities during temple feasts) with superbly carved doors and adjoining pavilions used for preparing offerings or reciting prayers. The tiered *meru* are dedicated to Bali's various mountain, sea and rice gods, to Mengwi's royal ancestors and even to the ancestral gods of the Majapahits.

Mengwi lies on the Ubud–Tanah Lot tourist trail, and so every afternoon is invaded by buses *en route* to Tanah Lot's sunset rendezvous. If possible, visit this otherwise harmonious temple setting in the morning.

▶▶ Nusa Dua　　　　　　141D1

Bali's third major tourist resort (after Kuta and Sanur) lies on the eastern tip of the southern Bukit Peninsula. Pristine Nusa Dua was developed in the mid-1980s when Sanur's coastline was reaching asphyxiation point, and is aimed at a well-heeled clientele ostensibly trying to get away from it all. Traditionally designed, luxury hotels are set in spacious, landscaped gardens that open on to a beautiful white-sand beach. Amenities are seemingly infinite and Balinese staff *do* smile here, but this carefully planned resort, a city unto itself, is a sterilised haven with a packaged taste of the island culture, a clone of every luxury development from the Caribbean to the Indian Ocean.

▶▶ Nusa Lembongan　　　141D1

This small (8 sq km), palm-fringed and coral-edged island offers the mainly unspoilt attractions of excellent swimming, surfing, snorkelling and diving, a peaceful atmosphere and budget accommodation. Rather than latching on to tourists, the island's 2,000-odd inhabitants are profitably employed in harvesting seaweed which, after it has been dried in the sun, is exported to Japan, Hong Kong and Singapore for processing into crackers and cosmetics. The pretty beach of **Jungutbatu** thus sees snorkellers just a few metres from fishermen raking the bottom for seaweed. Access to Nusa Lembongan is by morning boat from Sanur (about 2 hours).

▶▶ Nusa Penida　　　141E1

This sister island to Lembongan is saddled with a reputation for malevolent spirits and adepts of black magic, but makes a quiet get-away for surfing and diving. The rugged, arid, limestone island, once a penal colony for the Klungkung kingdom, has some lovely beaches, a dramatic south coast indented with creeks, sheer white cliffs and the temple domain of the demon king – Pura Peed (see panel, page 156). Regular boat services operate from Padangbai and Kusamba, taking about an hour for the crossing. Limited accommodation is available at Sampalan.

Gamelan music
Whether you are in a luxury hotel or at a temple ceremony in Bali you will soon hear the melodious echo of the gamelan. All music, whether for pleasure or for divine entertainment, is sacred to the Balinese. A full gamelan orchestra consists of over 25 seated men playing bronze-keyed xylophones, double-ended drums, gongs and cymbals, together producing a five-tone melody which is heightened by rhythm and changes in tempo. Over the last decades older, more sedate styles of playing have developed into *kebyar*, a faster, syncopated style first created in north Bali. Gamelan orchestras are formed within neighbourhoods or villages and actively seek to improve their talents through competitions and government-sponsored festivals.

157

Even the luxury resort of Nusa Dua incorporates stone-carvings of Hindu deities

BALI

Balinese markets
In Bali the word for market is *peken*, usually followed by the name of the regency or village in which it is held. A unique feature of these markets is the *laapan*, or small shrine which is found in almost every stall, yet another aspect of the seemingly ineradicable importance of Balinese Hinduism in everyday life. A short distance east of Singaraja lies the picturesque village of Sawan, where the night market unfolds in kerosene-lamp splendour to display a bountiful array of local fruit and vegetables.

Outriggers on Sanur beach await high tide

▶▶ **Padangbai** *141E2*

Padangbai is essentially a launching pad for ferries to Lombok, but it is also a pleasant little resort in its own right with a pretty crescent-shaped beach, colourful fishing boats and some excellent diving off shore. Clustered behind the jetty and along the main road are strings of souvenir shops aimed at the cruise-ship hordes that descend sporadically on the port when their liners anchor in the bay. Otherwise, the restaurants and accommodation fronting the bay are small, relaxed and friendly. Immediately south of the port over the headland is the more secluded and very picturesque beach of **Pantai Kecil**, while to the north stands the sea temple of **Pura Silayukti**. The ferries to the port of Lembar on Lombok leave every 3 hours throughout the day.

▶ **Penelokan** *141D3*

Perched high above Gunung Batur's crater lake (see page 150) at an altitude of 1,200m is the village of Penelokan, offering the first astonishing panorama of the area if you arrive from the south – the name does not mean 'Place to Look' for nothing. If you manage to escape tour-group visiting hours this is the perfect spot for meditating on shifting cloud formations and lava flows. Panoramic restaurants cling to the crater rim along the road to Kintamani, but those intent on climbing Mount Batur or touring the lake should turn right down the twisting road to Kedisan. On entering Penelokan from the south, a side-road takes off to the right through thick pine-woods interspersed with more scenic views of the lake, and skirts Mount Abang before eventually arriving at Besakih. This little-used road offers beautiful rural vistas and an alternative route to Bali's mother temple.

▶ **Sanur** *141D1*

Once famous for its priests and demons, as well as being the point where the Dutch landed in 1906, Sanur became

one of the first areas in Bali to be colonised by foreigners when both Walter Spies and Margaret Mead sojourned here in the 1930s. Today, the 3km beach is fronted by luxury hotels, while shops and restaurants are concentrated along the parallel Jalan Danau Tamblingan. The atmosphere is monied and cosmopolitan, a far cry from the beer-swilling of Kuta across the peninsula, although touts still proliferate and the beach has its scruffy moments. Watersports are plentiful (at a price), but at low tide the sea recedes to the horizon to leave a somewhat unenticing coral and rock perspective.

Sanur's one cultural destination is the **Museum Le Mayeur►►** (*open*: mornings; closed on Monday), former home to a Belgian artist who lived here from 1932 to 1958. Le Mayeur's Post-Impressionist works feature scenes from much of the globe and his densely coloured pictures of Balinese life have inspired many a local artist. Although now sandwiched between hotels, this dark, atmospheric old building has a lot of charm.

Boat tours can be made from Sanur to nearby **Pulau Serangan** where turtles are raised for their precious meat and offshore coral offers good snorkelling.

► **Singaraja** *140C3*

Bali's second-largest town offers little in the way of sights but is a mandatory stop-over along the north coast. The original rajas of Singaraja were a splinter group of east Bali's powerful Gelgel Dynasty, and at one time their power extended as far south as Kintamani. In the early 19th century Dutch colonisation began here and, following their 1882 conquest of north Bali, Singaraja became the seat of government for the entire Nusa Tenggara province until 1953. The dry lands of the north have since been tamed to produce coffee, vanilla and cloves, but the former bustle of Singaraja's port has been diluted into a peaceful seaside centre of administration. Bali seems far away in this town where mosques and Chinese temples are common, yet the town does claim the island's best collection of *lontar* (illustrated palm-leaf books) at the **Gedong Kirtya►►** on Jalan Veteran, a library founded by the Dutch in 1928. The tourist office is located next door.

A bas-relief at Pura Beji in Sangsit, near Singaraja, exemplifies northern Balinese style

Household temples
Visible in every village throughout the island are rows of family temple compounds. The degree of ornamentation of the shrines varies according to the family caste. Each compound has a family temple oriented towards holy Mount Agung that may contain shrines dedicated to the god Sanghyang Widhi but which focuses mainly on the family's deified ancestors. Every compound also contains a roofed shrine (*kemulan*) with three openings said to be for the Hindu triad of Siva, Brahma and Vishnu, or alternatively for Sanghyang Widhi flanked by male and female characteristics. The roof of the *kemulan* is usually of thatched *duk*, a tough black fibre from the sugar palm. Other shrines are devoted respectively to guardian spirits, the god of the breadwinner's profession (or talent) or to Kala Raksa, the demon god of peace.

Balinese arts and crafts

■ The centuries-old Balinese craft tradition is deeply embedded in the people's philosophy of life, and despite strong external pressure is probably one of the keys to the island's survival. In amongst the ubiquitous kites, temple umbrellas, puppets and masks lies an astonishing range of exquisite and unusual items worth searching out.....■

Kris

In Indonesia a man's *kris* (sword) was always his most important accessory, symbolising his family and himself as an individual. A few examples can be found in antique shops, but usually they are clung to as precious family heirlooms. The *kris* revealed a man's economic status and the most extravagant, ruby-studded royal versions seen in museums today are glittering reflections of the metalsmith's craft. In Bali, *kris*-makers belonged to a special guild called *pande wesi* and were deemed to be magicians, as anyone working with metal was assumed to have mastered the art of sorcery. Their élite group was regarded as aristocratic, thus usurping the caste system, and even the proud Brahmanas had to address them in high Balinese.

A lizard takes form

For the Balinese every art form is sacred and every man or woman an artist. All babies are born with a 'talent', a gift from the gods, that they will spend their whole life developing, be it music, dance, painting, carving or weaving. The Balinese craftsman works in a group, thus identifying himself with his village or workshop and sharing profits with the community. This tradition of creating beauty in service to religion or society, formerly nurtured by the island's royal courts, has now found a new audience in the tourist industry. Commercial inroads may have changed the essence of many crafts, but they have certainly not affected those most closely associated with Balinese life. Zoomorphic coffins and elaborately crafted cremation towers remain perfect examples of such 'sacred' though ephemeral craftsmanship.

Painting Traditional Balinese painting was developed at Klungklung under the Gelgel Dynasty in imitation of the flat profiles of *wayang kulit* (shadow puppets). Peopled by heroes of the Hindu epics, the *Ramayana* and *Mahabharata*, these graphic, soberly coloured images (their hues are limited to red, brown, blue, yellow and ochre) were destined for royal temples and palaces, and were aimed at educating the masses about good and evil forces. Today *wayang* painters are based at Kamasan, just outside Klungklung, where they continue to produce work in traditional style.

Bali's most commercialised centre of painting is in and around Ubud (see panel on page 164), where several schools produce Western-influenced works depicting idealised village life, paddy-fields, Balinese dancers, birds and butterflies, all executed in naive style, and not always skilful or inspired.

Sculpture and carving Bali's sculptors and carvers have, so to speak, their work cut out for them. Temples and dance groups, joined today by hotels and restaurants, provide an endless market for statues of gods and demons, mythical beasts and ferocious masks.

In the village of Batubulan, craftsmen traditionally specialise in working basalt for decorating new temples or restoring weathered ones (temple guardians are in constant demand), but their sculptural energy now extends to gorgons, deer, frogs and anything else deemed fit to grace a hotel swimming-pool. At nearby Mas, woodcarvers also happily split their talents between sacred statues and dance masks on the one hand and, on

Woods
Materials used by Balinese woodcarvers range from costly tropical hardwoods to softwoods of the acacia family whose malleability and cheapness make them ideal for carving small items. Ebony, imported from Sulawesi, is a tough, dense wood while sandalwood, imported from Timor, is equally resistant but its fine trunk only lends itself to small-scale carvings. The *nangka* (jackfruit) tree, the frangipani tree and the coconut palm are also used for their density and light colour. Unless treated chemically and dried out thoroughly, however, all tropical woods will crack slightly when transported to a cooler, drier climate.

161

A Peliatan wood-carver with a freshly chiselled naga *(mythical snake)*

the other, more profane renderings of bare-breasted Balinese dancers price-tagged in US dollars. Despite the dubious taste of much of their contemporary works, the Mas craftsmen still produce some technically fine pieces.

Intricately carved wooden screens and panels are produced at the village of Batuan (half-way between Batubulan and Mas), although, as everywhere in Bali, the village specialisation is disappearing in a cloud of mass-produced souvenirs, from wind chimes to ducks.

Infinite cornucopia Balinese artistry is seemingly innate and its bounds infinite. While traditional forms such as buffalo-hide *wayang* puppets continue to be profitable merchandise, Balinese craftsmen are far from stagnating – the combination of Western demands and available natural materials inspires constant diversification and innovation. Dazzling gold and silver jewellery made at Celuk (see panel on page 144), for example, has developed with stylish new designs, subtle *ata* basketware made at Tenganan is adapted to 20th-century Western lifestyle and even textiles used for Kuta's latest hip fashions are a product of time-consuming experimentation. Where to next?

The rock temple of Tanah Lot remains oblivious to hundreds of lens-snappers every sunset

▶▶▶ Tanah Lot   140C1

This is Bali's most photographed sight, a towering rock temple that is transformed into an island battered by dramatic surf at high tide. The 15th-century temple is one of Bali's six holiest shrines and is dedicated to the gods of the sea, but is strictly reserved for worshippers. The cliché of sunsets at Tanah Lot has been so well marketed that the cliff facing the temple is now lined with restaurants cashing in on the spectacle. The setting is certainly stunning and if you head for the clifftop at the far end of the beach you will escape the masses.

▶▶ Tenganan   141E2

A road winds north from Candi Dasa through shady banana and palm groves to reach the fortified village of Tenganan, until recently one of the most conservative villages of the Bali Aga, the island's 'original' pre-Hindu people. The aristocratic Tenganese have a rich crafts tradition due to the fact that their communally owned land was worked by hired Balinese labour. Today the village's inhabitants have been sucked into the vortex of commercialism and many of their compounds, arranged around a central paved area, are showrooms for examples of their exceptional *kamben gringsing* (double-ikat weavings – see panel), *lontar* (illustrated palm-leaf books) and finely woven *ata* (palm-fibre basketware).

Tenganese double-*ikat*
The famous 'flaming' cloth of *kamben gringsing* was woven by the women of Tenganan and supposedly had the power to immunise the wearer against evil vibrations. This complex cotton weaving was originally made exclusively for ritual and priestly purposes, but today the tourist market has elbowed its way in and only the finest pieces are reserved for Tenganese ceremonial dress. Prices are high, as the intricate process of weaving and dyeing a single piece can take anything up to five years to complete and traditionally involved an entire family.

▶▶ Tirtagangga   141E2

This exceptionally beautiful area of west Bali offers picture-postcard views of terraced paddy-fields and, at its centre, a tranquil water palace. The Indian-inspired complex of pools (*tirta* means 'blessed water' and *gangga* derives from Ganges) was built by the raja of Karangasem in 1948 to tap a freshwater spring, and offers one of Bali's most regal, scenic and cooling swims. A restaurant and hotel bungalows (run by the rajah's grandchildren) overlook the area from a hill where the rajah's country house once stood. Although numerous *warungs* (food-stalls), souvenir-stalls and low-key *losmen* (budget inns) lie around the main car-park, Tirtagangga lies off the main tourist beat and offers a real taste of rural Bali.

Drive **Around Mount Agung**

See map on pages 140–1.

This route skirts the eastern slopes of Gunung Agung, passing through some of Bali's most picturesque rural landscapes before following the island's north coast and terminating at the holy lake of Danau Bratan. There are several ideal spots for a cooling dip along the way.

From Candi Dasa or Amlapura, follow the main road to **Tirtagangga** and its elegantly structured spring-water pools surrounded by rolling rice-fields. The road twists north towards Abang, climbing through sweeping valleys that are graphically and tightly terraced, offering a completely unspoilt vision of rural Bali.

A constant visual companion as you drive along is the looming volcanic peak of **Gunung Agung,** which rises in menacing splendour to the west and then, after the road veers around the coast at Culik, to the south. The landscape now assumes a volcanic identity, a hangover from the 1963 eruption. The road passes dry river beds and lava flows, and only a few cattle and palm trees break the monotony of the arid slopes. At the village of **Tulamben** you can stop for a snorkelling tour around a World War II wreck which lies in its watery grave a short distance off shore. Tulamben is now a popular diving centre, and beach accommodation is developing.

The vegetation gradually becomes greener as you continue, bamboo groves appearing as the road passes through numerous coastal fishing villages. More diving and accommodation are available at Sambirenteng, where the profile of Mount Batur takes over from Agung; by the time you reach Bukit the road is actually directly above the volcanic black-sand beaches. Stop at **Air Sanih** for another freshwater dip, detour inland to the temple at Jagaraga, then continue to **Singaraja**. From here the main road inland through Sukasada climbs fast, with superb sea panoramas all the way to the mountain pass just beyond the waterfall village of Gitgit. Mount Catur accompanies you to the east and Lake Buyan is visible to the west as the road finally descends to magical **Danau Bratan**.

Underground springs feed the cool pools of Air Sanih

BALI

Ubud art
Ubud's flourishing modern art movement leapt into action in the 1930s when Walter Spies and Rudolf Bonnet set up residence at Campunan. Spies, the homosexual son of a German diplomat, was invited to Bali by the prince of Ubud and was soon entranced by the place. He set up a co-operative for local artists in 1936 with the Dutchman Bonnet. The foreigners' genuine interest brought with it encouragement, materials and patronage, as well as the imposition of a Western aesthetic. Spies was also notable for his art collection, his recordings of Balinese music and the founding of the Bali Museum in Denpasar. Both artists died during World War II.

This acknowledged centre of Balinese arts throbs with Westerners intent on discovering the authentic Bali. Sadly, it is no longer here, but none the less the town has a unique amalgam of tranquillity and liveliness.

Orientation Forming the centre of Ubud is a large rectangle composed of two steep parallel roads, Monkey Forest Road and Jalan Hanoman, which are joined in the north by the main market and restaurant street, Jalan Raya. The famous **Monkey Forest** (watch out – the inmates can be vicious) lies in the southwest corner. Up-market hotels are concentrated on Monkey Forest Road or well outside the town, while budget accommodation can be found in every possible location from paddy-fields to family compounds. All tourist needs are catered for, from transport rental to massages or bird walks, while aesthetics remain high in most restaurant or hotel priorities. The well-organised tourist office is located centrally on Jalan Raya virtually opposite Ubud's beautiful 16th-century palace, the intricately carved **Puri Saren**.

Art? Ubud's role in nurturing modern Balinese art is well illustrated in the collection displayed at the **Puri Lukisan Museum**▶▶ on Jalan Raya (*open*: 8–4). The museum is surrounded by luxuriant gardens replete with fountains and statues, and is reached via a bridge over a river, its setting as attractive as its contents. About 1km north of the Campuan suspension bridge is the **Museum Neka**▶▶, which houses a large collection of modern Indonesian painting as well as the works of countless foreign artists who have elected to live in Bali over the years – from Le Mayeur to Walter Spies, Rudolf Bonnet and

An example of modern Balinese art at the Museum Neka

Arie Smit. The rollercoasting quality of the works does not detract from the fact that Ubud has played a unique role in blending Eastern and Western influences. The town still attracts Western artists who believe in a never-never land of tropically inspired kitsch and you are cordially invited to see the worst of this at the gaudy temple erected by - erotica artist Antonio Blanco to his own genius. 'Artists' are thick on the ground in Ubud and quick to open their homes or studios to the public; sales talk is equally fast so be certain you like a painting before actually investing in it.

Beyond Ubud Leisurely strolls through rice-fields and forests are part of Ubud's offerings, and with a rented bike you can also tour the outlying villages which are now virtually joined to Ubud. Immediately east of the centre lies **Peliatan**, famed for its active dance group and gamelan orchestra, and also home to numerous crafts galleries. In the paddy-fields to the south lies the artists' community of **Pengosekan** and, further east, the temple-rich village of **Bedulu**. Of most interest here is the **Pura Penataran Sasih**, thought to be 1,000 years old and home to a superlative 'moon' bronze kettledrum and a collection of 11th-century stone sculptures. **Goa Gajah** (see page 149) lies immediately south.

West of Ubud, up a steep forested road from Campuan, lies **Penestanan**, centre for the 1960s Young Artists' Movement (more galleries). Beyond this is the spectacular terraced gorge of Yeh Agung at **Sayan**, focus for some discreet luxury hotels.

▶▶ Uluwatu 140C1

The small sea temple of Uluwatu balances dramatically on a sheer cliff edge in the extreme southwest corner of the rugged Bukit Peninsula. Like Tanah Lot (see page 162) it is dedicated to the protective spirits of the sea and for centuries was reserved for the prince of Badung's annual offerings, although today a friendly tribe of macaques has taken over. Uluwatu's other highlight is its popular surfing beach, Panti Suluban, accessible only by motor bike.

Peliatan's highly regarded gamelan musicians prepare for a procession

Legong
Ubud is renowned for its evening dance performances held in atmospheric temple or palace settings. One of the most commonly staged is the *Legong Kraton*, the quintessential 'heavenly' dance of femininity and grace formerly only held in the royal *puri* (temples) of each village. Dancers are recruited among the prettiest and most talented girls, who start at the age of five and retire at 14. Three dancers perform this highly stylised drama based on a historical romance that took place in East Java around the 12th century. The girls' tiny supple bodies, glittering in gold brocade and floral head-dresses, enact the story with bewitching control, flowing from one character to another as the accompanying gamelan orchestra changes rhythm.

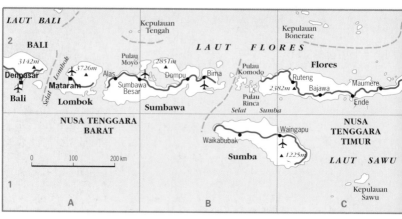

Pulau
Adonara

Larantuka

Pulau
Solor

Pulau
Lommlen

Pulau
Pantar

Pulau
Alor
(Ombaii)

Selat Ombai

Pulau
Wetar

Pulau
Atauuo

Dili

2963m

Timor

▲
2427m Kefamenanu

Pulau
Semau

Kupang

Pulau Roti

D

Selat Wetar

Pulau
Romann

Kepulauan
Leti

Baukau

Tutuala

TIMOR TIMUR

LAUT   TIMOR

E

NUSA TENGGARA

Nusa Tenggara This extraordinarily diverse region encompasses hundreds of islands and islets straggling 1,500km across the Indian Ocean, which from Lombok eastwards to Timor become progressively arid and consequently impoverished. It consists of two provinces: West Nusa Tenggara, composed of Lombok and Sumbawa; and East Nusa Tenggara, made up of Komodo, Flores, Sumba, West Timor and 562 smaller islands. East Timor is the latest province, integrated in 1975, and remains a continuing political and human rights embarrassment. A trip through these islands offers a wealth of ethnographic interest, skilful crafts traditions, some fabulous beaches, captivating landscapes and a population that, beyond Lombok's tourist centres, is glad to meet a rare visitor.

Historical diversity Nusa Tenggara's history varies from island to island. Natural resources were limited to the fragrant sandalwood forests of Timor and Sumba, and so it was only Portuguese missionaries in Flores and Timor that left any lasting European impact. Until the 1970s East Nusa Tenggara led an isolated existence, its bad communications coupled with primitive farming methods and rain shortages all contributing to severe poverty.

Lombok's past is more intensely coloured, first by Balinese princes and then, in 1894, by the arrival of the Dutch, neither of whom were appreciated by the indigenous Sasaks. Sumbawa, meanwhile, kept a low Islamic profile from its 17th-century conversion until a short-lived colonial period. The diverse backgrounds of the islands create a socio-cultural divide, with Islam dominating the more prosperous west and Christianity the poorer east.

Animism Lying below the surface of or parallel to the acquired religions is an authentic belief in animisim. Lombok's Sasaks, Flores' Ngada, Timor's Atoni, the people of Sumbawa's Bima region and, above all, the *merapu* culture of Sumba's inhabitants, all produce extraordinary forms of symbolic rural architecture, echoed in some

Transport
Regular flights from Darwin in Australia to Kupang on West Timor are opening up East Nusa Tenggara, but despite recent improvements bussing across both Timor and Flores continues to be a bone-shaking experience. Car hire is non-existent except in Lombok; the most you'll get elsewhere is a chartered *bemo* (minibus). But this is, after all, the land of the loudest and most colourful *bemos* (compare the decorations of those in Kupang with Maumere), closely followed by the fastest and most heavily pomponned *bendis* (pony traps) in Sumbawa. Ferries between Flores, Komodo, Sumbawa and Lombok keep to regular schedules and island boats ply the waves of the Savu Sea. Airstrips dot the terrain but flights are infrequent and unreliable except to Kupang, Maumere and Mataram.

Dancing at a Para ceremony in Soa, near Bajawa, Flores

cases by animist rites, sacrifices, carved megaliths and even, in the case of Sumba, mock battles on horseback that occasionally become homicidal.

Lombok's villages have mostly adapted to the tourist trade, but in the more remote parts of East Nusa Tenggara rituals and inhabitants remain untainted. It is not by chance either that these islands produce Indonesia's best *ikat*; each region or even village specialises in specific colours, overall designs and motifs, and it is hard not to become fascinated by the laborious techniques that often constitute a family's only revenue. In a different vein, the crafts of Lombok, much influenced by commercialism, are becoming increasingly inventive.

Natural attractions Alfred R Wallace, the Victorian naturalist, drew an imaginary line between Bali and Lombok dividing the flora and fauna of Asia and Australasia. Although this theory has since been revised, there is certainly a marked transformation from the rich tropical vegetation west of Bali to the barren scrubland of Timor, where only *lontar* palms dare to grow. Fauna follows the same equation, as elephants and rhinoceroses, formerly common as far east as Bali, are replaced in Nusa Tenggara by marsupials, monitor lizards and cockatoos.

Rainfall is one of the reasons for the variations: the wet season (October to March) sees barely a quarter of the annual downpours that drown Sumatra and Sulawesi and the sun is noticeably fiercer. In amongst the savannah there are, however, some spectacular natural sights, with Flores' multi-coloured Kelimutu lakes top of the table, closely followed by Komodo's carnivorous 'dragons', Lombok's towering volcano, Rinjani, and Sumbawa's nature reserve on Pulau Moyo. Blissful, reef-lined beaches are to be found everywhere, but getting to them can be a problem as adequate infrastructures exist only in Lombok, at Flores' Maumere and Labuanbajo, and at Kupang in Timor. South coast beaches on all the islands claim the big rollers, those of Lombok, Sumba and Sumbawa now pulling in surfers looking for a thrill.

A deserted valley near Ende in central Flores

Betel-nut
Red splashes on pavements and in marketplaces point to one thing only – the betel-nut *(sirih)* habit. This stimulant produces red-stained gums and lips as well as blackened teeth, but custom prevails and the practice is common throughout most of the outer islands.

The women of Flores openly display their dowries

FLORES

The long, thin, volcanic, impoverished island of Flores can boast some of the worst roads in Indonesia. The speed along its 'highway' averages 25kph, but the recompenses are great, as scenery evolves from the lush, tropical coastline of banana, coconut palm and bamboo groves up through spectacular ravines to misty, highland villages set among pine trees. When the Portuguese rounded the eastern cape in 1512, they were so struck by the island's beauty that they dubbed it Cabo das Flores ('Cape of Flowers'), and the name, still appropriate today, has stuck. Although the Dutch moved into Ende in 1670, their impact was minimal, and 85 per cent of the population remains devoutly Catholic. The two island highlights are the crater lakes of Kelimutu and the fabulous coral reefs off Maumere, but Flores also offers fascinating animist villages near Bajawa, picturesque old Portuguese churches, an expanding beach resort at Labuanbajo and some of Indonesia's best *ikat*-weaving.

Going to market at Boawae

▶▶ **Bajawa**   170B1

This cool, friendly mountain village reeking of wood smoke lies in the west of Flores. It serves as a base to visit nearby Ngada villages such as Bena or Wogo, whose animist traditions have curiously blended with Catholicism. To the south of Bajawa looms the perfect cone of **Gunung Inerie** (2,131m) which last erupted in 1980, while the nearest towns are Ruteng to the west and Ende to the east, both 5–6 hours away by road. An alternative is to use the very rural airfield which offers occasional flights to other Nusa Tenggara destinations. Bajawa radiates from its small market, church and mosque, and offers numerous budget hotels and restaurants all within walking distance of one another. Evening entertainment is limited to a lone billiard hall.

▶▶ **Bena**   170B1

A bumpy but beautiful 1-hour drive south of Bajawa around Gunung Inerie takes you to Bena, the best preserved and, therefore, most popular of the Ngada villages. High-gabled, thatched houses climb up a steep slope which rises to a look-out point over the Savu Sea, *ikat* (not

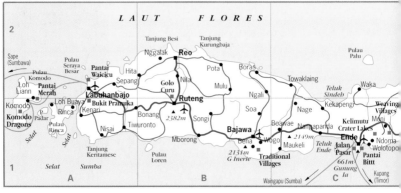

the best) is displayed for sale, an entrance fee is charged, and the villagers in general look as if life has passed them by. However, what is unique about Bena is the presence of Christian graves and a simple chapel beside megaliths and *ngadhu* and *bhaga* shrines which respectively symbolise male and female ancestral forces (see panel opposite). Each house is also topped by another male or female emblem. Energetic walkers can continue downhill to the even older Ngada village of **Gurusina**, about 7km away.

►► Boawae   170C1

About 40km east of Bajawa on the Ende road is the village of Boawae, known above all for its *ikat* and its gory buffalo sacrifices. The weaving is characterised by white horse designs on a dark background and is sold at the lively daily market. The local Nage-Keo people also indulge in a traditional form of boxing known as *etu*, which takes place after the harvest between May and August.

Dowries
Even the Catholic inhabitants of Flores have to face up to the probem of dowries. Marriage is by no means easy as it requires a dowry equivalent to Rp2–3 million (US$1,000–1,500), payable in ivory, horses or *ikat* – no mean figure in a rural society where agriculture barely covers subsistence. Tourism is still in its early days here and some mountain villages are painfully dispossessed.

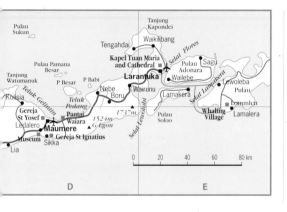

House-building at Bena is preceded by a buffalo or pig sacrifice

Colour change

The phenomenon of the evolving colours of Kelimutu's lakes has baffled scientists for years. Explanations suggest the existence of interconnecting channels deep down in the volcano, but the accepted opinion is that different chemical and mineral mixes in the water cause the transformations. The earliest reports say that the lakes were white, red and black; a decade ago they became dark red, green and blue. Colour changes, which can take place within a year, are interpreted by locals as a sign from the spirits, and they believe the three lakes resting places for the old (received by the lake that lies separate from the other two – also a favourite for suicides), the young and the evil.

Whale-harpooning

The village of Lamalera on Pulau Lembata (or Lomblen), which lies beyond Pulau Adonara to the east of Larantuka, is renowned for its spectacular whale-harpooning, a centuries-old practice which is allowed to continue despite international whaling bans. Only 20 or so sperm whales are killed every season (roughly runnng from May to September) and the meat is divided carefully among village families. Wooden whaling boats traditionally use palm-leaf sails, but when a whale is sighted and the hunt is on, oarsmen take over. The climax comes when the boat arrives close to the whale and a harpooner leaps on to the creature's back to accomplish the death blow.

Old houses on Larantuka's main street

► **Ende** *170C1*

Flores' largest town of 66,000 inhabitants (many of whom are Muslim) is an unavoidable stop-over. It is located at the neck of a small peninsula backed by the two volcanoes of Gunung Meja and Gunung Ia (the last eruption was in 1969), both of which can easily be climbed. On the west coast the busy commercial port (spectacular at night when it sparkles with illuminated fishing boats) is backed by a huge market area along **Jalan Pasar**. The rest of the town sprawls west and north over the hills.

The only historic site is **Sukarno's House and Museum** on Jalan Perwira, where he was exiled in 1934–8, but this is stretching a point. Cross the peninsula to the east side and you soon reach some good, though rocky beaches. **Pantai Bitta** is particularly scenic, edged by palm groves and enlivened by local fishermen. **Wolotopo**, 7km east of Ende, is a beautifully sited village of traditional houses that is famed for its weavings. The neighbouring village of **Ndoma** also produces its own intricate and abstract *ikat* designs.

▶▶▶ Kelimutu   170C1

The star of the island is an extraordinary natural wonder consisting of three crater lakes, each of a different and evolving colour (see panel opposite). Kelimutu is easily comparable to the magnificence of Java's Bromo, yet sees only a limited number of tourists. At dawn, swirling cloud rises beside a blood-red sun from the valleys below to surround these perfect jewels. Civilisation seems far away – and it is! The easiest way to get there is to take a pre-dawn truck ride from the village of Moni, up a painfully twisting track to the park entrance 12km above. Two lakes lie side by side, offering a stunning juxtaposition of brilliant turquoise and pale jade, while behind a crag lies the mysterious third lake, 50m below its walls and turning slowly from maroon to black. Kelimutu tours are also arranged from Ende and Maumere, but the early morning call is consequently even earlier.

One of Kelimutu's spectacular triad of contrasting lakes

▶▶ Labuhanbajo   170A2

This predominantly Muslim fishing village lies at the western end of Flores and looks out on a sapphire-blue sea sprinkled with islands. It is the easiest launching pad for visiting Komodo, but as it also possesses some excellent snorkelling beaches and good accommodation it makes an ideal base simply for relaxing.

The town straggles along one road that runs parallel to the seashore, from the harbour in the north past the market to the airport and the Ruteng road. **Pantai Waicicu**, the most popular weekend beach, is a 15-minute boat ride north of town and is equalled by **Batugosok** (both have accommodation), but more inspiring still are the deserted white sands and coral reefs of **Pulau Bidadari**, **Sabolo Besar** and **Sabolo Kecil**, easily reached by chartered boat. For panoramic views over the bay, especially beautiful at sunset, climb **Bukit Pramuka** just behind the town. Labuhanbajo is the departure point for budget boat tours to Komodo and Sumbawa which end at Lombok.

Portuguese traditions run deep in Larantuka's churches

▶ Larantuka   171E2

At Flores' eastern extremity is this staunchly Catholic town which long held strategic importance as a stop-over port on the way to Maluku and Timor. Larantuka huddles at the base of a volcano, separated by a narrow strait from the islands of the Solor and Alor Archipelago with which it shares Lamaholot culture and language. By the early 17th century Dominicans had established 20 missions here which later developed in isolation, preserving prayers in Latin and old Portuguese, as well as a considerable community of *Topasses*, the half-caste descendants of the Portuguese. Their deeply ingrained beliefs come to the fore during Easter week, which sees processions worthy of Seville. Of the many churches, the most revered are the **Kapel Perawan Maria (Chapel of the Virgin Mary)** and the century-old **Larantuka Cathedral**.

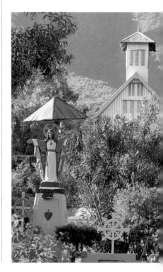

NUSA TENGGARA

Lone museum
The Jesuit Seminary Museum at Ledalero is unique in Flores as it exhibits the only collection of artefacts from the island. Displays assembled by Father Piet Petu over the last 25-odd years cover archaeology, crafts (several photo albums detail regional *ikat* techniques and designs) and ethnography. Some pieces even come from Irian Jaya, but all lie beneath a thick layer of dust. Leave a generous donation for this one-man museum.

Taking the pig to market in Ruteng

▶▶ **Maumere**   *171D1*

Maumere used to be a pleasant market town that thrived on fishing and a reasonable flow of tourists heading for its pristine coral reefs. Then in December 1992 disaster struck in the form of a tidal wave and earthquake, leaving some 2,000 dead, an entire district wrecked and the upper part of the reef shattered (see panel opposite). Despite reconstruction, Maumere retains a bombed-out look, hotels are mediocre and the only bank offers what must be the worst exchange rates in Indonesia. The still ramshackle market does, however, offer a good selection of Flores *ikat* and there are some reasonable restaurants.

Catholicism is embodied by the badly damaged cathedral and the lovely old wooden church of **St Yosef**, where paintings depict an Indonesian Christ. About 8km west at **Ledalero** (along Flores' best stretch of road thanks to a papal visit in 1989) is a mission museum displaying a jumbled but very rich ethnographic collection (see panel).

If little appeals in town, head out east to the beaches edging the magnificent Teluk Pedang and its offshore coral islands. Plans are afoot to develop a resort about 30km away, but for the moment facilities are mainly limited to **Pantai Waiara**, about 12km east of Maumere beyond the airport. Bungalow accommodation designed for divers is of a high standard and hotels organise boats to the outlying coral reef, though at a price. The arresting landscape here is dominated by the active cone of **Gunung Egon** and fishing villages line the road. Villagers can be seen pounding broken coral to create limewash or drying cocoa beans along the main road, and trips up into the nearby hill villages are scenically rewarding.

▶ **Moni**   *170C1*

This pretty little village in the lush hills below Kelimutu now depends very much on tourists heading for the crater lakes. Accommodation, mostly homestays, remains basic and is concentrated opposite a dilapidated church and playing field. There are some scenic walks in the area, one of which leads to a waterfall and hot springs, or you can visit Moni's own traditional carved and thatched house. Villagers hold a permanent *ikat* market on the main road as Moni and other villages east of here (**Wolowaru**, **Nggela** and **Jopu**) are renowned for their stunning weaving techniques, mostly using dark, earthy, natural dyes.

▶ **Ruteng**   *170B2*

Ruteng is the main market town of western Flores, a gathering point for the Manggarai people of the surrounding fertile hills. Luminous-green rice-fields dominate the landscape, and for a striking panorama of terraced slopes and valleys head for the hill of **Golo Curu**, just north of town. Maize and coffee is also cultivated, and buffaloes and ponies used extensively. Catholicism predominates but some Manggarai traditions survive, including *caci*, an enthralling combat between two masked men who attempt in turn to whip each other, encouraged by drums and gongs. Ruteng offers reasonable accommodation and a fair selection of weavings, including the local embroidered black sarongs.

▶▶ Sikka   *171D1*

About 30km south of Maumere lies the coastal village of Sikka, again famed for its weavings. Fishing boats and thatched wooden houses line the black-sand beach (the rough southern sea is referred to by locals as the 'man's sea', in contrast to the calm waters of the north coast which are known as the 'woman's sea'), and the village centre is dominated by the huge church of **St Ignatius** (1899). This white and green wooden construction boasts a remarkable interior, but you may have to search out the church warden for the key. The church is a clear symbol of Sikka's former power as, together with Solor and Ende, the town was a major early 17th-century Portuguese settlement which dominated the region until this century. Any visitor who sets foot in Sikka will be welcomed by an instant *ikat* market; women materialise within minutes to display their superb maroon and indigo weavings.

175

Natural disaster
On 12 December 1992 an earthquake which registered 7.5 on the Richter scale, and with an epicentre about 30km northeast of Maumere, devastated much of eastern Flores. A few minutes later it was followed by a 15m-high tidal wave which swept over the islands of Pulau Babi, Besar, Kambing and Pamana, scooping up fishing boats and dumping them in the streets of Maumere, destroying numerous villages and killing some 2,000 people. Most of the damage centred on the islands which broke the back of the wave, leaving survivors severely traumatised, but the magnificent coral reef also suffered. The damaged coral is now growing again and tropical fish are as numerous as ever.

Women in Moni sell a wide range of ikat *styles from nearby villages*

■ **The Komodo dragon advances, raises its head out of the grass and flicks its forked orange tongue. A scene from the best horror movie can be witnessed live in and around Komodo, home to these fearsome remnants of the dinosaur age.....■**

Precautions

A commemorative plaque on Komodo reminds visitors of their potential fate. It is dedicated to a Swiss baron who 'disappeared on this island' in 1974, aged 79. Visitors are advised not to wear red as, despite the Komodo's bad eyesight, it is thought to associate this colour with blood and therefore is attracted to it. Following a similar logic, menstruating women or anyone with a wound is advised not to visit the islands. If you are faced with a Komodo in attacking mode (hissing and raising its back), you are advised to push a stick or a handful of stones into the creature's mouth. Easier said than done, no doubt.

The world's largest living reptile, top in the predator stakes, fearlessly attacks buffaloes, horses, deer and pigs

The Komodo dragon (*Varanus komodoensis*), a living example of prehistory, has survived for over 10 million years but only became known to the West in 1910 when a Dutch expedition chanced upon one. Although monitor lizards exist in Asia, Africa and Australia, this giant version has developed in isolation on the islands of Komodo and Rinca, and on the west coast of Flores. Estimates of the creature's size have been wildly exaggerated in the past, a factor that may even have inspired the Chinese myth of the dragon. At the most, the Komodo dragon reaches a length of 3m. It does, however, move remarkably fast, is an aggressive predator, and in one day can consume a good three-quarters of its body-weight (which approaches 150kg).

No trifle The life span of this carnivore is about 60 years, an impressive duration which may have something to do with the fact that it devours some 13 different animal species. Nor is the reptile averse to cannibalising dead members of its own species, as any rotting meat is its preferred meal. When it attacks, the dragon presents a terrifying spectacle, inflating its neck, opening its jaw, sticking its tongue out and hissing while advancing on its hind legs. Sharp teeth and ferocious claws combine with the whiplash effect of its tail to overcome goats, buffaloes and, on occasion, even humans – a Komodo is not to be trifled with.

Although the Komodo has poor hearing and weak sight, it makes up for this with a phenomenal sense of smell and touch, helped by a 50cm-long tongue. The creatures can also run, climb, swim, dive and dig. Mating generally takes place in June or July, after which the females lay up to 20 huge eggs which they bury in the sand. On hatching, a baby Komodo will already measure 50cm.

KOMODO

Komodo is known for one thing only – its dragon. This top predator of the reptile kingdom is only found in the Komodo National Park, an area of 170,000 hectares which incorporates the islands of **Komodo**, **Rinca** and **Padar**, and which was established in 1980. These islands are home to some 3,000 of the giant lizards but also offer good though hot trekking through the savannah.

Tours to see the monster are arranged from as far afield as Bali, so don't think you'll be alone at feeding time. The nearest port for Rinca or Komodo is Labuanbajo in Flores, from where boats take 2–4 hours. An alternative is to take the morning ferry from Sape in Sumbawa (Monday, Wednesday and Saturday), which only stops at Komodo and takes over 6 hours. Currents in these straits are ferocious so only charter reliable-looking boats.

Before setting off for Komodo, visit either of the PHPA offices in Labuanbajo or Sape. They issue permits and can

Sardonic grin
'There, facing me... crouched the dragon. He was enormous...He was standing high on his four bowed legs, his heavy body lifted clear of the ground, his head erect and menacing. The line of his savage mouth curved upwards in a fixed sardonic grin and from between his half-closed jaws an enormous yellow-pink forked tongue slid in and out.'
– From *Zoo Quest for a Dragon* by David Attenborough (1957).

book you in at the ranger's camp situated at **Loh Liang**, an essential move in the peak summer months (June to September) when the island's limited accommodation is much in demand. The PHPA office at Loh Liang itself can organise chartered boats to other islands and beaches; there is superb snorkelling near by at **Pantai Merah** but take your own equipment. Guides are obligatory during the summer months if you want to hike off the main marked trails. Feeding time (Wednesday and Saturday) is a gory affair which takes place at a dry river bed about 30 minutes' walk from Loh Liang. Rangers hang dead goats on a tree, the dragons devouring these with alacrity.

Rinca, less touristry than Komodo, offers better chances of spotting wildlife such as monkeys, deer, wild horses, boar and water buffalo. Dragons can be seen here, too, and there are PHPA bungalows at **Loh Buaya**.

The barren, ochre-coloured slopes of Komodo are protected as a national park

LOMBOK

Hard life
Over the centuries, Lombok's Sasak population has undergone conversion to Islam, endured harsh Balinese overlords and heavy handed Dutch colonial rule, and faced countless famines which as recently as 1966 resulted in thousands of deaths. Rice is the agricultural mainstay, but harvests are insufficient for a burgeoning population of over 2.5 million squeezed into an area of 5,600 sq km. Crafts – from pottery to weaving and fine basketwork – are becoming an important trade, but inhabitants of the more arid south remain noticeably impoverished. Tourism is possibly the only answer, so go there before it's too late.

Immediately to the east of Bali lies Lombok, a predominantly Muslim island with magnificent beaches, Hindu temples, a sacred volcano and indigenous Sasak culture. For the moment only Senggigi claims a sophisticated infrastructure, leaving Kuta in the hands of surfers and beach-addicts, and the Gili Islands for divers and snorkellers.

One good road cuts across the middle of the island, dividing the fertile slopes of Gunung Rinjani from the Sasak crafts villages of the south, and connecting the capital of Mataram with the port for Sumbawa. With its adequate facilities and less frenetic pace than Bali, though lacking the latter's cultural intensity, Lombok makes a peaceful and rewarding alternative.

▶▶▶ Gili Islands 178A2

The three idyllic coral-rimmed islands of Gili Air, Gili Meno and Gili Trawangan off Lombok's northwest coast are easily reached by ferry from **Bangsal**, also the destination for a direct boat service from Bali's Padangbai, and diving packages are organised from Senggigi or on Trawangan itself. There are no banks on the Gilis, so take cash with you. Most of the accommodation and low-key nightlife is concentrated along the east beach of Trawangan, while Meno appeals to those seeking peace and quiet. Air, a 20-minute boat ride from Bangsal and with the largest local population, offers facilities between the extremes.

All three islands offer mainly budget bungalow accommodation and excellent seafood, but the word is out and Trawangan in particular becomes overcrowded in the

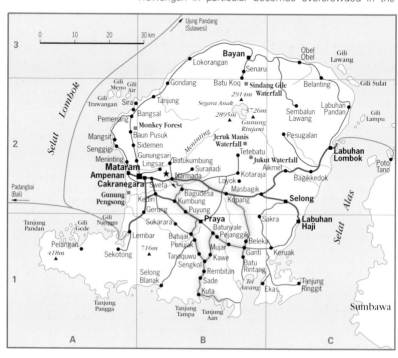

high season. The reef between Trawangan and Meno is a favourite with snorkellers as strong (sometimes wild) currents carry you southwards along the coral wall. Meno's northeast coast offers spectacular blue-coral landscapes.

▶▶▶ Gunung Rinjani   178B2

An ascent of this 3,726m volcano is one of the greatest experiences Indonesia has to offer, but it is an arduous, 3-day climb that should only be undertaken by the very fit. Few people make it to the actual summit, contenting themselves instead with the breathtakingly beautiful emerald-green crater lake which lies at 2,900m. Mist-shrouded Rinjani, now a 40,000-hectare reserve, is Indonesia's third-highest mountain and much revered by both Muslim Sasaks and Hindu Balinese. Sasaks climb to the crater every full moon during the dry season, while Balinese make twice-yearly pilgrimages to throw goldfish and rice cakes into the lake.

The best place to start your climb is from the fascinating Sasak village of **Bayan** on the north slope (the last *bemo*, or minibus stop), then walk to **Batu Koq** or **Senaru** where the essential guides and tents can be hired and basic accommodation is located. From here it is a 7- or 8-hour trek to the base camp at 2,100m, up through rainforest and past the thundering **Sindang Gile** waterfall and alpine landscapes, followed by another 2 hours of hiking through a moonscape to the caldera rim. Cloud may obscure the lake of **Segara Anak**, but views across Lombok to Bali's Mount Agung are exceptional and the cold can be kept at bay by trekking down to hot mineral springs just below the lake. Camping shelters (not well maintained) dot Rinjani's slopes and the crater rim itself. An alternative, less-used route up Rinjani starts from **Sembalun Lawang** on the east slope, from where it takes about 9 hours to reach the crater.

Gili Trawangan's beaches are becoming increasingly popular with divers and snorkellers enjoying the coral reefs

Wektu Telu
Lombok claims two branches of Islam: Wektu Lima, which observes Koranic law strictly and is followed by about two-thirds of the population; and Wektu Telu, a syncretic religion which combines aspects of animism, Hinduism and Islam and is practised by mountain people in the centre and north of the island. The only Muslim belief of the latter is in Allah and in Muhammad as his prophet, but they reject the Islamic observances of five daily prayers (their shrine at Lingsar is called 'three times' in reference to their three daily prayers), Ramadan fasting and the pilgrimage to Mecca. Their caste system strongly resembles that of Bali and ceremonies are closely linked with nature.

Bau Nyale
This annual festival, also celebrated in Java, is conceived of by Lombok's Sasaks as a prayer for rain. The rice-fields of central and south Lombok are often desperately dry and the night-long vigil on Kuta beach aims to encourage the heavens to open – usually the case in February/March. Heavy dawn rain brings out thousands of *nyale* (seaworms) from their home beneath the coral to the surface. Sasak legend recounts the story of a princess, Mandalika, who confounded her rival princely suitors by announcing that she would marry all of them – then promptly threw herself into the Indian Ocean and was transformed into a *nyale*.

The sacred eel-pond at Pura Lingsar

►► Kuta 178B1

Despite the fact that this beach village carries the same name as Bali's infamous resort, it could not be more different. Some 7km of spectacular indented coastline offer empty, white-sand beaches, plenty of scenic walks, and bays where rolling surf alternates with calmer waters to cater to all aquatic tastes – from swimming to windsurfing and surfing. Bungalow accommodation is low key and visitors youthful. Locals also know Kuta as Putri Nyale in honour of an annual all-night festival which usually takes place in February or March (see panel).

Tanjung Aan (to the east) is the best, most secluded swimming beach and, to the west, **Selong Blanak** (accessible only by a separate road from Praya) is quite simply paradise. On the road northwest of Kuta are caves and a look-out point with sweeping views.

► Labuhan Lombok 178C2

This rather scruffy village is the disembarkation point for Sumbawa. The crossing takes about 1½ hours and ferries leave five times a day, but if you get stuck Labuhan Lombok has a few basic *losmen* (budget inns). Further north up the coast there is a small tourist development at **Labuhan Pandan**, from where you can charter boats to reach the lovely, unspoilt islands of **Gili Lampu**, **Sulat** and **Lawang**, all of which have beautiful beaches and excellent snorkelling.

►► Lingsar 178B2

Just 9km northeast of Mataram is a large Hindu temple which stands next to a shrine devoted to Wektu Telu, an unofficial branch of Islam unique to Lombok (see panel on page 179). This rarity was erected in 1714 and rebuilt in 1878 to symbolise the harmony between the two communities.

First in the complex is the Hindu temple comprising four shrines, one dedicated to Bali's Gunung Agung, one to Gunung Rinjani, Lombok's home of the gods, and between them a double-sided shrine dedicated to the union of the two islands. On the adjoining terraces below are the Wektu Telu precincts, one of which contains an altar stacked with stones wrapped in yellow cloth which represent dead ancestors. Below this again is a series of bathing-pools, home to sacred eels.

► Mataram 178B2

The island's administrative capital of Mataram merges west to the old port of **Ampenan** and east to the former royal seat of **Cakranegara**. The latter is now Lombok's rather unattractive commercial crossroads and in turn spills into the transport hub of

Sweta. All Lombok's Hindu monuments are located near here, as are an informative tourist office, a vast, enticing market and a good museum.

First stop should be the **Museum Negeri**►► (*open*: Tuesday to Thursday, 8–2; Friday, 8–11; weekends, 8–1), which has a well laid out and labelled ethnographic collection including some dazzling examples of gold and silver, studded royal *kris* (swords), *songket*, costumes, terracotta, basketware and a rich display of *lontar*-leaf manuscripts. At Sweta's labyrinthine **market**, next to the *bemo* (minibus) station, tourist-oriented handicrafts and an extraordinarily diverse array of food are on sale. Weaving is demonstrated at a number of workshops, including Selamat Riyadi on Jalan Tenun and Rinjani Handwoven on Jalan Pejanggik, both in Cakranegara.

The jewels of Lombok's Balinese Hindu era are located in Cakranegara on opposite sides of Jalan Selaparang. The **Mayura Water Palace**►► was built in 1744 by the Balinese king of Lombok, who placed his *Bale Kambang* (a 'floating pavilion' used as a court and meeting-place) in the centre of an artificial lake, flanked by landscaped gardens. Across the road loom the tiered towers of the **Pura Meru**, the royal temple erected in 1720 and dedicated to the Hindu trinity of Siva, Vishnu and Brahma.

Lombok's Sasak architecture is used in hotel and restaurant constructions, as here on Gili Trawangan

Circumcision
One of the showcases in Ampenan's Museum Negeri contains pegs and knives used for circumcision. All young Muslim boys are circumcised. The occasion is particularly solemn and sees boys being carried through village streets on painted wooden horses with palm-leaf tails. Family celebrations follow. The circumcision is carried out without an anaesthetic as the boys are supposed to suffer pain for Allah.

Sasak architecture

Typical Sasak architecture is closely connected with their *adat* (traditional law). Each building must be constructed on a particular day and the wooden frame completed before dusk, otherwise bad luck follows. The largest are the rectangular *beruga* (community halls) with their low walls and steep, thatched pyramidal roofs, a form that is repeated on a smaller scale for *bale tani* (family houses). Some buildings are raised on stilts, all have walls made of lime and grass, and villages are generally surrounded by a high fence. *Lumbung* (rice-barns) have the same horseshoe shape as in Bali, an architectural curiosity now being used in the design of new hotels.

Naga snakes and an errant dog greet worshippers at Suranadi's temple

▶ **Narmada** *178B2*

A royal pleasure garden and place of worship are combined at Taman Narmada, 11km east of Mataram. The terraced park, built in 1801 by the king of Karangasem (East Bali), descends to an artificial lake designed to resemble the sacred crater lake on Gunung Rinjani which the ageing king could no longer ascend. Fact or fiction continues to relate that the king would install himself in the pavilion above the lake and select his concubines from among the women bathing. The lake is now, less lyrically, home to pleasure boats shaped like ducks, one pool has become a public swimming-pool and the entire park is a popular weekend promenading area. The temple, **Pura Kalasa**, sees an annual celebration in honour of Batara, the god who dwells on Rinjani, when gold is thrown into the lake.

▶ **Senggigi** *178A2*

Senggigi is one of several villages lining the coast north of Ampenan, but in reality the resort bearing this name stretches 5km on either side. This beautiful coastline is thick with tall coconut palms and banana groves, where development remains tasteful and aimed at the top end of the market, though not exclusively so.

From **Meninting** in the south, site of a small tourist office, the road follows the coast through **Batu Layar** and past the overrated **Pura Batu Bolong** (a Hindu temple facing Gunung Agung across the straits, popular at sunset) to the main promontory at Senggigi, where a cluster of restaurants, diving shops, craft shops, night-clubs and hotels are located. Beyond this the road reaches **Mangsit**, then climbs north along the cliffs before plunging down to **Bangsal**. For real escapists there is a magnificent beach at **Sira** overlooking the Gili Islands, reached by a rough road just north of Bangsal. Senggigi activities are self-evident, as the fine stretches of sand and headlands offer good swimming with plenty of watersports laid on by the luxury hotels.

Monkey business If you want a break from the beach, make a circuit from Pemenang in the north which circles back via a scenic inland road through Lombok's **Monkey Forest** at Baum Pusuk, where troops of macaques scamper beside the road. To the east loom the twin peaks of Tampole and Punikan, and there are some lovely valley views at Sidemen, the local centre for palm-sugar production. From here the landscape flattens out before reaching Gunungsari, known for its old temple, lively market and bamboo crafts. A right turn here takes you back to Meninting and Senggigi beyond.

▶ **Suranadi** *178B2*

The temple at Suranadi, 7km north of Narmada, is considered one of the holiest on the island and consists mainly of freshwater pools. The pools contain sacred eels which slink around on the look-out for hard-boiled eggs donated by well-wishers. There are several Balinese-style elevated shrines behind this small bathing area, and the main altar is indicated by *naga* (sacred snake) sculptures which adorn the steps. The lush setting extends to an adjoining botanical garden.

▶▶ Tetebatu 178B2

This tiny village, high on the southern slopes of Rinjani and surrounded by brilliant swathes of terraced paddy-fields, is becoming a popular retreat for those seeking cool air and mountain walks. A cluster of low-budget hotels lies at the entrance to the village, and a colonial-style establishment that offers panoramic views is up a hill beyond. Walks can take in the **Jeruk Manis Waterfall**, 2km to the north in a lush tropical setting, whose waters are believed by locals to encourage hair-growth, and the **Jukut Waterfall** 6km east. A few kilometres to the north-west is a forest inhabited by vociferous, jet-black monkeys. The access road from the south passes through **Kotaraja** ('Town of Kings') which, together with nearby Loyok, served as a refuge for the central Lombok Sasak rulers fleeing from Balinese invaders in the 18th century.

Peresean
If you hear gamelan music and see a demonstrative crowd of men, it is probably for a *peresean* contest. These usually take place in the late afternoon after work. Contestants, picked by two costumed 'experts', use rattan sticks and cow-hide shields. The prize is a sarong or, more common today, a T-shirt.

Tetebatu is Lombok's scenic rice bowl

Drive Lombok

See map on page 178.
This drive takes you on a circuit around southern Lombok, where Sasak villagers work the fields or concentrate on a growing crafts industry. Rural vistas and tiny villages combine with the dramatic scenery of the south coast to offer a rounded vision of Lombok's attractions. Allow a leisurely day for this circuit, which takes in a swim and a siesta on the beach at Kuta.

Starting from **Narmada**, take the main turn-off south towards Praya. This twists around a shady, lush river gorge thick with bamboo to Bagudesa, then continues through extensive rice-fields to **Kumbung**. Turn left here on to Lombok's second main road and continue to Praya, passing through agricultural land which uses sophisticated irrigation systems and the occasional brick-making village. **Praya** itself is a non-descript administrative and market town, the centre of a web of roads which covers southern Lombok.

From here turn left towards Batujai and continue to **Penujak**. Villagers here are mainly employed in making superb terracotta storage jars, urns, cooking vessels and bowls. Some forms are adapted for the tourist market but decoration remains sober – pieces are unglazed or splashed with a black-pigment wash. A few kilometres further on, the village of **Tanaquwu** displays a similar craft tradition. Continue towards **Sengkol**, a Sasak market town which comes alives on Thursdays when straw-hatted men and saronged women sell weavings, sugar-cane, baskets, beans and rice, resulting in a serious *bendi* (pony trap) traffic jam.

Left: a typical roadside scene. Right: sugar-cane for sale at Sengkol

From this crossroads town follow the main road south through increasingly arid landscapes towards **Rembitan**, a pretty little village claiming a 17th-century mosque, then **Sade**, where tall, thatched *lumbung* (rice-barns) climb the slopes. This traditional Sasak village sees a number of tour groups and has adapted itself accordingly, but offers a good view of domestic architecture as well as displays of weavings. The road south of here soon twists up through Lombok's southern mountain range before descending to **Kuta**, with some arresting views *en route*. Stop for lunch and a swim at Kuta or drive 4km east to **Tanjung Aan**, a protected bay edged with white sand.

Retrace your steps as far as Sengkol where a road leads northeast towards Kawe, then on to Batunyale. Turn right here towards **Pejanggik**, a village famed for its handwoven cloths where you can watch the shuttles flying back and forth. Continue through Mujar to Ganti, where a short detour to the right (south) takes you to **Batu Rintang** which, like Sade, is a traditional Sasak village but is far less visited. North of Ganti lies **Beleka** where crafts production focuses on rattan and fine basketwork. There are numerous workshops located down the backstreets and no shortage of willing 'guides' to lead you around; prices are

considerably lower than in Mataram or Senggigi. From Beleka the road continues north, rejoining the main east–west axis near Kopang, about 30km east of Mataram.

One of many stunning beaches on Lombok's south coast

185

SUMBA

Sumba claims what is perhaps Indonesia's most authentic and widespread animist culture (*merapu*), symbolised by huge megalithic tombs, rituals, costumes and village structures. This remote and intriguing island is also renowned for its boldly designed *ikat* (see pages 194–5), sturdy horses and varied scenery. Although small in comparison to Flores, Timor or Sumbawa, Sumba has two distinct topographies and cultures: the dry and barren east survives on livestock and weaving; and the more isolated, fertile and agricultural west sees fortified villages steeped in tradition. When visiting villages, remember that inhabitants appreciate gifts (betel-nuts) or money and may even demand payment for photos.

East Sumba The tranquil base of **Waingapu▶**, with its airport and harbour, is the inevitable entry point for Sumba. *Ikat* maintains a high profile in numerous stores and hotels, or is simply draped over the bicycles of itinerant traders, but to see it being made you need to head out of town. **Prailiu** is the closest weaving village, while the arid coast road east soon reaches **Kawangu**, then continues to the oasis of **Melolo** which claims a *losmen* (budget inn) and a good beach.

To the south, interest at the striking village of **Pau** focuses on a group of stone sculptures, tombs and huge communal houses. East of Melolo lies **Rende**, whose superbly carved royal tombs are overshadowed by sales of *ikat*, firmly targeting tour groups. Last stop on this circuit is **Kaliuda**, about 40km south, where weaving motifs consist of blue and white cocks and horses. Cool but rough surf is the final offering at **Pantai Kalala**.

West Sumba Some 137km west of Waingapu through undulating and increasingly tropical countryside lies **Waikabubak▶▶**, a charming hill town where horses outnumber cars and whose adequate facilities include the airstrip of Tambolaka, 42km to the north. The lovely

186

One of Sumba's striking horsemen

Getting around
Local transport is reliable between Waingapu and Waikabubak (5–6 hours) and around the east coast, but the best option for touring villages is to charter a jeep, *bemo* (minibus) or motor bike. A guide is a considerable asset. Hotels are the best source for both, though bargaining is essential.

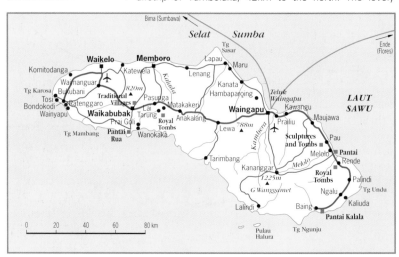

Stone reti *(tombs) in west Sumba*

surroundings are peppered with traditional villages where steep, thatched roofs hold out against corrugated iron, particularly in and around **Anakalang**, 22km to the east. At **Lai Tarung** a thatched pavilion elevated on 12 pillars, symbol of the unity of the 12 tribes of the Anakalang kingdom, stands near the sacred hilltop lake where dozens of tombs form a monumental staircase. **Pasunga** houses a unique tomb containing lifesize statues of its occupants – not quite a Torajan *tau tau* (see panel on page 207), but almost. A short distance further on, at **Matakakeri**, stands Sumba's heaviest megalith (said to weigh 70 tonnes), the tomb of an Anakalang king.

Beach villages The road leading south from Waikabubak winds through more verdant hills offering brilliant sapphire flashes of the Indian Ocean. Fascinating villages surround **Wanokaka**, particularly **Prai Goli** which claims the oldest megaliths of the region – and they are superb. **Pantai Rua**, a few kilometres to the southwest, is good for surfing, but swimmers should aim for **Bondokodi▶▶**, a village situated about 60km west of Waikabubak through bucolic paddy, cornfield and buffalo-inhabited landscapes. Some basic *losmen* make it possible to spend a few days in this idyllic region. Village styles are different here yet again, roofs becoming increasingly pointed and tombs sometimes positioned outside the walls, the most picturesque actually facing the deep blue sea from among clusters of coconut palms. The most interesting villages in the area are Tosi, Ratenggaro and, above all, **Wainyapu**.

Pasola
Hundreds of massed horsemen from two villages thunder towards each other flinging spears (blunted by central government edict!) in an ebullient day-long ritual. This stirring battle is a remnant from the days when Sumba's rival kingdoms were in semi-permanent conflict. In theory, it is performed to celebrate the hatching season of *nyale* (sea-worms), whose numbers are supposed to predict the quality of the harvest. However, in reality it is a blood-curdling spectacle that as recently as 1991 degenerated into open warfare, leading to torched villages and several deaths. The Pasola is held in February at Bondokodi and in March at Wanokaka.

Sumba's death cult

■ **The fervently animist inhabitants of Sumba regard life on Earth as but a temporary prelude to an eternal existence in the heavenly domain of the spirits. This belief governs daily acts and worship as much as festivals and the creation of startling icons, and seems as strong as ever.....■**

Top: a buffalo is about to be sacrificed at a funeral
Above: Sumbanese ceremonial dress

Taboo month
West Sumba's inhabitants still maintain taboo months, the dates being determined by priests from a lunar calendar. During this period homage is paid to the spirits of the clan's ancestors. A week before the end of the month a dozen priests set off to the sacred and secret abode of the ancestors. Offerings are made before their sunset return, this marking the beginning of an all-night celebration.

Elaborate tombs at Pasunga, east of Waikabubak

Merapu (spirit) is the key to Sumbanese life and death concepts. The world of spirits is called *Prai Merapu*, nature teems with *merapu*, anyone with medium talents is *merapu*, the dead become *merapu*, and certain sites (such as forests and hilltops) and certain objects (such as weavings and stones) are *merapu*. Even the upper part of houses are *merapu* and every lunar year has a *merapu* month. This cult holds things as part supernatural, part sacred, and incorporates a complex network of rituals.

Equilibrium According to *merapu* belief, every spirit consists of two elements and happiness is achieved only by their correct balance. This is symbolised by the Great Mother and Great Father (*Ina Kalada* and *Ama Kalada*), who govern the universe in the form of the moon and the sun and are mythological parents to Sumbanese ancestors. To honour *merapu*, statues of carved wood are placed on stone altars in village yards where offerings of betel-nuts and cattle sacrifices are made. Effigies placed inside the house represent deified ancestors, while between the houses stand the tombs. Although these are obviously very *merapu*, the Sumbanese do not hesitate to use them for daily tasks.

Funerals A funeral forms the climax of Sumbanese ritual. Immediately after death, the deceased is buried with a simple sacrifice, usually of a dog. Months later, when the family has gathered and the tombstone been carved, the corpse, wrapped in precious *ikat* cloth, is transferred to a tomb. Friends and family make offerings and buffaloes and pigs are sacrificed and eaten. Not too long ago these animal sacrifices were accompanied by those of servants.

SUMBAWA

This little visited and sparsely populated island of two distinct regions connected by a narrow isthmus straddles the sea between Lombok and Flores. The rugged, mountainous interior descends through dry savannah to coastal fishing villages that are interspersed with deserted beaches – visually blissful but with no tourist infrastructure. Only Bima in the east and Sumbawa Besar in the west have reasonable facilities, but the 268km road between them requires a good 5 hours. Since the conversion of Bima's ruler in the early 17th century, Sumbawa has been devoutly Muslim and its lack of natural resources resulted in only short-lived Dutch control, thereby leaving traditions visibly intact.

East Sumbawa Visitors to Komodo aim for **Sape**, a pretty port near some good beaches and at the heart of a region where traditional thatched bamboo houses and rice-barns are much in evidence – visit **Sambori**. Some 50km to the west lies **Bima**►►, the administrative centre for east Sumbawa, which straggles along the shores of a large bay edged with salt-flats. Despite the town's small size, a harbour and medieval-looking market keep it alive, and its streets echo to the sounds of colourful, jingling *bendis* (pony traps) out to beat speed records. On the grassy square behind the market street stands the **Museum Asi Mbojo**►►, a former sultan's palace (1927) where displays range from Portuguese flintlock pistols to traditional costumes and a dilapidated royal bedroom. Excursions can be made to **Songgela**, a popular local beach, to **Wadu Pa'a**, a Hindu-Buddhist cave sanctuary across the bay, to the fascinating traditional villages of **Donggo** and **Maria**, and to **Dompu**, where Bima handweaving is made.

Huu, on the coast south of Dompu, offers the largest stretch of sand in West Nusa Tenggara, and its uncompromising surf and basic accommodation attract streams of Australian surfers.

West Sumbawa Ferries from Lombok arrive at Poto Tano, a 2-hour drive from the friendly, suburban-style town of **Sumbawa Besar**►. This is a real stop-over place

Sumbawans are strict Muslims

189

Krakatau's rival
Gunung Tambora towers 2,821m above Sumbawa's northernmost peninsula. Its 1815 eruption was one of the world's most powerful and could be heard 1,400km away in Ternate. Vivid orange sunsets were seen around the world and the resultant drop in northern hemisphere temperatures led to the famous 'year without a summer' of 1816. Some 12,000 people died in Sumbawa as a direct result of the eruption, the ensuing famine leading to a further 40,000 deaths.

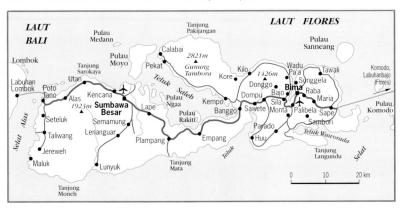

with one historic sight, the complex wooden palace of Dalam Loka (1931), also known as **Istana Tua**, which is raised on 99 pillars, a reflection of local belief in the 99 names for Allah. A project is afoot to transform the palace into a museum, but for the moment it functions as a cultural performance centre. About 80km southwest of Sumbawa Besar is the extensive lake of **Lebuk Taliwang**, choked with water lilies and rich in birdlife, its surface dotted with fishermen in vulnerable-looking canoes.

There is good snorkelling and diving 10km west of Sumbawa Besar at the beach of **Kencana**, which also offers comfortable accommodation and homestays in buildings designed in traditional Sumbawan style. Boats can be chartered from here or from Labuhan Sawo to the wildlife reserve of **Pulau Moyo►►**, home to endangered bird species, wild cattle, deer and boar, as well as some 6,000 hectares of magnificent coral gardens inhabited by shoals of technicoloured fish, sharks and even turtles. Accommodation here is either the ultimate in world luxury (Amanwana) or basic PHPA bungalows; obtain advance information on availability from the latter's office in Sumbawa Besar.

190

One of Bima's speedy bendi *(pony traps)*

Buffalo-racing
Sumbawa's buffalo-races are similar to Madura's bull-races but without the high speeds. These elaborate, ceremonial affairs take place annually in all districts just before the rice-planting season. A ploughed field serves as a racetrack where pairs of decorated buffaloes thunder along dragging a wooden sled which carries the jockey. The aim of this race is to bring down one of the bamboo poles on the finishing-line – no mean feat as buffaloes are not easily manoeuvrable beasts, and tend to be difficult to stop once they are launched.

Sumbawa's rural economy is based on timber, salt, rice, fish and horse-breeding

TIMOR

Timor's name is known the world over for the events that followed Indonesia's forceful annexation of East Timor in 1975. Estimates of up to 200,000 deaths (about one-third of the population) and recurring incidents have made East Timor Indonesia's blackest spot in terms of the republic's international reputation. For tourists, however, the only signs of government intervention are the massive amounts of money being poured in to rebuild confidence, coupled with a strong military presence.

The entire island has a wild, sometimes bleak beauty of vast, ochre landscapes that closely resemble those of neighbouring Australia and suffers from a long dry season which leaves river beds empty. Sandalwood still grows here, but in nothing like the quantities which brought the Portuguese to Timor's shores in 1514. Colonisation, inter-marriage and evangelisation followed, but in 1637 the strategic harbour of Kupang fell to the Dutch. A treaty in 1859 finally confirmed the division of colonial interests, leaving West Timor to the Dutch and East Timor to the Portuguese. The betel-nut-chewing West Timorese population is 95 per cent Christian, but maintains strong traditions in village structures, intricate *ikat*-weaving and in occasional animist practices.

West Timor The provincial capital of **Kupang▶▶** is Timor's transport hub, with a well-served airport and harbour, and an excellent tourist infrastructure catering above all for visitors from Australia's Darwin (less than 2 hours away). This dynamic, friendly town sprawls over the hills and teems with colourful *bemos* (minibuses).

The **Museum Nusa Tenggara Timur▶▶▶** gives an excellent introduction to the culture and history of Timor, Sumba and Flores but, together with the tourist office, is inconveniently located in a new administrative zone east of town. The town's market, **Pasar Inpres**, lies south on the road to the weaving village of Baun, but Kupang's

> **Guides**
> To make the most of Timor it is essential to employ a guide as, outside Kupang, the island sees few tourists. Kupang's tourist office is a good source for contacts and rates are generally quite reasonable. Otherwise, contact the lively and informative Willy Kadati, c/o Lavalon Backpackers, Jalan Sumatera 1 no 8, Tode-Kisar, Kupang.

Life invariably hovers at subsistence level

NUSA TENGGARA

A typical Atoni beehive house

Beehives

The region around Soe and Kefamenanu has a unique surviving culture, that of the Atoni who are thought to be Timor's earliest inhabitants and some of whom still practise forms of animism and ancestral worship, notably at Boti. Their houses (*ume*) are distinctive, beehive in shape, the thatch descending down to the ground with only one opening through a low arch. Although the government has tried to abolish these constructions, considering them unhealthy, many Atoni have rebuilt them as kitchens and storerooms. Particularly visible around Kefamenanu are the *lopo*, open-sided community halls built of four pillars with a circular roof in which sacred legacies are stored.

youth heads instead for the commercial downtown area along the seafront which comes alive as the sun sinks over the headland, tranquil **Pulau Semau** visible in the distance. The latter is a pretty, coral-fringed island and is Kupang's main beach resort, although others are growing at **Pantai Lasiana**, east of town. Diving is well catered for and boats can be organised through Teddy's Bar, located on the filthy beach below the *bemo* station. Sandalwood remains a major industry on Timor and the processing factory just outside town can be visited.

On the arid slopes of Gunung Mutis (2,427m) north-east of Kupang, the relaxed hill towns of **Soe** and **Kefamenanu**▶▶ (80km apart) make excellent bases for exploring unspoilt, traditional Atoni villages, markets and natural splendours such as the beautiful valley of Tamkesi or curiosities such as the raja's graves at Niki-Niki. Temperatures are cooler in these undulating hills dotted

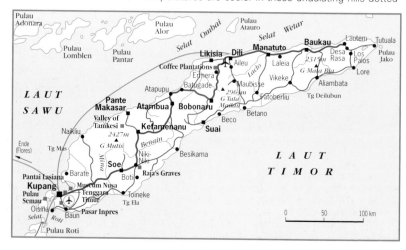

Fretilin
After the calamitous events of World War II when some 50,000 East Timorese died at the hands of the Japanese, by starvation or by Allied bombing, this seemingly blighted country again faced catastrophe when Portugal decided to relinquish its last colonies in 1974. Three political groups responded, the most radical of which, the ASDT, later known as Fretilin (Independent East Timor Revolutionary Front), advocated total independence. Fighting broke out and the Indonesian army, fearing that Communist and separatist sympathies would spread to other regions of the republic, soon moved in and annexed the province. This is still not recognised by the UN. In 1995, after continuing international pressure, President Suharto agreed to re-examine East Timor's political status.

with eucalyptus trees and *lontar* palms, so trekking is relatively painless, although local dialects necessitate a guide (see panel on page 191). Both towns have reasonable accommodation as well as frequent onward transport through Atambua to East Timor.

East Timor This province was closed to foreigners from 1975 until 1990, and again in 1992 following the 1991 Santa Cruz massacre. However, tensions have since eased and there is no control on tourists, although facilities remain very limited. The obvious and only major base is **Dili►**, a placid town characterised by old Portuguese churches and modern municipal buildings. Its location on a lovely bay backed by barren hills makes up for a lack of cultural interest and hotels aimed at local businessmen are of a reasonable standard.

The coast road east of Dili is stunningly beautiful, with sheer cliffs, deserted creeks and white-sand beaches. At the pottery centre of **Manatuto** (60km east) is East Timor's oldest church, and 35km further on is the rather decrepit colonial town of **Baukau** which overlooks spectacular beaches from its hilltop site. Projects are in the pipeline to make this a luxury resort served by an international airport that will target Asian tourists. The rough road ends at the far eastern point of **Tutuala**, which claims a cave covered with enigmatic handprints, while inland towards Los Palos there is some rare traditional village architecture, notably at Desa Rasa.

Some 55km south of Dili lies a magnificent mountainous region of coffee plantations centred on **Ermera►►**, famed for its weavings, where superb scenery unfolds across Gunung Tata Mailau (2,963m) as far as **Maubisse►►**. Panoramic views, fine *ikat*-weaving and a rare guesthouse make Maubisse an ideal base for trekking.

To the west, right on the former border, lies **Batugade** where the Balibo Fort played a dubious role as site for the declaration of East Timor's 'willingness to integrate' in 1976.

Older Timorese still cling to ikat *and the betel-nut habit*

■ **The rich, earthy colours and varied designs of *ikat* weavings that can be seen in villages throughout East Nusa Tenggara indicate that the craft is still alive and kicking. New techniques may have been adopted in the intricate fabrication process, but many of the traditional spiritually inspired motifs remain intact.....■**

Authentic?

Judging your *ikat* investment is tricky. Thread is perhaps the most easily identifiable component: when machine-spun it has a regular twist, while hand-spun cotton is more fibrous. Natural dyes can usually be recognised by their earthy tones, ranging from indigos to maroon, purple, rust, orange, yellow and red. Hand-woven cloth is generally stiffer than the machine-woven variety and the pattern may contain minor imperfections. Rayon, although made from natural fibres, is a much softer, commercially produced textile which creases easily and is chemically (often garishly) dyed.

The complex art of ikat-weaving

As mysterious in its symbolism as it is in its origins, *ikat*-weaving today thrives only in East Nusa Tenggara and, to a lesser extent, in Kalimantan, Maluku, Sumatra, Bali and Sulawesi. Flores, Sumba, Timor and Roti are the main centres of this laborious but fascinating craft, where centuries-old techniques of spinning, staining with vegetable dyes and handweaving still hold out against technology. This is a woman's craft, but the finished product is worn by both sexes – as a nonchalantly draped shawl (*selendang*), a blanket (*selimut*) or a sarong. Each pattern, colour and motif has a symbolism that is inextricably linked with pre-Hindu animist beliefs, each piece of cloth clearly designates social status or has a specific ceremonial function, and each village produces its own 'school'.

Techniques *Ikat*-weaving is thought to have been inspired by the Dongson culture from Vietnam around 700BC. Their intricate bronze designs stimulated existing weaving and led to a blossoming of geometric motifs (spirals, diamonds, hooks and meanders) created by binding and dyeing sections of the threads before weaving (*ikat* means 'tie' or 'bind' in Malay). Three types of *ikat*-weaving exist: warp *ikat*, when the ornamentation is applied to vertical warp threads, a technique which predominates in Nusa

Tenggara; weft *ikat*, where the horizontal weft threads are decorated, found mainly in Sumatra; and double-*ikat* (*gringsing*) in which both warp and weft threads are tied and dyed in patterns. The latter extremely complex procedure is found only in the Bali Aga village of Tenganan (see page 162).

All methods involve the same preliminary process in which cotton threads arranged on a loom are tightly bound with dye-resistant vegetable fibres in a pre-determined design. Successive plunges into a vat of vegetable dye bring different or deeper tones, new ties being added each time to create the required overall pattern. After this lengthy process the cloth is woven on a simple hand-loom.

Motifs The supernatural powers of nature have long inspired *ikat* motifs. Geometrical renderings of magical animals include crocodiles, lizards and gheckos to represent the underworld, and birds to symbolise the upperworld. The tree of life represents the afterlife, while much-venerated ancestors (deemed to have special powers) are usually represented with arms and legs extended and often with ghoulish faces.

Overlaps between animist symbols and imports from early foreign cultures (China and India) include the isosceles triangle; for the Hindus this designated Dewi Sri, the goddess of rice and prosperity, but it also represents the bamboo shoot, symbol of power from within. Dutch influence brought coats of arms and floral patterns, while late 20th-century tourist interest in *ikat* has led to a blossoming of representational designs.

Not only sarongs The uses of *ikat* cloth are manifold. For some it is merely a sarong, but for others it has deep spiritual significance – for example, a particular weaving will be reserved for life-cycle rituals, be they birth (Timor), teeth-filing (Bali), circumcision, weddings (in Flores in particular treasured *ikat* is included in the dowry, along with gold, ivory and cattle) or death (some Sumba *hinggi* or blankets, are designed as shrouds). Until fairly recently Sumba's hierarchical society only allowed the noble classes to wear *ikat*, and in other areas specific designs are reserved for shamans.

Colours also have their significance: black or indigo is typically used in funerary rites, while reds and terracottas are associated with battles or weddings. According to extreme tradition, the making of *ikat* is a divine inspiration, and prayers, recitations, meditation, fasting and numerous taboos would accompany the painstaking process. Today, with the advent of chemical dyes, machine-spun cotton or rayon, machine-weaving and even printed *ikat* fabrics, the taboos remain with the buyer as determining an authentic piece requires extensive preliminary groundwork (see panel opposite).

Sumba's large hinggi *(ikat* blankets) *often incorporate figurative designs and are worn exclusively by men*

Roti special
The three islands of Roti, Savu and tiny Ndao, lying between Sumba and Timor, all place as much importance on textile weaving as on house-building skills, respectively male and female god-given talents. Of the three, Roti underwent most external influence, from 17th-century Portuguese missionaries and contact with Indian traders from Gujarat. The latter brought with them double-*ikat* *patola* cloths whose geometric designs were soon incorporated into noblemen's sarongs. The motifs and colours (red and blue) of Savu's *ikat* have remained more isolated and reflect their hierarchical social system. Ndao textile designs incorporate elements from both these islands and today their weavers often work for the more commercial Rotinese.

SULAWESI

LAUT
CELEBES

KALIMANTAN

Tarakan
(Kalimantan)

Santigi
Tanjung
Arus
Benteng
Tolitoli
Tanjung Kandi
Lanu
Biau
Pulau Simatang
Teluk
Dondo
Pegunungan
Mikapa
G Tentolomatinan
2207m
Minahas
Paguyaman
Lais
2490m
Moutong
3000m
G Sonjol
Siboa
Tomini
Tinombo
Tanjung
Panjang Reserve
Marisa

Balikpapan
(Kalimantan)

Makasar

Selat

Sibayu
Sigenti
Teluk
Tomini
Kepulauan
Togian
Pulau
Una-Una
P Malenge
Katupat
Pulau
Waleabba
P Talatakoh
P Togian
Wakai
Pulau
Batudaka
Selat
Walea
Oti
Kasimbar
2100m
G Sidole
Pantoloan
Tawaeli

Tanjung Karang
Towale
Beach
Donggala
Palu
Pobova
Reserve
Sausu
Tanjung
Pandendelisa
Ampana
Tanjung Api
Reserve
Peg
Balinggara
2400m
G Tumpu
Pangian
Souraja
2355m
G Nokilalaki
Teluk
Poso
Poso
2835m
Gunung
Katoposa
Bongka
Batui

Lariang
Lariang
Peg
Takolekaju
2480m
Danau Lindu
Taman Nasional
Lore Lindu
Gimpu
Tentena
Gua Pamona
Pantai
Mutako
Tagolu
2563m
Morowali
Reserve
2628m
Donggi
Momo
Kuma
Bada
Valley
Gintu
Danau
Poso
Taripa
Kolonodale
Morowali
Tanjung Onematubu

Babana
2960m
Bancea
Orchid Park
Pendolo
Peruhumpenai
Reserve
Teluk
Tomori
Teluk
Tolo

Sampaga
Karama
Buta
Wono
Rongkong
3016m
G Balease
Saroake
Danau
Matana
Wata

Mamuju
3074m
G Gandadiwata
Tana
Toraja
Masamba
Wotu
Malili
Timampu
Losoni
Danau
Towuti

Peg
Quarles
Mantalinga
Larona

Malunda
Mamasa
Rantepao
Palopo
Lelewau
1782m
Buleleng
Kep
Salabangk

Balikpapan
(Kalimantan)

Masawa
Makale
Teluk
Tanjung
Jenemejai
Kuete
Bayu

Somba
Polewali
3440m
G Rantemario
Cimpu
Malamala
Pulau
Labeng

Majene
Tanjung
Rangasa
Teluk
Mandar
Bamba Pua
Valley
Siwa
Pegunungan
Abuki
Pulau
Bahubulu
Lembo

Pinrang
Sadang
Rapang
Pangkajene
Bone
2790m
G Mekongga
Pegunungan
Konaweha
Waimenda
Wawotobi
Kendari

Parepare
Museum
D
Tempe
Anabanua
Jalang
Pulau
Padamarang
Kolaka
Motaha
Sampara

Sumpangbinangae
Batu
Batu
Sengkang
Silk Weaving
Torobul

Watusoopeng
Gua Mampu
Museum Lapawawoi
Taman Nasional
Rawa Aopa
Watumohae

Segeri
Takalala
Watampone
(Bone)
Towari
Daule
Selat Tiwor

Ujunglamuru
Marek
Bugingkalo
Laora
Wanasabari

Lembar
(Lombok)
Maros
Bantimurung
Reserve
Watdan
Napabale
Lagoon
Pulau
Muna

Ujung Pandang
Benteng Rotterdam
Museum
Caves
Sinjai
Pulau
Kabaena
1570m
Mawasangka

Surabaya
(Jawa)
Sungguminasa
Museum
Balla
Lompoa
2876m
G Lompobatang
Reserve
Bira
Tanjung Kokoe
Baubau
Pulau
Siumpu
Benter
Patae
Wohi

Pulau
Kayangan
Bulukumba
Bontosunggu
Tanjung Lasa
Jeneponto
Pulau Tanakeke
Selat
Selayar

Tanjung
Malasoro
Bonelohe
Pulau
Selayar

Bima
(Sumbawa)
Benteng

A
B
C

5
4
3
2
1

0°

Kepulauan Sangihe

Pulau Bangka

Pulau Mantehge Selat Bangka

Pulau Bunaken

Pulau Manado Tua

Tangkoko-Batuangus Reserve

Manado

Bitung

Sawangan

Gunung Lokon 1580m

Tondano

Tara-tara

Tomohon

Pinabetengen

D. Tondano

Amurong

1830m

G Soputan

Gunung Ambang Reserve

Belang

Inobonto

Tanjung Samia

Boroko

Kuandang

Semenau djung Peg Buludawa

Danowa

Kotamobagu

Gorontalo

Taman Nasional Bone Dumoga

Nuangan

Molibagu

Tanjung Flesko

Benteng Otanaha

1970m

Gunung Bulaca

Pulau Tidore

Equator

LAUT

MALUKU

Boalemo

Poh

Luwuk

Peleng

Balo

Tanjung Santigi

Basiano

Pulau Peleng

Pelei

Kembani

Pulau Banggi

Pulau Taliabu

Pulau Mangole

Pulau angkulu

Pulau Labobo

Selat Salu Timpaus

Kepulauan Banggai

P. Salue

Kepulauan Sula

Pulau Sanana

Kepulauan Bowokan

Pulau Padea Besar

Pulau Manui

Pulau Wowoni

Watunea

awowa

Tanjung Butung

Pulau Ambon

Buton Utara Reserve

Pulau Buton (Butung)

Tanjung Goram

Waogena

Kapantareh

Wokole

Pulau Wangiwangi

Pulau Kaledupa

0   50   100   150 km

Tanjung Pemali

Kepulauan Tukangbesi

Pulau Tomea

Marine Reserve

Pulau Binongko

D

E

Palu street scene

When to visit
Sulawesi's baffling and uneven climate, further affected by its mountain ridges, means that rain falls throughout most of the year. Theoretically the heaviest rainfall takes place between December and February, but don't believe it. Merciless week-long downpours can take place even in June, right in the middle of the so-called dry season. The safest time to visit is between August and October, and the driest area is around Palu.

Restless currents
'Except for some of the highest and narrowest ledges near the bungalow, all these terraces were flooded and so reflected the blushing sky and the delicate birds that wavered across it... From the shining lakes of the fjord floor, criss-crossed by narrow bridge-like paths, rose promontories and hillocks edged with cliffs of red soil and crowned with bamboo groves that were restless currents of fresh green foliage, ceaselessly ebbing and flowing like gently troubled waters. Here and there I could see the golden gable of a high, boat-like roof as the bamboos swung dreamily apart in the dawn breezes.'
– From *Six Moons in Sulawesi* by Harry Wilcox (1949).

Sulawesi The deformed octopus-shape of Sulawesi, sometimes compared more poetically to a spider orchid, unfolds its magnificent tentacles across the Celebes Sea between Kalimantan and the Spice Islands of Maluku. International fame came late to the island compared with Bali or Java, but it now attracts jetloads of visitors who come to soak up the fascinating Toraja culture or to glide through the underwater delights of Manado's coral reefs. Yet the tourist invasion has reached no further, leaving the rest of this beautiful island relatively untouched.

Naturalist's dream Sulawesi's four tentacles, crossed by the Equator in the north and mostly composed of mountains, are renowned for their climatic variations and for their isolated species of flora and fauna. Some 90 per cent of the island's mammals and nearly 40 per cent of its birds are endemic, while insects, butterflies and reptiles are here in abundance. Sightings are best at the nature reserves of Tangkoko-Batuangus in the north, Lore Lindu and Morowali in the centre, and at Bantimurung in the south.

Nautical history No point in Sulawesi lies more than 100km from the sea, so it is logical that the island's history revolved around the waves. The inhospitable mountainous interior nevertheless preserved cultures such as the Toraja (bar a period which saw marauding Bugis) until the turn of this century when missionaries started their work. In the north, Portuguese missionaries left their mark as early as the 1560s, following the first sighting of the fertile Minahasa land by Magellan's fleet in 1524.

The south saw rival trading kingdoms develop from the 13th century onwards, the Gowa sultanate in Makassar (Ujung Pandang) eventually dominating Bugis Bone (Watampone). Then followed European, Asian and Arab traders bartering spices, slaves and sharks' fins. Finally, in 1605, came Gowa's official acceptance of Islam.

Spicy rule Dutch commercial ambitions during the 17th century became increasingly focused on the lucrative spice trade, sporadic conflicts with Gowa leading to a successful alliance with the Bugis and the consequent capitulation of the sultan of Gowa in 1669. The ensuing militaristic and repressive Bugis rule prompted many to flee the country, this leading to the aggressive forays that plagued the seas as far as Siam well into the 18th century. The Dutch colonisation of the north, sealed by an alliance with the Minahasans in 1679, went smoothly, but they had a harder time in Makassar (governed with the aid of Bugis Bone) and had to deal with intermittent uprisings – including a civil war in the 1750s.

Another region, another culture The 159,000 sq km of Sulawesi are divided into four administrative regions, each corresponding to a 'tentacle'. The 13 million inhabitants are roughly divided between the Muslim Makassarese and Bugis, the Christian-animist Toraja, the devoutly Christian Minahasans, the coast-dwelling Bajau, a sprinkling of prosperous Chinese and a few secluded tribes in the interior. The island is also receiving an increasing number of Balinese transmigrants, adding a further dimension to this patchwork of cultures.

▶▶   Danau Poso   *196B3*

Indonesia's fourth-largest lake covers an area of over 32,000 hectares in mountainous Central Sulawesi. The cool climate, gentle landscapes, lakeside beaches and clean water make it an ideal stop-over on the gruelling overland trail between Tana Toraja and the reserves of Lore Lindu or Morowali. Accommodation is available at Pendolo in the south or Tentena in the north; daily lake ferries connect the two (3-hour crossing). Carp- and eel-fishing, swimming and trekking are the main activities in this tranquil oasis.

From **Pendolo** a road runs through jungle along the western shore to the flourishing **Bancea orchid park**, fronted by a sandy beach. **Tentena**, the livelier of the two main lake towns, is surrounded by rocky limestone banks riddled with caves. The network of **Gua Pamona** descends below the lake's surface and was formerly used as a burial ground; human bones and primitive coffins have been found here. Otherwise, Tentena's main feature is a 210m roofed wooden bridge that shelters eel-traps. Jungle treks can be taken to the stepped waterfall of Salopa (1 day away) or to the Bada Valley megaliths (2 days away; see panel, page 200).

▶▶   Donggala   *196B4*

This sleepy town, 35km north of Palu, was once Central Sulawesi's most active trading port and administrative centre but has now fallen on less illustrious times. The tropical forest that clad the surrounding hills has been completely logged and the resultant silting caused the port to be shifted across the bay to Pantoloan. However, Donggala remains picturesque and its superb beaches and coral reefs attract snorkellers and divers.

At the end of the cape is **Tanjung Karang**, an hour's drive from Palu airport, which has a beautiful white beach, low-key accommodation, sailing and diving (there are some fantastic drop-offs), and proboscis monkeys. Boat trips can be organised from here to unspoilt turtle islands off Sulawesi's northern tentacle, where the absence of fishing or river outflows leaves the waters perfectly transparent. South of Donggala is **Towale** beach, a local favourite.

The picturesque port of Donggala is now used only by smaller vessels – you can catch a boat from here to Pare-Pare

Lake Poso mysteries
The hornbills, hawks and menacing-looking eagles swooping over the often choppy waters of Lake Poso could indicate the presence of other types of currents, and the lake is in fact considered sacred by locals. According to a far from modest legend, the lake is the pivot around which heaven and Earth revolve and a rope connecting the two once existed on the shore. Another belief is that the fossilised remains of a dragon lie in the lake's depths and are visible when it is calm. A curious existing feature is the *batu gong*, a stone which when struck makes a hollow sound similar to a gong. And, apart from the burial caves near Tentena, there are graves in the hills of the west bank which still contain skeletons and objects for the afterlife.

Bada Valley megaliths
Central Sulawesi's megaliths are most numerous in and around Lore Lindu National Park in the Bada, Besoa and Napu valleys. The origins and function of these megaliths remain a mystery, and their date of construction has been estimated at anything from 3000BC to AD1300. One hypothesis is that the menhirs (upright stones) were associated with human sacrifice and ancestor worship, while the *kalemba* (vast stone cisterns) may have been used as baths or aristocratic burial chambers. The Bada Valley statues vary in height from 1m to 4m yet are stylistically similar to one another, with roughly hewn faces and lightly etched limbs. Most celebrated is the 4m-high Raksas Sepe which gazes impassively westward – a further clue to suggest that the Bada people were associated with the Toraja, for whom west is the direction of death.

Trekking in Lore Lindu is not without strange encounters

▶▶ Gorontalo 197D5

Half-way along Sulawesi's northern arm lies the friendly, peaceful town of Gorontalo, famed for its fine *krawang* embroidery. This small port has regular connections with Poso, Bitung and the Togian Islands, possesses a reasonable beach at Pantai Indah and has plentiful *bendis* (pony traps).

Sights include traditional local architecture, Dutch art deco buildings and the hillside **Otanaha Fort** which overlooks Danau Limboto to the west. To the east, fertile rice- and cornfields soon make way for the **Bone-Dumoga National Park**▶▶, a densely forested, mountainous area that harbours maleo birds, hornbills, *anoa* (dwarf buffalo), boar and giant fruit-bats, as well as orchids, palms and rattan. The Dumoga Valley is the site of a large irrigation and transmigration project that receives technical and financial assistance from the World Bank.

▶▶▶ Lore Lindu, Taman Nasional 196B3

Wild savannah, deep river gorges and virgin rainforest cover the rugged 250,000 hectares of this national park. Also here are mysterious megaliths, indigenous tribes, the 2,355m Mount Nokilalaki and Danau Lindu. Wildlife ranges from gigantic exotic butterflies to *anoa*, *babi rusa* (hairless wild boar), macaques and tarsiers, while the varied birdlife counts as many as 19 species of waterfowl around the lake. Over 100 carved megaliths and cisterns are scattered around the Besoa and Bada valleys, the greatest concentration being located near Gintu (see panel).

Access to this vast and magnificent park is either from Tentena via Gintu or from Palu via Gimpu and can be undertaken on local missionary flights and/or by ponies and jeeps. Few tourists reach this inaccessible area, but the rewards are great and basic facilities range from a special bird-watching guest-house at Kamamora to a *losmen* (budget inn) at Gintu. Permits and guides (essential to track down the megaliths) can be obtained through the PHPA office in Palu or at Tentena. Allow a good 5 days and avoid the very rainy season (as opposed to the slightly rainy season) between January and April.

► **Makale** 196B2

Makale is the capital of the Toraja district, and also serves as a tourist overflow and alternative to Rantepao, 18km to the north (see pages 206–7). It is surrounded by rocky mountains and laid out around a small artifical lake, and has a distinctly rural atmosphere with an interesting market, Toraja-style buildings and comfortable accommodation on the outskirts but lacks the tourist facilities of Rantepao. Around 60km to the south on the main highway stretches the magnificent **Bamba Pua Valley►►►**, a green cleavage descending between cloud-shrouded limestone peaks that constitutes a deserted no man's land between Muslim Bugis territory and Christian Toraja land.

►► **Mamasa** 196A3

About 100km west of Rantepao across the mountains lies the town of Mamasa, a far less visited outpost of Tana Toraja. Although devoid of the burial culture of Rantepao's Sa'dan tribe, the town offers rich traditional architecture, woodcarving and costumes, and above all remains less tainted by the tourist invasion. For the moment telephones do not exist here (although satellite television does) and the market town, which survives on coffee, cloves and rice, makes a good base for scenic trekking to nearby mountain villages (Mamasa itself is at a cool 1,200m). Local villages of interest include **Buntu Kasissi**, with a soaring 400-year-old house, **Rantebuda►►►**, monopolised by a massive, beautifully carved chief's house, and **Minanga Karassik**, with its 16 buffalo-head coffins. Access to Mamasa is from Parepare via Polewali and then up a twisting mountain road.

Sorting live fish at Makale market

Sulawesi fauna and flora
Sulawesi's natural isolation has endowed it with rainforests which are dominated by *Agathis* trees rather than the dipterocarps that are common to Kalimantan, Sumatra and Java. There is also a high proportion of palms, a special type of rhododendron and the rare *anggrek serat* (fibre orchid). Endemic creatures include the *anoa* (dwarf buffalo), the *babi rusa* (a hairless wild boar sporting four tusks), the black Sulawesi macaque, pygmy squirrels, the *tangkasi* or spectral tarsier, a variety of phalanger (a marsupial) and maleo birds. Four areas have been designated to protect these species: Lore Lindu, Morowali, Tanjung Api and Bangkiriang, the latter being particularly good for spotting maleo birds (see panel, page 210).

Carved waruga *tombs at Sawangan's cemetery*

▶▶ **Manado** *197E5*

Tourists come here for two purposes: to dive and snorkel around the blissful marine park of Pulau Bunaken (see page 205) or to use the town as a base for exploring the fascinating and beautiful Minahasa land. Manado is a loud, thriving, cosmopolitan city which saw Portuguese and Spanish galleons back in the 16th century, followed closely by missionaries, and which by 1679 had embraced Dutch colonisation. Close collaboration resulted, the former animist Minahasans happily converted, the region developed, and by 1958 they were sufficiently independently minded to rebel against Sukarno. Harsh government reprisals included the bombing of Manado – the reason for its modern centre.

Urban straggle The main action in this buzzing town of 320,000 inhabitants is centred around the crossroads of Jalan Sam Ratulangi (which runs parallel to the seafront) and Jalan Sudirman which runs out east towards the airport. Here are shopping centres, cinemas, banks, market stands and the terminus of the city's fleet of turquoise *mikrolets* (minibuses). Immediately north, between the small harbour and the Tondano river, is the **Pasar 45** market surrounded by old shophouses and close to the colourfully restored 19th-century Chinese temple of **Ban Hin Kiong**. Manado's diving centres are located in rural settings north of the river towards Molas or south of town around **Malalayang**, where the best beaches are found. Artefacts relating to North Sulawesi's four ethnic groups are displayed at the **Museum Negeri Propinsi Sulawesi Utara (North Sulawesi Provincial Museum)**▶ on Jalan WR Supratman (*open*: mornings only).

Minahasa territory The word Minahasa (*esa* means 'one') derives from the 15th-century unification of the seven tribes that occupied the forested hills south of Manado. The village of **Sawangan**▶▶▶, near Airmadidi, is home to an exceptional cemetery containing 144 *waruga*, carved stone tombs which were built to contain bodies in sitting, foetal positions (see panel). The *waruga* are unique to this region and are thought to be about 500 years old; other less numerous examples can be seen at Airmadidi, Tomohon and Tara-tara. A small museum at the cemetery entrance exhibits artefacts from the tombs.

South of here past steep limestone cliffs dotted with Japanese wartime caves lies the town of **Tondano**, notable for its bizarre church constructions, hefty monuments and surrounding rice-fields and duck-farms. **Danau Tondano**▶▶ itself, a southern landmark for the Minahasa, is edged with fishermen's shacks and the occasional low-key resort offering watersports and fishing. The area is rich in hot springs, notably at Karumenga, Tamaska Hijau and Ranopaso, close to the pretty bougainvillaea-clad village of Tataaran.

Volcanic zone Southwest of Danau Tondano rises the active volcano of **Soputan** (1,830m). Climbers usually camp half-way up the volcano in a casuarina forest before attacking the summit early the next day. At the village of **Pinabetengen**, near more Japanese wartime caves at Kawangkoan, stands another remnant of Minahasa

Waruga
The pre-Christian Minahasan belief was that as the foetus sits curled up in the mother's womb, so must man pass on to eternity in the same position. And to prevent offence to the earth god Makawalang, corpses had to remain above ground. As a result, Minahasan tombs developed into vertical stone chambers with prism-shaped lids, some able to accommodate three bodies. Each one is carved to depict the cause of death and the pastime or occupation of the deceased, and is further decorated with serpentine, floral or geometric motifs, animals, and even, in some cases, frock-coated Europeans.

history in the form of a large boulder carved with undeci-phered pictograms. Further north, the church-studded missionary town of **Tomohon** lies on a plateau between the twin peaks of **Gunung Lokon** (1,580m) and **Gunung Mahawu** (1,311m), both of which claim steaming crater lakes and can be climbed, although advance information is essential (one woman climber died in 1992). The walk up the more spectacular Gunung Lokon starts from Kakaskasen, not far from the village of **Tara-tara**, where Minahasan dance and music is performed. The road twist-ing north from here to Manado offers fabulous views over the city and outlying islands.

►► Morowali Nature Reserve 196C3

Some 160,000 hectares of virgin rainforest bordering pris-tine Tomori Bay were saved from being turned into a transmigration destination in the 1980s after a survey identified their uniquely isolated plant, animal and marine life. Five rivers flow through the reserve and the moun-tainous hinterland is inhabited by the semi-nomadic Wana tribe, who still hunt with blowpipes and practise shifting cultivation. *Losmen* (budget inn) accommodation is avail-able on the bay at **Kolonodale**, about 4 hours by road from Danau Poso, and inside the reserve in Wana bam-boo huts or tents. Guides and tours should be arranged through the tourist office at Poso.

Ready for rain at Manado's night market

Minahasa gourmet food
Beware if you are faint of heart, for in this region dog is considered a local spe-ciality, tossed into a frying-pan and dished up in a thick and spicy brown sauce. It is known locally as *rintek wuuk* (RW for short) and is apparently much appreciated by Japanese tourists. Other local specialities range from *kawaok* (fried field-rat) to *lawa pangang* (stewed fruit-bat). But do not despair. Seafood is plentiful in Manado itself and the expressway edging the sea-wall (Jalan Piere Tendean) is dotted with lively establishments where fish, rice and beer form the staple diet.

The extrovert and resourceful Minahasans are one of north Sulawesi's four ethnic groups, together numbering 2.5 million

SULAWESI

Deep-sea future
Bunaken's myriad marine species include the giant Napoleon wrasse, stingrays, manta-rays, turtles, barracuda, dolphins, reef sharks (harmless), brilliantly patterned parrot-fish and clownfish, groupers, snappers, blue ribbon eels and sea snakes. Thriving in the coral reef itself are red and orange encrusting sponges, Christmas-tree worms, basket and tube sponges, anemones, seawhips and Spanish dancers, as well as thousands of molluscs. Yet visitors to the world's most beautiful sea gardens are already causing its destruction, barely 15 years after its discovery. Anchors are gradually breaking up the fragile coral and certain fish species, once abundant, are now disappearing.

Fishermen mending nets on Pulau Bunaken

▶ **Palu** *196B4*

The town of Palu, rich from the revenue of ebony, rattan and copra, sprawls around the mouth of a dramatic estuary backed by mercilessly logged hills. Its only interest is as a gateway to the still undiscovered natural splendours of Central Sulawesi, and as such it serves its purpose, with an airport, plenty of money and ticketing facilities, a tourist office, a beach with a view but no swimming, excellent night *warungs* (food-stalls), reasonable Chinese restaurants, but overpriced and characterless accommodation. Another drawback is the high incidence of malaria in this region.

One saving grace is the **Souraja (King's House)**, an imposing construction on carved wooden stilts which houses calligraphic carvings in Farsi and Kufi scripts. The **Museum Negeri Sulawesi Tengah (Museum of Central Sulawesi)** at Jalan Sapiri 23 displays models of regional traditional architecture plus natural history and ethnographic exhibits, and is fronted by replicas of the Bada Valley megaliths. Palu is also blessed with abundant, jingling *bendis* (pony traps).

Short excursions can be made to the **Poboya Nature Reserve**, 7km east and located in a hillside sandalwood forest with sweeping views over the bay, or 20km north to the silk-weaving village of **Tawaeli** where double-*ikat* is still made. The mountain pass east of here to Toboli offers a tortuous but magnificent route through dense primary jungle. For beaches and underwater life, head for Donggala (see page 199).

▶ **Parepare** *196B2*

South Sulawesi's half-way staging-post between Ujung Pandang and Tana Toraja lies in a lovely coastal site. Its large bay is dotted with outriggers and backed by rolling

hills, the intervening skyline dominated by corrugated-iron roofs, palm trees and mosques. There is little to do here except indulge in the excellent local seafood, gaze at the gold-jewellery shops, visit the diminutive Bangenge Ethnographic Museum south of town at Cappa Galung, or watch port activities, but it makes a friendly, relaxed place for a short stop-over.

▶ Poso 196B3

This small port on the south side of immense Tomini Bay is a surprisingly clean, prosperous-looking place and offers travellers reasonable facilities before they set out into Sulawesi's great unknown. Hotels and restaurants are mainly concentrated east of the Poso river, with administrative buildings (including an informative tourist office) and a bountiful market on Jalan Sumatera to the west. Fishing and sailing boats can be hired at the beaches outside town, the best being some 25km east at **Matako**. A few kilometres south of Poso at the village of **Tagolu** is a cluster of ebony-carving workshops, many of them manned by Balinese transmigrants whose Hindu temples can be seen along the coastal road that runs out to the northwest.

▶▶▶ Pulau Bunaken Marine Park 197E5

This 75,000-hectare park off Manado surrounds five islands: Pulau Bunaken; the half-submerged volcano of Manado Tua; Siladen; Mantehage; and Nain. This (with Manado) is slated as one of Indonesia's fastest-growing tourist centres, the islands hovering between their present unspoilt state and an uncertain future monopolised by tourists from Singapore, Taiwan and Japan. For the moment, however, all is well.

Bunaken itself remains unspoilt, its coastal mangroves only cleared in a few spots to make way for low-key beach accommodation, its fishermen still busy with their outriggers and, above all, its coral reefs still teeming with marine life. The safest and most popular diving spot is at **Teluk Liang**, where a flat reef slopes down to underwater valleys and steep drop-offs of several hundred metres. Visibility often exceeds 30m. Bunaken village, on the west coast, is a sleepy place where domestic dogs, chickens and goats are more active than the inhabitants and two imposing churches provide spiritual guidance. **Manado Tua** and **Manehage** offer equally spectacular coral formations, while **Siladen**'s tranquil white beaches make a superb snorkelling and swimming outpost. Public boats leave Manado's Pasar 45 market for Bunaken daily around 2pm and return with the early morning tide. Diving trips can be arranged through any of Manado's diving centres.

Poso's Mr Amir
An inimitable figure around Poso is that of the local tourist information officer, Mr Amir. Whether it is 5am or 10pm he is out on the job, tracking down tourists on night ferries or buses, inviting them to his home for dawn breakfast and a shower or putting them on the right departing bus. Mr Amir is a mine of information about the region and is totally dedicated to his job. Search him out (if he doesn't find you first) at the Tourist Information Centre, Jalan Kalimantan 15 (tel: 0452 21211) during office hours.

Increased diving activity around Pulau Bunaken is having destructive effects on the magnificent reefs

This scene from everyday life in a Rantepao barber's shop contrasts sharply with the animist rituals of neighbouring Torajan villagers

Getting around
Many Torajan sights can be visited using public transport, particularly those lying off the road south to Makale, but these are the most touristy and anything further afield involves a really bone-shattering, crowded ride by *bemo* (minibus). It is far more rewarding to invest in a good guide with transport even if only for a day to see more distant sights and understand the basics of this complex culture, then explore on foot to experience the peaceful landscapes. The recently opened Jet Tourist Service on Jalan Landorundun 1 (tel: 423 21145) offers a team of excellent, multi-lingual guides, efficient service and reasonable, negotiable rates.

▶▶▶ **Rantepao**   *196B3*

Tana Toraja (Toraja land) is one of Indonesia's greatest 'ethno-tourist' attractions, and the small market town of Rantepao lies at its centre. Rantepao makes an ideal and cool base, situated in stunningly beautiful landscapes peppered with traditional Torajan villages where the cult of the dead is, so to speak, alive and well. The town offers a good range of accommodation, reasonable restaurants, antique/souvenir shops, transport rental and a host of hustling guides. Its main feature is its lively market-place, full of regional produce, handicrafts, *tuak* (palm-wine) and local specialities cooked in bamboo or in buffalo blood. Outside the crowded high season (July to August) the town even has a pleasant, relaxed atmosphere, but avoid the rainy season (November to April) when most of the badly maintained Toraja roads become impassable mud-baths. The funeral 'season' starts after the harvest in June and generally lasts until October.

South A circuit can be made south of Rantepao taking in much visited **Londa▶**, a cavernous burial site stacked with coffins, skulls and bones, **Lemo▶▶**, a small, commercialised village in a valley of paddy-fields overlooked by densely inhabited *tau tau* cliffs (see panel opposite), then, east of Makale, the village of **Suaya▶▶▶**. The latter, less touristy, is the site of seven royal graves and the *tau tau* here are original. At the base of the cliff stands a glass-fronted building containing carved coffins of exceptional quality, some 300 years old, inspired by buffalo and boat forms. These are joined by two separate graves, respectively Muslim and Christian. A path climbs up to the right to a viewpoint overlooking the fabulous valley.

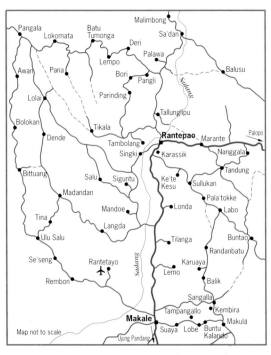

A short distance from Suaya through paddy-fields is Tampangallo▶▶, which claims superb old boat coffins, bones and new *tau tau*. Next stop east along the potholed road is **Lobe**, a field of megaliths used for buffalo sacrifices and, close by, the small private museum of **Buntu Kalando**▶, partly housed in a soaring Torajan house. Beyond this lies the much-vaunted baby grave of **Kembira**▶, consisting of niches hewn in trees where dead babies were buried. A short detour off the road north from here leads you to **Karuaya**▶▶, a typical example of a Torajan family hamlet in a magnificent lush setting. Last stop on the circuit before you return to Rantepao is **Ke'te Kesu**▶▶▶, with perfectly aligned, lavishly carved prow-like houses and rice-barns nestling in bamboo and palm groves, and with a cliff-face of suspended boat-coffins, skulls and *tau tau* (part old, part new) behind the village.

North, east and west Off the main road east of Rantepao lies **Marante**▶▶, another stunningly sited Torajan village with cliff and cave graves, and, 8km further on, **Nanggala**▶▶▶, a royal village containing a huge and ancient hunting house faced by superbly carved rice-barns. Torajan interest continues to the less-visited north, in particular at **Palawa**▶▶ which although commercialised offers more spectacular constructions, and beyond this **Sa'dan**▶, where much of the Torajan weaving is made. The rapidly deteriorating road west from Pangli climbs into dramatic mountains offering good trekking with accommodation at **Batu Tumonga**, numerous cliff graves at Lokomata and increasingly dense primary forest beyond.

Tau tau
Many of the startling *tau tau* effigies that gaze out from niches in the region's limestone cliffs have been stolen for profit and since replaced by new versions. Only a few villages possess the more soulful originals in higher, less accessible niches. Each of these almost life-size wooden statues represents a dead person, the quality of carving and wood reflecting that person's wealth and status. A minimum sacrifice of 24 buffaloes and 59 pigs must accompany the installation. Once the deceased's coffin has been fitted into a natural cave or niche hewn in the rock (a custom apparently developed to preserve the contents from plundering Bugis invaders in the 17th century), the *tau tau* is placed in front behind a protective balcony.

207

Tau tau at Lemo gaze out over paddy-fields

The Toraja

■ **The beautiful high valleys of Tana Toraja are home to a flourishing ethnic group that still maintains unique and fascinating death rituals. Meanwhile, living Torajans continue to inhabit astonishing carved masterpieces whose ethereal roofs hover above fertile rice-terraces.....**■

Torajan names
'A baby Toraja is called after just anything... What about Deppa (cake), Koto (wrinkle), Lelang (auction) and Pong' Masa'aga (wicked)? Karak's mother, they told me, was called Lai' Sapeda (bicycle), and there was a woman in Makale named Lai' Oto (automobile).'
– From *Six Moons in Sulawesi* by Harry Wilcox (1949).

At the funeral, close relatives of the deceased wear black

For centuries the Toraja led a completely isolated existence in a veritable land of milk and honey. Nothing interrupted the cycle of their peaceful agricultural existence until the 17th century when aggressive Bugis arrived from the south to ransack their graves and occupy their territory. This seven-year period ended with a Torajan rebellion and a subsequent return to self-sufficiency for another three centuries until the Dutch penetrated their mountains. Subjection did not come easily, but by 1906 all resistance had been overcome and Protestant missionaries soon moved in.

Yet the strongly animist Torajans were not easy to convert; at Independence only an estimated 10 per cent were Christian and it has been mainly the fear of Muslim dominance that has provoked further conversions to today's figure of 70 per cent. However, traditional beliefs and structures continue to hold out and the Torajans, not the greatest believers in birth control, show no signs of disappearing into the Indonesian melting-pot: some 400,000 inhabit Tana Toraja today and a million or so have moved further afield.

Stuff of life The rulers of Torajan life are rice and buffaloes, the former endowed with a high spiritual value and the latter acting as the symbolic unit of wealth. For the Torajans a buffalo is no mere agricultural tool; it is a valuable symbol of wealth and prestige, and as such is pampered respectfully until its sacrificial dooms-day. Buffalo horns adorn houses to signify the owner's wealth or, more precisely, how many of the beasts were sacrificed at the last family funeral. Buffalo images are carved on houses and rice-barns, their relative merits are discussed endlessly in the market-place, and 24 are necessary as compensation in a divorce.

Rice is venerated to such an extent that its store, the sacred rice-barn (*alang*), may be more elaborately decorated than the owner's house, its lower platform considered an honoured spot for socialising and its superstructure prow-roof extending

The Toraja

towards the heavens. The latter remarkable feature of Torajan architecture, comparable to the extravagant roofs of Sumatra's Batak and Minangkabau houses, is said to have been inspired by the boats that brought the first Torajans up the Sadang river from the coast.

East and west In Torajan philosophy rice is of the east and of life, while death comes from the west. All Torajan rituals are based on placating the complementary opposites of life and death, east and west, sunrise and sunset, right and left, lightness and darkness. House layout, clothing colour and the timing of ceremonies are determined by whether the object is life-giving or death-causing. Animist beliefs in the spiritual force of elements – whether rice, a buffalo or a man's head (the Torajans were head-hunters when the Dutch arrived) – rule the massive death feasts (*tomate*) that dominate the Torajan calendar; when buffalo-meat is eaten the consumer is thought to be injected with magical strength. These prolonged and highly energetic ceremonies vary in scale and duration according to whether the deceased was of the noble 'gold rod' caste, the second 'iron rod' class, or the 'palm-tree heart' class of commoners.

Funeral fury Gold-rod funerals are magnificent affairs that are prepared for months or even years in advance. A rock-face is dug out by hand, temporary houses are erected for guests from far afield, a *tau tau* is made and, above all, finances for the ceremony are amassed (it can cost up to Rp100 million, or US$50,000). Traditionally, the corpse remains enveloped in a shroud in the family house to await its big day. Up to 1,000 guests may arrive for the week laden with pigs, sacks of rice or, better still, a buffalo. Processions, buffalo-fights, dances, sacrifices, *tuak* (palm-wine) consumption and feasting start at midday and continue well into the night for several days until the final family procession sees the installation of the deceased in his or her cliff tomb, from where the soul will watch eternally over the family and its rice-fields.

A funeral guest

Microcosms
Traditional Torajan houses are raised on sturdy piles, with stairs leading from the east side (the side of life) into three interior rooms. The three levels are a microcosm of the Torajan universe, with clear divisions between the underworld, the middle or earthly world, and the upper world of the spirits. Here the northern 'prow' of the swooping roof is considered the most sacred, for this is where the gods enter the home.

209

*Elaborately carved
Torajan houses*

SULAWESI

Maleo birds
The *Macrocephalon maleo*, a member of the Megapode family, is native to Sulawesi. This bald, scrawny necked, black and white striped bird, about the size of a domestic hen, buries its huge eggs in mounds of solar- or volcanically heated soil for incubation purposes, then takes off. Three months later a single chick hatches, works its way out of the sand and is able to fly immediately thanks to its size. Much prized as a delicacy, the eggs are now protected in nesting grounds, the most important of these being Bangkiriang Reserve on the arid south coast of the Banggai Peninsula (east of Luwuk).

Danau Tempe at Sengkang, an angler's and birdwatcher's paradise

▶▶ **Sengkang**   196B2

This Bugis silk-weaving centre on the shores of scenic Danau Tempe lies well off the Trans-Sulawesi Highway and is therefore little visited. Much of the town is built on marshes edging the lake, and so consists of a network of stilt-houses with interconnecting walkways. The 4m seasonal variation in water-level means that a lakeside mosque is visited either by car or canoe depending on the time of year. The **Pasar Senteral**, a gloomy market building on the main street, offers the best selection of fine, handwoven silk, although the use of chemical dyes generates some lurid hues. Walk down any side-street to the lake and you will hear the rattle of looms, these usually placed in the shade beneath a raised house. More silk-weaving can be seen at **Sempang**, 5km away, and at **Watusoppeng**, 40km southwest.

Danau Tempe▶▶▶ itself can be toured by motorised longboats (hired through Sengkang's few hotels). This bird-lovers' paradise teems with winged creatures, from kingfishers to huge black herons, while the rampant mauve-flowered weed that cloaks the tranquil waters is a magnet for fish. A stop can be made at Batu Batu, a Bugis fishing village on the opposite shore.

▶▶ **Tangkoko Batuangus**
       Nature Reserve   197E5

This 3,000-hectare reserve crowning Sulawesi's northern tentacle is located immediately north of Bitung, about 65km east of Manado in the foothills of Gunung Dua Sudara. The undulating grassland environment nurtures tarsiers, black apes, maleo birds, *babi rusa* (hairless wild boar), cuscus and plenty of snakes, and the reserve also incorporates the coral-fringed coastline. Entrance to the park is at **Danowudu**, and basic accommodation is available here and at Tangkoko. Contact the PHPA office in Manado for permits and further information.

▶ **Tanjung Api Nature Reserve**   196C4

Some 156km east of Poso on a headland jutting into Tomini Bay is the tiny reserve of Tanjung Api ('Fire Cape'). It is home to many of Sulawesi's endemic species (such

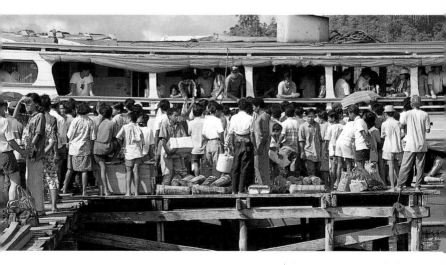

as black macaques, tarsiers and *babi rusa*), as well as deer, wild boar and pythons, and is named after a series of jets of natural gas which catch light as they come into contact with the air. The coastal forest is crossed by an easy trail which offers occasional views north to the outlying Togian Islands. The nearest accommodation is at the small port of **Ampana**.

►►► Togian Islands   *196C4*

Seven main islands and myriad atolls make up this tropical paradise that lies scattered over immense Tomini Bay. The lava and limestone islands are still blissfully untouched by tourists and have no telephones, although there is the odd satellite television dish. On offer are rich coral landscapes, white beaches, fishing shacks in mid-sea, dolphins, turtles, dugongs (sea cows), sharks and even whales. Accommodation is limited to one hotel and one *losmen* (budget inn), but by far the best way to experience the islands is by organised boat trip. Public ferries between Gorontalo, Ampana and Poso stop off twice a week in both directions at the main island ports.

Coral The uninhabited volcanic island of **Pulau Una-Una** (which last erupted in 1983) rises in the north, while the main villages are located on a string of adjacent islands to the south. **Wakai**, at the eastern end of Batudaka, and **Katupat**, on the northern coast of Togian, offer the only accommodation and are both served by the island ferry. To the east, tiny **Pulau Malenge** offers a dense concentration of Sulawesi wildlife. Endless reefs edge the islands, where giant platter-, mushroom- and cacti-shaped corals teem with brilliantly coloured fish.

Parts of the reef have been destroyed by fish-bombs, once widely used but now heavily policed and threatened with hefty fines. The Bajau fishermen, who live off both their fresh catch and dried fish, commute between island water-villages and precarious-looking bamboo shacks erected in the shallow seas. Palm sugar, dessicated coconut and profitable gourmet terrapins, sharks' fins and coconut crabs form the rest of the local economy.

Finding a space on the ferry at Wakai in the Togian Islands

The Bajau
This tribe of former sea-gypsies can be found scattered around the Celebes Sea, from Sulawesi to Borneo and the Philippines. Their origins may remain obscure, but their lives and beliefs are closely linked to the sea. In Sulawesi they have settled in coastal water-villages, maintaining maritime links through their offshore stilt-houses.

Island tour
For a blissful boat tour of the Togian Islands, best undertaken in the driest season between September and November, contact Rudy Ruus through the Hotel Wasantara in Tentena (tel: 0458 21345), or write to him in advance at Jalan Pulau Seram, Nusa Indah 8, Poso, Sulawesi Tengah. His basic wooden boat can sleep up to four people and he also arranges accommodation with families in Bajau fishing shacks ('coral houses') and at island homestays. Rudy's knowledge of the reefs and his semi-mystical approach is hard to beat.

Prehistoric paintings at the Leang-Leang cave, 30km northeast of Ujung Pandang

Butterflies at Maros
Maros, about 30km to the north of Ujang Pandang, is home to the world's largest number of butterfly species, now protected in the adjoining park of Bantimurung where there is a museum and breeding centre. The area's attractions were first recognised back in the mid-1800s by the naturalist Alfred R Wallace. Today, the park attracts weekend crowds for its lush vegetation, dramatic limestone outcrops and cascading waterfall.

Bantimurung's cooling cascades, near Maros's butterfly park

 **Ujung Pandang** *196A1*

The steamy port of Ujung Pandang, formerly known as Makassar, has a colourful history that is barely apparent in today's rather characterless sprawl. The city's strategic position once made it a natural hub for the spice traders who were encouraged by the powerful sultanate of Gowa (13th to 15th centuries), and the Makassarese were renowned as great seafarers. It took over 50 years of political manoeuvring and open conflict for the Dutch to finally force a treaty on Gowa in 1667 (see panel on page 213). Even then the sultan did not capitulate for two more years. Ujung Pandang's present status still stems from its geographical location, and the airport has become one of Indonesia's busiest transit crossroads.

On the waterfront Most points of interest are situated just south of the harbour in and around the port's main commercial centre. The crumbling and unimpressive remains of **Benteng (Fort) Rotterdam►** (*open:* Tuesday to Sunday, 9–4), dating from 1545 but rebuilt by the Dutch, contain gardens flanked by the **Museum La Galigo (State Museum)►►**. Exhibits in the left wing focus on the Gowa kingdom, a badly labelled ceramics collection, photos and coins, while on the right of the gardens the museum concentrates on Sulawesi ethnography. There are some impressive models of typical Makassarese schooners and fishing boats, and a good display of textiles and weaving techniques upstairs.

The streets immediately north of the fort (around Jalan Sulawesi) make up Ujung Pandang's Chinatown and contain some colourful old temples. On Jalan Diponegoro stands **Prince Diponegoro's Tomb**, the last resting place of the Indonesian rebel hero who spent his last 26 years imprisoned by the Dutch in Fort Rotterdam.

Sea shells Down the main sea-front road of Jalan Penghibur is the embarkation point for outlying islands (Pulau Kayangan has a good beach), a cluster of hotels and the old shopping area one street inland on Jalan Sumbaopu. The waterfront stretch here is a popular promenading area where night *warungs* (food-stalls) come alive as the sun sets on the horizon. Along a leafy

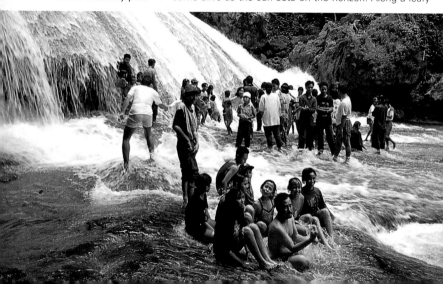

A pristine orchid specimen at Clara Bundt's nursery

Treaty of Bungaya
The terms of the Bungaya Treaty, signed by the Dutch and the Makassar government in 1667, give a clear idea of Dutch ambitions. The Dutch United East India Company got complete monopoly on the spice trade; all Portuguese and British were to be expelled from Gowa; no Indians, Javanese, Achenese, Malays or Siamese were allowed to trade in cloth; Bugis sailors required passes from the Dutch government; Dutch coinage was introduced; the king of Gowa was to send 1,000 slaves to Batavia (Jakarta).

213

side-street lies the former **home of Clara Bundt▶▶** (Jalan Mochtar Lufti 15), which maintains a fascinating display of her collection of sea shells and other marine pickings, plus an orchid nursery garden. It looks permanently closed, but someone is always around to let you in.

Old Gowa Ujung Pandang spreads east of Jalan Hasanuddin into a grid of residential streets, but the main place of cultural interest lies at **Sungguminasa**, about 10km south. This is the site of the old Gowa kingdom, dominated by the sultan's palace (now the **Museum Balla Lompoa▶▶**) on the main square. The imposing wooden building, built in 1936 for the 35th raja, houses a collection of royal costumes and photos, as well as the *pusaka* (royal treasure) which you must ask to have unlocked.

On the way back to the city centre lies a Muslim pilgrimage spot consisting of the Mesjid Syech Yusuf, the Mesjid Katangka (one of Sulawesi's oldest mosques) and, perhaps most interesting, the tomb of Syech Yusuf, a 17th-century Muslim scholar and later rebel. Here, too, are the royal graves of the Gowa sultanate.

▶   Watampone   *196B2*
This former capital of the much-feared Bugis kingdom of Bone, 175km across the mountainous peninsula from Ujung Pandang, has shrunk into a neglected and rarely visited town. The Bugis, long-time rivals to the kingdom of Gowa, finally capitulated to their neighbours in 1611, bowed to Islam, then subsequently allied with the Dutch to break Gowanese power. Bone remained a bustling trading hub well into the 19th century.

The **Museum Lapawawoi▶▶** houses some interesting Bugis ethnographic and royal exhibits (including the royal cigar collection), but Watampone's main sight is **Gua Mampu▶▶**, 34km northwest of town. This is Sulawesi's largest cave and is thick with bats, bizarre stalagmites and stalactites, and human and animal rock-carvings.

Ujung Padang is home to numerous Chinese temples

KALIMANTAN

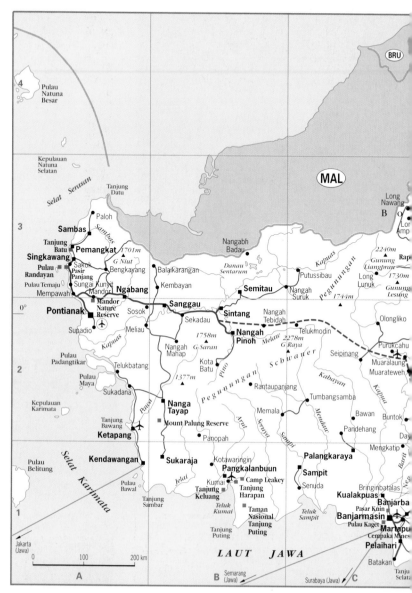

BRU

MAL

4 Pulau
Natuna
Besar

Kepulauan
Natuna
Selatan

Selat Serasan

Tanjung
Datu

Paloh

Sambas

Long
Nawang

B

3

**Tanjung
Batu** **Pemangkat**

Singkawang
**Pulau
Randayan**

Sambas

1701m
G Niut
Bengkayang

Balaikarangan

Nangabh
Badau

Danau
Sentarum

Kapuas

Putussibau

2240m
Gunung
Liangpran Rap

Long
Lunuk

1730m
Gunung
Lesung

Pegunungan

Lor
Amp

Pulau Temaju
Mempawah

Sakok
Pasir
Panjang
Sungai Kunyit
Mandor

Ngabang

Kembayan

1744m

Pontianak

Mandor
Nature
Reserve

Sosok

Sanggau

Semitau

Nangah
Suruk

Olongliko

0°

Supadio

Meliau

Sekadau

Sintang

Nangah
Tebidah

Telukmodin

Purukcahu

Kapuas

Nangah
Mahap

G Saran
1758m

**Nangah
Pinoh**

Melaw

2278m
G Raya

Seipinang

Muaralaung
Muarateweh

2

Pulau
Padangtikar

Pulau
Maya

Telukbatang

Pino

Schwaner

Kabayan

Kapua

Kepulauan
Karimata

Sukadana

1377m

Pegunungan

Rantaupanjang

Tumbangsamba

Bawan

Buntok

Pawan

Memala

Mendau

Pandehang

Day

**Nanga
Tayap**

Mount Palung Reserve

Seruyu

Mengkatip

Tanjung
Bawang

Panopah

Sampi

Ketapang

Pulau
Belitung

Kendawangan

Sukaraja

Kotawaringin

Palangkaraya

Barit

Nee

1

Selat Karimata

Pulau
Bawal

Tanjung
Sambar

Jelai

Kumai

Pangkalanbuun

Camp Leakey

**Tanjung
Keluang**

**Tanjung
Harapan**

Senuda

Sampit

Bringinbatalas

Kualakpuas

Banjarba

Pasar Kuin

Banjarmasin

Marbapu

Jakarta
(Jawa)

0   100   200 km

Teluk
Kumai

Tanjung
Puting

Taman
Nasional
Tanjung
Puting

Teluk
Sampit

Pulau Kaget

Cempaka Mines

Pelaihari

A

LAUT   JAWA

B

Semarang
(Jawa)

Surabaya (Jawa)

C

Batakan

Tanju
Selata

Map labels (Kalimantan / Borneo region):

RP

2160m
Gunung Harden (Harun)
Lumbis
Ulu Ulu
Pulau Sebatik
Teluk Sebuku
Pulau Mandul
Longmalinau
Sembakun
Sesayap
Pulau Bunyu
Kubuang
Sabalanung
Tarakan
Teluk Sekatak
Besah
Muarapangean
Tanjungselor
Longjelai
Longagung
Telukbayur
Tanjungredeb
Tanjung Batu
Pulau Maratua
Tolitoli (Sulawesi)
Pura
2053m
Gunung Kemal
Kelai
1390m
Semurut
n e o
Kubumesaai
Peg. Sambaliung
Domaring
Brahim
2000m
Gunung Menyapa
Pelawanbesar
Sepinang
Long Bangun
Muarawahau
Tanjung Mangkalihat
Rukun Damai
Belayan
Telen
Kembangjanggut
Kutai Reserve
Sepasu
Long Iram
Kersik Luwai
Danau Semayang
Klampo
Bontang
Equator
Mahakam
Danau Melintang
Muara Muntai
Kotabangun
Tenggarong
Melak
Danau Jempang
Tanjungbalai
Mancong
Tanjung Isui
Samarinda
Sangasanga
Teweh
1223m
Tanjung Pemarung
Samboja
Palu
Paring
Beraspapan
Penajam
Balikpapan
Ampah
Bebulu
Teluk Adang
Riya
Tanjung
Kerang
Tanjung Aru
Tanahgrogot
Amuntai
Barabai
Sungaidurian
SULAWESI
Loksado
1892m
Tanjungbatu
Mamuju
Kandangan Rantau
Pegunungan
Kotabaru
Batuamparan
Majene
Pagatan
Pulau Sebuku
Satui
Karambu
Parepare
Pulau Laut
D / Surabaya (Jawa)
E
Ujung Pandang (Sulawesi)
Selat Makasar

Kalimantan The classic preconception of Kalimantan as a wild land cloaked in impenetrable jungle and peopled by blowpipe-sporting Dayaks is fast becoming a myth. Decades of logging and offshore oil drilling have transformed coastal areas into a prosperous yet monotonous belt of plantations and sawmills, with nondescript towns whose inhabitants are as likely to hail from Java, Sulawesi or China as from the interior.

To experience the true heart of Borneo, the world's third-largest island, treks need to be made at least 400km inland to the mountainous core. Here, at last, where river transport is the only option, are primary rainforests, longhouse-

KALIMANTAN

Pontianak, capital of West Kalimantan

dwelling Dayaks and unique species of wildlife. However, such expeditions do not come cheap; guides and chartered boats are essential, and as a result most visitors opt for a more economical tour from either Banjarmasin, Samarinda or Pontianak. All these 'adventure' trips also require good physical condition, a tolerance for rough living and an appreciation of the glowering skies that characterise Borneo. Rain becomes scarcer from July to September, but as it is a permanent feature from December to February this season is best avoided.

Transformation Kalimantan did not always present this face. The various Dayak peoples, forced inland by Malay coastal settlers, lived undisturbed in their communal longhouses, hunting, fishing and practising shifting cultivation, and carrying out their animist rituals and taboos. Head-hunting was common, as were inter-tribal conflicts.

Coastal settlements presented a different picture, as Kalimantan was a stop-over for traders sailing between China, the Philippines and Java. Hinduism reached the island's southern shores as early as AD400, and by the 15th and 16th centuries Islam was making strong inroads; the sultanates of Kutai (near Samarinda) and Banjarmasin became important Muslim cultural and trading crossroads. In West Kalimantan the 18th century saw a flood of Chinese immigrants who came to work the gold-mines of Sambas and who subsequently spread south to trade.

British and Dutch colonial interests had, by the mid- to late 19th century, carved out their respective territories in Borneo – although internal conflicts were certainly not over – and plantations of rubber, coffee and pepper were soon followed by the discovery of oil. Since the 1970s timber has joined the list of diminishing natural riches.

▶ **Balikpapan** *215D2*

The symbol of the featureless sprawl of Balikpapan is an eternally burning flame flickering above the immense Pertamina oil refinery that dominates the northwest part of the city. Unfortunately, it is difficult to avoid transiting here as the harbour, the brand-new airport and the distinctly less impressive bus stations together form major crossroads for transport in all directions.

The hilly town is skirted by a wide estuary to the west and the Makassar Strait to the east (source of East Kalimantan's immense oil wealth) with old colonial villas occupying the more scenic hilltops. The main north–south axis, Jalan Jend A Yani, winds down to a seafront junction which is rapidly becoming a desperately needed town centre. A plethora of restaurants, banks, travel agents, modern hotels (mainly overpriced or not for foreigners) and a shopping centre form the hub, with a few craft shops dotted up the road to the north. Spend a night here if you really have to, then head out fast. Buses to Samarinda (2 hours) leave from the Batu Ampar terminal, 4km north of town, and for Banjarmasin (12 hours) from Penajam, which is reached via a boat ride across the bay.

▶▶ **Banjarbaru** *214C1*

This small town, about 35km east of Banjarmasin near Martapura, is notable for one thing, the **Lambung Mangkurat State Museum** (*open*: Tuesday to Sunday, 8:30–2; Friday, 8:30–11). This traditional Banjarese-style building of carved *ulin* wood (ironwood), with a steep, tiled roof, houses an interesting, well-presented collection of South Kalimantan ethnographic artefacts. These include Hindu statues excavated at Candi Laras and Candi Agung, Dayak and Bukit gongs and jewellery, traditional and Dutch weapons, costumes, models of river boats, gamelan instruments, Chinese porcelain and some royal furniture. The collection is divided between the upper floor and a 'history room', located beneath the staircase and consequently easy to miss.

Panning for precious stones at Cempaka, near Martapura

The Banjarese
Banjarese culture is an assimilation of Dayak, Malay and Javanese cultures, and although these people were originally Hindu, they were converted to Islam by the Javanese kingdom of Demak in the mid-16th century. Today, the Banjarese population numbers 2.5 million and, despite the adoption of numerous non-Banjarese words, the Banjarese can often be heard speaking their local dialect. Pride in their culture runs deep. Traditional steep-roofed houses are being reproduced as public buildings (look out for the brand-new public library near Banjarmasin's Terminal Induk on the Martapura road) and the Banjarese themselves continue to make *sasirangan*, a unique tie-dyed fabric unlike any other in Indonesia.

The highlight of Banjarmasin is its unique floating market, at its busiest early in the morning

Proboscis monkey
These very shy monkeys (*Nasalis larvatus*), native to Borneo, live only in coastal or riverine forests and mangrove swamps. Mature male proboscis reach enormous proportions, but their outstanding feature is an outsized, pendulous, cucumber-like nose. Their Kalimantan nickname is *orang belanda* ('Dutchman'). Unlike the more solitary orang-utan, proboscis monkeys move around in groups, generally one male and his numerous 'wives' and offspring. They are notoriously difficult, even on Pulau Kembang, but the best time is around sundown when they rustle around the shoreline looking for fresh young leaves.

This is by far Kalimantan's most stimulating and picturesque city, a 400-year-old community where life revolves around a network of canals running off the Barito and Martapura rivers. Banjarmasin is also the capital of a strongly Muslim province (93 per cent are Muslims), claims Indonesia's second-largest mosque, and has a skyline that is punctuated by onion domes. There is a well-frequented Islamic school at nearby Martapura. The Banjarese cling firmly to their traditions, but they are outgoing and friendly. The dynamic town centre offers very adequate tourist facilities and makes an excellent base for adventure tours and trekking into the interior; public transport is also good.

Water visit The most popular activity here is a river tour along the Martapura then through narrow canals to Indonesia's longest and widest river, the Barito, where morning activity is focused on the floating market of **Pasar Kuin▶▶▶**. A *klotok* (motorised longboat) can be hired cheaply at the wharf behind the market on Jalan Ujung Murung; leave at dawn to catch the floating market at its liveliest (it stops around 9am) and to observe Banjarmasin awakening in the early light *en route*. Zealous toothbrushing and washing takes place from rickety wooden and bamboo houses, while the canal itself buzzes with canoes piled high with bananas, coconuts, firewood, melons and mandarins. Women vendors and shoppers are often hidden beneath broad palm-leaf *tanggui* (sun-hats), and at the market itself floating *warungs* (food-stalls), sell a delectable array of Banjarese cakes, rice and satay.

Islands Plywood factories and sawmills line the banks of the Barito, while to the south two midstream islands offer a glimpse of wildlife. The nearest is **Pulau Kembang▶**, renowned for its long-tailed macaques. Some 12km further lies the swampy island reserve of **Pulau Kaget▶▶**, which harbours proboscis monkeys (see panel, page 218), black long-tailed macaques and flocks of egrets. Back along the Martapura river towards the town centre is the **Pelabuhan Lama Martapura▶▶**, a harbour dating from colonial days with a wonderful line-up of Bugis schooners.

Dry land Banjarmasin's main land-based area of interest lies west of a curve in the Martapura river. **Jalan Samudra**, the busy main axis running east to end at the Pasar Malabar by Antasari Bridge, has a concentration of shops, restaurants and hotels, with night markets enlivening its sidestreets. Immediately north in Jalan Hasanuddin are airline offices, money changers and travel agents. Beyond that is the Pasar Baru food market. From A Yani Bridge, Jalan Pos (a riverside area slated for redevelopment) curls round to join Jalan Sudirman, dominated by the city's pride and joy, the **Mesjid Sabilal Muhtadin▶**. Five lofty minarets overlook the mosque's gold-plated dome (completed 1979).

▶▶   Kutai Nature Reserve   215D3

This 200,000-hectare reserve, 100km north of Samarinda, is visited from Bontang or Samarinda (see panel). Massive logging has left much of East Kalimantan desolate, but here dense rainforest is populated by orang-utans, gibbons and leaf-monkeys, plus an estimated 239 species of birds.

Swimming buffalo
Another of South Kalimantan's peculiarities is its swimming buffaloes. These are raised in the swamplands which lie between the rivers that flow into the Java Sea. Herds of the curiously aquatic buffaloes swim from one grazing area to the next, occasionally heaving themselves on to log platforms built for them by farmers. The buffaloes' superior size and quality of meat brings in high prices at local markets. The nearest herds to Banjarmasin are in the vicinity of Bati-Bati, about an hour's drive southeast.

Visiting Kutai Nature Reserve
Facilities at the park are basic, but accommodation, boats and guides can be arranged at the PHPA office in Bontang. The most economic way to visit the park is by organised tour from Samarinda.

The rare black orchid at the Kersik Luwai reserve near Melak

The black orchid
This rare orchid (*Coelogyne pandurata*) originates from the forests of East Kalimantan, and is named after the black colour found on one violin-shaped furrow in the middle of the labia and on its curly edges, these remaining black from the moment it blooms until it dries up. No other variety of orchid has this colour.

Banjarese house near Martapura

► **Loksado**   215D1

Some 100km northeast of Banjarmasin, in the foothills of the Muratus Range, lies a region of traditional Dayak longhouses (*balai*). The village of Loksado is becoming increasingly popular as a base for white-water rafting on the Amandit river, and for trekking around villages and longhouses. Numerous tours target this area, and can arrange accommodation in longhouses, but independent travellers may resort to some basic *losmen* (budget inns) in the main town of Kandangan. The Banjarese Hill Dayaks practise shifting cultivation, and on Wednesdays a colourful crowd laden with produce homes in on the market.

► **Long Iram**   215D2

Long Iram lies over 400km west of Samarinda in Kenyah Dayak country and is often the last outpost for travellers on the Mahakam river. In 1908 the town had the status of being the furthest Dutch administrative post upriver; the post office dates from this era. The town is divided into twos, one side inhabited by Kutai people and other newcomers, the other by Bahau Dayaks. A minor gold-rush took place recently, changing the profile of the backwater town with an increase in basic accommodation, restaurants and local 'girls'. Traditions are few here, but to visit really authentic Kenyah longhouses and meet settled Punans, go upstream to Rukun Damai. In certain seasons boat services upstream from here may grind to a halt, and chartered boats are the only option beyond Long Bangun.

►► **Martapura**   214C1

South Kalimantan's trading centre for semi-precious and precious stones, mostly mined at Cempaka (10km away), lies 35km east of Banjarmasin. Jewellery shops and diamond polishers line the road, but most of the business goes on at the central market, where diamonds, emeralds, rubies, sapphires, topaz, amethysts, jade, turquoise and tourmalines sparkle at traders and tourists. A reputable shop is Kayu Tangi on Jalan Sukaramai 4/J at the

back of the main square, but remember to bargain.

The 'mines' of **Cempaka**▶▶▶ are an incredible sight, consisting of rickety shafts and sifting areas scattered across muddy fields. Each shaft, which can be up to 15m deep, is manned by a family team of 10 to 20 male and female members who pass up baskets of soil from the depths. This is then washed carefully, sieved and screened in four stages to try to find a *galuh* ('girl'), the fond local name for a diamond. Conditions and methods have hardly changed over the centuries, myths and taboos of the process extending to shamanist ceremonies for determining new shaft locations. Each shaft is exploited for up to two months, depending on its yield.

▶   **Melak**   215D2
This small Dayak town is located about half-way along the Mahakam river between the three lakes around Muara Muntai and the town of Long Iram. There is some *losmen* accommodation and mainly modernised longhouses near by. The town offers little of interest other than the famous orchid reserve of **Kersik Luwai**, about 16km away and accessible by *ojek* (motor-cycle taxi) or jeep. Some 30 species of orchid exist here, including the rare black orchid (see panel opposite). Some Tanjung Dayaks in this area are still devout animists and if you visit during a festival or ceremony you may witness a ritual trance.

        Pangkalanbuun   214B1
This town is located in the swampy, southwestern corner of Central Kalimantan and serves as a launch pad for visiting the Tanjung Puting Nature Reserve (see page 228). It can be reached by air from Banjarmasin, Pontianak or Semarang, but is accessible only by river at ground-level. Cargo and passenger ships stop at its harbour, while all its facilities (small hotels, airline offices, a PHPA office, banks and restaurants) are concentrated along two streets running parallel to the Arut river. The entrance to the reserve is at Kumai, 25km away along one of Central Kalimantan's rare roads.

Martapura's gold-cutting and polishing methods have barely evolved

Diamonds are forever
The largest diamond ever unearthed in Cempaka's fields (116 carats) was found in 1965 and baptised the *Trisakti* ('Triple Power'). This was a rare find; more common are 12-carat *galuhs*, such as the one found in May 1994 which fetched Rp52 million (US$26,000), not considered a brilliant sale as such stones can go for up to twice that value. About 2,000 workers are involved in the laborious mining business, men working at the base of the shaft (ventilated from above by a primitive foot pump), and women and children taking turns in the narrow middle section and at the top. Cleaning soil in wooden troughs and sieving are male preserves. The salary for a ten-hour day is a miserable Rp3,000 (US$1.50).

The Dayaks

■ **Change is coming to Borneo's Dayaks. Longhouses, blowpipes and animism are fast disappearing as Kalimantan's timber boom and the march of the 20th century irretrievably transform communications and thus traditions in the region. Only in the less-accessible hinterland do communities still cling to the old way of life.....■**

Longhouses

Traditionally, all Dayaks (except the Ngajus of the centre), live in longhouses (*betang*) built for 30–40 families. A covered veranda runs along one side or across the middle between individual family quarters. As a defensive and functional measure the houses are raised some 3m above the ground.

Entrance is by a steep, notched log which leads to a communal, outer terrace where washing or rice is dried. The inner communal gallery is used for social gatherings and as an area where women can weave. Although the main structure is of ironwood, floors are creaky bamboo and roofs increasingly made of corrugated iron.

Top: Dayak beadwork
Right: carved totems protect longhouses and sacred sites
Below: a Kenyah Dayak in full ceremonial attire

The indigenous Dayaks today form barely a quarter of Kalimantan's population. The term itself, meaning loosely 'people of the interior', encompasses several dozen ethnic groups, each with its own dialect, culture and social structure, some of whom have spread over the border into Sarawak. These are Borneo's original inhabitants (their origins date back to 30,000BC) who were gradually forced into the forested mountains of the interior by subsequent immigrants. However, with the arrival of 'progress', individual houses are now replacing communal longhouses, T-shirts and jeans are worn instead of loincloths, and jobs in towns, mines and logging camps appeal more than hunting and agricultural activities. As a result, many Dayaks find themselves suspended between two worlds, one eye on the satellite television and the other on an animist ritual.

Natural gods Christianity may have made strong inroads, leaving posters of Christ pinned to longhouse walls, but the basis of Dayak beliefs is inescapably linked to the spirits of the all-powerful and bountiful forest. Every aspect of the Dayaks' natural environment is identified with ambivalent spirits and demons, giving rise to seasonal ceremonies, rituals, taboos, tattoos, superbly crafted symbolic objects (totems, statues, weavings and beadwork) and headhunting. Although this ritual 'sport' was theoretically wiped out earlier this century by colonial rulings, the Ibans in particular are known to have renewed their passion for headhunting during the Japanese occupation in World War II.

In the past, Dayak survival depended entirely on their relationship with nature and even today, when many are forced to leave their communities to work elsewhere, their knowledge of the forest's infinite offerings is remarkable. A Dayak guide or porter knows the properties of every plant in the forest, the 'spirit' of every bird or beast and the feasibility of every river rapid.

Dayak groups

The main Dayak ethnic groups are the Kenyahs, concentrated north of the Mahakam river; the Kayans, on East Kalimantan's remote Apo Kayan Plateau; the Iban, grouped far along the Kapuas river near the Sarawak border; the Ngajus and Ot Danums in Central Kalimantan; and the Bukit Dayaks of South Kalimantan's Muratus Mountains. Smaller groups such as the Tanjungs and Benuaqs live along the middle reaches of the Mahakam, while the formerly nomadic Punans (or Penans) have mostly abandoned their forest roaming to settle near the Kenyahs and Kayans.

The Punans, simple, shy, stockily built people, are perhaps the saddest symbols of Borneo's recent mutation. Once expert hunter-gatherers who rarely set foot outside the jungle (as a result they have much paler skins), they shunned sedentary lives and external contact except to trade their exquisitely woven baskets with the Kenyah-Kayans. However, diminishing forests and government directives are now forcing the Punans into settlements, while inbreeding (they number only 10,000–20,000) has also left its mark.

Long ears

The much photographed Kenyahs form Kalimantan's most obviously colourful ethnic group as these are the famous 'long-ears'. The pendulous ear lobes of Kenyah women, stretched by weighty brass or gold ornaments since childhood, sometimes hang below their shoulders; this exoticism is further accentuated by tattoos, brightly beaded baby-carriers and patchwork conical hats. Unlike other Dayaks, the Kenyahs and their close relatives the Kayans have a strict hierarchical social structure with a respected aristocracy. Most have adopted Catholicism and in some cases have even trimmed their ear lobes as a sign of conversion. This is in stark contrast to their former enemies, the Ibans, who maintain an egalitarian community and are loath to abandon their animist beliefs. These gregarious people were once fearsome head-hunters and pirates, and their great mobility has led many of them over the mountains into Sarawak.

Top: Tanjung Dayak longhouse
Above: Kenyah women are known as 'long-ears' – for obvious reasons

Dayak handicrafts

The semi-nomadic Punans are masters at producing intricately woven baskets of *Pandanus* leaves or rattan, usually designed as backpacks and decorated with geometric patterns. Traditional Dayak *hampatong*, woodcarvings of humans, animals or mythical creatures, have been developed into decorative Western-style bowls and plates. The best woodcarving is the preserve of the Kenyah-Kayans, who are also experts in intricate beadwork. *Ikat*-weavings are perfected by the Ibans, while Benuaq Dayaks make *doyo* grass-weavings

KALIMANTAN

Kite-flying in front of the 18th-century Mesjid Jami

►► Pontianak

214A2

The burgeoning capital of the province of West Kalimantan straddles the confluence of the Kapuas and Landak rivers in a low-lying coastal region bang on the Equator. The city's population of 450,000 (unofficially said to number 700,000 due to the influx of rural Javanese transmigrants and Dayaks desperate for work) has a large proportion of Chinese, many of them descendants of Hakka immigrants who joined the 18th-century gold-rush to Sambas. Timber, rubber, coffee and pepper form the backbone of the provincial economy, and Pontianak acts as the main processing and transport hub.

The city makes a comfortable base for organising excursions into the interior along the Kapuas river (see page 227), north along the coast to Singkawang or across the border into Sarawak. International flights from Kuching and Singapore bring in streams of shoppers and nightlife enthusiasts, but otherwise West Kalimantan is little visited by Westerners.

Downtown Pontianak's commercial heart lies on the south bank of the Kapuas in an orderly area surrounding the central market and *bemo* (minibus) station of **Kapuas Indah** on Jalan Tanjung Pura. **Sa Seng Keng**, the city's oldest Chinese temple (17th century), stands on the waterfront here. Immediately to the east is one of the city's pungent old canal areas, packed with small houses but soon to be redeveloped as it presents a significant health hazard. Behind it, on the banks of the river, is the old harbour lined with Bugis schooners that face the mosque and palace opposite. Public boats ply the river and others are available for hire to cross to these two monuments, situated in the original Bugis settlement. The **Kraton Kadriyah**►► dates from the founding of the city in 1771, although it has been extensively renovated since. This elegant ironwood palace incorporates numerous 1920s features and displays regal paraphernalia ranging from a canopied throne to silver, porcelain and old photos. The son of the last sultan still lives in the palace. A short walk from here across a canal stands the tiered green **Mesjid Jami**►►, another beautiful construction erected by the first sultan. The site was apparently chosen by firing a cannon-ball.

Beyond the centre Southeast of the centre in a newly developed administrative zone which terminates at the university stands the **Museum Negeri (State Museum)**►► (*open*: Monday to Sunday, 9–4; Friday, 9–11). Although the museum is laid out somewhat erratically, it offers a good introduction to local Dayak culture, with exhibits of weapons, *ikat*, elaborate brassware, models of

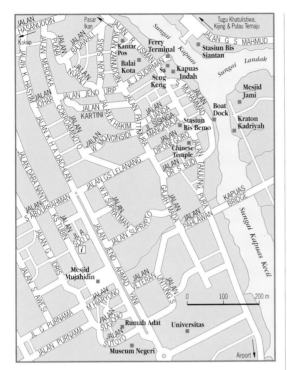

Seafood special

If you feel like escaping Pontianak's steamy nightlife of karaoke bars and call-girl line-ups, head 20km west to the picturesque coastal fishing village of Kakap, famous for its floating seafood restaurants and glorious sunsets. A daytime visit will reveal nearby fisheries, some of which specialise in crab, and could include a short boat trip to the Kwan Im Buddhist temple in the bay.

Tours inland

Pontianak's best tour agency is Ateng Tour on Jalan Gajah Mada 201 (tel: 561 32683; fax: 561 36620). The knowledgeable staff organise jungle expeditions, longhouse accommodation, riding the rapids and virtually anything else that West Kalimantan has to offer. All trips into the interior start with flights on a Cessna plane, thereby cutting out the less interesting plantation areas near the coast.

West Kalimantan's largest palace, the Keraton Kadriyah

longhouses and West Kalimantan's various *kraton* (palaces), Chinese lacquer and a large section devoted to local ceramics made by Chinese immigrants around Singkawang and Batulayang. In a parallel street stands the rather forlorn-looking **Rumah Adat►**, a replica of a Dayak longhouse. Pontianak's pride and joy, the **Equator Monument►**, lies diametrically opposite this quarter in an industrial zone across the river. This was dubiously restructured in 1991, and a new concrete bunker now surrounds the original four ironwood columns that are surmounted by a globe and directional arrow.

When the sun really hits its equatorial zenith and you thirst for a cooling dip, head 85km or so north to Sungai Kunyit, where you can hire a boat to go across to the beaches of **Pulau Temaju►►**, or collapse on the popular mainland beach at **Kijing**, near Mempawah and its palace.

Samarinda 215D2

▶ **Samarinda**

Despite its evocative-sounding name, Samarinda is a rough, hard-edged port which over the last decade has prospered and expanded on the back of the timber industry. The town is strategically positioned on the muddy Mahakam river and is the main gateway to the interior of East Kalimantan for tourists, logging concessions and gold-miners alike.

The town centre rises from the main commercial zone that hugs the waterfront, the latter home to the unmistakably renovated **Mesjid Raya** and the **Pasar Pagi** (market), into a hilly residential district where a luxury hotel and the tourist office are located. The town has numerous banks and mid-range hotels, as well as plenty of handicraft and antique shops along the riverside road (Jalan Gajah Mada). Public and private boats leave from the jetty in front of the Pasar Pagi.

▶▶ **Singkawang** 214A3

▶▶ **Singkawang**

This rural trading town, 145km northwest of Pontianak, was founded by Hakka Chinese following the 18th-century gold-rush to Sambas and, later, Monterado. It is a

Dayak weavings

Traditional Dayak weaving continues today, and even more tourist-oriented pieces have a complexity of design and subtlety of colours that make them tempting buys. *Doyo* fibres, spun from a type of grass or sometimes from the pineapple leaf, are woven into *ikats* by the Benuaq Dayaks. These are widely sold in the lower Mahakam area, at Tanjung Isui and Samarinda.

Riverside structures at Samarinda

well-kept, pleasant place characterised by Chinese shop-houses, but its greatest attraction lies at **Pasir Panjang►►**, a beautiful palm-fringed beach south of town on the Pontianak road that is equipped with cottage accommodation, watersports facilities and *warungs* (food-stalls). More good beaches lie on the outlying coral island of **Pulau Randayan** and to the north around Pemangkat (**Tanjung Batu**).

Singkawang is also famed for the traditional Chinese ceramics fired at the village of **Sakok**, 7km south, and for rare sightings of the *Rafflesia* flower on the slopes of Gunung Puting, immediately to the east. Further afield is the gold-mining town of **Sambas**, site of an impressive royal mosque and a palace which houses a few antiques, and close to the traditional weaving villages of Pendawan, Manggis and Semberang.

► **Sungai Kapuas** *214A2*

The Kapuas river meanders some 1,100km west from its source in the Müller Range in the mountainous heart of Borneo to enter the sea near Pontianak. Loggers and Christian missionaries have left their marks on the region, though tourism has yet to come. It is only beyond Sintang (8–9 hours by bus or 2 days by boat from Pontianak) that primary forest and Kenatyan Dayak traditions really become noticeable and justify the trip.

Sintang►► makes a good base for exploring, offering basic hotels, boats heading south down Sungai Melawi or onwards along the Kapuas through Iban country around Semitau to Putussibau, and treks into the Bening Forest Reserve or up Bukit Kelam, about 18km from town. **Putussibau**, where Dayak longhouses are numerous, is the last stop for the Kapuas public boat service. From here the really adventurous can head up into the mountains to reach the Mahakam river, but guides are essential for such a major expedition.

►► **Sungai Mahakam** *215D3*

This 920km waterway is Kalimantan's most frequented river, tourists having a high profile as far as **Tanjung Isui** (see page 228). The last stop for public boats is **Long Bangun**, over 100km northwest of Long Iram (see page 220), although fluctuating water levels often curtail the journey. The best time to travel here is between September and December. Around **Rukun Damai** (between the two towns) is a spectacular region of primary rainforest where numerous highly decorated longhouses and their inhabitants offer vivid insights into Kenyah Dayak traditions and lifestyle. Beyond Long Bangun it is necessary to charter boats and guides, a costly business, and rapids enliven the adventure.

The entire trip by public boat along the Mahakam from Samarinda to Long Iram takes about 30 hours, and to Long Bangun about 40 hours. Accommodation is in *losmen* (budget inns) or longhouses, although most visitors opt for organised tours which provide comfortable houseboats. An alternative which cuts out the most populated part of the Mahakam is to take a small plane from Samarinda to **Long Lunuk** (also called **Data Dawai**), a settlement high in the Müller Range where you can negotiate boat hire with local Dayaks.

After the rain near Long Bangun on the Mahakam river

Logs
A familiar sight along the Mahakam are enormous rafts of loosely assembled logs being floated downstream for processing at Samarinda. East Kalimantan has the dubious status of being Indonesia's largest timber-producing province, and the effects of this are strikingly visible in the more accessible coastal regions. Shorn hillsides are more common than large tracts of virgin rainforest, a result of years of uncontrolled felling which is now, however, pricking a few consciences. In 1985 the export of whole logs was prohibited, a move which greatly boosted the sawmill industry and which has made Indonesia the world's second producer of tropical plywood. Further measures include a tax of Rp32,000 (US$16) per cu m of hardwood, money that is supposed to finance replanting.

Forest threats

Perladangan berpindah is the Indonesian term for shifting cultivation, long practised by the Dayaks. A patch of forest is cleared, dried out and the tree trunks burned, then rice is planted. Six months later harvesting takes place, followed theoretically by a two-year fallow period before replanting. If this method is carried out scrupulously, no harm is done, but this is not often the case with recent migrants. Bad shifting cultivation practices are often used as an argument by logging companies to justify their own destruction of the forest. Far more harmful are the catastrophic fires which have destroyed millions of hectares in the last 15 years. In 1982–3 some 29,000 sq km of forest went up in smoke in Kalimantan and in 1991 much of East and South Kalimantan disappeared into a thick haze for weeks. Last but not least in the destructive stakes is the uncontrollable practice of illegal logging.

Dayak woodcarving at Tenggarong's museum

► **Tanjung Isui**   *215D2*

East Kalimantan's main Dayak tourist centre is found in this scenic village, which has been almost entirely converted to the needs of foreign visitors. It is located beyond Muara Muntai near the shores of Danau Jempang, the last of a series of lakes strung along the marshes of the lower Mahakam. Preferring individual stilt-houses, villagers have abandoned their traditional long-houses; instead these are now used for cultural performances, handicraft displays (this is a good source of *doyo* weavings) and tourist accommodation. An older, less touristy longhouse can be visited 8km away at Mancong, easily reached by road or by river, with others a few kilometres further on. Wildlife at the three large lakes of Semayang, Melintang and Jembang includes easily sighted freshwater dolphins. Tanjung Isui is about 14 hours by public boat from Samarinda.

►►► **Tanjung Puting, Taman Nasional**   *214B1*

The 305,000 hectares of this long-established reserve on the south coast of Kalimantan are known above all for their orang-utan rehabilitation centres at Camp Leakey and at Tanjung Harapan. The reserve progresses from nipa palm, mangrove and peat swamps near the coast to lowland dipterocarp forest further inland, all of which claim a fantastic variety of wildlife. The Sekonyer river, which crosses the park, offers good sightings of salt-water dolphins at its mouth in Kumai Bay, as well as proboscis monkeys, gibbons, deer, crab-eating macaques, monitor lizards and crocodiles along its forested banks. Some 200 bird species include herons, storks, egrets, hornbills, kingfishers, flycatchers and bulbuls.

Wild and rehabilitated orang-utans are occasionally seen, but the best place to observe them is at the rehabilitation centres. **Camp Leakey**, the original centre, was set up in 1971 by the Canadian Dr Biruté Galdikas, and incorporates a 3,000-hectare study area criss-crossed by trails. The shaggy, rusty coated apes can easily be seen here outside feeding times (late afternoon). The more accessible **Tanjung Harapan** station was developed later to cope with increased visitor numbers.

Police and park permits are essential for visiting the Tanjung Puting reserve. The first is obtained from the Kantor Polisi in Pangkalanbuun and a copy should be presented with your passport on arrival at Kumai before registering at the PHPA office. Kumai is where *klotok* (motorised longboats) can be chartered to start the 4- or 5-hour trip up the Sekonyer river. It is possible to immerse yourself in jungle sounds by sleeping in a boat, but accommodation is available at Tanjung Harapan or, more comfortably, at an up-market hotel across the river.

A good way to recover from the hot and humid jungle is to finish the trip with a detour to either of two white-sand beaches, **Tanjung Keluang** or **Teluk Kubu**. The fishing village at the latter provides abundant fresh fish.

► **Tenggarong**   *215D2*

First stop up the Mahakam from Samarinda, or an hour away by road, is the former capital of the sultanate of Kutai, which moved here in 1872. Tenggarong's main sight lies right opposite the jetty – the **Museum Mulawarman**►

(*open*: Tuesday to Sunday, 10–2), an incongruous, pristine-white art deco building which stands out starkly in a land of corrugated-iron roofs and murky river water. The collection dwells heavily on royal memorabilia, including a re-created royal bedroom, the sultan's throne, his numerous *kris* (swords), clothes and photos. Chinese ceramics and local Dayak costumes and handicrafts complete the offerings. Next to the museum is a newly built *warung* (food-stall) and souvenir-shop complex, in high contrast to the older buildings toppling over the river banks.

Once a year in late September this dozy little town springs to life with the Erau Festival, which celebrates Tenggarong's illustrious past. Dayaks stream in from the surrounding region to indulge in traditional food, sports, music and dance, the proceedings culminating in the ceremonial throwing of a mock dragon into the Mahakam.

Boat passengers travelling along the Mahakam river never go hungry

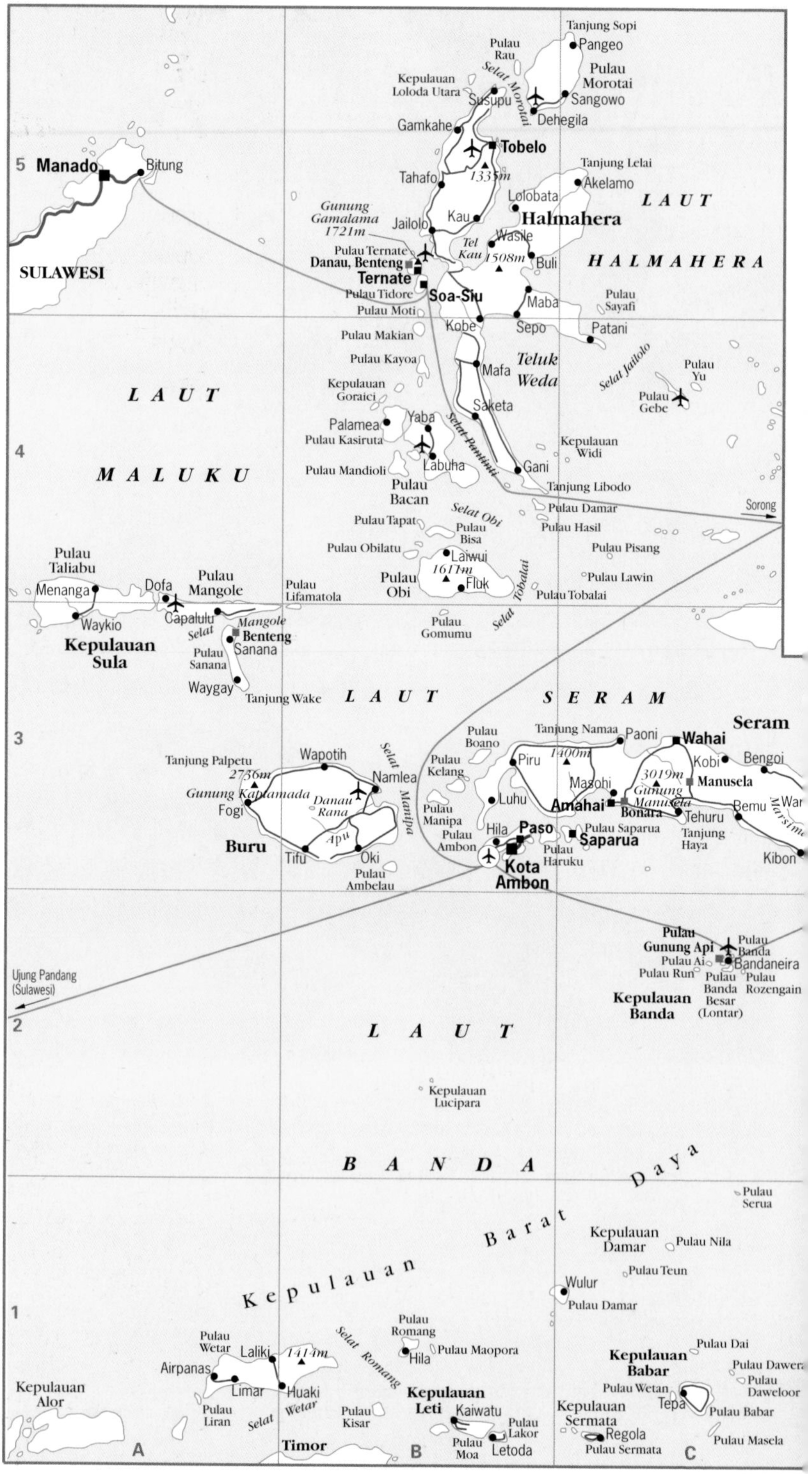

MALUKU

Tanjung Sopi
Pangeo
Pulau Rau
Pulau Morotai
Selat Morotai
Sangowo
Kepulauan
Loloda Utara
Susupu
Dehegila
Gamkahe
Tobelo
Tanjung Lelai
LAUT
Tahafo
1335m
Akelamo
Manado
Bitung
Jailolo
Kau
Lofobata
Gunung
Gamalama
1721m
Halmahera
HALMAHERA
SULAWESI
Pulau Ternate
Danau, Benteng
Ternate
Tel
Kau
Wasile
Buli
Pulau Tidore
Soa-Siu
1508m
Pulau Moti
Maba
Pulau Makian
Kobe
Sepo
Pulau
Sayafi
Patani
Pulau Kayoa
Mafa
Teluk
Weda
Kepulauan
Goraici
Saketa
Selat Jailolo
Pulau
Yu
Palamea
Yaba
Pulau Kasiruta
Gani
Pulau
Gebe
Pulau Mandioli
Labuha
Kepulauan
Widi
Pulau
Bacan
Tanjung Libodo
Selat Obi
Pulau Damar
Sorong
Pulau Tapat
Pulau
Bisa
Pulau Hasil
Pulau Obilatu
Lawui
Pulau Pisang
Pulau
Taliabu
Pulau
Mangole
Pulau
Lifamatola
Pulau
Obi
1611m
Fluk
Pulau Lawin
Menanga
Dofa
Pulau Tobalai
Waykio
Mangole
Selat
Benteng
Sanana
Pulau
Gomumu
Selat
Kepulauan
Sula
Pulau
Sanana
Waygay
Tanjung Wake
LAUT
SERAM
Seram
Tanjung Palpetu
Wapotih
Tanjung Namaa
Paoni
Wahai
2736m
Namlea
Pulau
Boano
1400m
Piru
Kobi
Bengoi
Gunung Kapalamada
Selat
Pulau
Kelang
Magohi
3019m
Manusela
Fogi
Danau
Rana
Manipa
Luhu
Gunung
Manusela
Bemu
War
Buru
Apu
Pulau
Manipa
Amahai
Bonara
Tehuru
Tifu
Oki
Hila
Paso
Pulau Saparua
Tanjung
Haya
Pulau
Ambelau
Pulau
Ambon
Saparua
Kibon
Kota
Ambon
Pulau
Haruku
Pulau
Gunung Api
Banda
Pulau Ai
Bandaneira
Ujung Pandang
(Sulawesi)
Pulau Run
Pulau
Banda
Besar
(Lontar)
Pulau
Rozengain
Kepulauan
Banda
LAUT
Kepulauan
Lucipara
BANDA
Daya
Barat
Pulau
Serua
Kepulauan
Damar
Pulau Nila
Wulur
Pulau Teun
Pulau Damar
Kepulauan
Pulau
Romang
Hila
Pulau Maopora
Pulau Dai
Pulau
Wetar
Laliki
1414m
Pulau Dawera
Kepulauan
Babar
Airpanas
Selat
Romang
Pulau
Daweloor
Kepulauan
Alor
Limar
Huaki
Wetar
Pulau Wetan
Tepa
Pulau Babar
Pulau
Liran
Selat
Pulau
Kisar
Kepulauan
Leti
Kaiwatu
Kepulauan
Sermata
Timor
Pulau
Moa
Pulau
Lakor
Letoda
Regola
Pulau Masela
Pulau Sermata

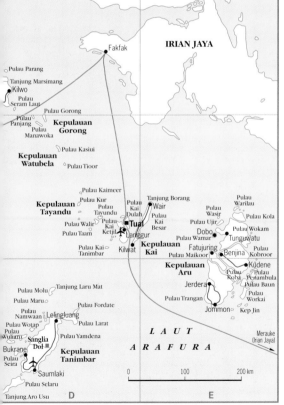

IRIAN JAYA

Fakfak

Pulau Parang

Tanjung Marsimang
Kilwo
Pulau
Seram Laut

Pulau Gorong

Pulau
Panjang
Pulau
Manawoka

**Kepulauan
Gorong**

**Kepulauan
Watubela**

Pulau Kasiui

Pulau Tioor

Pulau Kaimeer

Pulau Kur
Pulau
Tayundu

**Kepulauan
Tayandu**

Pulau
Kai
Dulah

Tanjung Borang
Wair

Pulau
Warilau

Pulau
Wasir

Pulau Kola

Pulau Walir
Pulau Taam

Pulau
Kai
Ketjil

Pulau
Kai
Besar

Pulau Ujir

Pulau Wokam

Tual
Langgur

Dobo

Tunguwatu

Pulau Wamar

Pulau Kai
Tanimbar

Kilwat

**Kepulauan
Kai**

Fatujuring

Pulau Maikoor

Benjina

Pulau
Kobroor

**Kepulauan
Aru**

Kudene

Pulau
Koba
Pulau
Penambula
Pulau Baun

Jerdera

Pulau
Workai

Pulau Trangan

Jommon
Kep Jin

Pulau Molu
Tanjung Laru Mat

Pulau Maru

Pulau
Namwaan
Lelingluang

Pulau Fordate

Pulau Wotap
Wuliaru

Pulau Larat

**Sanglia
Dol**

Pulau Yamdena

Bukrane

**Kepulauan
Tanimbar**

Pulau
Seira

Saumlaki

Pulau Selaru

Tanjung Aro Usu

*LAUT
ARAFURA*

Merauke
(Irian Jaya)

0   100   200 km

D   E

MALUKU

When it rains

Maluku is one of those tricky Indonesian regions which has an inverted and self-contradictory rainy season. The equatorial area of north and central Maluku (Ternate, Ambon, Seram and Banda) is best visited from October to March when temperatures hit a sticky 38°C but rains are scarce (although winds can be very strong in February). From April to September, deluges are virtually ceaseless, peaking in May to July and creating havoc with transport. In the southern Maluku Islands the climate is closer to that of Nusa Tenggara, with a much lower rainfall and fine weather from May to September. Seram further complicates the pattern, the weather along its south coast in tune with that of central Maluku but its north coast experiencing rain and winds from September to March.

Maluku's geographical isolation ensures an unhurried existence

Maluku Imagine an area measuring 850,000 sq km, of which 90 per cent consists of the deep-blue sea. This is Maluku, once known as the Moluccas, an erratic chain of over 1,000 volcanic, coral and limestone islands curving down the map between the Philippines and Timor. This lush archipelago forms a geological and biological transition zone between Asia and Australia, a factor that is reflected in its flora and fauna, in its underwater life and in its indigenous people. Equally noticeable is the source of its former fame: spices.

Tourism is in its early days here and comfortable accommodation is limited to Ambon, Banda and Ternate. And while opportunities for exploring are endless, you need plenty of spare time as frequently cancelled flights mean that inter-island boats become the only option.

Spice Wars The Portuguese who anchored off Banda in 1511 set into motion three centuries of dispute, conflict, rebellion and misery known as the Spice Wars. After the Portuguese came the Spanish under Magellan (who died *en route*) in 1521, followed by the English under Sir Francis Drake in 1579 and finally Cornelius de Houtman's Dutch fleet in 1599. With the fading of Portuguese maritime power and the founding of the VOC (Dutch United East India Company) in 1602, European trading knives were officially drawn.

By 1621, guided by ruthless Governor-General Jan Pieterszoon Coen, the Dutch had secured their aim of a total monopoly of the spice trade. Machiavellian to the extreme, Dutch methods included rape, torture and massacre, as well as the destruction of any spice-bearing trees that lay outside their control. This monopoly spelled economic disaster for local Moluccan traders and farmers before itself dying out when clove plantations were set up in Zanzibar in the late 19th century, so turning the Moluccas into the backwater they remain today.

Surviving traditions Maluku's population of 1.8 million, about 45 per cent Christian and 55 per cent Muslim, is a mixture of indigenous Austropolynesians with marked Papuan influence, and Bugis, Makassarese and Javanese along the coasts. Traditional societies survive in the hinterland of larger islands such as Pulau Seram, while other islands such as Ternate and Tidore maintain strong bonds with their powerful sultanate pasts; even Ambon, bristling with church spires, continues to witness esoteric rites and black magic.

Banda Islands

This minuscule group of coral-fringed islands, flung into the limpid depths of the Banda Sea, is recognised as one of the world's finest scuba- and skin-diving destinations. Six main islands and various atolls surround **Pulau Banda** itself, where the airstrip, harbour and accommodation (but no banks) focus on the tiny capital of Bandaneira. Looming opposite is the majestic island volcano of **Gunung Api** (650m), still smoking after its last major eruption in 1988 but offering fabulous summit panoramas into its crater and over the surrounding islands. Between Gunung Api and Pulau Banda is a beautiful natural lagoon, while to the south lies the largest island in the group, **Banda Besar** (also called **Lontar**). Further out to the west are **Pulau Ai** (which has a few homestays) and **Pulau Run**, and to the east **Pulau Rozengain**. Canoes or motorboats can easily be rented from Bandaneira to reach deserted beaches, snorkel over bewitching underwater landscapes or dive into paradise itself.

Nutmeg and forts Lush tropical vegetation and coconut palms combine with nutmeg and mace groves to cloak the islands, while old Dutch forts indicate their former economic significance. Banda itself claims two forts overlooking the harbour. The restored **Fort Belgica** (1611), built by Governor-General Jan Pieterszoon Coen, is linked by an underground tunnel to **Fort Nassau** (1609) which crumbles elegantly below. Banda Besar's **Fort Concordia** and **Fort Hollandia** (1624) were mostly destroyed by an earthquake, but their hilltop remains offer ever more superb views of the archipelago. Another earthquake victim is **Fort Revengil** (1616) on Pulau Ai, which was rebuilt in 1753 and still sports a few Dutch cannon.

Bandaneira's gracefully fading past is echoed by numerous colonial villas, some of which are now being carefully restored. Colonial memorabilia, weapons and antiques are exhibited at the **Museum Rumah Budaya** in Bandaneira. Next door is the **Rumah Pengasingan (Exile Home)**, devoted to Indonesian nationalist leaders Sutan Sjahrir and Mohammed Hatta, both exiled here by the Dutch in the 1930s.

Banda's landmark, Gunung Api

Beneath the surface
Some 176 types of coral and over 120 varieties of fish are found in the transparent sea surrounding the Bandas, a fact that is attracting increasing numbers of divers. Diving equipment is available from the more up-market hotels run by Des Alwi, an enterprising local who, almost single-handedly, has saved the islands from sinking into oblivion. However, check your season before even approaching the Bandas: the rainy season can start in April and last until August, sometimes leaving tourists stranded as aircraft cannot land (see also panel opposite).

Nutmeg is obtained from the seed of Myristica fragrans and mace from the coating

233

Pulau Ambon

Cloves were used in China as early as the 3rd century AD

Ambon is Maluku's unavoidable transit island as all flights to more far-flung islands start and end here. Whether you arrive by ship or by plane and whatever your port of embarkation, the change in tempo is noticeable. You are now a long way from anywhere and the underlying sense of desolation in some run-down villages is heightened by the curious ethnic mix – part Polynesian, part Papuan, part Bugis and part Javanese.

The island is divided neatly into two parts, these joined by a narrow spit of land to create the huge, mountain-backed Ambon Bay. The airport, rather illogically, lies about 40km from the capital of Kota Ambon on the northern side of the bay, and most villages are dotted around the coast.

▶▶ Hila

234B2

A bumpy, potholed ride north from Kota Ambon takes you over the hilly spine of the Hitu Peninsula and down to the north coast at **Hitu**. Since pre-colonial days this area has been staunchly Muslim, and villagers today are fairly impoverished. Hila lies about 10km west along a beautiful, lush shore where thatched shacks topple on stilts over the water and children paddle around in canoes. The village of Hila has three major claims to fame: immaculately restored **Fort Amsterdam**, built in the 17th century on Portuguese foundations; nearby **Imanuel Church** which, though dating from 1780, suffered from earthquake damage and was rebuilt in the 1930s; and Maluku's oldest mosque, **Mesjid Wapauwe**, said to date from 1414, much rebuilt in 1664 and recently restored. Less monumental but equally significant is the **Rumah Kakehang**, an old meeting-house once used by a male-only village sect whose initiation ritual included bringing back a human head. If you intend travelling to Hila by *bemo* (minibus), allow an hour to get there and remember that the last *bemos* return at around 4pm.

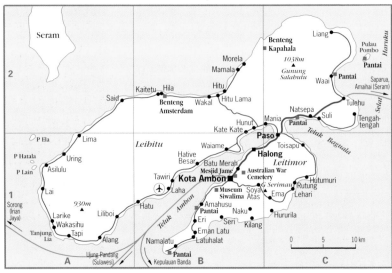

Drying cloves at Hila

Ambon's overpriced hotels are situated in the bustling but surprisingly ordered capital where even *becaks* (trishaws) obey one-way regulations. This uninspired immigrant port of over 200,000 inhabitants was mostly rebuilt after it was bombed during World War II, and its only real sight is the graceful old **Mesjid Jame** down near the main harbour, now repainted in tropical green. From here the main commercial street of **Jalan AJ Patty**, chock-a-block with craft and souvenir shops, runs east to the **Pasar Mardika** covered market and gigantic *bemo* station. Half-way along is the old market area, which spills across Jalan Yos Sudarso to the bay. This is where Bugis schooners and small inter-island boats dock, while larger cargo and passenger ships use the main harbour in front of the mosque. *Bemos* to north coast villages leave from the Batuh Merah terminal further east.

The capital's main cultural institution, the **Museum Siwalima▶▶▶** (*open*: Tuesday to Sunday, 8–2:30; Friday, 8–1) is located 3km west of town up a steep access road. It presents a well-organised and captioned (in English) background to Maluku history, crafts and ethnography, with a fascinating section on head-hunting rituals, black magic and animist carvings. A poignant Allied Forces **War Cemetery** is located a few kilometres east of town at Tantui on the airport road. Over 2,000 Australian, New Zealand, British, Indian and Dutch servicemen are buried here in a beautifully tended tropical garden overlooking the bay.

Clove craft
The most spectacular of Ambon's crafts are the superb model ships made entirely of cloves mounted on to a wire structure, intricate and fragrant creations sometimes even peopled by miniature sailors. Many of these ships are made at the village of Latuhalat. Less subtle are the kitsch landscape collages of iridescent mother-of-pearl and shell. Shell crafts extend to lamps, trays and boxes, and there is plenty of pearl and coral jewellery. While you will also see items made from dugong tusks and tortoise shells, do not buy these as the animals are now classed as endangered species.

Becak special

Kota Ambon's *becaks* (trishaws) come in either white, yellow, or red. Tuesdays and Fridays are reserved for white *becaks*, Mondays and Thursdays for yellow, and Wednesdays and Saturdays for red. Sundays see *becaks* of all three colours. The reason for this? It is an inspired attempt by the local government at job-sharing, thus multiplying career openings for Ambon's youth. However, many *becak*-drivers get around these restrictions by owning more than one *becak*, each of a different colour!

▶▶ Latuhalat/Namalatu 234B1

The only alternative to staying in Kota Ambon is to head south to these adjoining coastal villages where bungalow accommodation, homestays and a diving centre are located. The rocky coast, interspersed with some secluded beaches, is edged with palm groves and there is reasonable snorkelling and diving along the offshore reefs. These reefs, as well as those off the northeast coast, have suffered considerable damage from fish-bombing, but none the less the fish are spectacular. The dirt road continues to the end of the point where a short scramble across rocks takes you to a spot offering sweeping views over Ambon Bay.

▶▶ Soya Atas 234B1

Soya's importance is firmly linked with the arrival of Christianity as it was here that St Francis Xavier, the Jesuit missionary, preached in 1546. The tidy villages bordering the typically lush road winding up to Soya are bastions of Catholicism and on a Sunday outing up here you will witness crowds of well-dressed churchgoers. Soya's raja once controlled Kota Ambon and his house stands opposite a quaint little church on the main village square. Up behind the village is an ancient ceremonial meeting-place (*balileo*) and, further up the hill, a sacred stone megalith whose site offers magnificent 360-degree views of the island.

▶ Tulehu 234C2

Some 25km from Kota Ambon on the northeast coast is the pretty fishing village of Tulehu, the departure point for ferries to Seram and Saparua. Its beach claims hot sulphurous wells, a simple homestay and reasonable swimming. Most people come here to visit **Waai**, just 5km north, where the local raja's former bathing-pools are now inhabited by a family of giant 'holy' eels which are fed eggs regularly by a keeper. Not surprisingly, Waai is imbued with legends and is much revered by the local Ambonese.

Coconut groves line the coast at Namalatu

Pulau Seram

Maluku's largest island completely dwarfs Pulau Ambon in scale, claims the region's highest mountain (Gunung Manusela, at 3,019m), yet rarely sees Westerners. Settlements are limited to the coastline, leaving a rugged, sparsely populated interior of dense forest, waterfalls and generous rivers. Portuguese missionaries visiting in the 16th century and subsequent Dutch control did little to change some of the extraordinary habits of Seram's indigenous inhabitants. Head-hunting is said to have stopped (although only recently), but the Bati tribe of the southern mountains maintain their reputation for being able to fly. More probable airborne sightings are of Seram's fantastic birds, including cockatoos, kingfishers, parrots, hornbills, honey-eaters and megapodes.

Secret Seram
The indigenous tribes of Seram's wild interior, collectively known as Alfuro, were long feared by the Ambonese for their black-magic powers, their ability to 'fly' and to make themselves invisible, and their propensity for head-hunting. The Naulu, above all, were respected warriors and were often employed to defend coastal villages against Papuan raids from Irian Jaya.

Harvesting sago

Animist rites remain central to Naulu life

South coast Frequent boats from Ambon dock at **Amahai** on the south coast where the airstrip is also located, although accommodation is concentrated at **Masohi**, about 15km north on vast Elpaputih Bay. This entire area offers little charm, but there are some interesting traditional villages near by. Easiest of access is **Bonara**, a cluster of thatched stilt-houses surrounded by sago palms and cassava fields where Naulu men, identifiable by their red headbands, will stage a *Cakalele* war dance for a fee. Other Naulu villages, such as Watane and Janeero, lie within walking distance of Bonara.

Manusela National Park This 100,000-hectare swathe of forest commences in the coastal plains of the south, rises to a high central valley, then rolls down to the north coast just west of **Wahai**. The PHPA office is located at this small port, which can be reached directly from Kota Ambon. If entering the park from the south near **Tehuru** (again, best reached by ferry), register with the police before setting off. The entire, arduous trek across the centre takes at least a week and a guide is essential.

■ **Maluku's varied and unusual flora and fauna will astound those that strike out into its tropical forests or plunge beneath its enticing waters. And if you meet a long-toothed dugong, try to believe (as mariners once did) that it is a mermaid.....■**

Those that don't fly
Two flightless birds of Maluku, the scrub-fowl and the cassowary, are unfortunately both favoured victuals of local inhabitants. The balding scrub-fowl can also be found burying its eggs in Sulawesi's sands (see panel on page 210), while the extraordinary cassowary is a typically Australasian species whose feathers are greatly prized by Irian Jaya's Asmats. The bird's aggressive defence mechanism is embodied in ferocious claws, an impressive height (approaching 2m) and protruding black quills which replace wings.

One of the 200-odd species of the Heliconia *family, which also includes the banana palm*

As Indonesia's large land masses splinter off into the thousand-odd islands of Maluku scattered across the Banda Sea, so the flora and fauna changes. For Darwin's contemporary, Alfred R Wallace, 'The glorious birds and insects render the Moluccas a classic ground in the eyes of the naturalist, and characterise its fauna as one of the most beautiful and beautiful in the world.' Wallace's theory of a divisional ecological line cutting down the Makassar Strait may have been proved erroneous, but Maluku certainly represents a transitional zone between the dominant mammals of Asia and the marsupials of Australasia. Numerous Moluccan bird and insect species overlap with those of neighbouring Irian Jaya and Sulawesi, but selective migration and geographical isolation have also created unique species and hybrids.

Island foliage The basic vegetation of Maluku is monsoon forest, a partly seasonal mixed tropical forest which is considerably lower in height, less dense and less varied than the dipterocarp forest found in Borneo and Sumatra. Maluku's luxuriant landscapes also see Australian eucalyptus trees, sago, coconut and banana palms, and, of course, groves of clove and nutmeg trees that brought the region its ephemeral glory. These beautiful, fragrant trees which thrive on high humidity are a characteristic sight in Banda, Ambon, Ternate and Tidore.

Ubiquitous throughout the islands is the multi-purpose sago palm, which provides Maluku's staple diet as well as fibre for rope and mats, leaves for thatch, and sap, which is turned into the local alcoholic tipple. Another bonus is the ease with which sago is harvested, ten days' work producing a year's food supply. Less functional though more aesthetic are the wild orchids that proliferate in Pulau Ambon and the Tanimbar Islands, most famous being the deep violet or white *anggrek Larat* (*Dendrobium phalaenopsis*) from Larat Island.

Winged beauties Wallace's endless treks through Maluku's forests produced a count of 265 bird species, many of which exist in Irian Jaya. Most famed, and for centuries most sought after, are the spectacular birds of paradise which are found in the Aru Islands in the far southeast of the archipelago. A total of 26 species of this magnificent bird exist, the ornamental silky plumage changing according to their mating instincts. The late 19th-century fashion for their feathers saw thousands of these creatures succumb to hunters' arrows. And the practice is not over, despite the fact that the birds are theoretically endangered species. Other vivid birds include kingfishers, pigeons and some 25 species of

The cassowary: with quills instead of wings, it is a bird that cannot fly. Its kick, however, may be fatal

Pungent fruit
Common throughout Southeast Asia and grown abundantly in Maluku is the notorious durian, the 'king of fruits', which possesses the remarkable qualities of combining a sewer-like odour with an addictively ambivalent flavour. The green skin is covered with a thorny coating, painful if your penknife slips, but the rewards of its creamy white interior are great. No description has yet managed to pinpoint the durian's taste, which combines aspects of the avocado, custard, almonds, onions, yoghurt and cheese. You'll either love it or loathe it.

239

parrot, from red-crested cockatoos to crimson lories and the garish Amboina king parrot.

Land and sea beasts Few land mammals made it to Maluku (Wallace counted ten, most of these introduced by man). Indigenous wildlife is mainly limited to marsupials, from the agile opossum to the bandicoot and the slow-moving tree-dwelling cuscus, an endearing furry creature with huge saucer eyes that is an easy target for hunters. The islands of Aru and Kai share fauna with Irian Jaya, such as tree kangaroos, crocodiles and monitor lizards, as well as an astonishing wealth of insect life. Brightly coloured butterflies are thick in the air, and in the case of the green and blue great bird-wing butterfly their span reaches 20cm. Closer to the ground are armies of beetles and spiders.

Out in the waves is the increasingly rare dugong, super-ficially similar but unrelated to the walrus that is said (incredibly) to have inspired sailors' tales of seductive mermaids. The dugong's teeth have long been favourites for necklaces and it is now an endangered species. Meanwhile, beneath the surface of the seas teems one of the world's greatest concentrations of tropical fish.

The cuscus, one of Maluku's indigenous marsupials

A shady pitch at Ternate's market

Pulau Ternate's small size is dominated by the volcano of Gunung Gamalama

Pulau Ternate

This perfect volcanic cone rising out of the Maluku Sea was once home to the most powerful sultanate of the region, whose influence extended to Sulawesi and Irian Jaya. With the 1521 arrival of the Portuguese, Ternate's lucrative cloves were siphoned off to the West, a habit that continued under the period of Spanish control and, finally, the Dutch monopoly.

Today the fervently Muslim island still has a foothold in the clove and nutmeg trade, but its economy has diversified to pearls, fish, cocoa and copra. Visitors will find Pulau Ternate a stunningly beautiful though limited destination, with ruined forts, lakes, lava flows and the omnipresent volcanic peak of Gunung Gamalama all contained within an area barely 10km in diameter.

▶▶▶   Gunung Gamalama   230B5

An ascent of this active 1,721m volcano is best undertaken with a guide from the village of Marikrobo on its eastern flank. The tough, 1-day trek can also take in the **Afo ('Giant') clove tree**, said to be the world's oldest at about 400 years and once producer of 360kg per harvest. Gamalama's summit is topped by a smouldering crater and offers spectacular views. The last eruptions were as recent as 1987 and 1990, so it is essential to obtain advance information from the tourist office in town.

▶▶   Pulau Tidore   230B5

This neighbouring and once rival island can be visited on a day-trip by taking the ferry from Bastiong (just south of Ternate town) to **Rum** on Tidore's north coast. Although slightly larger than Ternate, Tidore is less developed and its turbulent history, which saw it as a pawn tossed between colonial powers, left it with a marked Papuan influence and two ruined forts. Cloves, coffee, fruit and tobacco are cultivated in the fertile volcanic soil on the lower slopes of **Gunung Matabu** (1,730m), this agricultural abundance best witnessed on market days (check at

Arriving

All visitors arriving in Indonesia must have a passport valid for six months and proof of onward passage – either a return flight or through-tickets to another destination. Immigration officials often demand to see such proof, particularly at Denpasar airport in Bali.

Visas

No visa is required for nationals of the following countries to spend up to two months in Indonesia: UK or any other European country, Australia, Canada, New Zealand, USA. Passports are stamped on entry, and woe

betide any tourist who overstays his or her welcome. For those who wish to stay longer, the solution is to leave Indonesia and return via one of the shortest foreign routes (Bali–Singapore, Kupang– Darwin, Pontianak–Sarawak, Medan–Kuala Lumpur or Medan– Singapore).

Customs regulations

Customs allowances are 2 litres of alcohol, 200 cigarettes or 50 cigars or 100g of tobacco, and a 'reasonable amount' of perfume. Radios, cassette recorders, television sets, pornographic material, arms, ammunition, narcotics and printed matter in Chinese are all prohibited. There is no restriction on import or export of foreign currencies and traveller's cheques, but Indonesian currency is limited to Rp50,000 whether you are coming or going.

Travel insurance

It is essential to take out a reliable travel insurance before arriving in

The mythical garuda eagle logo of the national airline

PK-GAO

Indonesia. Make sure it covers repatriation for any emergency health problems, and also so-called 'dangerous sports' such as white-water rafting if you intend doing any. Most travel agencies will offer recommendable policies.

Arriving by air The majority of international flights to Indonesia arrive at Jakarta (Java), Denpasar (Bali) or Medan (Sumatra), with a lesser number arriving at the foreign entry points of Manado (Sulawesi), Pulau Ambon (Maluku), Pulau Batam (Riau Archipelago), Pulau Biak (Irian Jaya), Kupang (Timor), Pontianak or Balikpapan (Kalimantan), Pekanbaru (Sumatra) and Surabaya (Java). Choose your arrival airport carefully according to what region you intend to explore – the archipelago is large and internal transport often poor.

Jakarta's **Sukarno-Hatta Airport**, an impressive Javanese-style construction, is over 30km from the city centre, a distance which may take at least an hour to cover during morning and evening rush hours. Taxis are plentiful (though they may attempt to impose a flat fee instead of using the meter) and there are regular Damri airport buses which serve different points in Jakarta (Kemayoran, Gambir, Rawamangun, Blok M and Kebayoran Baru). Money-changers, duty-free shops, telephones, fax machines, telex facilities, hotel reservation desks, car-rental desks, tourist information desks and coffee-shops can be found in Terminal II, serving international and Garuda domestic flights at its sub-terminals D, E and F. Terminal I (sub-terminals A, B and C) concentrates on domestic flights but has the same facilities. For departure and arrival information at Sukarno-Hatta Airport, tel: 021 550 5307/9.

Bali's **Ngurah Rai Airport** lies at Denpasar on the southwest coast, only a few kilometres from Kuta. Inevitably, it abounds in taxi-sharks at the ready to spirit you anywhere on the island; take your time and bargain hard as there is no shortage. The two adjoining terminals (international and domestic), both in inspired Balinese architectural style, are efficient and offer all necessary facilities. For Ngurah Rai Airport information, tel: 0361 25662/3.

Indonesia's third main international airport is **Polonia Airport** at Medan in Sumatra (tel: 061 512444). It lies on the edge of the city and can even be reached by trishaw if you are desperate. Here the facilities and style are more basic, matching those you will meet at most provincial airports throughout Indonesia.

Arriving by sea Few visitors arrive by sea unless coming from Pulau Pinang (Malaysia) or Singapore. From Pinang there are regular catamaran and hydrofoil services (Selesa Express) which take 4–5 hours and arrive at Medan's port of Belawan, 25km north of the city. Tickets can be bought in Medan at **Selesa Express**, Jalan Brig Jend Katamso 35C (tel: 061 514888).

From Singapore there are frequent express boats to the islands of Batam (30 minutes) and Bintan (4 hours) in the Riau Archipelago, from where connecting boats or planes continue to Sumatra, Java and Kalimantan. Another sea route exists between Melaka (Malaysia) and Dumai (Sumatra), but this is not an international entry point. For those cargo-boat-hopping around the Indian Ocean, the seaports which allow international entry are: Belawan (Medan, Sumatra); Batu Ampar and Sekupang (Pulau Batam,Riau Archipelago); Tanjung Pinang (Pulau Bintan, Riau Archipelago); Tanjung Priok (Jakarta); Tanjung Perak (Surabaya, Java); Tanjung Emas (Semarang, Java); Benoa (Bali); and Padangbai (Bali).

Departure
Airport departure taxes are charged for both domestic and international flights, although the former should be included in your ticket price. Check on purchase, as many regional airports do a lucrative trade in charging extra taxes; if you know it has been paid with your ticket, be adamant and refuse to pay again. International departure tax is currently Rp21,000 (US$10). Always reconfirm your international flight 72 hours in

Climate

Theoretically, most of Indonesia experiences the West Monsoon (rainy season) which starts in November/December and continues into April. However, many regions offer contrasts and surprising micro-climates. The only stable factor is the temperature, which is 27–33°C at sea-level with daily variations of about 6°C, but diminishes as you scale the volcanic heights. High humidity is also a constant companion (75–100 per cent), although island breezes often offset this.

Broadly speaking, the wettest parts of Indonesia are equatorial Sumatra, Kalimantan and central Irian Jaya. Sumatra's west coast hardly sees a month without downpours (the driest months are June and July), but the central valleys and plateaux have far less rain. Kalimantan varies from north to south, being noticeably drier in the southern regions and much wetter in the central mountains (40 per cent of the island experiences some nine months of rain which only lets up in July to September). Irian Jaya's climate varies from the dry southern coast (particularly dry from June to November) to the wet mountainous centre.

Java and Bali share a more predictable pattern, with a dry season lasting from May to October, but as you move east through Nusa Tenggara this season is markedly longer and temperatures rise as the effects of the hot South Pacific trade winds are felt. Sulawesi abounds in microclimatic anomalies but sees less rain in August to October.

Downpours keep the rivers flowing

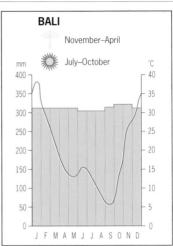

BALI

November–April

July–October

Maluku sees the greatest contrasts of all, with a reversed rainy season taking place in May to October, although there are even variants to this within the region.

National holidays

● New Year's Day
1 January
● Isra' Mi'raj (movable Muslim festival for Muhammad's Ascension)
January/February
● Nyepi (movable Hindu 'day of silence' at spring equinox)
March
● Good Friday
March/April
● Kartini Day (women's day)
21 April
● Waisak Day (movable Buddhist festival)
May
● Idul Adha (movable Muslim 'festival of sacrifice')
May/June
● Muharram (movable Muslim New Year)
June/July
● Independence Day
17 August
● Garebeg Maulud (movable Muslim celebration of Muhammad's birthday)
August/September
● Christmas Day
25 December

The all-important fasting month of Ramadan falls in the ninth month of

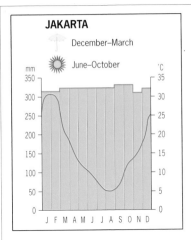

JAKARTA

December–March

June–October

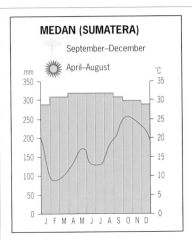

MEDAN (SUMATERA)

September–December

April–August

the Muslim calendar and terminates with two days of extensive celebrations (called dul Fitri). Travelling during Ramadan can be tricky in more orthodox areas as you may have to participate in the fast.

Time differences
The archipelago spreads over three time zones. Western Indonesia Standard Time covers Sumatra, Java, Madura, and West and Central Kalimantan, and is 7 hours ahead of GMT. Central Indonesia Standard Time covers East and South Kalimantan, Sulawesi, Bali and Nusa Tenggara, and is 8 hours ahead of GMT. Eastern Indonesia Standard Time, which covers Maluku and Irian Jaya, is 9 hours ahead of GMT.

Opening times
Business office hours are usually Monday to Friday, 8/9–4/5 with a 1-hour lunch break, and some companies also open on Saturday mornings. Government office hours are Monday to Thursday, 7–4; Friday, 7–4:30. Normal banking hours are Monday to Friday, 8–2:30. Shops keep longer hours, often 9–9, and some open on Sunday although in smaller towns many close daily, 1–5. Museums tend to follow government office hours, but remain open on Saturday and Sunday mornings and close on Monday. There are, however, plenty of local permutations; any unusual opening times of places of interest are listed in the A–Z

section of this guide, but as these may change it is best to check with the local tourist office before making a special journey.

Money matters
The Indonesian currency is the rupiah (Rp), with notes starting at Rp100 and ending at Rp50,000. Large denomination notes may be difficult to change in small towns, so always hoard small notes and change for *becaks* (trishaws), buses and *warungs* (food-stalls). Travelling in Indonesia requires cash as credit cards are accepted only in large hotels, top restaurants and for purchasing airline tickets.

If you intend sticking to the main tourist centres of Java and Bali you will have no problem changing major currencies at banks or money-changers, but in more obscure parts of the archipelago rates are poor and US dollars may be the only answer. In this case take a mixture of traveller's cheques and US dollars (in good condition otherwise they may be refused). On remote islands there are often no money-changing facilities so arm yourself with wads of rupiah. Banks which give reasonable rates are Bank Dagang Negara, Bank Negara Indonesia, Bank Exim and Bank Danamon (which also gives cash advances on credit cards). The worst rates are offered by Bank Rakyat Indonesia. Cash exchange rates are marginally better than those for traveller's cheques.

Car rental

Few regions in Indonesia are suitable for self-drive cars, the only ones being Java, Bali and Lombok. In other regions it is more common to hire a car with driver, more often than not a *bemo* (minibus) or, if you are lucky, a four-wheel drive. Enquire at local travel agents or tourist offices for details. Rental rates on Bali and Lombok are very reasonable and include unlimited mileage, but make sure all existing damage to the car is marked clearly on your rental contract. An international driving licence is required but not always asked for in Bali.

Petrol is cheap but in more rural areas it is not always easy to find; fill up at petrol stations as the roadside stalls which sell it in recycled bottles (occasionally artistically displayed) are not known for their quality. Ask your car-rental company for a contact number in case of breakdown.

Jakarta
● Avis (tel: 021 334495).
● Bluebird (tel: 021 314 3000/ 325607).
● Hertz (tel: 021 570 3683).
● Nasional (tel: 021 333423); branches in Bandung, Yogyakarta, Medan, Surabaya and Denpasar.
● Toyota Rentacar (tel: 021 362672/799 3207).

Minibuses are numerous

Surabaya
● Globe Renting Car (tel: 031 576900).
● Melani Taxi (tel: 031 817 5569).
● Rejeki Taxi (tel: 031 69553/69368).

Bali
● Bagus Car Rental Sanur (tel: 0361 287794/288329).
● Bali Car Rental Service Ngurah Rai (tel: 0361 88539/88550).
● Bali Wisata Motor Co Kuta (tel: 0361 51474).
● Samudra Car Rental Sanur (tel: 0361 88471).
● Toyota Rentacar (tel: 0361 751282/751356).

Lombok
● Metro Car Rental Mataram (tel: 0364 32146/33288).
● Rinjani Rent Car Mataram (tel: 0364 21400).
● Surya Car & Motorbike Rental Senggigi (tel: 0364 93076).

Driving tips Always drive more slowly than you would in your home country. Roads are not well maintained and errant rocks and pot-holes are worth watching out for, particularly if you are on a motor bike. During torrential rains roads suffer from mud-pools, flooding and/or landslides, while stray animals are a constant problem. Manic lorry- and bus-drivers can be dangerous, so don't tempt fate and keep a safe

distance. Signposts are not common and a detailed map is therefore essential to find your way. Avoid driving after nightfall when turn-offs, animals and village cyclists become invisible. In the case of an accident always contact the local police station (there is one in every village). Life-sized models of traffic-policemen grace every crossroads as a permanent deterrent to bad driving, though this seems to have little effect on locals.

Public transport

By train Railways are restricted to Java and southern Sumatra. The main lines connect Jakarta (Kota station) with Cirebon, Semarang and Surabaya, or with Bandung, Yogyakarta, Surakarta (Solo) and Surabaya. The northern route via Cirebon to Surabaya has one air-conditioned sleeper service (the **Mutiara**) which takes a flexible 12 hours, and an evening service as far as Semarang (the non air-conditioned **Senja Utama**) which takes approximately 8 hours.

The central route is used daily by the comfortable **Bima** express sleeper which completes the entire journey to Surabaya in about 14 hours. Less convenient is the **Senja Utama Solo** which leaves Jakarta in the evening and terminates at Solo

Becaks (trishaws) offer slow-paced touring at negotiable rates

some 11 hours later. Nine trains a day link Jakarta with Bandung. Three classes (economy, business and executive) offer varying levels of comfort. Reservations can be made painlessly at Jakarta's Gambir station or through travel agents.

By air Indonesia's domestic airlines have improved considerably with growing private competition, but **Merpati** (a subsidiary of the national airline **Garuda**) still monopolises many obscure routes so that you are entirely at its mercy. Merpati's 'commercial flights' are reasonably efficient but their 'pioneer flights', which operate in remote parts of Kalimantan, Sulawesi, Maluku and Irian Jaya, operate to standards well below the norm and should not in any sense be relied upon. Be prepared for the fact that flights may be delayed, if not cancelled outright, and that it will only be with calm forcefulness that you manage to get any kind of compensation for missed connections (food and a hotel).

Bouraq, currently undergoing a new look, operates mainly in Nusa Tenggara, Kalimantan and Sulawesi, while the ultra-efficient **Sempati** (owned by one of President

Suharto's sons) concentrates on major business routes. In Kalimantan, Sulawesi and Irian Jaya you can also fly with the non-commercial missionary flights of **Missionary Aviation Fellowship** (MAF) or **Associated Missions Aviation** (AMA), but they are under no obligation to take you and seats are not cheap (flight information can be obtained at local airstrips). If purchasing domestic tickets in Indonesia, book through a travel agent who should find the best price and option for your route.

Substantial discounts (25–50 per cent) are available on Garuda and Merpati domestic fights if you make your international flight with Garuda, but this is only really viable if you intend to fly extensively as the basic international tariff rises to accommodate the discount. The flights must be booked and paid for in your country of origin.

Another discount system is the **Visit Indonesia Pass**, valid for all Garuda/Merpati domestic flights. This is a flight coupon system (minimum three flights, maximum ten flights over 5–60 days) but routes must be pre-booked – in your country of origin if making your international flight with Garuda or, if arriving with

Passenger ferries ply Indonesia's rivers and seas

another airline, in Indonesia within 14 days of arrival.

Airline head offices in Jakarta:
- **Bouraq** Jalan Angkasa 1–3, Kemayoran (tel: 021 629 5150/ 659 5179).
- **Garuda** Jalan Merdeka Selatan 13 (tel: 021 380 1901).
- **Mandala** Jalan Garuda 76 (tel: 021 420 6645).
- **Merpati** Jalan Angkasa 2, Kemayoran (tel: 021 417404/ 413608).
- **Sempati** Jalan Merdeka Timur 7 (tel: 021 384 8760).

By ship Plying their way through the seas of the archipelago are seven large **PELNI** (Pelayaran Nasional Indonesia) passenger ships which cover fortnightly routes. The boats vary in modernity and size but all have four classes of cabin and one deck class. Meals are included in the fares, as are endless videos in deck class. If the schedule fits your own (PELNI ships are more punctual than Merpati planes), sailing makes a very pleasurable and more relaxing alternative to flying. The main office is at Jalan Gajah Mada 14, Jakarta (tel: 021 343307; fax: 021 381 0341) and every port has a branch.

Apart from these ships there are countless smaller craft, ferries and cargo boats that connect islands; ask at the local port for information.

By bus Long-distance buses do not always offer a comfortable ride but often they are the only option. It is advisable to buy your ticket in advance for infrequent routes. Luxury express buses with reclining seats, air-conditioning and videos cover unbelievable distances – for example, from Jakarta to Bima on the island of Sumbawa, or Banda Aceh in Sumatra to Bali – taking in ferries and food stops along the way. Night buses are not always advisable for safety or for comfort reasons. At the bottom of the ladder are the *bis kayu*, quite simply trucks with benches at the back, although these are only used now in Flores on unsealed roads. In Bali, parts of Java and Sumatra, comfortable and fast tourist buses operate extensively; enquire at local tourist offices.

City buses and short-distance buses offer endless variants on the *bemo* theme. These Toyota (or equivalent) minibuses theoretically take up to 12 passengers but in reality will squeeze in as many bodies as possible. Fares may be signposted and are usually paid to the driver's offsider or, in some cases, to the driver himself. Variously named *opelets*, *mikrolets*, *colts* or *angkutans*, they can offer excruciatingly

How many Sumbans can you fit into a bis kayu?

uncomfortable journeys unless you charter one. Other drawbacks are the time-consuming *keliling* (circling the town to look for passengers) and the high-decibel music. Despite these negative aspects, this is the best way of getting to know Indonesians.

Miscellaneous means Transport is never a problem in Indonesia, whether by taxi, *ojek* (motor-cycle taxis which in Medan even have side-cars), *becak* (trishaws), *dokar* or *bendi* (horse-drawn carts).

Student and youth travel
Railways offer student discounts of up to 25 per cent on production of an International Student Identity Card plus a back-up letter from your educational institution. Domestic airlines give a 50 per cent reduction for children under ten.

Permits
These are necessary for travelling into the interior of Irian Jaya. Take several passport photos and your passport to the police station at Biak or Jayapura, where the permits are issued quickly and efficiently.

Media

Approximately 7 million newspapers and magazines circulate daily throughout Indonesia. These include 126 dailies, 85 weeklies (minus the three 'outspoken' titles that were banned in June 1994), 35 fortnightlies and 62 monthly magazines. Although government control is nothing like that of neighbouring Singapore and Malaysia, the Indonesian press is expected to toe the line and respect the president and his family.

Three English-language newspapers are published in Jakarta, the most readable being the *Jakarta Post*, which can be found in all major towns and which occasionally produces some probing political comment. An English-language weekly, *Review Indonesia*, covers economic and financial news. Foreign newspapers are generally limited to the *International Herald Tribune* and the *Asian Wall Street Journal*, while *Time*, *Newsweek*, *The Economist* and the *Far Eastern Economic Review* are all distributed throughout the big cities.

The state-controlled Radio Republik Indonesia (RRI) broadcasts through 49 regional stations and there are also some 900 private stations, both commercial and non-commercial. Satellite television is now received even by the Papuans of Irian Jaya and Sulawesi's Bajau fishermen, and includes the government-run news and entertainment channel, Televisi Republik Indonesia (TVRI) and an

The local papers

educational channel, as well as four privately owned channels.

Depending on where you are in the archipelago it is also possible to watch CNN, Australian television or even a French overseas channel beamed at its territories in the Pacific Ocean.

Overseas mail and poste restante services are slow but reliable

Post offices and postal services

Kantor pos (post offices) are found in every Indonesian town and are open Monday to Friday, 8–4, and Saturday, 8–1pm. The postal service is reasonably reliable, although delivery time varies considerably and any important mail should be sent registered. Parcels up to 10kg can be sent by sea mail. Incoming poste restante mail is kept at every main post office and should be addressed to the addressee, Poste Restante, Kantor Pos, town name, region name. Such letters are generally kept unsorted in boxes which you are then left to sift through.

Telephone and fax

Telecom offices (*kantor telepon dan telegrap*) are run efficiently and nearly all offer fax and telex services. An alternative is to use the private chain of Wartel or Warpostel offices which are generally open until midnight.

Card-phones are a relatively new phenomenon, so you cannot rely on finding them outside big cities.
- Domestic operator 100.
- International operator 101.
- International enquiries 102.
- Regional enquiries 106.
- Jakarta enquiries 108.

For overseas calls, first dial 00, then the country and town codes, then the desired number. The code for Indonesia from abroad is 62.

Note that many phone numbers in Jakarta and other cities are changing, as they move from six digits to seven.

Language guide

Bahasa Indonesia is a fairly easy language which is well worth studying if you plan to go off the tourist track. English is the first foreign language spoken but is not widespread, so basic vocabulary is often essential – particularly numbers or prices. C is pronounced 'ch', the r is rolled; otherwise pronunciation follows spelling.

good morning (until 11am) selamat pagi
good-day (11–3) selamat siang
good afternoon (3–6) selamat sore
good evening selamat malam
goodnight selamat tidur
goodbye (to those leaving) selamat jalan
goodbye (to those staying) selamat tinggal
yes/no ya/tidak
please tolong
thank you terima kasih
you're welcome sama sama
excuse me permisi
much, many, very banyak
OK, fine baik
good, nice bagus
big/small besar/kecil
open/closed buka/tutup
where? where to? di mana? ke mana?
how much? how many? berapa?
how much (price)? berapa harga?
what is this/that? apa ini/itu?
is it far? apa jauh?
what time...? jam berapa...?
4 o'clock jam empat
4 hours empat jam
today/tomorrow hari ini/besok
week/month minggu/bulan

ticket karcis/tiket
bus station/train station stasiun bis/stasiun kereta api
what is your name? siapa nama anda?
my name is... nama saya...
I want to go to... saya mau pergi ke...
turn left/right belok kiri/kanan
straight on terus saja
I don't understand saya tidak mengerti
bedroom/private bathroom kamar/kamar mandi didalam
towel/soap handuk/sabun
toilet paper kertas WC ('way-say')
I want to see the room saya mau lihat kamar
laundry cuci

1	satu
2	dua
3	tiga
4	empat
5	lima
6	enam
7	tujuh
8	delapan
9	sembilan
10	sepuluh
11	sebelas
12	duabelas
13	tigabelas
20	duapuluh
21	duapuluh satu
30	tiga puluh
100	seratus
200	duaratus
250	duaratus limapuluh
1,000	seribu
2,000	duaribu
half-kilo	setengah kilo

Fatma Raksasa Raflesia Arnoldi Puspa Langka

Kartu Telepon 100 Unit Pulsa

KEHIDUPAN NELAYAN DI PANGANDARAN JAWA BARAT

KARTU TELEPON 100

CONVERSION CHARTS

FROM	TO	MULTIPLY BY
Inches	Centimetres	2.54
Centimetres	Inches	0.3937
Feet	Metres	0.3048
Metres	Feet	3.2810
Yards	Metres	0.9144
Metres	Yards	1.0940
Miles	Kilometres	1.6090
Kilometres	Miles	0.6214
Acres	Hectares	0.4047
Hectares	Acres	2.4710
Gallons	Litres	4.5460
Litres	Gallons	0.2200
Ounces	Grams	28.35
Grams	Ounces	0.0353
Pounds	Grams	453.6
Grams	Pounds	0.0022
Pounds	Kilograms	0.4536
Kilograms	Pounds	2.205
Tons	Tonnes	1.0160
Tonnes	Tons	0.9842

MEN'S SUITS

UK	36	38	40	42	44	46	48
Rest of Europe	46	48	50	52	54	56	58
US	36	38	40	42	44	46	48

DRESS SIZES

UK	8	10	12	14	16	18
France	36	38	40	42	44	46
Italy	38	40	42	44	46	48
Rest of Europe	34	36	38	40	42	44
US	6	8	10	12	14	16

MEN'S SHIRTS

UK	14	14.5	15	15.5	16	16.5	17
Rest of Europe	36	37	38	39/40	41	42	43
US	14	14.5	15	15.5	16	16.5	17

MEN'S SHOES

UK	7	7.5	8.5	9.5	10.5	11
Rest of Europe	41	42	43	44	45	46
US	8	8.5	9.5	10.5	11.5	12

WOMEN'S SHOES

UK	4.5	5	5.5	6	6.5	7
Rest of Europe	38	38	39	39	40	41
US	6	6.5	7	7.5	8	8.5

Crime and police

Indonesia is a fairly safe country for travellers, and petty crime is generally limited to Jakarta and other large cities. However, this does not mean that you should be relaxed about your valuables. Keep cash, traveller's cheques, passport and tickets in a safe place, preferably on your person, or use hotel safes when they are available. Market-places and public transport (particularly night trains and buses) are the dodgiest places, so be on your guard. Keep cameras and the like locked in your bag in the hotel room when not using them. If you are pickpocketed or robbed, report the incident to the police station for insurance purposes.

Embassies and consulates

● **Australian Embassy** Jalan HR Rasuna Said Kav C 15–16 Jakarta Selatan (tel: 021 522 7111; fax: 021 522 7101).
● **Australian Consulate** Jalan Raya Sanur 146, Tanjung Bungkak Denpasar, Bali (tel: 0361 35092/3).
● **British Embassy** Jalan MH Thamrin 75, Jakarta Pusat (tel: 021 330904; fax: 021 314 1824/390 2726).
● **Canadian Embassy**, Wisma Metropolitan I, 5th floor, Jalan Jend Sudirman Kav-29, Jakarta 12920 (tel: 021 510709; fax: 021 578 2251).
● **New Zealand Embassy** Jalan Diponegoro 41, Menteng, Jakarta 10310 (tel: 021 330680; fax: 021 310 4866).
● **US Embassy** Jalan Merdeka Selatan 5, Jakarta Pusat (tel: 021 360360; fax: 021 386 2259).

Emergency telephone numbers

● Police   110
● Fire   113
● Ambulance   118

Lost property

If you lose essential items such as your passport or traveller's cheques, report this to your embassy or consulate and to the issuing bank (keep cheque numbers and contact phone numbers in a separate place from the cheques themselves). Other losses (tickets, cameras and the like) should be reported to the local police station for insurance purposes, but you will need someone who speaks good Bahasa Indonesia.

Health and vaccinations

No vaccinations are required for entering Indonesia unless you have been in an area infected with cholera, smallpox or yellow fever. Health hazards come mainly in the form of malaria and a number of hygiene-related illnesses. Make sure your typhoid, tetanus and polio vaccinations are up to date (boosters are needed every five years), but note that cholera jabs are now recognised to be ineffective. Hepatitis A can be warded off with a new vaccination, Havrix, which needs two jabs spaced over two weeks before departure and, six months later, a further two jabs. This inoculates for ten years so is a good investment.

Preventive malaria treatment should be started at least one week before entering a malarial zone and continued for six weeks after leaving it. Low-lying areas of Irian Jaya, Central Sulawesi, Central Kalimantan and parts of Nusa Tenggara are the main danger spots. Prophylactic drugs can have strong side-effects so avoid taking them for very long periods (several months). Mosquito-coils and repellent are widely available and should be used, particularly during the rainy season.

Never drink tap-water; always stick to bottled or boiled water and be wary of ice. Avoid raw vegetables, salads and fruit unless you can peel them yourself. If you suffer from an attack of diarrhoea, drink lots of fluids (not coffee or fruit juice, although Coca Cola is beneficial) and above all take in water mixed with oral rehydration salts (*bubuk glukosa elektrolit*; the main brand is Oralit). It is best not to eat at all and only break yourself in gradually with dry toast, bananas, yoghurt or boiled rice. Anti-diarrhoea tablets such as Lomotil can be taken to relieve stomach cramps, but if the symptoms persist for over a week you should consult a doctor immediately as you may be suffering from dysentery.

Dehydration and sunburn are not obvious hazards but they can be seriously debilitating, while excessive perspiration also leads to loss of essential salts. Always drink lots of water, use sunblock liberally, wear a hat if trekking or if by the sea and keep up your salt intake. Another illness that is easy to pick up and hard to get rid of in this tropical climate is the common cold, usually caused by air-conditioning; keep an extra layer of clothing with you when you take domestic flights and long-distance bus journeys.

While it is advisable to have a small medical kit with you (including antiseptic ointment, antihistamine cream for insect bites, anti-diarrhoea tablets, aspirin or Paracetamol, and plasters), pharmacies are numerous and stock all basic medication as well as sunscreens, tampons and mosquito repellent. Small towns and villages generally have a clinic which will help in the case of more serious problems (although attendants will not necessarily speak English), while large towns usually have hospitals.

Food from street-stalls is readily available and usually hygienic

265

Camping
Camping facilities exist in some of Indonesia's national parks and reserves, but they are not of a high standard. Contact the national parks' head office, the **PHPA** (Perlindungan Hutan dan Pelestanan Alam) in Bogor at Jalan IH Juanda 9 for further information. As accommodation is so cheap it is hardly worth carrying the extra baggage, but nothing will stop you pitching a tent where you please in rural areas. At altitudes above 1,000m you will need a sleeping bag, and rain can often be a problem.

Clothing
The constantly warm and humid climate demands loose cotton or linen clothing. Those aiming to head up a volcano or trek in highland areas should also pack a pullover, scarf and appropriate footwear. Aim to travel as light as possible, particularly if using local *bemos* (minibuses) where space is minimal, and if necessary buy extra shirts, T-shirts or pants on the spot (the choice is endless and prices very reasonable). Women should dress modestly away from beach resorts – trousers and tops which cover the shoulders are quite acceptable. If you visit a Balinese temple you will need a sarong; these can be hired or bought very cheaply.

Conversion charts See page 264.

Bemo *in Padang, West Sumatra*

Tipping
Major hotels add a 10 per cent service charge to the bill, but in mid-range and budget establishments tipping is not expected. The same applies to restaurants. It is normal to round off a taxi fare and to tip guides or hire-car drivers if they have provided a good service. However, as bargaining is such an integral part of negotiating the price in the first place, a tip is never essential.

Toilets
Public toilets are not particularly salubrious but all airports, bus stations, restaurants and museums do have them. Ask for the WC ('way-say') or *kamar kecil*.

Visitors with disabilities
Indonesia is not an easy destination for those with disabilities, except for Bali where some of the more up-market hotels have suitable facilities and access. Contact your local Indonesian tourist office (see page 269) for further information.

Places of worship
Freedom of worship is one of the principles of *Pancasila*, Indonesia's national ideology, so there is no shortage of temples, mosques and churches. Christian churches abound in certain areas: Batak country around Sumatra's Danau Toba; in and around Manado in Sulawesi's Minahasa territory and at Tana

Indonesia offers rich pickings for the photographer

Toraja; on Maluku's Pulau Ambon; on Flores; on Timor; and in the central region of Irian Jaya.

Jakarta's main churches are:
- **Methodist** Jemaat Anugerah, Jalan Daan Mogot 100.
- **Catholic** St Canisius, Jalan Menteng Raya; or St Patrick's Cathedral, Lapangan Banteng.
- **Anglican** All Saints, Jalan Prapatan.

Electricity
Power supply is usually 220V/50 cycles in large cities, but more remote areas still function on 110V. Normal outlets use plugs with two round pins.

Photography
Colour print film is easily available in hotels, airports and small towns, but slide film is generally sold only at specialist photographic shops in large towns. Black and white film is very hard to find. Prices are reasonable (similar to European levels but higher than in the US) and in Bali they can be negotiated. Always check the expiry date when purchasing film. Same-day developing and printing can be done in all large towns and the quality is very acceptable. Keep unexposed and exposed film as cool and as dry as possible and, if making several domestic flights, don't let it through the X-ray machine. Camera batteries expire faster in hot, humid conditions so keep a spare set handy; they are readily available.

Most Indonesians love having their photo taken, but be careful when photographing orthodox Muslims (particularly women) and always be discreet if you are taking pictures during any religious festival. The Papuans in Irian Jaya's Baliem Valley are wise to their photogenic value and often demand payment first.

Etiquette and local customs
Indonesians are a particularly friendly, outgoing race and it is rare not to be accosted cheerfully by children, adolescents or even adults with the ubiquitous *'Hullo Mister!'* With women this may change to *'Hullo Mrs!'*, but not always. However charming this habit may seem initially, your interest will soon decline as the cry echoes around you in every street, beach or seemingly deserted landscape. There is absolutely nothing you can do about it bar wearing ear-plugs. Otherwise the generous Indonesian spirit is one of the archipelago's greatest pleasures, and conversations are easily struck up with strangers.

One cardinal rule to remember, however annoying the situation may be (delayed or cancelled transport being the most common), is never to lose your temper, for doing so will actually have a negative effect and be of no use whatsoever. Remain calm and firm, throwing in the odd piece of humour (if you still have any), and you may be able to swing the situation to your advantage. Smiles are widespread and never go against the grain. In the same vein, never criticise someone publicly as this makes them lose face.

As in all Muslim countries, the head is considered sacred and should not be touched (avoid patting children), while feet should not be put on tables and shoes should be removed on entering a private home, mosque or even museum. The right hand is used for eating and handshaking – never use the left hand. Pointing is also considered impolite. Body contact here is particularly difficult for Westerners to understand. Although public displays of affection between men and women are frowned upon, the

Indonesians have no qualms about touching a perfect stranger to emphasise a point so don't be over-sensitive to this.

Women travellers

Women travellers will find Indonesia fairly easygoing if they dress reasonably modestly. This does not mean that they will not be pestered in some places, but in general this will be harmless banter and should be treated firmly but with humour. The worst areas for women travelling alone are South and East Kalimantan and Aceh in North Sumatra, all orthodox Muslim areas where solo Western women are considered easy game. Care should be taken in choosing your hotel in these regions, but perhaps the best advice is to avoid them altogether. Other parts of Indonesia will, at the most, leave you with memories of incessantly repeated questions about your marital status and the quantity of your offspring. In such cases, life can often be made much easier by inventing an imminently arriving husband.

An outrigger taxi collects passengers at Gili Trawangan, Lombok

Tourist offices outside Indonesia

- **Australia** Indonesia Tourist Promotion Office, Level 10, 5 Elizabeth Street, Sydney, NSW 2000 (tel: 02 233 3630; fax: 02 233 3629/357 3478).
- **UK** Indonesia Tourist Promotion Office, 3–4 Hanover Street, London W1 9HH (tel: 0171 493 0030/0034; fax: 0171 493 1747).
- **USA** Indonesia Tourist Promotion Office, 3457 Wilshire Boulevard, Los Angeles, CA 90010 (tel: 213/387 2078; fax: 213/380 4876).

Tourist offices inside Indonesia

Each of Indonesia's 27 provinces has its own regional tourist office, known by its acronym Diparda or generally identified as *kantor pariwisata* ('tourist office'). Many towns have an additional municipal tourist office with specific local information. Below is a list of Diparda by province, arranged in order of the A–Z section of this guide. Note that phone numbers in Jakarta and elsewhere are changing from six digits to seven.

- **Jakarta** Directorate General of Tourism, Jalan Kramat Raya 81 (tel: 021 310 3117; fax: 021 310 1146). Visitor Information Centre, Jakarta

The 'Hullo mister!' syndrome

Theatre Building, Jalan MH Thamrin 9 (tel: 021 354094/364093).
- **West Java** Diparda Jawa Barat, Jalan Cipaganti 151/3, Bandung (tel: 022 81490; fax: 022 87976).
- **Central Java** Diparda Jawa Tengah, Jalan Imam Bonjol 209, Semarang (tel: 024 510924/511773). Diparda Yogyakarta, Jalan Marlioboro 14, Yogyakarta (tel: 0274 62811).
- **East Java** Diparda Jawa Timur, Jalan Darmokali 35, Surabaya (tel: 031 575448/9).

- **Aceh** Diparda Aceh, Jalan TGK Chik Kuta Karang 3, Banda Aceh (tel: 0651 33723).
- **North Sumatra** Diparda Sumatra Utara, Jalan Jend A Yani 107, Medan (tel: 061 511101).
- **Riau Archipelago** Diparda Riau, Jalan Gajah Mada 200, Pekanbaru (tel: 0761 25301).
- **West Sumatra** Diparda Sumatra Barat, Jalan Jend Sudirman 43, Padang (tel: 0751 21716).
- **South Sumatra** Diparda Sumatra Selatan, Jalan Bay Salim 200, Palembang (tel: 0711 24981/28305). Diparda Bengkulu, Jalan Pembangunan 14, Bengkulu (tel:

0736 21272).
Diparda Lampung, Jalan WR Supratman 39, Gunung Mas, Bandar Lampung (tel: 0721 42565/ 61720).

● **Bali** Diparda Bali, Jalan S Parman, Niti Mandala, Denpasar (tel: 0361 22387/26313).

● **West Nusa Tenggara** Diparda Nusa Tenggara Barat, Jalan Langko 70, Ampenan, Lombok (tel: 0364 21730/21866).
● **East Nusa Tenggara** Diparda Nusa Tenggara Timur, Jalan Jend Basuki Rachmat 1, Kupang (tel: 0391 21540/21824).
● **East Timor** Diparda Timor Timur, Jalan Dr Yose Carvalite, Dili, East Timor (tel: 0390 21530; fax: 0390 21558).

● **South Sulawesi** Diparda Sulawesi Selatan, Jalan Sultan Alaudin 105b, Ujung Pandang (tel: 0411 83897).
● **Central Sulawesi** Diparda Sulawesi Tengah, Jalan Raja Moili 103, Palu (tel: 0451 21795).

Bon voyage!

● **North Sulawesi** Diparda Sulawesi Utara, Komplek Perkantoran, Jalan 17 Augustus, Manado (tel: 0341 64299).

● **West Kalimantan** Diparda Kalmantan Barat, Jalan Achmad Sood 25, Pontianak (tel: 0561 36712).
● **South Kalimantan** Diparda Kalimantan Selatan, Jalan Mayjen DI Panjaitan 23, Banjarmasin (tel: 0511 2982).
● **East Kalimantan** Diparda Kalimantan Timur, Jalan Al Suryani 1, Samarinda (tel: 0541 21669/22641; fax: 0541 22111).
● **Central Kalimantan** Diparda Kalimantan Tengah, Jalan Letjen S Parman 21, Palangkaraya (tel: 0514 21416).

● **Maluku** Diparda Maluku, Kantor Gubernur, Jalan Pattimura, Kota Ambon (tel: 0911 52471).

● **Irian Jaya** Diparda Irian Jaya, Jalan Soa Siu Dok II, Jayapura (tel: 0967 2138 ext 263).
Kanwil XVII Depparpostel Irian Jaya, Jalan Raya Abepura 17, Entrop, Jayapura (tel: 0967 32216; fax: 0967 31519).

HOTELS AND RESTAURANTS

HOTELS AND RESTAURANTS

Note: telephone numbers in Jakarta and other cities are changing, as they move from six digits to seven.

ACCOMMODATION

Indonesia's bargain-priced accommodation ranges from primitive beach-huts to *losmen* (budget inns) where the toilet and *mandi* (a cold-water bath from which you ladle water over yourself) may be shared, or comfortable, cheap hotels where rooms have a private *mandi* or shower plus television and telephone. Good, mid-range hotels are found in large towns and tourist areas, while luxury hotels abound above all in Bali, Lombok and the main cities of Sumatra, Java and Kalimantan. The further east you go, the less choice there is. The following hotels have been divided into three price categories:

- budget (£)
- moderate (££)
- expensive (£££)

JAKARTA

Borobudur Intercontinental (£££) Jalan Lapangan Banteng Selatan (tel: 021 380 5555; fax: 021 380 9595). Jakarta's largest luxury hotel just off Medan Merdeka. Plush and spacious; many facilities, garden, tennis-courts, pool.
Cikini Sofyan Hotel (££) Jalan Cikini Raya 79 (tel: 021 399938; fax: 021 310 0432). Good value and well located in an old colonial residential area.
Cipta Hotel (££) Jalan Wahid Hasyim 53 (tel: 021 421 4700; fax: 021 326531). Central location near Jalan Jaksa. Recently renovated air-conditioned rooms.
Djody Hotel (£) Jalan Jaksa 27 and 35 (tel: 021 384 6600). Smartest hotel in this street of budget accommo-

dation. Range of reasonable rooms around a central patio, some with air-conditioning.
Mandarin Oriental Jakarta (£££) Jalan Thamrin (tel: 021 321307; fax: 021 324669). Excellent, elegant hotel in heart of city centre. Spacious rooms and Jakarta's best French restaurant, the Club House.
Menteng Hotel 1 (££) Jalan Gondangdia Lama 28 (tel: 021 325208; fax: 021 314 4151). Reasonable value for Jakarta; has a small pool.
Wisma Ise (£) Jalan Wahid Hasyim 168, 3rd floor (tel: 021 333463). Quiet but central location. Friendly, very cheap guest-house.
Yannie International Guest House (££) Jalan Raden Saleh Raya 35 (tel: 021 320012; fax: 021 327005). Charming old 16-roomed family hotel in pretty street. Clean, air-conditioned rooms open on to a patio. Excellent value; often full.

JAVA
Bandung

Chedi Hotel (£££) Jalan Ranca Bentang 56/8, Ciumbuleuit (tel: 022 230333; fax: 022 230633). Innovatively designed hotel on northern edge of town. Japanese-style rooms, business centre, superb restaurant and pool.
Guntur Hotel (£) Jalan Oto Iskandar Dinata 20 (tel: 022 443763). Uninspired modern hotel just north of station; comfortable rooms with television and phone.
Santika Hotel (££) Jalan Sumatera 52/4 (tel: 022 441038; fax: 022 439601). Pleasant hotel with pool and well-appointed rooms. Bar, restaurant and sauna.
Savoy Homann (£££) Jalan Asia Afrika 112 (tel: 022 432244/430083; fax: 022 436187). One of Bandung's most striking art deco landmarks, located in the heart

of downtown. Excellent service, attractive scale and reasonable rates.

Blitar
Sri Lestari Hotel (£/££) Jalan Merdeka 173 (tel: 0342 81766/81687). Pleasant old colonial house with modern extension. Clean rooms, some with television, telephone and air-conditioning. Excellent restaurant.

Bogor
Bogor Inn (££), Jalan Kumbang 12 (tel: 0251 328134). Small, friendly family-owned hotel. Comfortable and convenient location.
Firman (£) Jalan Paledang 48 (tel: 0251 323246). Popular and friendly guesthouse near Botanical Gardens. Recently expanded but rooms remain small.
Pakuan Palace (££) Jalan Pakuan 5 (tel: 0251 323062; fax: 0251 311207). Businessman's hotel with well-appointed rooms.

Borobudur
Lotus Losmen (£) Jalan Medang Kamulan (no telephone). Basic, cheap rooms with attached *mandi* in friendly family *losmen*. Breezy terrace restaurant.
Pondok Tingal Hostel (£) Jalan Balaputradewa (tel: 0293 8245/8145; fax: 0293 8166). Large traditionally styled Javanese structure about 1km south of temple. Wide range of rooms. Gardens, restaurant.
Taman Borobudur Guesthouse (££) Komplek Taman Wisata (tel: 0293 8131/8266). Up-market hotel in park adjoining temple. Air-conditioned rooms with telephone and satellite television.

Bromo
Bromo Cottages (£££) Tosari, Pasuruan (tel: 031 515253; fax: 031 511811).

Luxury cottage hotel with fabulous views, tennis-courts and a good restaurant. Transport to crater.

Cemara Indah (£) Cemara Lawang, Ngadisari (tel: 0335 23457). Superbly situated hotel overlooking crater. Dormitory accommodation or comfortable rooms, tour facilities, restaurant.

Yoschi's (£) Jalan Wonokerto 1, Ngadisari (0335 23387). Located 2km downhill from Ngadisari; very reasonable rooms and an excellent restaurant. Transport to crater.

Carita

Carita Krakatau Beach Hotel (£/£££) Jalan Raya Labuhan, Pandeglang (tel: 0254 320252; fax: 0254 320848). Wide range of rates for spacious beach cottages or economy rooms. Avoid weekend crowds.

Cirebon

Asia Hotel (£) Jalan Kalibaru 15/17 (tel: 0231 22193). Quiet, atmospheric location. Reasonably priced clean rooms with *mandis*.

Grand Hotel Cirebon (££) Jalan Siliwangi 98 (tel: 0231 25457). Old colonial hotel, recently renovated. Good central location and comfortable rooms.

Dieng Plateau

Bu Djono (£) Dieng village (no telephone). At entrance to village from Wonosobo. Cheap, very basic rooms with freezing, communal *mandi*. Friendly, eccentric service and simple food.

Dieng Plateau Homestay (£) Dieng village (no telephone). Next door to above. Marginally better rooms and structure, but equally cold *mandi* and less character.

Hotel Nirvana (£) Jalan Resimen 18, Wonosobo (tel: 0286 21066). Clean rooms, hot water; excellent restaurant.

Gedung Songo

Rawa Pening (££) Jalan Pandanaran 33, Bandungan (tel: 0298 313338). Tranquil, traditional hotel with colonial charm and superb views. Restaurant, pool.

Madura

Camplong Beach Cottages (£) Jalan Raya Darmo, Camplong (tel: 0323 21586). Breezy beach cottages on flat palm-lined stretch 7km east of Sampang. Some cottages with telephone, television, attached bathroom. Restaurant.

Wijaya I (£) Jalan Wahid Hasyim 1, Sumenep (tel: 0323 21532). Clean though basic rooms, some with air-conditioning. Sister hotel (Wijaya II) on main street is of similar standard.

Malang

Hotel Helios (£) Jalan Pattimura 37 (tel: 0341 62741). Small family-run hotel in residential area. Clean rooms (some with attached *mandi*).

Splendid Inn Hotel (£/££) Jalan Mojopahit 4 (tel: 0341 66860; fax: 0341 63618). Rambling old 1920s hotel just off central Jalan Tugu. Well-equipped rooms with television, telephone, air-conditioning and bathroom at reasonable rates.

Tugu Park Hotel (£££) Jalan Tugu 3 (tel: 0341 63891; fax: 0341 62747). Tasteful new 36-room hotel designed around pool and garden. Excellent restaurant, attentive service and well-appointed rooms.

Mojokerto

Wisma Tenera (£) Jalan HOS Cokroaminto 3 (tel: 0321 21753). Well-situated small, modern hotel. Clean rooms with fan, telephone and private *mandi*; small garden.

Pangandaran

Adam's Homestay (£) Jalan Pamugaran, Bulak Laut (tel: 0265 379164/379343). Small German-owned hotel with immaculate rooms set around garden. Private bathrooms, fans and hotel bar.

Sunrise Beach Hotel (££) Jalan Kidang Pananjung 175 (tel: 0265 379220; fax: 0265 379425). Set in gardens opening on to east beach. Bungalows with verandas, air-conditioning, telephone and television. Wide price range. Pool.

Yuli Beach Resort (££) Jalan Pamugaran (tel/fax: 0265 379375). Secluded spot at far north end of west beach. Fan-cooled bungalows in garden, small pool. Rates drop for several days' stay.

Pelabuhanratu

Bayu Armta (£) Jalan Cisolok (tel: Bandung 022 50882). Basic bungalow accommodation on cliff edge. Good views and reasonable seafood restaurant.

Pondok Dewata (££) Jalan Kijang Kencana (tel: Carita 0254 410226; fax: 0254 02889). Comfortable air-conditioned beach cottages just west of village. Pool and restaurant.

Surabaya

Hotel Paviljoen (£) Jalan Genteng Besar 94–8 (tel: 031 43449). Wonderful old 1920s colonial house. Reasonable clean rooms, all with fan and attached *mandi*. Friendly and centrally located.

Majapahit Hotel (££/£££) Jalan Tunjungan 65 (tel: 031 43351; fax: 031 43599). Thoroughly renovated colonial hotel in central position with garden. Good facilities although rooms vary.

Tanjung Hotel (££) Jalan P Sudirman 43–5 (tel: 031 44031/32). Has 50 well-equipped air-conditioned rooms with television, telephone and bathroom. Conveniently situated. Restaurant.

HOTELS AND RESTAURANTS

Surakarta (Solo)

Hotel Dana (££) Jalan Slamet Riyadi 286 (tel: 0271 33890/1; fax: 0271 43880). Wide range of decent rooms in garden setting. Opposite museum and tourist office.

Hotel Wisata Indah (£/££) Jalan Slamet Riyadi 173 (tel: 0271 43753/44770). Friendly, modern hotel with good facilities and wide range of rooms, most with air-conditioning, television, telephone and bathroom.

Kusuma Sahid Hotel (£££) Jalan Sugiyopranoto 22 (tel: 0271 46356; fax: 0271 44788). Superb *kraton*-style hotel set in huge landscaped park close to centre. Very comfortable rooms; many facilities.

Relax Homestay (£) Gang Empu Sedah 28, Kemlayan (no telephone). Dilapidated old mansion under renovation with peaceful garden and good restaurant. Budget prices; most rooms share *mandi*.

Tretes

Natour Bath Hotel (££/£££) Jalan Pesanggrahan 2 (tel: 0343 81776/7; fax: 0343 81161). Overpriced resort hotel with pool, restaurant, tennis-courts and 70 rather spartan rooms. Avoid weekends. Good views.

Tanjung Plaza (££) Jalan Wilis 7 (tel: 0343 81102). Not very well maintained and again overpriced. Basic rooms with bathroom, telephone and television.

Yogyakarta

Agung Star (£) Jalan Parangtritis 42 (tel: 0274 71811). Cheap, acceptable rooms with fan and bathroom arranged around small pool.

Airlangga Guest House (££) Jalan Prawirotaman 6–8 (tel: 0274 63344; fax: 0274 71427). Guest-house with restaurant and small pool.

Immaculately maintained; friendly atmosphere.

Puri Artha (££) Jalan Cendrawasih 9 (tel: 0274 63288/65918; fax: 0274 62765). Outside city centre but delightful calm garden setting. Tastefully decorated rooms, good service and restaurant.

Santika (£££) Jalan Jend Sudirman 19 (tel: 0274 63036; fax: 0274 62047). Recent smart construction in city centre but remains quiet. Comfortable rooms, restaurant and pool.

Wisma Gajah (£) Jalan Prawirotaman 4 (tel: 0274 75659/72037; fax: 0274 72037). Pleasant hotel laid out around garden and pool. Rooms with fan or air-conditioning.

Wisma Persada (£) Jalan Dagen 6 (tel: 0274 63780; fax: 0274 63147). Clean, modern hotel at top of budget range. Rooms with fan or air-conditioning, television, some with small balconies.

SUMATRA

Banda Aceh

Hotel Sultan (££) Jalan Panglima Polim (tel: 0651 22581). Air-conditioned rooms with television and telephone in quiet central location. Good restaurant.

Losmen Aceh (£) Jalan Mohammed Jam 1 (tel: 0651 21354). Opposite grand mosque. Fading colonial hotel with a range of rooms, some with air-conditioning.

Bengkulu

Pantai Nala Samudra/ Horison Hotel (££/£££) Jalan Pantai Nala 142 (tel: 0736 21722/21114). Beachfront location 4km east of town. Well-appointed air-conditioned rooms, pool, restaurant, bar, night-club.

Samudera Dwinka (£) Jalan Jend Sudirman 246 (tel: 0736 21604). Close to centre

with clean rooms, fan-cooled or air-conditioned, and private *mandis*.

Berastagi

Brastagi Cottages (££) Jalan Gundaling (tel: 0628 20908). Has 34 spacious rooms in garden setting. Air-conditioning, restaurant.

Crispo Inn (£) Jalan Veteran 3 (tel: 0628 91023). Very smart lobby and adjoining antique shop, but offers room only with shared bathroom.

Hotel Bukit Kubu (££) Jalan Sempurna 2 (tel: 0628 20832). Lovely old colonial hotel just north of town centre and surrounded by golf-course. Good views, restaurant and facilities.

Bukit Lawang

Wisma Bukit Lawang Cottages (£) PO Box 20774 (no telephone). Bungalow accommodation garden setting. Varying standards and prices, although all have private *mandi* and balcony. Excellent restaurant.

Bukittinggi

Benteng Hotel (£/££) Jalan Benteng 1 (tel: 0752 21115; fax: 0752 22596). Excellent-value mid-range hotel with superb views. Wide price range but all rooms with hot-water shower, television and telephone.

Denai Hotel (££) Jalan Dr Rivai 26 (tel: 0752 21466/21511). Pleasantly designed hotel with some cottages in Minangkabau style. Comfortable rooms and good facilities.

Hotel Sari Bundo (££) Jalan Yos Sudarso 7a (tel: 0752 22953/22637). Modern Minangkabau-style hotel beside fort. Quiet but central. Well-appointed rooms, bar and restaurant.

Mountain View Guesthouse (£) Jalan Yos Sudarso 3 (tel: 0752 21621). Small budget hotel with reasonable rooms, private showers and outdoor sitting areas.

Danau Toba
Carolina's (£) Tuk Tuk, Pulau Samosir (tel: 0625 41520). Popular lakefront hotel on southern point of peninsula. Wide range of rooms. Bar, restaurant, beach; motor bikes for rent.
Marroan Hotel (£) Tuk Tuk, Pulau Samosir (no telephone). Basic but spacious rooms with shower and small veranda.
Silintong Hotel (££) Jalan Durian 5, Tuk Tuk, Pulau Samosir (tel: 0625 41345). Tuk Tuk's priciest hotel. Fresh, bright rooms, garden and restaurant.
Toba Beach Hotel (££) Tomok, Pulau Samosir (tel: 0622 41275; or Medan tel: 061 529265). Large, up-market hotel just south of Tomok. Lakeside position and comfortable rooms, but rather overpriced.
Wisma Danau Toba (££) Jalan Pulau Samosir 3–6, Parapat (tel: 0625 41302). Large lakeside hotel. Wide price range depending on location and amenities. Bar and restaurant.

Medan
Deli Raya Hotel (£) Jalan SM Raja 29 (tel: 061 712997). Friendly small-scale hotel. Budget rates include breakfast. Avoid noisy front rooms but try the restaurant.
Natour Dharma Deli Hotel (£££) Jalan Balai Kota 2 (tel: 061 327011; fax: 061 327153). Luxury colonial edifice in city centre with range of room rates. Gardens, pool, restaurant and bar.
Polonia Hotel (£££) Jalan Jend Sudirman 14 (tel: 061 325300/700; fax: 061 519553). Large 175-room hotel in exclusive part of Medan near airport. Well-appointed rooms,

restaurant, pool, health centre and Chinese restaurant.
Sumatera (£) Jalan Sisingamangaraja 21 (tel: 061 24973). Characterless hotel and rooms, but well located and good value.

Padang
Padang Hotel (£/££) Jalan Bagindo Aziz Chan 28 (tel: 0751 22653). Assorted room standards, some with air-conditioning and private bathrooms. Small garden.
Pangeran City Hotel (££) Jalan Dobi 3/5 (tel: 0751 32133; fax: 0751 27189). Popular 65-room air-conditioned hotel in central location. Rooms with television and telephone. Restaurant and bar.
Tiga Tiga (£) Jalan Pemuda 31 (tel: 0751 22635). Spartan but clean rooms with attached *mandis*, helpful staff, lush garden.

Palembang
Sari Hotel (£) Jalan Jend Sudirman 1301 (tel: 0711 313320). Fairly mediocre hotel with air-conditioned rooms and restaurant.
Swarna Dwipa (££) Jalan Tasik 2 (tel: 0711 313322/313157; fax: 0711 362992). Up-market hotel combining old colonial building with modern wing to west of centre. Gardens and pool. Average air-conditioned rooms.

Pulau Nias
Lagundi Bay (£). Numerous *losmen* charge similar budget rates but no specific recommendations as standards change frequently.
Wisma Soliga (£) Km 4, Gunungsitoli (no telephone). Efficiently run with spacious rooms and a good Chinese restaurant.

Riau Archipelago
Bukit Nagoya Hotel (££) Jalan Sultan

Abdurrachman, Nagoya, Pulau Batam (tel: 0761 458 646). Overpriced but pleasant hotel in town centre. Wide range of rooms.
Riau Holiday Inn (£££) Jalan Pelantar II 53, Tanjung Pinang, Pulau Bintan (tel: 0771 22573/22644). Built on stilts over water; specialises in watersports. Well-designed rooms with bathroom and television. Reasonable rates.
Turi Beach Resort (£££) PO Box 55, Batu Ampar, Pulau Batam (tel: 0778 310078; fax: 0778 310042). Swish resort hotel at Nongsa with luxury wooden chalets on beach. Pool and restaurant.
Wisma Riau (£) Jalan Yusuf Kahar 8, Tanjung Pinang, Pulau Bintan (tel: 0771 21023/21133). Clean and comfortable hillside hotel with restaurant. Rooms with private bathrooms.

BALI
Air Sanih
Sunset Graha Beach Cottages (£) Air Sanih (tel/fax: 0362 21108). Spacious bungalows overlooking pools and sea. Restaurant. Snorkelling and hiking tours arranged.

Candi Dasa
Ida Beach Village (££), Desa Samuh (tel: 0361 229041; fax: 0361 751934). Built like traditional Balinese village. Luxury private cottages or *lumpungs* (two-storeyed rice-barns) with fan or air-conditioning. Small pool; restaurant.
Rama Bungalows (£) Candi Dasa (tel/fax: 0361 33778). Right beside lagoon and beach. Two-storey fan-cooled bungalows with large bathrooms and balconies. Wide price range; restaurant.

Danau Bratan
Ashram Guesthouse (££) Candikuning–Bedugul road (tel: 0362 22439). Rather

overpriced rooms and bungalows but lakeside setting and gardens. Restaurant.

Lakeview Homestay (£) Penelokan, Kintamani (tel: 0362 23464). Hotel/restaurant perched on edge of crater and Lake Bratan. Economy and superior rooms, some with bath-tub and hot water. Restaurant.

Kuta/Legian

Fat Yogi (£) Poppies Lane I, Kuta (tel: 0361 751665). Large hotel complex designed around lush garden. Cheaper rooms popular with surfers. Rock-video restaurant; pool.

Poppies (££) Poppies Lane, Kuta (tel: 0361 751059; fax: 0361 752364). Secluded garden setting with thatched cottages, rock-pools and swimming-pool. Popular restaurant near by. Needs advance booking.

Sari Yasa Samudra Bungalows (££) Kuta Beach (tel: 0361 751562; fax: 0361 752948). Beachfront hotel with comfortable air-conditioned or fan-cooled rooms, large pool, restaurant, bar, garden. Central location.

Suji Bungalow (£) Poppies Lane II, Kuta (tel/fax: 0361 752483). Air-conditioned or fan-cooled bungalows with terrace and private shower. Small pool, restaurant and transport service.

Lovina

Bali Lovina Beach Cottages (£££) Kalibukbuk, Singaraja (tel: 0362 41385; fax: 0361 24909). Excellent service; comfortable air-conditioned bungalows and Lovina's best seafood restaurant. Beachfront location, pool.

Nirwana Seaside Cottages (£) Kalibukbuk, Singaraja (tel: 0362 22288; fax: 0362 21090). Superb beachfront location at centre of Lovina. Basic bungalows with shower and veranda, or

pricier two-storeyed cottages. Garden and pleasant open-air restaurant.

Rini Hotel (£) Kalibukbuk, Singaraja (no telephone). Well-run, friendly place with good restaurant. Spacious, clean, fan-cooled rooms with private *mandi*.

Nusa Dua

Mirage Hotel (£££) Jalan Pratama 72 (tel: 0361 72147; fax: 0361 72131). Slightly cheaper than Nusa Dua's other luxury mammoths. Very comfortable rooms. Restaurant and pool.

Nusa Dua Beach Hotel (£££) Lot N-4 (tel: 0361 71210; fax: 0361 71229). One of Indonesia's top hotels. Exceptional decorative features, traditional Balinese-style constructions and impeccable service. Pool, good sports facilities.

Padangbai

Rai Beach Inn (£) Jalan Silayukti 3 (tel: 0361 35520). Imaginatively designed two-storey bungalows with private shower in walled garden compounds. Restaurant. Arranges tours.

Sanur

Gazebo Cottages (££) Jalan Tanjung Sari 45 (tel/fax: 0361 88300). Comfortable air-conditioned bungalows aligned in attractive garden opening on to beach. Good pool and restaurant.

Puri Klapa Garden Cottages (££) Jalan Segara Ayu 1 (tel: 0361 88999; fax: 0361 25708). Spacious cottages set in landscaped garden 300m from beach. Large pool; restaurant. Peaceful but central location.

Tirtagangga

Dhangin Taman Inn (£) Tirtagangga Water Palace (no telephone). Located beside water palace. Simple, clean rooms with private *mandi*. Restaurant.

Ubud

Amandari (£££) Kedewatan (tel: 0361 71267/95333; fax: 0361 71266). For a real Balinese splurge this is where to stay. Has 29 luxury suites in traditional walled-village style, some with private pools.

Ananda Cottages (££) Campuhan (tel: 0361 95376; fax: 0361 95375). Peaceful setting 1km west of central Ubud. Rural views, open-air restaurant, spring-water pool. One- or two-storey bungalows with bathroom and veranda.

Kajeng Homestay (£) Jalan Kajeng 29 (tel: 0361 975018). Secluded location 150m north of Ubud's main road. Cheap, spacious rooms with private shower and veranda.

Sayan Terrace (££) PO Box 6 (tel/fax: 0361 975384). A few kilometres west of Ubud at Sayan. Superb location. Comfortable cottages, each priced differently for view/facilities and decorative appeal.

Ubud Inn (££) Monkey Forest Road (tel: 0361 975071; fax: 0361 975188). Traditionally designed cottage accommodation in garden with pool and snack bar. Clean, friendly and tranquil; central location.

NUSA TENGGARA FLORES

Bajawa

Hotel Kembang (£) Jalan Diponegoro 18 (no telephone). Unspectacular building but clean, spacious rooms with private *mandi*.

Ende

Dewi Putra (£) Jalan Yos Sudarso 23 (tel: 0381 21465). Large modern hotel set a few blocks back from harbour. Rooms with private shower and air-conditioning or fan. Well-disposed but inefficient service; restaurant.

Nirwana (£) Jalan Pahlawan 29 (tel: 0381 21199). Rather ramshackle place on hill above town. Some rooms with air-conditioning.

Labuanbajo

Bajo Beach Inn (£) Jalan Yos Sudarso (no telephone). Good-value town hotel with wide range of room rates. Pleasant open-air restaurant.

Waecicu Beach Hotel (£) Pawai Waeicicu (no telephone). Catch a morning boat out to this beach, about 20 minutes away. Decent bungalows with private *mandi*. Meals included in reasonable rates.

Maumere

Flores Froggies (£) Wair Terang (no telephone). An idyllic French-owned beach getaway, 28km east of Maumere. Simple huts, some with private showers. Open-air restaurant.

Flores Sao Resort (££) Pantai Waiara (tel: 0382 21555; fax: 0382 21666; or Jakarta tel: 021 370333; fax: 021 373858). Large landscaped beach resort geared to divers. Spacious air-conditioned bungalows with good bathrooms and verandas, large pool and beautiful dark-sand beach. Excellent restaurant.

Hotel Maiwali (£) Jalan Raja Don Tomas (tel: 0382 21220). Overpriced hotel in town centre. Basic rooms with fan or air-conditioning, tiny shower-room and balcony. Restaurant being rebuilt after earthquake.

Waiara Cottages/Sea World Club (££) Jalan Nai Roa, Km 13 (tel: 0382 21570). Beach resort with bungalow accommodation, air-conditioned or fan-cooled. Some cheaper rooms with shared bathroom.

Moni

Friendly Losmen (£) (no telephone). In centre of village. Basic rooms with private or shared *mandi*. Friendly staff.

Sao Ria Wisata Bungalows (£) Km 1.5 (no telephone). Perched on a hillside overlooking valley and village. Traditional cottages with *mandi* and veranda. Good restaurant next door.

Ruteng

Wisma Dahlia (£) Jalan Kartini (tel: 0385 377). Clean, well-run *losmen*. Rooms with shared or private *mandi* and hot water. Good Chinese restaurant.

LOMBOK

Gili Islands

Gazebo Resort (££) Gili Meno (tel: Bali 0361 88212; fax: 0361 88300). Tastefully decorated Balinese-style wooden bungalows on east coast. Good diving facilities.

Hans Bungalows (£) Gili Air (no telephone). On northern tip of island. Charming, tranquil site and comfortable bungalows.

Rainbow Cottages (£) Gili Trawangan (no telephone). Friendly, well-maintained beach cottages with private *mandi*.

Kuta

Rinjani Agung Beach Hotel (£) Jalan Pantai (tel: 0364 54849). Bungalows and restaurant in garden setting located in middle of Kuta's beach stretch. Reasonable rooms with mosquito nets and private *mandi*.

Segara Anak (£) Jalan Pantai (tel: 0364 54834/5). Thin-walled bungalows with mosquito nets and spacious private *mandi*. Large breezy restaurant with loud rock music.

Mataram

Granada Hotel (££) Jalan Bung Karno (tel: 0364 22275; fax: 0364 36015). Comfortable air-conditioned hotel with garden and pool.

Well-appointed rooms; central location.

Hotel Mataram (££) Jalan Pejanggik (tel/fax: 0364 23411). Small, very clean hotel with adequate rooms in central position.

Senggigi

Ida Beach Cottages (££) Jalan Raya Senggigi (tel: 0364 93013; fax: 0364 93286). Charming Sasak-style hotel set on hillside. Lavishly decorated air-conditioned rooms with terraces. Restaurant and pool.

Lombok Intan Laguna (£££) Jalan Senggigi (tel: 0364 93090; fax: 0364 93185). Prime location on Senggigi beach. Luxury hotel with endless amenities. Garden with pool, gym, restaurants and bars.

Senggigi Beach Hotel (£££) Batu Layar (tel: 0364 93210; fax: 0364 93200). Excellent facilities and location on land-spit between two beaches. Traditional Sasak-style architecture, good sports facilities.

Windy Beach Cottages (£/££) Mangsit (tel: 0364 93191/2; fax: 0364 93193). On water's edge at far northern end of Senggigi. One- or two-storey bungalows in garden. Tasteful rooms and good bathrooms. Open-air restaurant.

Suranadi

Suranadi Hotel (££) Jalan Raya Suranadi (tel: 0364 23686). Old colonial hotel next to temple. Basic rooms or better appointed garden cottages. Tennis-court and spring-water pool. Overpriced; ask for discount.

Tetebatu

Wisma Soedjono (£/££) (no telephone). Rural colonial retreat in foothills of Rinjani; good base for hikers. Wide range of rooms and bungalows, some with lovely views, private showers and hot water. Restaurant.

SUMBA
Waikabubak
Hotel Manandang (£) Jalan Pemuda 4 (tel: 0387 197). Relatively new hotel with clean rooms opening on to interior garden. Excellent source of information about region; jeeps for hire. Good restaurant.
Losmen Mona Lisa (£) Jalan Gajah Mada (tel: 0387 24). Reasonable hotel decorated with antiques and old photos. Some rooms with private bathroom. New extension 2km from town is popular with groups.

Waingapu
Hotel Elim (£) Jalan Jend A Yani 73 (tel: 0386 323). Adequate rooms with attached bathrooms and air-conditioning. Helpful staff, good restaurant.
Hotel Sandlewood (£) Jalan Panjaitan 23 (tel: 0386 199). Well-run hotel near bus terminal. Spacious rooms with or without air-conditioning and private bathroom. Restaurant is not of same standard.

SUMBAWA
Bima
Lawata Beach Hotel (££) Jalan Sultan Salahudin (tel: 0374 3696/7; fax: 0374 3698). Beautifully located hotel 2km south of town. Air-conditioned or fan-cooled bungalows, all with good bathrooms and veranda. Garden, pool and open-air restaurant.
Sang Yang Hotel (£) Jalan Hasanuddin 6 (tel: 0374 2788; fax: 0374 2017). Large, somewhat run-down hotel in town centre. Reasonable though overpriced air-conditioned rooms with bathroom and veranda overlooking small garden.

Pulau Moyo
Amanwana (£££) c/o Amanusa, Nusa Dua, Bali (tel: Bali 0361 71267; fax: 0361 71266). Extraordinary island retreat and jetsetters' paradise. Twenty vast luxury tents lie scattered in jungle beside secluded beach. Excellent open-air restaurant, diving facilities and trekking. All-in prices.

Sumbawa Besar
Hotel Dewi (£) Jalan Hasanuddin Nomor 60 (tel: 0371 21170). Brand new hotel in town centre. Reasonably priced, some rooms with air-conditioning, television and telephone. Spacious and bright, but front rooms are noisy.
Hotel Tambora (£) Jalan Kebayan 2 (tel: 0371 21555; fax: 0371 21624). Well-established hotel with wide price range. Helpful staff. Transport, garden, open-air television lounge and restaurant.

TIMOR
Dili
Hotel Dili (£) Jalan Av Sada Bandeira (tel: 0390 21871). Seafront hotel which has seen better days. Reasonable rooms, some with air-conditioning.
New Resende Inn (££) Jalan Av Bispo Medeiros (tel: 0390 22094). Good amenities and central location. Restaurant. Clean, air-conditioned rooms.

Kupang
Hotel Flobamor II (££) Jalan Jend Sudirman 21 (tel: 0391 33476; fax: 0391 32560). Uphill from seafront area. Modern hotel with good air-conditioned rooms, hot water, television and pool.
Hotel Maliana (£) Jalan Sumatera 35 (tel: 0391 21879). Spacious air-conditioned rooms with peeling attached *mandi* and

veranda. Central seafront location, pretty garden and friendly service.
Orchid Garden Hotel (££) Jalan Gunung Fatuleu (tel: 0391 32004; fax: 0391 31399). Plush new hotel with good facilities in central downtown location. Air-conditioned rooms with bathrooms. Pool; garden.

Soe
Mahkota Plaza (£) Jalan Jend Suharto 11 (tel: 0392 21168). Simple rooms with attached *mandi* in large, soulless hotel. Restaurant.

SULAWESI
Danau Poso
Hotel Pamona Indah Permai (£) Jalan Yos Sudarso 25, Tentena (tel: 0458 21245/6/7). Atmospheric wooden hotel on lakefront by ferry pier. Range of rooms and family cabins, some with television, bath and hot water. Restaurant.
Hotel Wasantara (£) Jalan Yos Sudarso, Tentena (tel: 0458 21345). Clean, basic rooms with private *mandi* and terrace overlooking lake. Restaurant.
Mulia Poso Lake Hotel (£) Jalan Pelabuhan Wisata, Pendolo (no telephone). Recently opened up-market hotel. Comfortable, clean rooms with private shower. Scenic restaurant/bar built on stilts over lake. Own transport essential.

Donggala
Prince John Dive Resort (£) Tanjung Karang, c/o Milano Icecream, Jalan Hasanuddin II No 78, Palu (tel: 0451 23857; fax: 0451 27127). Thatched bungalows on idyllic white beach just north of Donggala. All-in prices, sailing facilities and superb diving trips.

Gorontalo
Hotel Indah Ria (£) Jalan Jend A Yani 20 (tel: 0435

278

21296). Centrally located, pleasant hotel. Range of rooms, some with air-conditioning. All-in prices.

Hotel Saronde (£) Jalan Walanda Maramis (tel: 0435 21735). Very good value and helpful owner. Range of rooms set around courtyard, some spacious with air-conditioning and shower, others with fan.

Makale

Barana Hill Hotel (££), Jalan Pontiku 509 (tel: 0411 22251/6). Large Toraja-style hotel on outskirts of Makale. Good modern facilities.

Wisma Bungin (£) Jalan Nusantara 35 (tel: 0411 22255). Simple but adequate modern hotel in town centre near lake. Rooms with bathroom.

Mamasa

Mamasa Cottages (££) c/o Wisata Lestari, Jalan Butung 75, Ujung Pandang (tel: 0411 317799/282; fax: 0411 24099). Toraja-style thatched cottages with television, bathroom and spring water. Beautiful views, good Chinese restaurant.

Manado

Hotel Minahasa (£) Jalan Sam Ratulangi 199 (tel: 0431 62059/62559). Short distance south of centre with non-stop *bemo* (minibus) connections. Friendly, old-fashioned establishment. Avoid noisy front rooms. Fan or air-conditioning; private bathrooms.

Hotel New Queen (££) Jalan Wakeke 12/14 (tel: 0431 65979/64440; fax: 0431 65748). Claims to be 'cleanest hotel in Manado'. Air-conditioned, comfortable rooms with television and telephone. Restaurant and karaoke bar.

Manado Beach Hotel (£££) Jalan Raya Trans Sulawesi, Tasik Ria (tel: 0431 67001/5;

fax: 0431 67007). Manado's top hotel, on beach over 20km south of town. Good facilities with pool, but rather isolated.

Nusantara Diving Centre (££/£££) Pantai Molas (tel: 0431 63988; fax: 0431 60368). Sprawling bunga-low accommodation on beach 7km north of town. Restaurant, bar, pool, garden and diving facilities.

Rex Hotel (£) Jalan Sugiono 3 (tel: 0431 51136/67706; fax: 0431 67789). Spotless new hotel in central location. Small but cheap rooms with bathroom, fan-cooled or air-conditioned.

Palu

Central Hotel (£/££) Jalan Kartini 6 (tel: 0451 22418). Excellent value modern hotel; good service and centrally located. If full, try Hotel Buana next door.

Poso

Hotel Bambu Jaya (£) Jalan Agussalim 65 (tel: 0452 21570). Modern frontage; older rooms at back. Clean, comfortable suites or standard rooms, some with air-conditioning.

Pulau Bunaken Marine Park

Daniel's Homestay (£) (no telephone). Group of bamboo beach-huts in clearing on water's edge. Excellent food included in budget price. Catch a public boat from Manado's market at 2–3pm or find a fishing boat to take you there.

Rantepao

Indra Hotels (£/££) Jalan Landorundun 63 (tel: 0423 21060/ 21163/21583). Three well-run hotels under same management, ranging from basic but decent rooms on main square (City Hotel), to adjacent Toraja-style garden hotel with standard rooms (Indra I), and more

up-market, scenic facilities across river (Indra II).

Toraja Cottages (£££) Kampung Bolu (tel: 0423 21268/211475). Well-appointed cottage hotel spread over landscaped hill-side 3km north of Rantepao. Restaurant/bar and pool.

Wisma Irama (£) Jalan Abdul Gani 16 (tel: 0423 21371). Large, clean rooms with bathroom or *mandi*.

Wisma Maria (£) Jalan Ratulangi (tel: 0423 21162). Efficiently run and in tranquil location with garden. Choice of comfortable rooms with attached hot-water shower or *mandi*.

Sengkang

Hotel Apada (£) Jalan Durian 9 (tel: 0485 21053). Curious construction around garden owned by Bugis princess. Has 17 very different rooms, all comfortable with private bath or shower, some very spacious with veranda. Restaurant serves Bugis specialities.

Pondok Eka (£) Jalan Maluku 12 (tel: 0485 21296). Small family hotel close to bus terminal. Large, rather dark rooms with bathrooms. Friendly management; tours arranged.

Togian Islands

Losmen Bolilanga Indah (£) Katupat, Pulau Togian, Poso (no telephone). Friendly basic *losmen*. Easy boat access to nearby coral reefs; snorkelling masks for hire.

Togian Islands Hotel (£/££) Wakai, Kec Una-Una, Poso (no telephone). Imaginatively designed wooden hotel on stilts. Good open-air restaurant, but sporadic electricity. Comfortable rooms with bath, television or shared *mandi*. Owner runs dive tours and also has two beach-huts on idyllic, uninhabited island near by. Boat transport can be arranged from Ampana.

Ujung Pandang

Makassar Beach Hotel (£££) Jalan Penghibur 10 (tel: 0411 326062; fax: 0411 319611). Efficiently run modern hotel. Fully air-conditioned, well-equipped rooms with sea views, television, telephone and good bathrooms. Restaurant, bar, car hire.

Makassar Sunset Hotel (££) Jalan Somba Opu 297 (tel: 0411 852442/854218). Older hotel situated on main seafront road. Large rooms with television, telephone and tiled bathrooms. Fully air-conditioned; restaurant.

Marina Inn (££) Jalan Haji Bau 30 (tel: 0411 872324; fax: 0411 874255). Small family hotel in quiet street south of city centre. Air-conditioned rooms with tiled bathrooms. Small terrace and garden. Overpriced; ask for discount.

KALIMANTAN

Balikpapan

Altea Benakutai Hotel (£££) Jalan Pangeran Antasari (tel: 0542 31896; fax: 0542 31823). Towering modern block in downtown seafront area. Large well-appointed rooms, pool, sauna, bar and restaurants.

Mirama Hotel (££) Jalan Mayjen Sutoyo IIA/16 (tel: 0542 22960; fax: 0542 34230). Somewhat past its prime, but comfortable '1st class' rooms are spacious with good views, bathrooms and satellite television.

Banjarmasin

Borneo Homestay (£) Jalan Pos 87 (tel/fax: 0511 66545). Popular budget homestay by river. Most rooms with shared *mandi*, but new annexe under construction should have slightly

upgraded rooms and rooftop restaurant.

Hotel Perdana (£/££) Jalan BJ Katamso 3 (tel: 0511 53276/68029). Central location and pleasant layout. Restaurant. Big drawback is sealed windows, so only pricier air-conditioned rooms are viable. Private television and shower.

Kalimantan Hotel (£££) Jalan Lambung Mangkurat (tel: 0511 66818; fax: 0511 67345). Well-appointed modern hotel. Pool, restaurant, bar, business centre.

Pontianak

Hotel Mahkota (£££) Jalan Sidas 8 (tel: 0561 36022/3; fax: 0561 36200). Luxury modern construction in central spot. Has 100 air-conditioned rooms with telephone, satellite television and good bathrooms. Wide price range, good facilities.

Kapuas Palace Hotel (££) Jalan Imam Bonjol (tel: 0561 36122/3; fax: 0561 34374). Well-established hotel with pool and restaurant. Spacious rooms and suites with television, telephone and bathroom.

Wisma Patria (£) Jalan HOS Cokroaminoto 497 (tel: 0561 6063). Large and friendly homestay with reasonable rooms (some air-conditioned) and restaurant.

Samarinda

Hotel Hayani (£) Jalan Pirus 31 (tel: 0541 42653). Reasonably priced spacious rooms with fan and bath or shower. Quiet, central location, helpful staff.

Hotel Hidaya I (£) Jalan Mas Temenggung (tel: 0541 21712; fax: 0541 37761). Well-maintained hotel beside market. Wide range of rooms with *mandi*, shower or bath, fan-cooled or air-conditioned.

Hotel Mesra (££/£££) Jalan Pahlawan 1 (tel: 0541 21011;

fax: 0541 35453). Spacious hilltop hotel north of centre with fine views over town. Cottage or room accommodation, fitness centre, restaurant, tennis-courts.

Singkawang

Mahkota Singkawang Hotel (££) Jalan P Diponegoro 1 (tel: 0562 31244; fax: 0562 31491). A 40-room modern hotel under same management as Pontianak's Mahkota. Well-appointed rooms with balcony. Pool, tennis-courts, restaurant, bar and disco.

Palapa Hotel (£) Jalan Ismail Tahir 41 (tel: 0562 31449/32021). Reasonable air-conditioned rooms with private shower or bath. Restaurant.

Tanjung Puting Nature Reserve

Blue Kecubung (£) Jalan Domba, Palangkaraya (no telephone). Reasonable rooms with fan or air-conditioning and private *mandi*. Restaurant and helpful guide service.

Dandang Matingang (£) Jalan Yos Sudarso 11, Palangkaraya (tel: 0514 21805). Air-conditioned rooms. Restaurant.

Hotel Rimba (££) Sekonyer, Tanjung Harapan (no telephone). Half-way up the Sekonyer river towards Camp Leakey. Comfortable rooms with private *mandi*; meals included.

MALUKU
BANDA ISLANDS

Pulau Banda

Delfika (£) Jalan Nusantara (no telephone). Friendly family guest-house in an atmospheric old Dutch mansion with garden.

Laguna Inn (££) Jalan Pelabuhan (no telephone). This and the nearby

Maulana Inn (££/£££) are owned by Des Alwi, Banda's undisputed tourism king. Both are run efficiently with good rooms. Excellent diving trips arranged.

PULAU AMBON
Kota Ambon

Amboina Hotel (££) Jalan Kapitan Ulupaha 5a, (tel: 0911 41725/12; fax: 0911 53354). Large modern hotel in town centre. Several room categories, all with bathroom, air-conditioning, television and telephone. Restaurant and bar.

Manise Hotel (££) Jalan WR Supratman 1 (tel: 0911 41445; fax: 0911 41054). Rather worn modern hotel but with excellent service. Well-equipped pricier rooms are very comfortable but 'economy' rooms are airless. Central location.

Wisata (£) Jalan Mutiara 15 (tel: 0911 3298/3592). Air-conditioned rooms with television and telephone. Restaurant.

Latuhalat/Namalatu

Lelisa Beach Resort (££) Jalan Namalatu 1, Latuhalat (tel: 0911 51989/90; fax: 0911 51988). Comfortable air-conditioned rooms in palm grove facing beach. Good open-air restaurant, relaxed atmosphere, helpful service, close to a diving centre.

PULAU SERAM
Masohi

Nusa Ina (£) Jalan Banda 9 (tel: 0914 221). Basic accommodation with attached *mandi*. Meals optional.

Sri Lestari (£) Jalan Abd Soulissa 5 (tel: 0914 178). Basic rooms with attached *mandi*. Meals included.

PULAU TERNATE
Ternate

Chrysant Hotel (£) Jalan Jend A Yani 131 (tel: 0921 21245/21580). Quiet place at southern end of centre. Decent fan-cooled or air-conditioned rooms with pri-

vate *mandi*. Overpriced. Full board available.

Hotel Neraca (££) Jalan Pahlawan Revolusi 30 (tel: 0921 21668). New up-market hotel in town centre. Good clean rooms; wide price range.

Nirwana Hotel (£) Jalan Pahlawan Revolusi 58 (tel: 0921 21787; fax: 0921 21487). Good-value, well-equipped hotel in town centre. Air-conditioned rooms with television and telephone. Restaurant, bar, night-club, sauna.

IRIAN JAYA
Baliem Valley

Baliem Palace Hotel (££) Jalan Trikora 114, Wamena (tel: 0969 31043). On main street close to market. Clean, bright rooms around small garden, some with hot water and bath-tub.

Nayak Hotel (£) Jalan Gatot Subroto 1, Wamena (tel: 0969 31067/31030). Directly opposite airstrip terminal. Rather dark rooms with windows looking on to corridor, but have private *mandi*. Restaurant.

Wio Silimo Tradisional Hotel (£) On other side of airstrip from Nayak Hotel, Wamena (no telephone). The only hotel in the Baliem Valley owned and run by Danis. Traditional thatched huts with oddly shaped rooms and basic private *mandi*. Set in lovely garden. Free transport into town. Cheap for Wamena.

Danau Sentani

Hotel Mansapurrani (£) Jalan Yabaso 113, Sentani (tel: 0967 91219). Pleasant, spacious rooms with fan, private *mandi* and terrace. Friendly management.

Hotel Semeru (£) Jalan Yabaso, Sentani (tel: 0967 91447). Clean rooms with private shower, fan-cooled or air-conditioned. Restaurant.

Jayapura

Hotel Dafonsoro (££) Jalan Percetakan 20 (tel: 0967 31695/6; fax: 0967 34056). Uninspired modern hotel. Reasonable air-conditioned rooms with bathroom and balcony. Good restaurant.

Hotel Irian Plaza (£/££) Jalan Setiapura 11 (tel: 0967 34649). Wide price range for clean rooms, all with attached *mandi*.

Hotel Matoa (£££) Jalan A Yani 14 (tel: 0967 31633; fax: 0967 31437). Priciest place in Jayapura. Well-appointed rooms but facilities limited.

Pulau Biak

Airport Beach Hotel (££) Jalan M Yamin, Biak (tel: 0961 22345/22311; fax: 0961 21496). Well-maintained rooms with shower, telephone and air-conditioning. Prices inclusive of meals.

Arumbai Hotel (££) Jalan Selat Makasser 3, Biak (tel: 0961 21835; fax: 0961 22501). New wing added to former Hotel Titiwaka with bar and restaurant. Well-equipped though rather small rooms with hot showers. Pool, plus car and motor bike rental.

Hotel Irian (££) Jalan Moh Yamin, Biak (tel: 0961 21139; fax: 0961 21458). Superb remnant from Dutch colonial days opposite airport. Large garden. Reasonable rooms with air-conditioning, shower, television and balcony. Rates include three meals.

Sorong

Cendrawasih Hotel (££) Jalan Sam Ratulangi 54 (tel: 0951 22361; fax: 0951 23269). Comfortable rooms with television, telephone and private shower.

Irian Beach Hotel (£) Jalan Yos Sudarso (tel: 0951 22713/4). Close to airport. Air-conditioned rooms with television, telephone and shower. Restaurant.

RESTAURANTS

For authentic regional specialities, the best places to head for are the *warungs* (food-stalls) which spring into action at nightfall. Always aim for the most crowded – a sure sign of quality. Otherwise, in towns the best restaurants are often in top- or mid-range hotels (see Accommodation). Below is a list of a few exceptional or good-value restaurants throughout the archipelago, divided into three price categories:

- ● budget (£)
- ● moderate (££)
- ● expensive (£££)

JAKARTA

Café Batavia (££) Jalan Pintu Besar Utara 32A, Taman Fatahillah, Kota (tel: 021 692 3842). Impressively renovated 1805 structure. Functions as art gallery. Snacks and *dim sum*.

Jakarta Restaurant (£) Jalan Thamrin 3 (tel: 021 323883). Opposite Sarinah department store. Top of budget range for Cantonese and Szechuan dishes.

Kuningan (££) Jalan HOS Cokroaminoto 122 (tel: 021 390 0384). Up-market seafood restaurant with lavish Thai and Chinese menu.

Le Bistro (££) Jalan KH Wahid Hasyim 75 (tel: 021 390 9249). Slightly musty but atmospheric. Mainly French menu includes seafood specialities.

Nelayan (££) Manggala Wanabakti Building, Jalan Gatot Subroto (tel: 021 570 0235). Local atmosphere and abundant seafood.

Oasis (£££) Jalan Raden Saleh 47 (tel: 021 327818). Essential to book at this ritzy restaurant in a historic Dutch mansion. Superb *rijstaffel*, live music.

Ratu Bahari (£££) Jalan Melawai VII 4, Blok M (tel:

021 774115). Well-regarded Chinese seafood restaurant.

Sarinah Food Court (££), Jalan Thamrin 11 (tel: 021 390 2774/5). Air-conditioned basement restaurant with regional dishes.

Sate House Senayan (££) Jalan Kebon Sirih 31a and Jalan HOS Cokroaminoto 78 (tel: 02 326238). Popular for satay and seafood.

Summer Palace (£££) Tedjabuana Building, 8th Floor, Jalan Menteng Raya 29 (tel: 021 314 2970). Grandiose setting for Szechuan and Cantonese specialities. *Dim sum* on Sundays.

Tokyo Garden (£££) Lippo Life Building, Jalan HR Rasuna Said 10 (tel: 021 572868). Expensive but excellent Japanese food.

JAVA
Bandung

Babakan Siliwangi (££) Jalan Siliwangi 7 (no telephone). Popular family restaurant in open-air setting. Sundanese dishes.

Handayani (££) Jalan Sukajadi 153 (tel: 022 83424). Located in old colonial house north of centre. Excellent Sundanese and Chinese cuisine.

Sindang Restaurant (£) Jalan Naripan 9 (tel: 022 443440). Large Sundanese restaurant, best on Saturdays during *wayang golek* puppet performance.

Cirebon

Maxim's (££) Jalan Bahagia 45/7 (no telephone). Most popular local Chinese restaurant with bustling atmosphere. Seafood delicacies.

Pangandaran

Rumah Makan Laut Biru (£) Jalan Kidang Pananjung 228 (tel: 0265 379046). Sizzling seafood in outdoor restaurant.

Surakarta (Solo)

Sari Restaurant (£) Jalan Slamet Riyadi 421 (no telephone). Considered by locals to be the best place for Javanese food.

Warung Baru (£) Jalan Ahmad Dhalan 23 (no telephone). Cheap travellers' meals; good atmosphere and large portions.

Yogyakarta

Baleanda Restaurant (££) Jalan Tirtodipu 3 (tel: 0274 76114). Delightful tropical garden setting. Imaginative Western and Indonesian dishes, friendly service.

Cirebon Restaurant (£) Jalan Marlioboro/Jalan Jend A Yani 15 (tel: 0274 2227). Old-fashioned restaurant. Indonesian, Chinese and Western dishes, snacks, delicious fresh fruit juices.

Pesta Perak (££) Jalan Tentara Rakyat Mataram 8 (tel: 0274 86255). Vast buffets of Javanese dishes, served in palatial setting.

SUMATRA
Berastagi

Brastagi Seafood Restaurant (£) Jalan Veteran 23 (tel: 0628 91339). Simple restaurant offering a wide selection of dishes and snacks. Good source of trekking information.

Bukittinggi

Restaurant Sari (£) Jalan Yos Sudarso 31 (tel: 0752 31720). Indoor and outdoor seating, with good mountain views. Seafood specialities and wide choice of Western and Indonesian dishes. Also in Padang at Jalan Thamrin 71b.

The Coffee Shop (£) Jalan A Yani 105 (no telephone). Congenial atmosphere with good, cheap Western and Indonesian fare.

Danau Toba

Restaurant Hongkong (£) Jalan Haranggaol 9–11

Parapat (tel: 0625 41895). Popular Chinese family restaurant. Indonesian and Chinese dishes.

Medan

Lyn's Restaurant (££) Jalan Jend A Yani 98a (no telephone). Favourite haunt for expats; lively bar and restaurant with Western menu.
Restaurant Garuda (£) Jalan Pemuda 20 (tel: 061 327692). A 24-hour restaurant near textile market. Offers juices, snacks and main courses.

BALI
Kuta/Legian

Goa 2001 (££) Jalan Seminyak (tel: 0361 753922). Spectacularly designed bar/restaurant in lofty traditional style. Sushi, plus Western and Indonesian dishes. Late-night bar. Check your bill.
Kopi Pot (££) Jalan Legian (tel: 0361 752614). A pleasant open-air restaurant which serves continental cuisine, salads, and vegetarian and seafood dishes.
Poppies (££) Poppies Lane (tel: 0361 51059). Atmospheric garden restaurant. Quite expensive Indonesian and Western dishes. Booking essential.

Ubud

Café Lotus (££) Main Street (tel: 0361 925660). Magical setting plus live gamelan music. Indonesian and Western dishes.
Café Wayan (££) Monkey Forest Road (tel: 0361 95447). Popular restaurant in garden setting. Balinese buffet on Sunday nights, otherwise Western and Indonesian menu.
Murni's Warung (££) Campuhan (tel: 0361 975223). Slickly designed restaurant with good Indonesian and Western food. A long-standing favourite.

NUSA TENGGARA
FLORES
Maumere

Sarinah Restaurant (£) Jalan Raja Centis 46 (tel: 0382 21592). Excellent Chinese cuisine but omnipresent television.

LOMBOK
Senggigi

Dynasty Restaurant (££) Jalan Senggigi (no telephone). International and local dishes at this lively seaside restaurant.

TIMOR
Kupang

Palembang International (£) Jalan Moch Hatta 54 (no telephone). Excellent Indonesian and Chinese dishes and pleasant semi-open-air setting.

SULAWESI
Manado

Manado Hill Top (££) Off Jalan 17 Augustus (tel: 0431 66581). Up-market restaurant with superb views. Indonesian, Chinese and Western cuisine.

Palu

Depot Ramayana (£) Jalan Dr Wahidin 58 (tel: 0451 22246). Open until midnight. Good Chinese soups, prawn, crab and fish dishes.

Rantepao

Setia Kawan (£) Jalan Andi Mappanyuki 32 (tel: 0423 21264). Wide range of Indonesian and Torajan dishes. Popular hang-out for local guides.

Ujung Pandang

Restaurant Ujung Pandang (£) Jalan Irian 42 (tel: 0411 317193). Efficient and popular seafood and Chinese restaurant.

KALIMANTAN
Balikpapan

Bondy Restaurant (££) Jalan Mayjen Sutoyo 7 (tel: 0542 23646). Pleasant open-air restaurant. Western and seafood specialities plus vast ice-cream menu. Own bakery.

Banjarmasin

Lezat Baru (££) Jalan Pangeran Samudra 22 (tel: 0511 53191). Bustling, good-value Chinese restaurant. Menu includes seafood, pigeon and frog.

Samarinda

Haur Gading (£) Jalan Pulau Sulawesi 4 (tel: 0541 21043). Quiet Dayak-style restaurant. Limited but excellent fresh seafood menu.
Lezat Baru Brothers (££) Jalan Mulawarman 56 (tel: 0541 43031). Popular Chinese restaurant serving generous portions.

MALUKU
PULAU AMBON
Kota Ambon

Restaurant Kakatoe (££) Jalan Said Perintah 20 Kota Ambon (tel: 0911 56142). European-owned restaurant serving Western and Indonesian food. Good breakfasts, music and book exchange service.
Tip-Top Restaurant (£) Jalan Sultan Hairun 12, Kota Ambon (tel: 0911 54324). Friendly local place with some seating outside. Excellent Indonesian and Chinese dishes.

IRIAN JAYA
Baliem Valley

Rumah Makan Lumayan (£) Jalan Trikora 87, Wamena (no telephone). Right next to the market. Hole-in-the-wall restaurant with reasonable Indonesian food.

Pulau Biak

Restaurant Mega Ria (££) Jalan Jend Sudirman 5, Biak (tel: 0961 21756). Chinese-owned restaurant; uninspired décor but wide range of seafood dishes.

Index

INDEX

287

INDEX/PICTURE CREDITS/CONTRIBUTORS

Picture credits

The Automobile Assocation wishes to thank the following photographers, libraries and museums for their assistance in the preparation of this book.

J ALLAN CASH PHOTOLIBRARY 67 Baluran fisherman, 88 Meru Betiri Reserve, 201 Makale market; BIOFOTOS/PAUL SIMONS 126a Rafflesia; FIONA DUNLOP 2a Timok, coconuts, 9b Madura, traditional headgear, 26a coral, 28a Dani village, 28b Dani village, 34b mosque, Kota Ambon, 64a Dieng Plateau, 64b preparing pineapple, 65 Dokar Madura, 71 Borobudur, 76a Mt Bromo & Mt Batok, 83 mosque at Sumenep, 90 Pangandaran, 93a Prambanan, 121 man carrying bamboo, 121c bamboo wall, 130a Pangaruyung Palace, 138 local fishermen, 163 Airsanih, 173a Kelimutu lake, 185a Sengkol market, 185b Belong Blanak beach, 191b Timor, 194a *ikat*, Sikka, 206 Rantepao, barber, 210 Sengkang, 211 Togian islands ferry, 238b banana flower, 242 Baliem Valley, 243 Irian Jaya, women, 244 Baliem Valley, 245 woman on path to Kuriema, 246a cinema, Irian Jaya, 246b Jiwika Baliem, 247 market at Pyramid, 248a Danis, Baliem, 248b Dani villages, 248c Dani and son, 250 Biak Korem, 250/1 Bosnik, WWII playground; MARY EVANS PICTURE LIBRARY 10a East Indies map, 36b Matelieff attack Malacca, 39a Dutch colony in East Indies, 77a Krakatoa, tidal wave, 139 pirate attack on galleon; MICHAEL HOLFORD canoe prow; THE HUTCHISON LIBRARY 30 Nias, 31 megalith at Bawamataluo, 134, Nias, initiation leap, 135 Nias, Bawamataluo, 136 Nias, 137 Nias, dancers, 249 Siberut, woman with fishing nets; Bali; FRANK LANE PICTURE AGENCY LTD 126b mitred Leaf monkey; THE MANSELL COLLECTION LTD 37 Frances Xavier, 38a Dutch Trade with East, 76b Krakatoa volcano; MUSEUM VOOR VOLKENKUNDE, ROTTERDAM (MUSEUM OF ETHNOLOGY) 252b carving; NATURE PHOTOGRAPHERS LTD 26b (P. Sterry) common dolphin, 27 (S C Bisserot) clownfish with anemone, 103 (H Miles) leopard; OXFORD SCIENTIFIC FILMS 127 (B. Bennett) Sumatran tiger; PICTURES COLOUR LIBRARY 4a Java, Bandung taxis; PLANET EARTH PICTURES 239 (K Lucas) cassowary; POPPERFOTO 77b earthquake, tuna fish; RIJKSMUSEUM-STICHTING, AMSTERDAM Jeronimus Becx II, 40a Dipo Negoro, 40b Herman Willem Daendels; SPECTRUM COLOUR LIBRARY 156 Mengwi, temple; TOPHAM/PICTUREPOINT 42a Indonesian Communist Party 1925, 42b Surabaya, bombed and blasted, 43 Dutch East Indies troops, 44a Dutch troops go into action, 44b Dutch troops, 45a ceremony in Royal Palace

The remaining photographs are held in the Association's own photo library (AA PHOTO LIBRARY) and were taken by Dirk Buwalda with the exception of pages 2b, 5b, 6/7, 13, 14a, 15, 18a, 20a, 29b, 33, 41, 45b, 46, 52, 53a, 56, 57a, 63, 91, 92, 98, 101c, 106b, 109a, 153, 157, 159, 164, 181b, 183, 184, 253b, 262a, 265, 267, 269, 270, 271a taken by Ben Davies, page 117a taken by Ken Paterson and page 262b taken by Wyn Voysey.

Captions Page 9 Traditional wedding head-dress, East Madura. **Page 29** Painting, Kertha Gosa pavilion; Balinese statue. **Pages 46–7** Puppet, Jakarta Wayang Museum; mango seller. **Pages 62–3** Paddy-fields, Java; *becap* driver. **Page 111** Traditional Batak head-gear. **Pages 140–1** Gunung Agung; priest, Pura Kehen Shrine, Bangli. **Pages 166–7** Lubuhanbajo, Flores; village elder, Nusa Tenggara. **Page 197** Woman carrying basket, Tidore Ternata. **Pages 214–15** Washing in the canal, Banjarmasin; Dayak man wearing *bluko*. **Page 231** Banda schoolgirl. **Pages 242–3** Dani men and woman. **Page 253** Palembang; Balinese street trader. **Page 271** hotel, Dation; Hard Rock Café, Legian, Bali

Acknowledgements

The Author is grateful for the assistance of Den Zachrie, Directorate General of Tourism, Gigi Schiemann, David Gourlay, Frances B Affandy, Anhar Setjadibrata and Manggus Haryono.

The Publishers would like to acknowledge the assistance given by Garuda Indonesia in the preparation of this book.

Contributors

Series adviser: Christopher Catling   **Copy editor:** Susi Bailey
Designer: Tony Truscott Designs   **Indexer:** Marie Lorimer